East Asia and the West

East Asia and the West

An Entangled History

Xiaobing Li, Yi Sun, and Wynn Gadkar-Wilcox

cognella®

SAN DIEGO

Bassim Hamadeh, CEO and Publisher
David Miano, Acquisitions Editor
Michelle Piehl, Senior Project Editor
Berenice Quirino, Associate Production Editor
Jess Estrella, Senior Graphic Designer
Stephanie Kohl, Licensing Associate
Natalie Piccotti, Senior Marketing Manager
Kassie Graves, Vice President of Editorial
Jamie Giganti, Director of Academic Publishing

Cover images:
Copyright © 2014 iStockphoto LP/EyeOfPaul.
Copyright © 2015 iStockphoto LP/Thampapon.
Giuseppe Castiglione, "The Qianlong Emperor in Ceremonial Armour on Horseback," https://commons.wiki-media.org/wiki/File:The_Qianlong_Emperor_in_Ceremonial_Armour_on_Horseback.jpg, 1758.
Copyright © 2015 Depositphotos/Kilroy.

Printed in the United States of America.

3970 Sorrento Valley Blvd., Ste. 500, San Diego, CA 92121

Brief Contents

Detailed Contents

Acknowledgments

Many people at the University of Central Oklahoma (UCO) have contributed to this volume and deserve recognition. First, Xiaobing Li would like to thank President Don Betz, Provost John F. Barthell, Dean of the College of Liberal Arts Catherine S. Webster, and Chairperson of the Department of History and Geography Katrina Lacher. They have been very supportive of the project over the past three years. The UCO faculty merit-credit program sponsored by the Office of Academic Affairs, as well as travel funds from the College of Liberal Arts, provided funding for our research and trips to conferences. The UCO Research, Creative, and Scholarly Activities (RCSA) grants sponsored by the Office of High-impact Practice, led by Director Michael Springer, made student research assistants available for the project during the past five years. UCO graduate students Ann Riley-Adams and Travis Chambers edited all the chapters. Brad Watkins prepared all the maps. Annamaria Martucci provided secretarial assistance. Li's special thanks go to Director Peter D. Hershock, Asian Studies Development Program, East-West Center, and Dr. Shana Brown, Department of History, University of Hawaii, as codirectors of the 2017 and 2018 Faculty Development Seminars of the USDoE/UISFL. The program offers a prized addition to the existing literature on the most important topics of East Asian Studies. Li is deeply indebted to his wife, Tran, and their two kids, Kevin and Christina, who shared the burden of overseas traveling to East Asia in 2014–2017.

At the University of San Diego, Yi Sun wishes to express her profound gratitude to all her colleagues in the History Department for their continuous and immeasurable support; their collective scholarly productivity has been forever inspiring. She would also like to thank Dr. Noelle Norton, dean of the College of Arts and Sciences, for providing travel funds that enabled her to further her collaborative efforts with her coauthors at several academic conferences during the past few years. Alma Ortega and Christopher Marcum, two remarkable librarians at USD's Copley Library, have both offered valuable and expeditious assistance in locating research resources. She is grateful to her students whose intellectual curiosity and thought-provoking questions on East Asia prompted her to select and analyze meaningful materials for this book. Meanwhile, she owes special thanks to her husband, Gary Boggs, for his indispensable support and understanding on the home front.

At the Western Connecticut State University, Wynn Gadkar-Wilcox would like to thank the Office of Academic Affairs and the local AAUP chapter for funding the research and writing of this book and for funding reassigned time for background research in 2015. He would also like to thank Joanne Elpern in the Interlibrary Loan Office at WCSU's Haas library and Rich Richie with Yale University Libraries, without whom he would not have had access to the materials needed for this book. He would also like to thank the members of the Department of History and Non-Western cultures, Katherine Allocco, Surekha Davies, Jennifer Duffy, Kevin Gutzman, Leslie Lindenauer, Martha May, Michael Nolan, Joshua Rosenthal, and Abubaker Saad for their suggestions and support. A special thank you is owed to the Department's secretary, Patricia Lerner, who is entirely invaluable. Finally, he would like to thank his family, especially his wife, Sujata, and daughters, Ishika and Aksita, for their support.

Finally, the three authors offer thanks to Dr. David Miano for his unfailing professionalism and his always-timely support during the editorial progress of this book. Of course, we are grateful to the editors, copyeditors, and staff at Cognella Academic Publishing for their first-class editorial expertise, without which this book could not have been completed.

Xiaobing Li, University of Central Oklahoma

Yi Sun, University of San Diego

Wynn Gadkar-Wilcox, Western Connecticut State University

Preface: How to Use This Textbook

The world was surprised when in 2014 the International Monetary Fund ranked China the number one economic superpower in the world as the country was surpassing even the United States in its share of the world's Gross Domestic Product. The American public remains concerned about North Korea's continuing nuclear threat, Japan's nuclear meltdown, and the ongoing conflict over disputed islands in the South China Sea that are claimed by multiple countries, including Vietnam and China. Americans increasingly interact with East Asians in the realms of global trade, international relations, and our everyday life. In education, Confucius Institutes are generating both educational opportunities and political controversy on college campuses throughout the United States. Increasingly, Asian-related classes are being offered at American universities, and more grade schools in the United States are providing classes for students to study the Chinese language. In the realm of popular culture, people can easily find Japanese sushi bars almost everywhere in urban areas, and sushi lunch boxes are available in many local supermarkets. In our neighborhood shopping centers, Korean Tai Kong Dao martial arts academies, Vietnamese pho restaurants, and Japan's Hello Kitty products have become ubiquitous and are increasingly part of the cultural life of urban youth in the United States. Naturally, these economic and cultural shifts are fueling ever-increasing interest in East Asia among educators, policymakers, and young people.

Globalization has done more than merely narrow the gap between the United States and East Asia. Today it is impossible to understand domestic politics in the United States without reference to economic and cultural changes in Asia. From defense to finance to technology and the environment, major policy issues in the United States are incomprehensible without reference to developments in East Asia. American college students have both academic and professional reasons to study East Asia, since knowledge of this area of the world will be an indispensable asset for major employers in the future. Sensing this change, this generation's students grasp the need to understand economic and technological changes in East Asia.

East Asia and the West: An Entangled History is designed to offer an accessible, but carefully documented and academically rigorous, general introduction to the history of modern East Asia to undergraduate students and interested readers in the general public. It offers a particular emphasis on the way in which the development of modern East Asia is inextricably tied to intellectual and political developments in Europe and North America, without reducing East Asians to mere puppets of European political developments. This book functions as a one-semester survey of relations between East Asia and Europe and North America from about 1600 to 2010. It is designed to serve the needs of both introductory and more advanced courses at the college and university levels. It introduces the sources, the persistence, and the flexibility of cultures and traditions in China, Japan, Korea, and Vietnam in the face of new cultural, economic, and military challenges from European powers in the 1700s and 1800s. It will demonstrate how East Asian rulers and intellectuals, along with ordinary people, localized and adapted Western practices to craft their own particular versions of modernity. The primary objective of the book is to provide college students and general readers with a better understanding of the origins and development of modern East Asia in the context of these relations.

This textbook and its accompanying sources are designed for modern college and university history classes on East Asia, including China, Japan, Korea, and Vietnam. It can also serve as a history survey for area studies, topic classes, and policy seminars, with coverage on issues such as Christian missionaries in Korea and U.S.-Japan relations in the twentieth century. Students will find the book's primary sources, many of which were not readily available in English, of great interest, and will study intriguing and important issues that have been previously overlooked.

East Asia and the West is a college textbook that presents both diachronic coverage of modern East Asia and a synchronic focus on major topics in modern East Asian history. These topics include philosophy, religion, economics, demographics, politics, military affairs, diplomacy, literature, and education. This book presents a narrative of the origins and development of East Asian modernity into the twenty-first century. It is designed to capture for students the human drama of anecdotes about the past while simultaneously illuminating larger themes and patterns in the development of East Asian modernity. Told with an emphasis on Asian perspectives, the volume explores how East Asians—from emperors to presidents to officials to ordinary people—made decisions to join, adapt to, or fight against Western powers. It provides insights into East Asian views of the world and perceptions of the West, and popular attitudes toward Christianity and technology.

Some conventional world history textbooks interpret East Asian modernization either primarily as a story of Western aggression and East Asian response, or as a story of Westernization bringing a stable and unchanging East Asia abruptly into a modern world. In these narratives, capitalist economies and advanced technologies led to Western imperialism and colonization in East Asia, and some nationalist leaders mobilized the masses for the long and often violent anticolonial resistance that gained popular support. The flaw in these narratives is that they view European actions as the motivating force in East Asian modernity. While military confrontations with European powers, along with cultural exchange, play a considerable role in the development of modern East Asia, these transformations need to be understood in the context of already existing modernist movements in these countries and in the contest of local economic and political changes.

This book questions the Eurocentric narrative in several ways. First, it considers the East Asian countries as active actors in their modernization rather than passive actors or even victims of industrialization. Each chapter studies patterns of decision-making indigenous to particular East Asian countries. Political and social elites acted according to their own tradition and incorporated Western concepts and technologies consistent with their own interests in national and international affairs. Because their interactions with the West were influenced by the demands of domestic politics, the results often changed the direction of East Asian countries while having a strong impact on their economy, politics, culture, and society.

Second, this book endeavors to understand relations between particular East Asian regions and European and North American ones in a specific historical context, while simultaneously trying to elucidate certain common patterns. Above all, it recognizes that "the West" is a problematic label, since it refers to a clear geographic body and can be used only vaguely to refer to a set of ideas. For example, the imperial and financial strategies of the Dutch, English, Portuguese, French, and Spanish in East Asia were not identical, nor were the missionizing efforts of Jesuits, Dominicans, Franciscans, Foreign Mission Society, or Protestant priests. Similarly, the East Asian countries in this volume have highly specific experiences with the military, financial, and cultural influences of Europe. Some were formally colonized to one extent or another, while others were not, resulting in vastly different relationships.

The notion that Western traders and missionaries from the seventeenth century onwards suddenly and fundamentally changed a hopelessly traditional East Asia is another problematic narrative. From the Silk Road to Mongol Contacts to Marco Polo, East Asians had interacted with Europeans for centuries. The modern encounter with the West was not new. Likewise, the Western missionaries and traders who encountered East Asian civilizations in the seventeenth century did not find a closed, hermetic East Asia permanently fixed to unchanging traditional values. The innovations of the Song dynasty (960–1279), including gunpowder, the printing press, and paper-based currency, show the dynamic nature of these civilizations in premodern times. In order to avoid problematic over-generalizations, this volume treats the experience of peoples throughout East Asia in all of their unique specificity.

Nevertheless, these caveats notwithstanding, it is possible to notice patterns in the history of relations between East Asian countries and the West. Though contact with Europe had persisted since ancient times, the economics of global maritime empires in the sixteenth and seventeenth centuries fundamentally changed the character of these interactions. Though each missionary group had their own unique features, the cultural encounter with missionaries—encompassing not just Christianity but also features of Western art, literature, and astronomy—shared common features in Vietnam, Korea, China, and Japan.

In comparison to the West, the study of East Asian history offers several different approaches to modernization. The book details the most important and influential events, people, and ideas in modern East Asian history. It provides a comprehensive resource on East Asian experiences of modernization from the seventeenth to the twenty-first centuries. Three authors divide the chapters by the countries of their specialties. Dr. Xiaobing Li is the primary author of the sections on China and Korea, Dr. Yi Sun of those on Japan, and Dr. Wynn Gadkar-Wilcox of those on Vietnam and Indochina. Through the chapters we have developed three analytical approaches to our overview of modern East Asia. First, we analyze general patterns in East Asian history in the context of relations with the West, to elucidate what common themes persist throughout this history. Secondly, we compare these general themes across nations and cultures in East Asia to consider the specific and localized reception of the West and the differences in the experiences of modernity throughout the region, as it affected the political, economic, social, and cultural spheres. Finally, we examine how both the general and the particular experiences change over time.

This book covers the major developments of the principal civilizations of East Asia. It situates East Asian experiences of modernization in the indigenous context of each of these societies while taking into account their patterns, progress, and challenges. This volume divides modern East Asia into five sections and fourteen chapters, along with a conclusion.

The first section, "East Asia before European Expansion," includes two chapters. The first chapter "Ancient Kingdoms, Centralized Empires, and Foundational Concepts," provides an overview and historical background of premodern East Asia by examining the early history of the four countries as unique entities, and then considering two trends that held East Asia together even in the premodern era: the Confucian-Mencian paradigm and the tribute system. Chapter Two, "The Emergence of the Early East Asian Modern," covers the development of trade networks, technology, and innovation in these four countries from the 1500s to the 1800s, and suggests that these trends mark the development of indigenous notions of modernity.

The second section, "Early Modern Contact with the West," includes two chapters, explaining why the Chinese Qing emperors continued their unsuccessful isolationist policy, while the Meiji leaders changed their policy and believed that only the open-door policy provided a better future for their people. Chapter Three, "Adjusting to the West: Trade, Technology, and Christianity" discusses why Eastern countries carried out an isolationist policy against Western influence, and how the conflict between the East and the West began in the 1800s. Chapter Four, "Fending off the West," examines East Asia at the critical juncture of the late eighteenth and early nineteenth century, when cultural conflicts with Western nations were on the rise.

The third section is entitled is entitled "Confrontation and Westernization." Chapter Five focuses on the Opium Wars between China and Great Britain in the 1840s and 1850s and their impact, which led to the collapse of the Qing dynasty in 1911. Chapter Six examines the successful case of the Meiji Transformation, explaining why Japan's economic growth in the 1880s to the 1900s soon turned into an imperialist aggression in East Asia at the turn of the century. Chapter Seven details the causes, origins, and execution of French colonization in Indochina from the 1850s to the 1940s with a particular emphasis on how that colonization affected Vietnam.

The fourth section, "Wars and Revolutions," includes three chapters and covers World War II and the communist movements in East Asia during the war. Chapter Eight looks into World War II in the Pacific, including the major events such as the attacks at Pearl Harbor, the Allied island hopping campaigns, atomic bombs, and the American occupation of Japan from 1945–1951. Chapter Nine discusses the Cold War in East Asia by focusing on the communist movement in China, the founding of the People's Republic of China (PRC), and the war between China and the United States in Korea from 1950–1953. Chapter Nine also continues the discussion of the hot conflicts in the Cold War in East Asia by examining the French Indochina War in 1946–1954. Chapter Ten provides the details of the major political movements in the PRC, such as the Cultural Revolution of 1966–1976 and Deng Xiaoping's return in 1978.

The fifth section, "The East Wind Prevails over the West Wind," includes four chapters and examines the competition and confrontation between the capitalist and communist systems in the Cold War in East Asia. Chapter Eleven analyzes Japan's economic miracle in the 1970s while exploring the economic and social problems during that time. Chapter Twelve focuses on the Vietnam Wars from the late 1950s to the 1980s in Indochina. Chapter Thirteen details China's and Vietnam's reforms and transformations from third-world countries to increasingly industrialized economies in the 1990s. Chapter Fourteen looks at China as an evolving economic superpower in the 2000s. The conclusion summarizes the semester-long class by emphasizing that understanding East Asia's modernization history and the challenges it faces is one of the most important tasks of the twenty-first century.

Even though they have the world's highest economic growth rate, East Asian countries must face their own problems, which include human rights violations, political corruption, and inconsistency in legal practices. These factors impede the improvement of their relations with the world in general, and with the West in particular. Conversely, western governments must understand these factors and work with East Asian countries on developing shared objectives, interests, and values, thereby drawing them into the international system. China, North Korea, and Vietnam, in turn, must live up to their respective international obligations and engage in constructive relations in a globalized world.

PART ONE

East Asia before European Expansion

Introduction to Part One

Only in the past hundred years has the possibility of a regional coherence of "East Asia" become a familiar concept. In the premodern past, the areas now known as China, Korea, Japan, and Vietnam all took different paths to construct kingdoms. It is important to remember the regional and even subnational distinctiveness of premodern East Asian cultures so as to not assume that the national units we understand in East Asia today existed in the ancient past. Yet while each of these areas had distinctive features, they nevertheless shared certain ideas. One of those is Confucianism, a theory of the world shared throughout East Asia in premodern times based on the thinking of scholars such as Confucius (551–478 BCE) and Mencius (372–289 BCE). In the context of an era of great division in China, these scholars wanted to devise a means to organize society that would require less use of military force and legal coercion. They proposed that people should become well educated through reading a set of common and important texts from the past and developing a series of common behavioral expectations, or rituals. These texts and rituals were the source for a social order based on the application of virtues, such as humaneness, known in Chinese as *ren*. Confucius and Mencius believed that through applying proper educational and ritual principles, a society could be produced in which people conducted themselves appropriately, thereby limiting the need to rely on law and punishment to maintain social order. Understanding the wide application of the ideas of Confucius and Mencius is important, because it can help us make comparisons across East Asian civilizations.

1

Chapter One also discusses a related concept—the tribute system. The tribute system was a means to organize relations between polities that grew out of the Confucian-Mencian paradigm. The tribute system was a means to organize relations between polities that grew out of the Confucian-Mencian paradigm and one of codifying relationships between China and other Asian states through the use of ritual protocol. On regularly scheduled occasions, smaller states would give the king of a larger state gifts that represented desirable products from their country, and the larger state would give back a series of larger gifts to symbolize the its superiority. This protocol would solidify a family-like relationship with the two sovereigns, and would mean that the two rulers incurred mutual obligations to defend one another.

A final premodern commonality between East Asian areas was Buddhism. Buddhism was introduced to East Asia in the second and third centuries CE, both overland from Central and South Asia via the trade routes conventionally known as the Silk Road, and via maritime routes from South and Southeast Asia. Buddhism, which provided a path to reduce human suffering through emphasizing the role that compassion could play in reducing selfish desires, provided a new and potentially egalitarian means for premodern East Asians to conceive of their relationship with others and with the cosmos.

As Chapter Two explains, by 1500 East Asian cultures had developed a version of early modernity. East Asian countries had established centralized bureaucracies that controlled territories, maintained social orders, and developed trade. They embraced technological and economic innovations. They had well-defined systems of territoriality and international relations, though those systems were markedly different from their European counterparts. Though these systems were well developed, they would alter, and be altered by, the political, economic, and international relations frameworks of Europeans, who by the sixteenth century would increasingly return to Asia to trade with East Asian countries and spread the Christian faith.

Chapter 1

Ancient Kingdoms, Centralized Empires, and Foundational Concepts

Though the term "Asia" was used in Greek and Roman times to refer to Turkey and more broadly what we might now call the "near East," most Japanese, Koreans, Chinese, or Vietnamese would have found the idea that they were "East Asian" a strange and foreign one until at least the last nineteenth century. Since "East Asia" is in many ways a modern construction, it should not be surprising that in prehistoric and ancient times, the areas we now consider a part of East Asia followed their own unique development. For example, early linguistic development differed in the areas now known as China, Korea, Vietnam, and Japan. The Vietnamese language developed historically out of Austroasiatic of Mon/Khmer languages of mainland Southeast Asia. Until little more than a millennium ago, it may not have been distinct from Muong or other Tai-related languages. Moreover, Vietnam's emergence out of Khmer and Cham polities and its historical and cultural links to other Southeast Asian cultures led to ultimately inconclusive and perhaps unproductive debates in the last decades of the twentieth century about whether or not Vietnam should be understood as an East Asian or a Southeast Asian country.

Korean appears most likely to be a linguistic singularity, lacking clear relation to any other language family, though some scholars still deem it an Altaic tongue related to other Turkic or Mongolian languages. The linguistic origins of Japanese are still obscure, though it may be distantly related to Korean and therefore possibly also Altaic. The origins of these three East Asian languages cannot be definitively linked to Sino-Tibetan languages like those spoken in China. This suggests that, at least in the ancient past, what is now East Asia did not share a common cultural heritage. Rather, Vietnam shared a cultural heritage with other polities in mainland Southeast Asia, and Korea and Japan shared a cultural heritage with one another and possibly with Mongolian and Turkic groups.

However, beginning around two millennia ago, a series of attempts at expansion and conquest from rulers in the North China Plain led to the diffusion of economic ideas, and these disparate places slowly evolved to share a common heritage. Over the course of many hundreds of years, East Asians in what are now China, Korea, Japan, and Vietnam developed patterns of social values, political sensibilities, institutional procedures, religious institutions, military strategies, and diplomatic behaviors, which have arisen through centuries of change, revolution, war, and reform. These patterns include commonalities in centralized political institutions, the dissemination of works describing the values and political theories of the Confucian-Mencian paradigm, the spread of Buddhism, and a system of uniquely East Asian diplomatic relations stemming from that paradigm. These civilizational patterns set a framework not only for the development and evolution of common premodern institutions but also for the modern development of East Asia. These common patterns in turn informed economic expansion and reform efforts in the seventeenth and eighteenth centuries as well as intellectual responses to Christianity, global trade, and European gunboats from the sixteenth century through the twentieth.

Ancient Kingdoms and Centralized Empires

China

In the territory now known as China, ancient hunters transitioned from living in small groups to tribal existence around 20000 BCE. Relics showing how primitive Chinese people lived communally have been found in many parts of central China along the Yellow River (*Huanghe*), the cradle of Chinese civilization. Warmer weather, improved tools, and domestication of some animals between 12000–8000 BCE led to significant agricultural

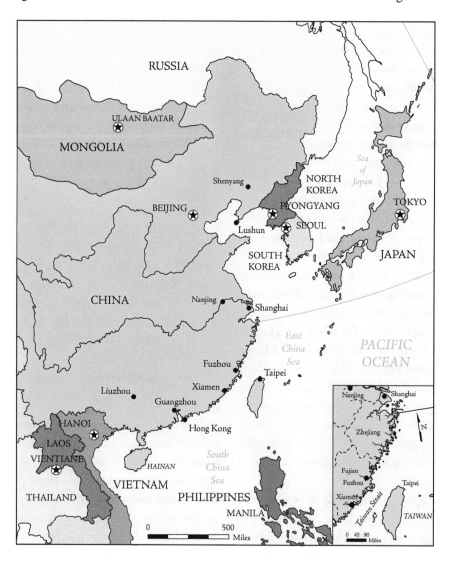

FIGURE 1.1 East Asia

development and an expanding population. The ancestors of today's Chinese had already acquired the skill of making stone and bone instruments and weapons. In approximately 3000 BCE, clans along the Yellow River developed patriarchal societies.

Historical records written by later scholars demonstrate that conflicts over arable land, slaves, and water resources evolved into large-scale warfare during the Five-Emperor period (*wudi*) (2600–2200 BCE), a period that marked the beginning of Chinese political history. However, no solid contemporaneous evidence exists to corroborate the existence of dynasties or emperors prior to the Shang dynasty (ca. 1600–1050 BCE). Nevertheless, the heroic legends of these purported rulers were important for later generations of Chinese, who used them to legitimize the rule of subsequent emperors. Among them was the tale of the Yellow Emperor (*Huangdi*), who led many tribes in the Hua-xia region along the western Yellow River to a series of victories, established a complex bureaucracy, and promoted the well-being of his subjects. Through three generations of military leadership: Yao, Shun, and Yu (or Great Yu), the Hua-xia group was celebrated by later Confucian scholars as brave and benevolent rulers who conquered territories and established a unified kingdom.

The Xia dynasty, which was reportedly established by the Great Yu (*Dayu*), lasted from 2205–1766 BCE. Chinese rice productivity along the Yellow River and Yangzi (Yangtze) River generated enough wealth and food to support a growing population. Although later Confucian scholars theorized that the Xia emperors developed a bureaucratic government with a large army, they imagined that revolts toppled the Xia Empire, leading to the creation of a new dynasty, the Shang.

The Shang dynasty is the first Chinese political entity whose existence is incontrovertible. The Shang established their capital first in Bo (modern Shangqiu, Henan Province), and then moved to Yin (Anyang, Henan). The Shang dynasty was able to expand politically, economically, and militarily in the North China Plain. Walled cities appeared along with bronze weapons. Inscriptions are visible on some early bronzes, but most Shang writings have been found incised on "dragon bones," that is, tortoise under-shells, the scapulae or shoulder blades of cattle, and other flattish bones.[1] These inscriptions reveal the concerns of Shang rulers with using priests to interpret cracks in these shells and bones for the purposes of establishing a relationship to their departed ancestors and in predicting the weather, the auspicious birth of royal children, or changes in royal fortune. Despite these earlier developments, by the late Shang period, continuous military expeditions, aristocratic factionalism, corruption, and public weariness of severe punishments had gravely weakened the dynasty.

As the Shang declined, the state of Zhou, one of the Shang's subordinate states in the west (modern Shaanxi Province), rose rapidly. By 1027 BCE, Zhou had defeated remaining Shang loyalists and established its own dynasty. The Zhou dynasty (1027–221 BCE) is historically divided into two periods: the Western Zhou (1027–771 BCE) with its capital in Hao (Xi'an, Shaanxi Province), and the Eastern Zhou (771–256 BCE) with its capital in Luoyi (Luoyang, Henan Province). In 771 BCE, the reigning king was killed by an alliance of Zhou vassals and people from regions to the west of the capital of Hao. Though one of the King's sons was established as the new ruler and a new capital established further East, the Zhou never again exercised its political dominance. Instead, the Zhou kings became figureheads and their territory became divided between de facto independent kingdoms.

---

1   Patricia Ebrey and Anne Walthall, *Pre-Modern East Asia: to 1800*, 3rd ed. (Boston, MA: Wadsworth Cengage Learning, 2014), 12–13.

This period of division in the Eastern Zhou can be further divided into two historical periods: the Spring and Autumn period (722–481 BCE) and the Warring States period (403–221 BCE). During the latter phase, the king of Qin embarked upon a dramatic conquest of ancient China's seven separate kingdoms. In 221 BCE, China was unified under Qin, from which emerged the nation's westernized name: China.

The Qin dynasty (221–206 BCE) built a highly centralized regime, the first of its kind in Chinese history. Having concentrated all power in his own hands, Qin Shi Huangdi (the first emperor of Qin who reigned from 221–210 BCE) headed a massive bureaucracy.[2] Though Qin Shi Huangdi was frequently remembered as a totalitarian emperor, aspects of his legal, military, administrative, and bureaucratic procedures remained key features of the Chinese imperial system through the end of the Qing dynasty (1644–1911 CE). For example, the establishment of a sophisticated and powerful army was necessary to secure the ruler's central control. Similarly, a centralized taxation system aided in drafting large numbers of peasants as laborers for the Qin's many infrastructure projects. The Qin also terminated the separate city-state system and transformed land ownership from dynastic families, relatives, and lords, to private owners.

Thus, the tax-paying peasants and landowners supported the entire imperial system. Farmers paid onerous taxes, both through donating portions of their crop yields and by being forced to provide manual labor for state projects. Regular taxes alone constituted two-thirds of an average farmer's harvest. Besides, the farmer was also required to spend one month per year working on roads, canals, palaces, imperial tombs, or military duties. With a total population of fifty-four million (at that time the population of the Roman Empire was no more than forty-six million), Shi Huangdi used two million peasants to build an initial section of the Great Wall in the frontiers. The heavy labor and ruthless recruiting required to meet the demands of the state led both farmers and scholars in China to revolt against the Qin regime.[3] The peasant rebellions played an important role in dynastic changes through Chinese history.

One of the peasant leaders, Liu Bang (256–195 BCE), eventually overthrew the Qin and established the Han dynasty (206 BCE–220 CE), thus beginning a cycle of dynastic changes in China that would continue for the next two thousand years. The successful military expeditions and territorial expansion during the Han dynasty convinced the Chinese people of the superiority of their civilization and institutions. The Chinese began to call themselves the "Han people" (Hanzu, or Han nationals, have historically constituted the demographic majority in China, and are ninety percent of its population today). The Han emperors believed that China (Zhongguo) was the "Central Kingdom," superior to any other people and nation under heaven, occupying a central position among countries in Asia.

---

2   Edward L. Dreyer, "Continuity and Chang," in *A Military History of China*, updated ed., eds. David A. Graff and Robin Higham, (Lexington: University Press of Kentucky, 2012), 23.

3   In 209 BCE, Chen Sheng and Wu Guang, together with nine hundred other peasants who were drafted and sent to Yuyang (today's Miyun County, Beijing) to perform military duties, staged an armed uprising at Daze and quickly occupied Chenxian (Huaiyang, Henan). They called upon all the peasants in China to revolt against the Qin regime. After the death of Chen and Wu, Liu Bang (256–195 BCE), one of the peasant leaders, eventually overthrew the Qin and established the Han dynasty (206 BCE–220 CE). See Xiaobing Li, *A History of the Modern Chinese Army* (Lexington: University Press of Kentucky, 2007), 306n16.

Japan

Lying off the eastern coast of the Asian continent, Japan is an archipelago surrounded by the Pacific Ocean to the east, the Sea of Japan to the west, the Philippine Sea to the south, and the Okhotsk Sea to the north. Separated by the Tsushima Strait from Korea, Japan consists of four main islands—Hokkaido, Honshu, Shikoku, and Kyushu—as well as thousands of smaller islands. Archaeological evidence suggests that the ancestors of modern Japanese likely traveled from the Korean peninsula to Japan by crossing a land bridge about 30,000–10,000 years ago during the glacial age.[4] They adapted to the island environment by engaging in hunting, gathering, fishing, and stone making. They later created the Jomon tribal society (8000–300 BCE), which was noted for its rather intricate cord-pattern pottery, seen in the clay figures and other vessels showing braided cord designs. In late Jomon, there was evidence of combined migration of settlers from both northern Asia and southern Pacific as well as early signs of rudimentary farming. During the subsequent Yayoi period (300 BCE–300 CE), life became much more sedentary as the settlers, whose existence stretched from northern Honshu to southern Kyushu, adopted agriculture by cultivating dried field grain and paddy rice, domesticating animals, and developing bronze products, such as bells and mirrors, and subsequently iron tools and weapons. In addition to creating more refined pottery products, compared to those during the preceding Jomon culture, the Yayoi period saw signs of trade with China, evidenced in the Chinese coins found at its sites. Most notably was its wet field rice cultivation that made it possible to support a growing population. The island existence and the mountainous land terrain made the Japanese civilization more conducive to developing decentralized entities and compartmentalized communities, which in turn fostered the growth of feudalism. The mid-third century saw the emergence of the Tomb culture in Japan, characterized by hundreds of earth mounds in various sizes and burial rituals, depending on the status of those the deceased. The tombs containing burial chambers were primarily used for the Uji elites, though during the late Tomb period toward the end of the fifth century, the burial practices were popular among the commoners as well.

The Yamato family, the largest hereditary aristocratic tribal group on the central plain near Osaka, founded the first cohesive government. After numerous intertribal conflicts, the Yamato group either defeated or established coalitional leadership with other tribes. As Japan's first emperor, in the sixth century CE, Yamato and his family ruled the country with more than three hundred tribes and two million people.[5] Despite the emergence of some level of political centralization and social stratification, early Yamato polity remained tribal in nature. The society was under the control of the Uji (clan) system, in which hereditary aristocratic family groups served in the government and military. The Uji varied in size and complexity, but they shared similarities in that each Uji had its elders serving as both secular and religious leaders in charge of managing tribal affairs and kami (spirits) worshipping. The Yamato government launched military expeditions into other islands and even sent missions to Korea. The Uji leaders identified themselves with Shinto, "the way of the Kami," an animist, local religion worshipping nature and the Sun Goddess, who was widely believed to be the creator of Japan.[6] In order to assert more political and administrative control in the midst of factional struggles at the court, the

---

4   Kenneth Henshall, *A History of Japan: From Stone Age to Superpower*, 2nd ed. (London, UK: Palgrave Macmillan, 2004), 10–12.

5   Anne Walthall, *Japan: A Cultural, Social, and Political History* (Boston, MA: Houghton Mifflin, 2004), 12–14.

6   Curtis Andressen, *A Short History of Japan: From Samurai to Sony* (Canberra, Australia: Allen & Unwin, 2002), 31–2.

Yamato family claimed a divine lineage from the Sun Goddess while engaging in Chinese learning, including the adoption of Chinese written language, music, and, most importantly, Confucianism. As a result, the all-encompassing Chinese philosophy helped the Yamato family establish an expanded bureaucracy with its elaborate code of moral conduct and its insistence on social order and political stability. Meanwhile, Buddhism, introduced to Japan from Korea, further injected religious morality into a country whose indigenous religion, Shintoism, was only concerned with nature worshipping and ritual cleanliness. As the Yamato family assumed growing power over other clans, the Yamato name became synonymous with Japan.

Korea

The Korean peninsula is approximately 620 miles in length from north to south and 130 miles wide at its narrowest; it is equivalent to the size of Great Britain at about 85,500 square miles. It is located on the eastern edge of the Asian continent, bordering China and Russia, and separated from the Japanese archipelago by the East China Sea and the Korean Strait, about 120 miles. At present, it remains divided into two parts: North Korea (Democratic People's Republic of Korea, DPRK) comprises 55 percent of the total land area, while South Korea (Republic of Korea, ROK) is slightly smaller, about 45 percent. As a mountainous terrain, its principal range runs through the peninsula from north to south with only one-fifth of the total area arable. The first migrants probably came to Korea from Manchuria (now a part of northeastern China) and settled in the north of the peninsula about 30,000 years ago. Hereditary aristocratic tribes were engaged in agriculture and fishing about 5000 BCE. Unearthed evidence reveals that bronze and iron tools, weapons, and ritual bells became

available in approximately 1000 BCE. The first unified government was founded at Pyongyang in 194 BCE, but it only controlled the northern half of the country. In 109 BCE Chinese emperor Wudi (Martial Emperor) of the Han dynasty (206 BCE–220 CE) conquered Pyongyang, establishing a Chinese military administration in Pyongyang and dividing the northern part of the country into twenty-five districts with 400,000.[7] The south was under the control of tribal chieftains and their warriors.

After the Chinese military administration at Pyongyang ended in 313 CE, Korea entered the Three Kingdoms period (340–668 CE) with Goguryeo as the largest kingdom in the north, Baekje in the southwest, and Silla in the southeast. During the Three Kingdoms period, Chinese monks introduced Confucianism and Buddhism first to Baekje and then to other kingdoms. These monks soon became cultural authorities, because they were among the few who could read and write in Korea at the time. Thus, the Chinese writing system spread to Korea with Buddhism and Confucianism. The kings and aristocratic families, or the *yangban* aristocracy, learned Chinese characters first, as knowledge of the Chinese language helped convey a sense of political superiority. After the Chinese Sui (581–618 CE) and Tang dynasties attacked Korea repeatedly, Goguryeo went into severe decline. Subsequently, Silla conquered the other kingdoms and unified the peninsula in 668 CE. Although Silla's native culture was the principal vehicle of Korean development through the middle age, Buddhism and Confucianism operated simultaneously and dominated Korean religious, cultural, political, and social institutions. Silla's kings sent their officials, monks, and royal family members to China to study Buddhism and Confucianism. Some Korean scholars even successfully passed Tang civil service examinations. Although Silla adopted the civil examination system in 788 CE to recruit

---

7   Michael J. Seth, *A Concise History of Korea: From the Neolithic Period through the Nineteenth Century* (Boulder, CO: Rowman & Littlefield, 2006), 18–20.

government officials in Korea, unlike the Tang, it allowed only aristocrats to take them.[8]

Vietnam

The Vietnamese shared a similar experience with Korea. Though Vietnamese nationalist historians have attempted to push the origins of Vietnamese civilization as far back in time as possible, very little is known for sure about the people we now see as Vietnamese prior to 207 BCE. At that time, General Zhao Tuo (d. 137 BCE), who had been sent south by Qin Shi Huangdi in an effort to expand Qin frontiers, established a kingdom of Nanyue (Nam Viet), which encompassed both most of the modern-day Guangdong province in China and a section of what is now the Northern part of Vietnam.

The history of the area, which is now Vietnam, prior to the time of Zhao Tuo is shrouded in myth and legend. Evidence found in caves located in Hoa Binh prefecture demonstrates the existence of a subsistence economy of people in Vietnam between 10000 and 2000 BCE. The people who lived near the Hoa Binh site, who may or may not be related to those living in Vietnam today, appear to have come from other parts of Southeast Asia to move into the Indochinese peninsula and settle in the north of today's Vietnam. Hereditary aristocratic tribes were engaged in agriculture by about 4000 BCE and by 1500 BCE made the Red River delta the "rice bowl" of Vietnam. Unearthed evidence reveals that bronze and iron tools, weapons, and ritual vessels were used, beginning about 1000 BCE.

Returning to the historical record, the court records of the Chinese Qin dynasty show border trade between China and Nanyue in 220 BCE, immediately prior to Zhao Tuo's appearance. This earlier record may be a reference to King An Duong, who fled from China to escape Qin rule and had established his own polity in the Guangdong/northern Vietnam area prior to Zhao Tuo. In 111 BCE, Chinese emperor Wudi (Martial Emperor) of the Han dynasty attacked Vietnam. The Han army integrated the far northern part of Vietnam as well as parts of what are now the Guangdong and Guangxi provinces in China as the province of Jiaozhi (Giao chi) and established several military outposts, including one near modern-day Hanoi.[9] Over the course of the next thousand years, military leaders from the North intermarried with locals and produced powerful Chinese-Vietnamese, Han-Viet families near modern-day Hanoi. These families adapted cultural and linguistic characteristics from the North, eventually producing the Vietnamese language, which is dominated by Sinitic vocabulary despite its being part of the Austroasiatic family of languages.

When the power of dynasties to the north was expanding, Chinese military officials, and the nascent Han-Viet elite near what is now Hanoi attempted to further codify their frontier administration and more effectively tax areas further south. When this happened, the population farther south, who may have been related to the people we call Muong today, resisted this administrative control. Examples of this phenomenon are the rebellion of the Trung sisters (40–43 CE), and that of Lady Trieu (248 CE).

When the fortunes of dynasties in China to the north waned, they found themselves unable to send troops to control this distant southern frontier. When that happened, local rulers, usually military leaders from Chinese dynasties who had previously exerted control over the area, filled the leadership void and established their own independent or quasi-independent regimes. Examples of this phenomenon are the regimes of Shi Xie (Vietnamese: *Si Nhiep*) (137–226 CE), Ly Nam De (503–548 CE), and Gao Pian (Vietnamese: *Cao Bien*) (821–887 CE).

---

8   Ibid., 52–6.

9   D. R. SarDesai, *Vietnam: Past and Present*, 4th ed. (Boulder, CO: Westview, 2005), 11–12.

One such void of imperial power from the North was the period between the end of the Tang dynasty (618–907) in China and the beginning of the Song dynasty (960–1279). In the intervening years between 907 CE and 960 CE, as powers vied for control of the North, various local rulers vied for power in the northern part of Vietnam. Many short-lived rulers took power in the tenth century; the one remembered by many Vietnamese as having created an independent Vietnam was Ngo Quyen in 939 CE. At this time, he led forces from an area to the south of modern-day Hanoi and, taking advantage of the civil war in China, defeated Chinese occupation troops and established an independent state.

Some historians describe the ancient history of East Asia as a series of dynastic cycles. In other words, the successive dynasties repeated the same story: a heroic founding, a period of great power followed by a long decline, and eventually total collapse. The founders of a new centralized dynasty believed that he and his people were superior to any other people and country under Heaven. This perception, combined with a moral cosmology, elevated the eastern emperor as the "Son of the Heaven" or the "Son of the Sun Goddess." As pointed out by Orville Schell and other scholars, such a claim granted the emperors supreme power derived from the "Mandate of Heaven."[10]

Confucianism in the Classic and Middle Periods

The centralized political control, or emperor-centered power, during the ancient age was supported by a classic East Asian philosophy: the Confucian-Mencian paradigm. Benjamin I.

Schwartz states that Confucianism has remained influential today in East Asian countries.[11] It is a humanistic philosophy with close ties between humans and nature. Confucius (551–478 BCE) as the founder pointed out humaneness (*ren*), righteousness (*yi*), proper behavior (*li*), inner integrity (*zhi*), and filial piety (*xiao*) as necessary qualities of a man of nobility. Mencius (Mengzi) (372–289 BCE) as one of the principal interpreters and the most important Confucian after Confucius emphasized good family relationships, social order, and moral government.

One of the primary goals of the Confucian-Mencian paradigm was social harmony, which was inculcated through the teaching of humaneness (*ren*). Both Confucius and Mencius avoided giving humaneness a formal definition, but they used the term in a way that suggested that to be human was to be concerned for others by cultivating proper relationships with them. Relationships were central to Confucianism; Mencius highlighted the five essential relationships that were most important to cultivate to achieve social harmony. These were ruler and subject, father and son, husband and wife, elder brother and younger brother, and friend and friend.

Specific duties were set down to each participant in these sets of relationships.[12] Everyone followed his or her role ethics to fulfill responsibilities, receive support and awards, and establish a unified society. In such a Confucian-Mencian country, peasants provided taxes and services, while the emperor in return promised opportunities and protection. According to the theory of "dynastic cycle," in the waning years of a dynasty, the rulers typically expand beyond their means and ability to tax their subjects, particularly the farmers. They therefore became more dependent

---

10   Orville Schell, *Mandate of Heaven: The Legacy of Tiananmen Square and the Next Generation of China's Leaders* (New York: Simon & Schuster, 1994), 21–2.

11   Benjamin I. Schwartz, *The World of Thought in Ancient China* (Cambridge, MA: Harvard University Press, 1985), chapter 3.

12   Zhang Dainian with Edmund Ryden, trans., *Key Concepts in Chinese Philosophy* (Beijing: Foreign Languages Press and New Haven, CT: Yale University Press, 2005), 339–40.

on military force and political corruption, indicating a departure from Confucian principles and thus a weakening of leadership. Such a decline would usually be made worse by natural disasters portending this dynasty's loss of the "Mandate of Heaven" (*Tianming*). Subsequently, aggrieved rebels would topple the existing dynasty and establish a new one, establishing their own governing apparatus and reinstalling social order according to the Confucian-Mencian paradigm.

In a Confucian society, while juniors are expected to respect their seniors, the latter also have duties and responsibilities toward the former. Displaying filial piety (*xiao*), children showing respect to their parents, including both the living and the dead, even remote ancestors, is considered among the greatest of virtues.[13] Confucianism also urges all people to become "elevated persons" who should act as moral leaders in society. A gentleman should cultivate himself morally, show filial piety and loyalty where these are due, and cultivate humanity. Confucius is regarded as the standard-bearer of the perfect gentleman.[14]

The Confucian-Mencian paradigm is a complex system of moral, social, political, philosophical, and quasi-religious thought. During the Han dynasty, it was adapted as the ruling ideology, and Confucian books became classics. The Confucian idea of meritocracy in part resulted in the introduction of the imperial examination system in traditional China, a system that can be traced back to 165 BCE. At that time, when the Han emperor called some candidates for public office to the capital for an examination of their knowledge of the classics, the examination was an irregular system of gaining office and an alternative to the existing system of appointment and recommendation of officials.

Upon the destruction of the Han dynasty in 220 CE, China entered a period of political uncertainty and instability known as the Era of Division (220–589 CE), during which several dynasties rose and fell in rapid succession. The promise of Confucianism, as exemplified by the nascent imperial examination system, was largely based on the idea that studying the classics would lead a person to gain stature as an official within the dynastic system. Yet the political chaos of the Era of Division made this kind of administrative career seem much less promising. In this context, the Chinese began to turn toward new interpretations of Daoism, an ideology that had gained favor in the Spring and Autumn period and stressed the importance of human attempts to live in harmony with the natural ebb and flow of things, the natural "way" (*dao*), as well as to other new religions and political ideologies. One of these was Buddhism, a religion associated with the story of the life of the Buddha Siddharta Gautama (*ca.* 480–*ca.* 400 BC), an heir to a local ruling clan called the Śakyas who controlled an area near the modern-day border of India and Nepal. Integral to the Buddha's teachings are the Four Noble Truths: namely, that life is full of pain and suffering; that our worldly desires are the cause of this pain and suffering; that if we are able to eliminate our desires, we can also eliminate these complications; and that the elimination of our worldly desires can be accomplished by compassionately following the "Eightfold Path" (right view, right intention, right speech, right action, right livelihood, right effort, right mindfulness, right concentration).

Though legend holds that Buddhism reached China in 68 CE after Emperor Ming of the Han dynasty had a dream that inspired him to establish and patronize the White Horse Monastery in Luoyang, little evidence exists to substantiate this tale. However, monks lived in Luoyang by about this

---

13   Yi Sun, "Explaining Female Suicides: An Analytical Study of the Cases at the Maple Women's Hotline Center," *American Review of China Studies* 5, nos. 1–2 (Spring and Fall 2004): 25–43.

14   Confucius, *Analects*, trans. Edward Slingerland (Indianapolis, IN: Hackett, 2006), xvii.

time, and images of the Buddha in the Mahao cave-tombs in Sichuan province and at Mount Kongwang in Jiangsu province point definitively to the existence of Buddhist iconography—if not concrete Buddhist doctrine—by the second century CE. Buddhist doctrine became integrated into Chinese political and cultural life during the time of the Emperor Sun Quan (182–252 CE) of the Eastern Wu kingdom (one of the Three Kingdoms, 222–280 CE). During this period, Kang Senghui (d. 280 CE), a merchant of Central Asian origins who had been born in Jiaozhi near modern-day Hanoi, travelled to the Eastern Wu capital at Jiankang and presented the emperor with sutras and relics. This Buddhist influence was further expanded in what is now the northern part of China during the time of Emperor Xiaowen of the Northern Wei dynasty (467–499 CE), during which large statues, stelae, and inscriptions were constructed in caves at Longmen, not far from the city of Luoyang.

However, by the time of the Sui dynasty (581–618 CE), Confucianism became more firmly reestablished and operated as an ideology alongside Buddhism. The national civil service examination system had been used to test knowledge of Confucianism. However, the Sui dynasty did not survive the second emperor, who continued construction of lavish palaces and foreign expeditions. Finding their burdens unbearable, the farmers rebelled, dealing a fatal blow to the Sui regime. Li Yuan, one of the rebel leaders, assumed the imperial title at Chang'an and called his new regime the Tang dynasty (618–907 CE).

The Tang emperors carried on the civil examination system to recruit officials for the central and local governments. They believed that this impersonal method of recruiting based on meritocracy would provide a large national pool for the administrative positions and allow "new talents" to rise in office.

The Tang dynasty, however, also represented the apogee of the transmission of Buddhism, which enjoyed considerable state support. Numerous Sinicized interpretations of Buddhism had proliferated. Though many of the basic texts were translated from Sanskrit and brought back from India through the work of Indian monks and Chinese travelers to India, such as Faxian (337–*ca.* 422 CE) and Xuanzang (602–664 CE), Chinese monks increasingly derived texts and doctrine in Chinese. They also encouraged the development of different sects of Buddhism, each roughly following the *Mahayana* (Greater Vehicle) interpretation of Buddhism, which afforded a greater place for lay participation in Buddhism than other interpretations of Buddhist doctrine. In this context, schools of Buddhism such as Chan (meditation) and Pure Land Buddhism thrived.

While the Tang dynasty became a haven for flourishing Buddhism, the Song dynasty was noted for its remarkable revival of Confucianism in the hands of Zhu Xi (1130–1200 CE), the greatest Confucian master of the day. He combined commentaries on classical Confucian texts with sensibilities and insights that may have been borrowed from Buddhism and Daoism. He developed methods and paths to achieve goodness or become a gentleman as Confucius and Mencius summarized in the Four Books.[15] His contemporaries' focus on the cultivation of virtue helped students to prepare for their civil service examination. The imperial examination system based on the Confucian-Mencian paradigm had been well established by the Song dynasty and continued until it was abolished in 1905. Theoretically, by passing this exam, anyone who wished to become an official would have that opportunity at the provincial or national level, bringing honor and wealth to his whole family. The Neo-Confucian emphasis on personal virtue and social order, strongly advocated by Zhu Xi, and strengthened

---

15 Ebrey and Walthall, *Pre-Modern East Asia*, 140–1.

through the civil exam system, led to the domination of the civilian bureaucracy in military affairs during the Song dynasty. Such a development, however, proved to be a double-edged sword, as it contributed to the Song army's defeats by the invading Mongol troops. In 1279, the Mongols destroyed the Chinese army, ended the Song dynasty, and established the Yuan dynasty (1279–1644 CE). Despite their aversion to Han Chinese traditions, the Mongol emperors of the Yuan court adopted Zhu Xi's commentaries on the Four Books for the civil service examinations in 1315.

The Confucian-Mencian paradigm not only influenced China, but also Korea, Japan, and Vietnam during their classic and Middle Ages through international trade, travel, and cultural exchanges in East Asia. During the Yamato period in Japan, several rulers sent their emissaries to China to gain Chinese confirmation of their dominance. Upon their return to Japan, they brought back knowledge of Confucianism, Buddhism, and the Chinese administrative system. In addition, after the Silla kingdom conquered its rivals in Korea, many war refugees refused to accept the unified Silla government and fled to Japan. Among them were many learned officials and the best-educated scholars, who brought the Confucian philosophy and imperial administrative experience to Japan.[16]

Japan started its classic period by accepting the Chinese elite culture, including the Sinicized version of Buddhism, Confucianism, Daoism, written language, literary arts, painting, and music through the Nara era (710–794 CE). By then Prince Shotoku had organized the writing of the first history book of Japan by following the Chinese imperial model. During the Heian era (794–1185 CE), Japanese pilgrims to Tang China brought back massive numbers of Chinese books.[17] With the spread of printing technology, Confucianism reached more Japanese

people, which reached 10 million by the end of the Fujiwara era (900–1050 CE), one that premodern Japanese historians described as a peaceful golden age of court culture. Confucianism continued to enjoy the support of Japanese rulers; it promoted aristocratic culture, strengthened the social hierarchy, and justified the inequality between men and women.

Tang, an exceedingly successful Chinese dynasty in both cultural advances and influence abroad, found Unified Silla a docile neighbor, unlike the defiant and militant Koguryo. Since most of Koguryo's northern territory was occupied by Tang and Balhae, Unified Silla was hardly in a position to challenge the power of Tang. As a result, a fairly stable equilibrium developed in the region, and normal relations between two states were restored. As exchanges between the two governments increased, Tang's cultural influence in Silla became even more pervasive. Korea's cultural sinicization had begun in earnest; sending offspring to Tang for study became popular in the ruling classes of the Unified Silla. It was during this period that Confucianism was formally introduced into Korea.

In 918 CE, the country was renamed Koryo. By the tenth century, a distinctively Korean type of state was firmly rooted. Koryo's fundamental policy was to maintain a friendly relationship with its powerful neighbor, as evidenced by its close diplomatic ties to the Five Dynasties and Song. Koryo resumed Silla's pro-China policy with little revision. During the early period of its dynasty, Koryo adopted militant policies toward the northern nomadic tribes. It intensified its defense along the northern border by adding garrisons. It also undertook the major construction of the old capital, Pyongyang. Despite later changes and the Mongol occupation from 1231 to 1392 CE, this Korean polity endured until modern times. Printing became popular during the Koryo

---

16   Conrad Totman, *Japan before Perry: A Short History* (Berkeley: University of California Press, 1981), 32–3.

17   Mikiso Hane, *Premodern Japan: A Historical Survey* (Boulder, CO: Westview, 1991), 48–9.

period and was adopted by both Confucians and Buddhists to make their books available. In 1344, the Four Books became a subject of study in Koryo. After the Mongols left, the Koreans established their own state, the Choson dynasty (1392–1910 CE), achieving one of the longest reigns by a single dynasty in world history.

Meanwhile, in 939 CE, Vietnamese forces under the leadership of Ngo Quyen took advantage of a civil war in China, and defeated Chinese occupation troops. Over the course of the next sixty years, several local strongmen vied to produce a lasting dynasty without success. Finally, in 1010 CE, the first Vietnamese dynasty, the Ly dynasty, was established. It ruled the country from 1010 to 1225 CE, followed by the Tran dynasty, which ruled between 1225 and 1400 CE. Ly and Tran kings were faced with numerous challenges in establishing consistent governance over what is now the northern part of Vietnam. First, they were always vulnerable to attack from Chinese or Mongol dynasties to the North who attempted to reintegrate Vietnam into a Chinese empire. Such attacks occurred in 1076 CE under the Song, and in 1258, 1285, and 1287 CE under the Yuan (Mongols). Second, they were reliant on the support of other powerful Han-Viet families of the Red River delta area for their continued existence. That support was usually codified through marriage alliances, but these brokered marriages made these dynasties vulnerable to the power accumulated by the maternal clans of the Kings. Third, they relied on the support and political legitimacy given to them by Buddhist monasteries, but maintaining such support required not only patronage of these monasteries but also tax exemptions for monastic landholdings, which increased the fiscal burdens on these regimes. Fourth, Ly and Tran kings sought to increase their territorial control

and taxation to make up for exemptions, but these moves made them vulnerable to populations in the South, possibly associated with what we would today call Muong people, who resisted the control of elite families from the Hanoi area. It also made them vulnerable to attack from the various Cham states, who were wary of Vietnamese encroachments into the areas of what is now central Vietnam that was previously their territory, resulting in multiple, long, and costly wars with the Chams, as occurred in 1075 to 1104 CE and again from 1367 to 1396 CE.

In the midst of these considerable challenges, Ly and Tran kings sought ideological legitimacy through positioning themselves as both Buddhist and Confucian monarchs. King Tran Thai Tong (1218–1277 CE) had read numerous texts of the Chan (Vietnamese: *Thien*) or meditation school of Buddhism, particularly the writings of the Chinese Chan patriarch Huineng (638–713 CE). In keeping with Chan ideas, but also integrating other current themes in Chinese Buddhism, he wrote a number of tracts and essays. Building on this material, Tran Thai Tong's grandson established a state-sponsored royal Buddhist sect called the Truc Lam (Bamboo Grove) School.[18] This further legitimated the Tran monarchs as powerful transmitters of the wisdom of the Buddha.

At the same time, the Ly and Tran dynasties sought legitimacy among the Han-Viet elites through establishing, if irregularly, civil service examinations. However, these examinations were not strictly Confucian. The imperial annals record that in 1075 CE, a "test of the three schools of Confucianism" was established for the primary purpose of recruiting literate officials.[19] This was followed by an examination on the "three religions" of Buddhism, Daoism, and Confucianism in 1096 CE. In total the Ly dynasty held seven events that

---

18   Keith W. Taylor, *A History of the Vietnamese* (New York: Cambridge University Press, 2013), 117.

19   The "three schools" being referred to here is likely the ancient tradition of the "five classics" tradition, the Zhu Xi school, and the Wang Yangming school. However, since Wang Yangming's birth was in the distant future at the time, perhaps "Three

could loosely be called civil service examinations, though their content varied widely. During the Tran dynasty, the civil service examinations became more consistent and became much more similar to the neo-Confucian examinations of Song dynasty China then the more loosely organized "three religions" examinations of the Ly. In 1246 CE the Tran dynasty declared that palace examinations, the highest of the civil service examinations, would be held once every seven years.[20] In 1253 CE the *Quoc Hoc* (National Academy) was established. It featured images of the Duke of Zhou, Confucius, Mencius, and the seventy-two disciples of Confucius for public veneration.

The influence of the Confucian-Mencian system throughout East Asia meant that a wide swath of the population established a common understanding of how to strive for humaneness, loyalty, sincerity, and benevolence, values that were taught not only by Confucian scholars but also by parents, grandparents, and relatives, and which provided norms for social conduct. Moreover, the dissemination of texts in classical Chinese ensured that the educated elite throughout East Asia could understand these ideas by reading the same texts in a common language. The common understanding of society provided by the Confucian-Mencian system, coupled with the possibility, at least for men, of being able to climb a "ladder of success" based on learning the classics, was a powerful legitimating ideology that was used by most subsequent governments in China, Japan, Korea, and Vietnam. Governments in East Asia used this idealization of past practices as a social and political ethos. The balanced nature of Confucianism may help explain its popularity and success

in East Asian during the past 2,500 years. The Confucian-Mencian paradigm also had an impact on Western Europe. The works of Confucius were translated into European languages through the agency of Jesuit scholars stationed in China. Matteo Ricci (1552–1610 CE) developed a positive view of Confucianism as a "natural religion" in order to legitimate his belief that Chinese intellectuals were ripe for conversion to Christianity, and the life and works of Confucius were translated into Latin in 1687 CE.

The Tribute System in East Asia

To cope with the international relations in East Asia, a tribute system was formed for conducting diplomatic and trade relations between China and other countries and steppe kingdoms such as Xiongnu from the third through eighteenth centuries. However, the outlines of this system were also evident in earlier times. Under this system exchanges of gifts between foreign rulers and the Chinese emperor were carried out. Foreign rulers, including Japanese, Koreans, and Vietnamese, saw advantages to seeking a mutual relationship with the Chinese empire. They sent their representatives to the Chinese capital to present their tributes (exotic luxury goods, local special products, or people) to the Chinese emperor, and in return, they were rewarded with promises and gifts from the Chinese emperor, such as political recognition, nonaggression agreements, and gifts like porcelain and silk.[21]

The symbolism of the tribute system ensured that the Chinese emperor and the Middle Kingdom

---

Schools" here refers to a Tang-style Examination, and perhaps the "three schools" reflect Buddhist and Daoist influence on the curriculum.

20   Ngô Sĩ Liên, ed., *Đại Việt Sử Ký Toàn Thư* [Complete Record of the History of Đại Việt] (Hanoi: Khoa Học Xã Hội, 1993), IV, 15a–15b.

21   David C. Kang, *East Asia before the West: Five Centuries of Trade and Tribute* (New York: Columbia University Press, 2012), chapters 1–2.

would be regarded as superior to their trading partners. Under this system the Chinese emperor recognized the authority and sovereignty of foreign monarchs. He conferred upon them the trappings of legitimacy. In exchange, rulers from foreign lands, adopting a posture of subjugation, recognized the supremacy of the Chinese emperor and the legitimacy of universal civilization as understood within the Confucian-Mencian paradigm. This suzerainty over neighboring lands afforded exclusive trading conditions between East Asian countries and implied military protection to the subordinate states on the part of China.

The system was not only to help establish the diplomatic relationship between China and other countries but also to promote large-scale commerce and trade between Chinese and foreign nations. The term "tribute" was different from the term "gift." Under such a system, the asymmetrical power relations between China as the Middle Kingdom and its surrounding subordinate states were clear. Power diminished with the cultural and geographical distance from the Middle Kingdom, so that Korea and Vietnam were placed higher than others, including Japan, the Ryukyus, and other Indochinese kingdoms that also gave tribute.[22]

Imperial China began to receive tribute from other kingdoms under the influence of Confucian-Mencian civilization. During the Han dynasty, the various tribes of Japan had already established the tribute relationships with China by the first century. During the reign of Han Wudi (the Martial Emperor, 141–87 BCE), the Western Han dynasty replaced a structure of diplomatic ties featuring intermarriage practices with neighboring steppe kingdoms, such as the Xiongnu, and they turned to an early variant of the tribute program. Under the system, the Xiongnu kings or a legitimate representative of them were committed to visit and express reverence to the Han emperors. In this process tribute was paid to China and in return, the Xiongnu kings received presents. Furthermore, the subordinate Xiongnu also was liable to relinquish a hostage from its royal family to the Han regime to ensure that the Xiongnu would not attack China.

The tribute relationship between Korea and China was established during the age of the Three Kingdoms of Korea in the fourth and fifth centuries. This relationship did not end until the Chinese were defeated by the Japanese in the first Sino-Japanese War of 1894–1895. During the Song dynasty, the Chinese court received more than three hundred tribute missions from other countries.

Under the Ming dynasty (1368–1644), countries that attempted to establish political, economic, and cultural relationships with the powerful Chinese empire had to enter the tribute system. Thus, tribute was often paid for practical objectives, instead of only as a sign of devotion to the Chinese emperor. To keep it official, for a short period, the tribute was actually the only existing element of foreign trade for China. Hongwu (reigned 1368–1398), the first Ming emperor, prohibited any private foreign trade in 1371. To increase the number of tribute states, the Yongle Emperor (1403–1424), expanded the tribute system by dispatching massive overseas missions to the South Seas in the early fifteenth century. Zheng He's (1371–1435) overseas expeditions carrying goods to build tribute relationships between the Ming and newly discovered kingdoms in Southeast Asia, South Asia, and Eastern Africa was one of the successful stories.

Between 1405 and 1433, as an imperial official, naval admiral, diplomat, and eunuch of the Ming dynasty, Zheng He made seven voyages to the Western seas. After the Yongle Emperor gained the throne in 1402, Zheng He was promoted to Grand Director of the Directorate of Palace Servants, the highest position of all eunuchs. In that year, Zheng was appointed as the admiral in charge of a huge

---

22 Andressen, *A Short History of Japan*, 62–3.

FIGURE 1.2 China

fleet, armed forces, and shipyards near Nanjing for undertaking the emperor's overseas expeditions.[23] Over two thousand vessels were built under Zheng He's command from 1404 to 1419, including a hundred big "treasure ships," approximately 370 to 440 feet in length and 150 to 180 feet abeam. The average loading capacity is estimated to have been about three thousand tons stern—post rudders,

they might have as many as fifty cabins and be capable of carrying 450 to 500 men each.

In June 1405, Admiral Zheng He embarked on his first voyage with over two hundred vessels, of which sixty-two were treasure ships, carrying silk, porcelain, gold, and 26,800 men. His fleet sailed west to Vietnam, Java, Bengal, and India. Between 1407 and 1411, Zheng made two more voyages to Central and West Asian countries. One of the principal functions of

---

23 Xiaobing Li, *Modern China: Understanding the Modern Nation* (Santa Barbara, CA: ABC-CLIO, 2015), history chapters.

his expeditions was to carry tribute envoys to China and back home. His fourth voyage from 1413 to 1415 CE reached many ports on the east coast of Africa, as far south as Malindi (near modern-day Mombasa, Kenya). From 1417 to 1422, he made two more voyages, visiting and revisiting thirty countries in East Africa, the Persian Gulf, Arabia, and the Red Sea. A year after Yongle died in 1424, his son the Hongxi Emperor discontinued the oversea voyages. Emperor Xuande (1426–1435) then resumed the expedition by ordering Zheng He to his seventh voyage into the "Western Ocean" (Indian Ocean). After making his seventh and final voyage from 1431 to 1433, Zheng He died in 1435.[24] It would be another thirty-seven years before Portuguese explorers on the west coast of Africa sailed as far south as the Gold Coast, and fifty-nine years before Christopher Columbus set sail with three small vessels totaling 450 tons.

The tribute system had been challenged and interrupted from time to time. During the Han dynasty, for example, Xiongnu came to regard the system as a fraudulent and empty agreement, and chose to utilize the act of tribute with frequency to such effect that it reaped enormous rewards for the subsidiary state. China recognized the disingenuous attitude on the part of Xiongnu and suspended the tribute relationship. Eventually, the tribute status of Xiongnu was restored, but China had displayed its unwillingness to have its diplomatic instrument abused, and acted in kind. In another case, Japan had its membership revoked by Ming China in the fifteenth century for failing to battle piracy effectively in the East China Sea.

In another situation, when there was a war between two tribute states, China was held to its own end of the bargain. The Japanese invasion of Korea in the 1500s is an example of this. Upon the landing of Japanese militants throughout southeast Korea, the vassal state requested prompt intervention on the part of Ming China in recognition of the binding tradition between the two. Korea had long been most faithful to the Chinese in the tribute system. The two countries had been closely connected since Korea became independent during the disunity of the third through fifth centuries, and China realized that the time had come to uphold its agreement. However, the Ming government was also in the tenuous position of needing to determine the actual nature of events. Was Korea participating in an act of intrigue and treachery? If this were so, China, in rushing to Korea's ostensible defense, risked walking into a devastating ambush on the long and channelized peninsula. Ming China also was grappling with an upheaval in Ningxia, on the northwestern border, which was represented by several treasonous Ming military officers.

The Ming emperor, Wanli, relented to the Korean calls for assistance by sending a precursory mercenary force to establish a presence in Korea and procure funds to be directed to the defense of the tribute state. In addition, Wanli ordered other elements of his standing military to begin preparation and training for the defense immediately. In time, the Chinese alliance made the difference on the peninsula after a long occupation. China's stout response may have been more robust in this particular circumstance than what would be observed at another place and time. As stated above, Japan had once been subordinate in China's tribute system but was expelled. China was adamant that Japan was to be punished for endeavoring to undermine its status on the mainland, and besides, an invasion of the Asian mainland was a direct challenge to China's own security in the event. After all, the tribute system was China's way of expressing suzerainty and being assured of its regional hegemony. It also was China's way of knowing its neighbors. Ming China's approach to official relations with the Portuguese specifically hinged upon knowledge it gained from a tribute vassal; because the Portuguese invaded

---

24 Gavin Menzies, *1421: The Year China Discovered America* (New York: Perennial, 2003), 64–5, 105–6, 455–6.

Malacca during its conquests in the sixteenth century, the Ming chose not to enter into a diplomatic agreement with them.

Doubtlessly, Korea's vassalage bought its fealty to China, as twice it refused to ally with Japan against the Chinese during Japan's late-sixteenth century invasion. Earlier, in 1373, Korea requested gunpowder from the Ming emperor for its coastal defense against Japanese pirates. These defenses were effective against seafaring threats for two decades. In addition, fourteenth-century Korean general Yi Songgye refused orders to attack Ming China from the sitting Korean king, acting in league with the Mongols.[25] Coincidentally the Choson dynasty (1392–1910), later founded by Songgye, came to be Korea's longest-lived governmental rule. Regardless of the leadership concerned, China profited from the stable society that rose from loyal vassalage and content neighbors, which in turn alleviated stress on its militaries, as was its goal with the tribute system.

The Chinese tribute system continued until the Qing dynasty (1644–1912) when European merchants began arriving in large numbers. Because the Confucian culture placed a greater reward on noneconomic functions than extra profit, the Chinese preferred to continue tribute customs even when the Western merchants began to arrive at the China coast to trade. China was willing and able to extend to Westerners, as "men from afar," a number of concessions and a certain amount of flexibility in meeting Qing requirements.[26] Since Westerners were used to the free market and free trade system, and the Imperial Chinese customs to control trade were not productive and noneconomic, the Europeans complained that they could not trade with Chinese merchants in such a way. The Europeans were not pleased with the tribute system, and the Chinese government refused to compromise with them, because the Qing dynasty did not see any clear advantage to establishing special relations with Europeans outside of the tribute system. Thus, Sino-Western trade was limited in the nineteenth century. Finally, the Europeans used military means to force the Qing government to open China's door to trade with the West in the First Opium War of 1839–1842.

---

25 Seth, *A Concise History of Korea*, 122–4.

26 James L. Hevia, *Cherishing Men from Afar: Qing Guest Ritual and the McCartney Embassy of 1793* (Durham, NC: Duke University Press, 1995).

Chapter 2

The Emergence of the Early East Asian Modern

Before the European expansion of the 1500s, East Asian countries had established centralized dynasties to control their territories, maintained certain social orders, and developed domestic and international trade. Territoriality played an important role for the monarchical governments in the 1500s–1800s, like the Qing dynasty in China, the Tokugawa Bakufu, the Trinh and Nguyen clans in Vietnam, and Choson Korea, to prove their legitimacy and authority, and justify their military expansion and social control. According to Charles S. Maier, the term *territoriality* can be defined historically as bordered space (and the properties) under certain political control.[1] In the modern European system of nation-states, "territoriality was the basis of establishing national identity, demarcating state boundaries, and conducting international relations." Yet, Xiaoyuan Liu asserts, "Territoriality did not start in modern time and was not a European specialty."[2]

In premodern East Asian history, before the full-scale incursion of Western powers, according to Liu, all East Asian states inside the Sino-centric tributary system possessed territoriality, even though such territoriality differed drastically from the modern/European type. After the mid-nineteenth century, Western powers achieved predominance in East Asia and thus an "era of negotiations" began, in which Western international relations and culture coexisted with, penetrated, oppressed, and eventually superseded the tributary system of East Asia's own.[3] In the meantime, modern transformation began for Japan, China, Vietnam, and Korea.

Therefore, although there are apparent resemblances between certain practices of ancient East Asian interstate systems and modern European international systems, their essential dissimilarities are more obvious. They have two modes of international conceptions of international relations based on totally

---

1 Charles S. Maier, "Consigning the Twentieth Century to History: Alternatives for the Modern Era," *American Historical Review* 105, no. 3 (June 2000): 807–31.

2 Xiaoyuan Liu, "From Five 'Imperial Domains' to a 'Chinese Nation': A Perceptual and Political Transformation in Recent History," in *Ethnic China: Identity, Assimilation, and Resistance*, eds. Xiaobing Li and Patrick Fuliang Shan (Lanham, MD: Lexington Books, 2015), 4.

3 Takeshi Hamashita, "Tribute and Treaties: Maritime Asia and Treaty Port Networks in the Era of Negotiation, 1800–1900," in *The Resurgence of East Asia: 500, 150 and 50 years perspectives*, eds. Giovanni Arrighi, Takeshi Hamashita, and Mark Selden (London, UK: Routledge, 2003): 17–50.

different conceptions. In the East Asian system, the varied ranking positions of states were associated with various conditions of territoriality. For China, a ruler could not establish his unified dynasty until he controlled the Central Plain, a vast fertile farming land from the Great Wall in the north to the Yangzi River delta in the south. When such a Central-Plain dynasty endured, Chinese territoriality, which some scholars call "the tribute system," featured not only the imperial government's direct control of people and land but also the emperor's awe and "fencing dependencies" along the outer margins of the dynastic power realm. Liu concludes, "Territoriality of pre-modern China emphasized ambiguous, unstable, and even arbitrary borderlines or frontier zones, marking only roughly the geographical reach of imperial influence. Such traditional boundaries were far from clear evidence to adequately demonstrate the nature of relations between the Qing dynasty and its peripheral regimes."[4]

Qing's Military and Territorial Expansion

The Qing dynasty, also known as the Manchu dynasty, was the last imperial dynasty of China, ruling from 1644 to 1911. It was preceded by the Ming dynasty (1368–1644) and followed by the Republic of China (ROC). The Manchu clan Aisin Gioro founded the dynasty in what is today northeastern China (also known as Manchuria). Originally established as the Later Jin, the dynasty changed its name to Qing in 1636. In 1644 Beijing, the capital city of the Ming dynasty, was sacked by a coalition of rebel forces led by Li Zicheng (1605–1645), a minor Ming official turned leader of the peasant revolt. The last Ming emperor Chongzhen (reigned 1628–1644) committed suicide when the city fell, marking the official end of the dynasty. The Manchus then allied with Ming general Wu Sangui and seized control of Beijing, overthrowing Li's peasant government. The Manchu Banner Army, two hundred thousand strong at the time, continued its military expeditions against uprisings, such as the Three Princes' Rebellion in 1681–1683 and the Eight Trigrams Rebellion in 1813–1815, and expanded into China proper and surrounding territories, including Taiwan, Tibet, Mongolia, and Xinjiang, through the seventeenth and eighteenth centuries.

The Qing emperors viewed political territory and territorial expansion as an outlet of imperial rulers' aspirations. The development of the Qing territory can be divided into two broad periods separated by the First Opium War. The early Qing emperors such as Kangxi (r. 1661–1722) and Qianlong (r. 1736–1795) adopted an aggressive policy toward neighboring kingdoms and continuously used military forces for territorial expansions in all the directions.

Having successfully suppressed the Three Princes' Rebellion in the south, Emperor Kangxi turned his attention to Taiwan, which Ming's troops had occupied since 1662. The Dutch colonized Taiwan in 1624, and called the island Formosa. In 1661, Zheng Chenggong, a Ming general who resisted the Qing army and fled the mainland with his troops, expelled the Dutch colonial administration. Zheng, however, died only four months after he took over Taiwan. His son, Zheng Jing, became the commander of the Ming's remnants on the island. In 1683 Kangxi assembled a fleet of three hundred vessels and appointed Admiral Shi Lang as the commander to attack Taiwan. Shi first destroyed Zheng's naval force around the Penghu Islands, and then landed at Taiwan. The garrison surrendered three months later. In 1684 Kangxi placed Taiwan under the Qing jurisdiction as a prefecture of Fujian Province.

---

4   Liu, "From Five 'Imperial Domains' to a 'Chinese Nation'," 7.

In the meantime the Qing army launched numerous offensive campaigns into Xinjiang and Mongolia. Toward the end of the seventeenth century, the Qing government sent troops three times to attack the Jungar (Dzungars) Mongolian tribes west of the desert land on the Mongolian Plateau. Kangxi gained control of Outer Mongolia, which became an important part of the Qing empire. Then the emperor launched several major expeditions to continue his war against the Jungars in Xinjiang. Eventually, Emperor Qianlong won the war after Kangxi. More than six hundred thousand Jungars died during the war. In 1759, the Qing took full control of the Tarim Basin in Xinjiang. Thereafter, more and more Han Chinese and Muslims settled in the Tarim Basin.

In the eighteenth century, the Qing dynasty established political and territorial control of Tibet in the west. By the 1700s, Tibetan Buddhism had been well established as a regional political, economic, religious, and social institution.[5] The political centralization resulted from the consequences of the Tibetan Buddhist conception of kingship, and it created a regional cult of royal authority. It was the role of the Dalai and Panchen Lamas to establish personal relationships of trust and loyalty with the numerous local leaders in order to incorporate them into the center. This integrated system worked for the Tibetans to choose their own leaders, maintain an independent religion, and sustain a self-supporting economy.[6]

In 1713 Emperor Kangxi granted the title of *Panchen Erdeni* ("Erdeni" meaning "treasure" in Manchu) to the Fifth Panchen Lama (1663–1737).[7] Kangxi also bestowed a gold-gilt album and a seal of authority to Panchen Erdeni. From then on, the status of the Panchen had always been authorized by the central government of the Qing regime, which also made a rule that all succeeding Panchens were to be legalized by going through these formalities.[8] Thus, the process of domesticating local spirits also served to enhance the political authority of the Tibetan government and its control over local powers. It was effective and strong enough for Lhasa to mobilize the Tibetans to defend their territory against British and Russian invasions in the 1880s and 1900s.[9] After the Chinese Nationalist Revolution in 1911, Tibet declared its independence.

As Qing power expanded further north and west in the early eighteenth century, the Banner military system was expanded by Hong Taiji to include Mongolian and Han Chinese Banners. Along its northern frontiers, the Qing government set up strings of *kalun* or checkpoints as a double-edged sword safeguarding both internally and externally. With its eastern neighbor Korea, the Qing government used the Yalu and Tumen Rivers as boundaries, enforcing a rule that "state borders did not permit willful crossing." In the south, along the boundaries with Vietnam running from Guangdong (Canton) to Guangxi to Yunnan, the Qing government established border control installments,

---

5   For more details on the theocratic system, see Jin Hui, ed., *Social History of Tibet; Documented and Illustrated History* (Beijing: China Intercontinental Press, 1995), 52–6.

6   Eva K. Dargyay, *Tibetan Village Community* (Warminster, UK: Aris and Phillips, 1982), 33.

7   Jin Hui, ed., *Social History of Tibet*, 25–6.

8   A complete line of the Panchen Lama from 1385 to the present is included in Appendices III in Wang Furen and Suo Wenqing, *Highlights of Tibetan History* (Beijing: New World Press, 1984), 183.

9   Among the major Tibetan defenses against the Western aggressions were the 1888–1889 battles against Great Britain at Mount Lung-Mdo; the 1904 battle against the British at Rgyal-rtse; and the 1905–1906 struggle against Russia. See Jin Binggao, *Zhongguo minzu yu minzu zhengce* [China's Nationalities and Ethnic Policy] (Beijing: Guojia xingzheng xueyuan chubanshe [State Administrative Studies University Press], 2013), 37.

including mountain passes, checkpoints, inspection dams, fortresses, and patrol camps.[10] Before the Western international system superimposed itself onto East Asia, Emperors Kangxi and Yongzheng had already partially demarcated Qing's northern borders with the Russian Empire with two bilateral treaties. The Treaty of Nerchinsk, signed by Qing and Russia in 1687, was the first treaty between the two disputing nations. The main purpose of the treaty was to restrict Russia from moving into Manchuria. In 1727 the Treaty of Kiakhta was signed between Qing and Russia to define the boundaries at and near Kiakhta.

The Qing dynasty reached its height in the eighteenth century, during which both its territory and population increased dramatically. With its new territorial expansions, the Qing government abandoned its old practice of segregating China proper from the ethnic frontiers and initiated drastic policy changes, including measures for integrating the four imperial constituencies of Manchuria, Mongolia, Xinjiang, and Tibet with China proper. More than fifty nationalities—the Han being the most numerous—lived within the boundary of China. The Qing government established in the capital the Board of Minority Nationalities Affairs for the administration of the frontiers and border regions where such nationalities were concentrated. Generals and ministers were dispatched there to handle military and administrative affairs on behalf of the central government.

Through its early success in unifying China and demarcating borders, the Qing dynasty established

by the Manchus expanded the Central-Plain Empire to well beyond earlier boundaries. As far as territorial control was concerned, the Great Qing Empire was innovative to a certain degree but continued territorial ambiguity as its dynastic predecessors. Differing from "Chinese empires," "Central-Plain Empires" were no longer confined to the Chinese homeland in the Central Plain. Centered in the Central Plain, it incorporated pastoral and forest areas beyond the Great Wall as well. Founders of such empires were no longer limited to the Han-Chinese stock but might come from peoples of the steppes who achieved mastery over the Central Plain. Qing's population reached 432 million in 1851, which constituted about one-third of the world's total population at the time.[11] Yet, such transformation did not end the instability of imperial territories, which expanded or shrunk frequently due to varying administrative policies, military strengths, and local conditions.

The Tokugawa Shogun and the Bakufu System

Japan enjoyed political stability from the 1600s to mid-1800s through the Tokugawa Bakufu system. Before the Tokugawa period (1600–1868), Japan had experienced a feudal agrarian economic system based on local clan alliances that in turn bred constant local warfare from the twelfth to sixteenth centuries. The Middle Period in Japan was an important era that saw the transformation of Japan from a governing bureaucracy loosely modeled after China to a Japanese form of feudalism.[12]

---

10 Li Huazi, *Qingchao yu Chaoxian Guanxishi* [Study of the Relations between the Qing Dynasty and Korea] (Hong Kong: Yazhou chubanshe [Asian Publishing House], 2006), 35–7; Xiao Dehao and Huang Zheng, eds., *Zhong Yue Bianjie Lishi Ziliao Xuanbian* [Selected Historical Materials on the Chinese-Vietnamese Borders] (Beijing: Shehui kexue wenxian chubanshe [Social Science Manuscript and Archival Publishing], 1992), 259–73.

11 The population of China increased from 150 million in 1600, to 300 million in 1800, and 432 million in 1851. See Fairbank, Reischauer, and Craig, *East Asian*, 241–2.

12 The utility of the concept of feudalism by historians generally, and for Japanese history specifically, remains a matter of active debate among historians. For a critique of feudalism that emphasizes the difficulty in arriving at a universally acceptable

FIGURE 2.1 Japan

The country warriors who had been instrumental in protecting the land for the absentee landlords that gathered around the imperial court evolved into an official class in Japanese history—the much-celebrated samurai. Departing from the Chinese system that exhorted the scholar gentry class as the social elites, Japan saw the glorified the samurai as its social elites. By 1600, with a population of twenty million, the Tokugawa social hierarchy clearly had the samurai standing at the very top, followed by peasants, artisans, and merchants.

Within the military rank, the Shogun or governor-general was in firm control, rendering the emperor a figurehead. The over 250 daimyo during

---

definition of the idea, see Elizabeth A. R. Brown, "The Tyranny of a Construction: Feudalism and Historians of Medieval Europe," *American Historical Review* 79, no. 4 (October 1974): 1063–88. For a defense of the utility of feudalism in comparing the history of Japan and Western nations, see Peter Duus, *Feudalism in Japan* (New York: McGraw Hill, 1993).

the Tokugawa period were local lords who functioned as regional governors, at the service of the Shogun. The daimyo owned land, controlled farming labor, and commanded a private force. A daimyo's prestige was measured by the size of the area he controlled and his wealth in terms of rice production and the tax yield of his villages. All lands in Japan were registered according to their productivity by *koku* (about 4.96 bushels). A daimyo had to have a domain of at least ten thousand *koku* by definition. The domain of a shogun/daimyo played the most important role by granting land ownership, recognizing property rights, and rewarding loyal members in the *shoen* (castle). The daimyo's domains became efficient units of local control in a semi-centralized feudalist structure, marking an important difference between Japanese feudalism and its European counterpart.

Dominant in Japanese society was the samurai class, warriors who provided security, ensured social order, and won victories for each shogun. The ethical code (*Bushido*) of samurai was an active force in Japanese society until World War II. Early feudalism's emphasis on loyalty, bravery, stoicism, and martial arts all survived until recent times. Loyalty was central to the whole system, because the feudal structure depended entirely on the personal loyalty of the vassal to his lord and his family. Death was preferred to surrender. The line between the samurai and commoners was strictly maintained. The samurai, who constituted 6 percent of the Japanese population, felt great pride in their status, symbolized by the wearing of two swords, one long and the other short, and an exclusive right to education. A samurai was considered superior to any commoner and had the right to kill a disrespectful commoner on the spot. The samurai system was not unlike European military systems, but it was quite different from military organization in China and other Eastern Asian countries.

Ranked below the samurai were the *kenin* (housemen), peasants who, with little or no land of their own, were the primary producers and the majority in a village. The daimyo derived their wealth from the *kenin* who nonetheless had to pay heavy agricultural taxes, often amounting to 45 or 50 percent of their annual crop yield. While shoguns, daimyo, and samurai lived in the castles, the peasants and other commoners lived in the villages as a semiautonomous tax-paying structure.

Beneath the peasants were the nonfarming laborers such as artisans, and at the very bottom of the hierarchy were the merchants. They were considered less valuable to society since their contribution to an agricultural society was minimal. As the lowest class of society, they belonged to a general "townsmen" category. During the second half of the Tokugawa shogunate, the peasants and merchants became the primary drivers of urban development and cultural life in Japan.

Unlike in European feudalism, no law in Japan required the head of the family to give his property to his oldest son. Instead, the father retained the right to choose any of his sons as heir and, if lacking one, to adopt a son. With over 200 local lords, the wars were mostly between rival nobles over land control and local leadership, though sometimes wars also took place within the same clan. From the thirteenth to the fifteenth century, Japan experienced constant warfare due to weak emperors, local military power, and family conflicts. Since the eighth century, Japanese imperial rule had embraced a convenient tradition: a reliable aristocratic family would take care of all administrative details in the name of the emperor. Although there was only one government, this family did all the practical work. The most well-known was the Fujiwara family whose success lay in its strategy to marry many of its women into the imperial households generation after generation. Consequently the Fujiwara influence over the emperors grew steadily from 794–1185. In the twelfth century, however, the Fujiwara family began to experience internal troubles and external rivalries for political power.

The Kamakura shogunate (1192–1333) and the Ashikaga shogunate (1333–1600) which followed established the Bakufu system, a shogun of all the shoguns, or a federation of shoguns as a military administration and a coalition of military families. In the Bakufu, all the families were to recognize the over-lordship of the leading family, respect each other, and set up some rules to avoid conflicts. However, the Ashikaga shogunate, failing to achieve full military control over Japan, saw the resumption of rampant warfare, eventually leading to the Tokugawa family winning the Battle of Sekigahara in 1600 and subsequently establishing an enduring system of centralized feudalism that lasted over 250 years.

The Tokugawa family owed its victory to the fact that it controlled the largest domain among approximately 245 to 295 different daimyo. Located in the Kanto Plain, the Tokugawa family was single-handedly responsible for a quarter of the rice farming production of the whole country. The Tokugawa shogunate controlled a total of seventeen thousand *kenins* (peasants) and five thousand samurai with firearms as a substantial military power.

In 1600, after Tokugawa Ieyasu crushed his opponents, he was authorized by the court to run the Bakufu with the title of Shogu. In 1603 Ieyasu decided to move the Bakufu to Edo (today's Tokyo) further away from Kyoto, the ancient capital, to make it easier for the Tokugawa to act as a real government. After his retirement in 1605, one of his sons, Tokugawa Hidetada, controlled the country by keeping a tight rein on the coalition of autonomous daimyo. Then, Tokugawa Iemitsu, son of Hidetada, took over in 1623 and continued his father's governing mechanism. After these first three shoguns, the Tokugawa system of government took full shape. In order to control the daimyo and society as a whole, Tokugawa created many rules and laws, rigid social classes, and a highly centralized Bakufu administration.

After almost two hundred years of warfare and prolonged disunity, Tokugawa eventually instituted a centralized control system and provided political and social stability in Japan for the next two hundred fifty years. The pattern of military and political rule established in the early 1600s continued with only minor modifications until the mid-nineteenth century. One of the reasons for the political and social stability was perhaps the relative remoteness of the islands, which made Japan less susceptible to external political pressure. Another is that the Tokugawa sought to insure political stability by limiting social mobility. The population increased from twenty million in 1600 to thirty million in 1721. There were few opportunities for class status changes among the daimyo, samurai, *kenins*, and artisans. All of them had specific hereditary status and subsistence incomes, which changed only under unusual circumstances. The whole feudal system depended on the clear functional division between the commoners and samurai. Meanwhile, the Japanese during the Tokugawa period seemed to develop a strong sense of honor, duty, and obligation. These characteristics spread from the samurai to commoners, and left Japan a legacy of inner discipline, personal drive, and social rigidity.

Nonetheless, the long period of peace and political stability led to the development of domestic trade and commerce. Social stability promoted arts, literature, education, and an urban culture. To some extent, the stringent, sophisticated, and clever control mechanisms ironically gave rise to unintended changes. For instance, the *sankin kotai* system required disloyal daimyo that had fought against the Tokugawa family prior to the Battle of Sekigahara, and deployed to the outskirts of Japan, to come to the Edo periodically for "alternative attendance" along with their samurai entourage, thus compelling them to spend valuable resources on the road and on maintaining a separate residence. The system, by mandating a staggered residence in Edo on the past of disloyal daimyo, and by holding their principal wives and children in Edo essentially as hostages when the daimyo went back to their home domains, was intended to prevent possible collusion among them and thus fend off organized rebellions. The successful implementation of the system, however, had unintended consequences by the second half of the eighteen century. The road system, kept in good repair by the daimyo due to their constant need to travel to Edo from the various parts of Japan, ended up facilitating the development of interregional trade as well as population migration. With the growth of cities, Tokugawa Japan began to experience a flourishing urban culture which, combined with widespread trade, made it possible for merchants to gain some economic clout and worse, yet, the gradual dilution of the class system, the very change that the Tokugawa shogunate tried hard to prevent from happening in the first place. The samurai class itself felt the impact of peace and political unity perhaps most strongly. Absence of warfare made it possible, if not necessary, for some of them to turn increasingly to the hereditary civil bureaucracy, martial arts academies, private schools, trade, and emergent manufacturing. Later, as Japan embarked on its road of modernization, the samurai became the first generation of manufacturing owners when they opened firms and factories in the cities.

Vietnam: Confucian Transformation, Civil War, and Nam Tien (the Southward March) (1407-1650)

Early modern Vietnamese history begins with a Chinese occupation. An expansionist Ming dynasty attacked Vietnam in 1407 and ruled the area until 1427. This occupation returned Vietnam, which then only occupied the northern third of Vietnam's geographic area today, to the situation that had existed for most of the thousand years between 111 BCE and 939 CE, when Vietnam was also administered by various dynasties from China.

This time, however, the Ming occupation continued a fundamental social transformation already underway in Vietnam during the time of the Ho dynasty (1400–1407), which the Ming had overthrown. In the previous four centuries of Vietnamese independent rule under the Ly (1009–1225) and Tran (1225–1400) dynasties, society and politics in the Red River delta area of northern Vietnam had come to be dominated by three groups. The first were powerful extended families (clans), many of whose origins could be traced to the intermarriage between Chinese officials and local indigenous elites in the earlier Chinese period. During the early years of Vietnamese independence, these groups solidified their control over large agricultural estates and secured authority for themselves through intermarriage into the royal line. The second powerful social entity were the religious orders, which played an instrumental role in placing the Ly monarchs in power under a flexible amalgamation of indigenous spirits as well as Confucian, and Buddhist beliefs that Keith Taylor has called "Ly dynasty religion."[13] In return for their support, the Ly and Tran dynasties offered royal patronage to certain sects, supported the construction of monasteries, worked to restore old temples and even offered prominent monks roles in the

---

13   Keith W. Taylor, "Authority and Legitimacy in 11th Century Vietnam," in *Southeast Asia in the 9th to 14th Centuries*, ed. David G. Marr and A.C. Milner (Singapore: Institute of Southeast Asian Studies, 1986), 143. For an updated evaluation of this concept, see Liam C. Kelley, "Constructing Local Narratives: Spirits, Dreams, and Prophecies in the Medieval Red River Delta," in *Chinese Encounters on the South and Southwest: Forging the Fiery Frontier over Two Millenia*, eds. James A. Anderson and John K. Whitmore (Leiden and Boston: Brill, 2015), 78–105.

imperial administration.[14] The third entity was the military, which was a crucial institution not just for securing the defense of the realm from China and from the Cham region but also for the governance of frontier areas.

Ultimately, these three institutions, which created the conditions for Ly and Tran governance, also undermined their ability to govern. Ly governance was decimated by the excessive influence of clans that had married into the imperial line, including their successors the Tran. The Tran attempted to avoid such clan politics by abandoning marriage alliances in favor of enforced royal incest and by devising a system to settle succession disputes while the previous king was still living. While still relying on Buddhist support, the Tran tried to stanch the excessive authority of the monasteries by seeking to produce orthodox Thien/Zen beliefs through the creation of a royal sect of Buddhism, the Truc Lam school. Despite these advances, Tran governance was eventually undermined by rivalry and corruption within their own clan, by the dissatisfaction of a growing Confucian scholar/elite, and by a powerful general, Ho Quy Ly (1336–1407).

Though the Ho dynasty would only last for seven years (1400–1407), it embarked on a series of reforms that would establish a new model for governance that would last through much of the early modern era. The Ho attempted to establish a much more rigorous version of the Confucian civil service examination, restricted the power of large landholders and nobility that had plagued the earlier administrations, and attempted to improve the fiscal health of the kingdom through financial reforms and an extension of the taxation system. These efforts triggered resistance to Ho rule, which could not withstand the onslaught of an expansionist Ming dynasty in China when the Chinese Emperor Yongle (r. 1402–1424) became convinced that the Vietnamese were rebels that needed to be brought under heel. When many of the great families of the Red River delta, who were suffering a decline of their fortunes under the more stringent Ho land and taxation policies, declared allegiance to the Ming, Ming forces won a relatively easy victory in 1407.

During the time of the Ming occupation, the transformation of Vietnamese society from one rooted in the power of Buddhist monasteries and powerful landholding clans in the Red River delta to one based on a Confucian bureaucratic elite continued. Ming administrators proved competent bureaucrats who restored the Vietnamese economy, continued Ho efforts to expand the taxation system, and afforded educated elites the prospect of participating through the civil service examination system in the wider world of Ming governance. These efforts brought the Ming some support among powerful clans, including that of the Mac family, who would become much more important a century later.

Ming rule, however, was not universally popular or beneficial. The Ming enforced orthodoxy in education and governance, leading them to burn "heterodox books," destroying many sources of indigenous Vietnamese knowledge in the process. Moreover, their expansion of taxation and administration into modern-day Thanh Hoa province and into the upland regions triggered a rebellion in those areas from people who had previously enjoyed de facto autonomy. This rebellion, coupled by a waning in Ming will to rule the area, brought the occupation to a close in 1427 under the military leadership of the founder of the Le dynasty, Le Loi (r. 1428–1433).

Under Le rule, the expansion of centralized administration and the Confucian scholar-elite that had been emphasized under the Ho and continued in the Ming occupation continued and gathered considerable momentum. Having gained the confidence of southern and upland peoples through

---

14 James Adams Anderson, "Creating a Border Between China and Vietnam," in *Eurasian Corridors of Interconnection: From the South China to the Caspian Sea*, eds. Susan M. Walcott and Corey Johnson (New York and London, UK: Routledge, 2015), 22.

maintaining the local power of their aristocratic clans, the Le were able to expand the educational system to benefit a much broader range of people and use Ming precedents to organize the government ministries effectively.[15] These developments reached their apex during the reign of Le Thanh Tong (r. 1460–1497); almost 25 percent of all the recipients of the highest degree in the Confucian examination system in Vietnamese history graduated during his reign.[16]

However, Le governance became ineffective after 1497. A series of weak emperors led to power devolving back into the hands of powerful clans. Vietnamese history in the sixteenth century is essentially the story of three of these clans: the Mac, the Trinh, and the Nguyen. The Mac clan, with connections to both the capital at Thang Long (modern-day Hanoi) and the coast, were able to rise to prominence under Mac Dang Dung (1483–1541, r. 1527–1541). At a time of Le political weakness and court intrigue, Mac Dang Dung, a military man and member of the palace guard who had ties to coastal merchants and to prominent intellectuals, was able to parlay that support into taking the throne and establishing the Mac dynasty in 1527. The Mac remain emperors in Hanoi until 1592, when they were ousted and the Le dynasty was restored, but they continued to operate in the far north of the country until at least 1677.

In establishing a new dynasty, the Mac faced competition from two powerful clans that remained loyal to the Le dynasty: the Trinh clan and the Nguyen clan. These two clans were natural allies with one another. Shortly after the Mac dynasty was proclaimed, the Nguyen clan, led by Nguyen Kim, a member of a prominent military family related to the Le dynasty through marriage, sought refuge in Laos to plan attacks against the Mac on behalf of the Le. There, he joined forces with Trinh Kiem, the leader of the Trinh clan. Trinh Kiem was a good strategist that rapidly became Nguyen Kim's most important general; the Trinh and Nguyen families became connected through marriage ties when Trinh Kiem married Nguyen Kim's daughter Ngoc Bao.

However, after Nguyen Kim died in 1545, Trinh Kiem attempted to take control of the pro-Le dynasty opposition to the Mac. He killed Nguyen Kim's eldest son, while allowing Nguyen Kim's younger son, Nguyen Hoang (1525–1613) to live, perhaps only because Nguyen Hoang feigned insanity. In 1558, fearful for her brother Nguyen Hoang's safety, Trinh Kiem's wife Ngoc Bao convinced Trinh Kiem to appoint Nguyen Hoang the governor of Thuan Hoa. Thuan Hoa province is modern-day central Vietnam, including the modern-day city of Hue which would become the Nguyen capital. But in the sixteenth century it was a distant frontier area that until recently had been controlled by various Cham polities.

Nguyen Hoang returned to the north when Trinh Tung forced the Mac to flee the capital and restored the Le dynasty in 1593. However, in 1600, Nguyen Hoang returned to the south permanently. By that time, there were effectively two separate Vietnams, both nominally loyal to the figurehead Le emperor: the southern regime of the Nguyen lords, called Cochinchina by Europeans, with a capital (by 1687) in modern-day Hue, and the northern regime of the Trinh lords, called Tonkin by Europeans, with its capital at modern-day Hanoi.

The Nguyen were able to benefit from a southward migration of Viet peoples seeking better economic opportunities that preceded Nguyen

---

15 John K. Whitmore, "Văn Đồn, the 'Mạc Gap,' and the End of the Jiaozhi Ocean System: Trade and State in Đại Việt, Circa 1450–1550," in *The Tongking Gulf through History*, ed. Nola Cooke, Li Tana, and James A. Anderson (Philadelphia: University of Pennsylvania Press, 2011), 107.

16 Taylor, *A History of the Vietnamese*, 206.

Hoang's move to the south in 1558 but likely accelerated with the Nguyen presence in the south. This southward migration, known as *nam tien* in Vietnamese, was not an organized plan but rather a series of responses to episodes in Vietnamese political and economic history.[17] This migration brought the Vietnamese into new lands with new economic and cultural opportunities. Viets mixed with Chinese, Chams, and Khmers and interacted with Portuguese, Dutch, Japanese, and other Southeast Asian merchants at the thriving commercial port of Hoi An. They enjoyed a government that, while initially run by the military, was much more informal and arguably much more efficient than the Confucian bureaucracy of the north. In Keith W. Taylor's words, the Nguyen inaugurated nothing short of "a new way of being Vietnamese," and this new way involved more profound engagement with Westerners and the wider world than the Vietnamese previously enjoyed.[18]

Meanwhile, society in northern parts of Vietnam was changing as well. After the restoration of the Le dynasty in 1593, the north featured a military government dominated by the Trinh clan, a military dominance necessitated by the warfare of the sixteenth and seventeenth centuries. As a result, Confucian literati declined in influence until the mid-seventeenth century, when they enjoyed an important revival. In the interim, however, new cultural features and religious movements appeared in northern Vietnam. The most significant were a revival of Buddhism and the introduction of Catholicism, which took hold amongst a substantial minority of northern Vietnamese and led to significant contacts with European missionaries.[19]

Between the 1620s, when the Nguyen stopped paying taxes to the north, and the 1670s, the Trinh and Nguyen clans fought an ultimately inconclusive war with one another. The war ended with the tacit acknowledgement that there were now two different regimes, and Vietnamese people in both polities continued to develop their own local practices until the outbreak of the Tay Son wars in the 1770s.

Choson Korea

After the Mongols were driven out of Korea in 1356, the Confucian elite class in Korea established their own state: the Choson (Yi) dynasty (1392–1910). "Their social and political structure withstood all challenges until the twentieth century, achieving one of the longest dominations by a single dynasty in world history."[20] The early period of the Choson dynasty was blessed by unusually productive reigns of several visionary monarchs: Kings Taejong (r. 1392–1398), Sejong, and Sejo (r. 1455–1468). They were all radical reformers and worked a revolution in Korean life. Under the visionary leadership of these kings, the Choson court was able to build a political foundation that supported the dynasty for some five hundred years. Particularly important was the invention of Hangul, the Korean alphabet, by King Sejong and his scholars.[21]

17   Li Tana, *Nguyễn Cochinchina: Southern Vietnam in the Seventeenth and Eighteenth Centuries* (Ithaca, NY: Cornell University Southeast Asia Program Publications, 1998), 19.

18   Keith W. Taylor, "Nguyen Hoang and the Beginning of Viet Nam's Southward Expansion," in *Southeast Asia in the Early Modern Era*, ed. Anthony Reid (Ithaca, NY: Cornell University Press, 1993), 42–65.

19   John K. Whitmore, "Literati Culture and Integration in Dai Viet, c. 1430-c. 1840," *Modern Asian Studies* 31:3 (July 1997): 671–5; K. W. Taylor, "The Literati Revival in Seventeenth-Century Vietnam," *Journal of Southeast Asian Studies* 18, no. 1 (March 1987): 4.

20   Charles K. Armstrong, *The Koreas*, 2nd ed. (London, UK: Routledge, 2014), 7–8.

21   Seth, *A Concise History of Korea*, 177–8.

King Sejong, the fourth monarch and one of the most brilliant in the history of the Chosen dynasty, sympathized with his subjects who were inconvenienced by not having their own alphabet. Contrary to the casual presumption that Korea may share the same language and characters with China, the Korean written language is entirely unrelated to its powerful neighbor. Yet the language did not have its own alphabet; the first Koran alphabets were invented during the Silla dynasty, but their use was restricted to a small number of commoners because of the popularity of the Chinese characters among the country's ruling classes and scholar-officials. Until the Chosen era, the Korean peoples were forced to learn the cumbersome Chinese ideogram if they intended ever to escape illiteracy. In 1443 the King recognized the problem and led his able scholars to invent the Korean alphabet, the *On Mun*, a purely phonetic alphabet that scarcely has its equal in the world for simplicity and phonetic power. Although there were objections from the ruling-scholar community, who monopolized the nation's literary prerogatives, the use of the *On Mun*, later renamed as the Hangul, gradually spread among underprivileged masses and then later to more resistant nobility groups.[22] Today Hangul is Korea's only written language and is used by its over eighty million citizens, making it one of the major alphabets in the world.

The early period of the Choson era turned out to be a precious respite for the Korean people. Not only was it free from characteristic external threats, but it was also replete with many nation-building programs. The early kings centralized state government by creating Confucian-style bureaucracy and offering the civil service examinations at local and national levels. The examination system brought in the great bulk of the bureaucracy and succeeded in recruiting the best talent of the country for government service. During this period, the nation's education system was upgraded and a new tax system was adopted along with various social programs. More and more aristocrats received Confucian education and served in high office. These aristocrats, known as *yangban*, became a power elite group who maintained their political and social predominance through the Choson era. According to Patricia Ebrey, "it was not until the early Joseon [Choson] period that centralization reached the point where magistrates in all of the three-hundred-odd local districts were appointed by the central government."[23]

Unfortunately, most of these programs were narrow in scope and slow in implementation. In spite of good intentions, the Choson court, like its Chinese counterpart, did not realize that it had barely enough time to improve its traditional society before the arrival of the threatening tide of the Europeans. By the time the Western powers were advancing into the region, Choson was still in an antiquated state, far from being able to effectively respond to critical international developments. Even under the leadership of the most knowledgeable Choson court, Korea was not yet fully prepared to utilize the unique geopolitical properties of the Korean peninsula. Still, the region's patent geopolitical game was to be resumed regardless of Korea's poor preparation. This time, however, the problem had become even more compounded by the presence of a strong Japan, and the consequence was more dramatic.

Upwardly mobile newcomers gradually inflated the elite class. Despite dramatic economic growth of the national market system, the complex changes severely strained Choson's political and social

---

22   Rhoads Murphey, *A History of Asia*, 3rd ed. (New York: Longman, 2000), 169.

23   Ebrey and Walthall, *Pre-Modern East Asia*, 250.

system.[24] In the traditional social hierarchy, a caste system divided Korean people into gentry, commoners, and slaves. Now the rise of affluent farmers, powerful merchants, and wealthy industrialists began to undermine the system and challenge the gentry as the ruling class.

After enduring the devastating invasions of both Japan in 1592–1598 and the Manchus in 1627–1629, Choson was given approximately two centuries of respite from foreign invasion. However, Korea "never fully recovered" from these invasions, and the Choson dynasty began to decline.[25] The country had to utilize this rare tranquility to dismantle its medieval society and to prepare itself for the even more rapacious foreign challenges the modern age brought to the region. Even before the Japanese invasion, Choson was experiencing severe economic stresses. The invasions of Japan and the Manchus greatly exacerbated the problems, leading both the court and the farmers into virtual financial collapse. The fact that Hideyoshi's invasion alone had reduced the size of the country's cultivated land to two-thirds of its prewar level clearly illustrates the severity of Choson's economic woes.

During the eighteenth century, domestic factional struggles occurred periodically. Some of the *yangban* scholar-bureaucrats emerged as willing and major participants in the factional political infighting. These conflicts were so intensified that the court was almost paralyzed by the middle of the eighteenth century. Soon the precarious political equilibrium collapsed and another dictatorial power emerged. This time a family related to royalty, the queen's family, grabbed power over contending political factions. Choson entered the fateful nineteenth century with an eleven-year-old monarch amid renewed factional fighting. The Kim family took advantage of the minor monarch by quickly maneuvering to dominate court politics and monopolize most high-level appointments for their family members.[26] The dictatorship of the Kim family represented a reactionary movement to the fragile socioeconomic reforms being pursued by social elite and Korean people.

The Choson court's profound failure to heed the masses was to haunt the entire country for a long time. The pitifully incapable monarchs and manipulative factional courtiers wasted the precious time needed to reform the country. Widespread and chronic corruption in public life, the zealous attachment to the past, and the antireform reactionary factions in the court were some prominent contributors to the failure. This failure, however, was more than a decline in the court's political power; in a sense, it represented a general default of the Choson society itself, particularly of the kingdom political and intellectual traditions. Many different elements of Choson society contributed to this failure, but the most significant may have been the decay of the Confucian tradition, which served as the Choson society's foremost political philosophy, family value, and social and ethical basis.

In traditional times, the prevailing influence of Confucianism shaped Korean women's lives, as well as those of women throughout East Asia. According to the historian Michael Seth, the status of Korean women underwent a period of lengthy decline during the Choson period "from the mid-fifteenth to the mid-eighteenth century largely due to the spread of Chinese Neo-Confucianism to the Korean Peninsula as they "lost the rights to divorce, remarry, and inherit property."[27] Neo-Confucianism, advocated

---

24 James Palais, *Confucian Statecraft and Korean Institutions: Yu Hyongwon and the Late Choson Dynasty* (Seattle: University of Washington Press, 1996), 181–3.

25 Murphey, *A History of Asia*, 170.

26 Seth, *A Concise History of Korea*, 212–13.

27 Michael J. Seth, *A History of Korea: From Antiquity to the Present* (Lanham, MD: Rowman & Littlefield, 2011), 161–4, 184.

by scholars and promoted by Korean rulers intent on maximizing social control, prescribed the "proper" code of conduct for women by emphasizing the need for them to demonstrate "virtue and chastity." It was defined as a woman's willingness to subordinate herself to the male figures in her life—father, husband, and eldest sons (in cases of widowhood), as well as to reject remarrying after the death of her husband in order to maintain her familial loyalty. During the Choson period, men and women lived in separate quarters in upper class households, though such an arrangement was less practical in lower-class families. Generally speaking, not only did the earlier evidence of women serving as heads of household disappear, it was replaced by unprecedented stringency that governed the lives of Korean women. Women's chastity was exhorted to such an extent that a woman was encouraged to commit suicide when confronted with a situation that might compromise her reputation, such as in the case of a sexual attack. It is worth noting that religious women who practiced shamanism and female entertainers were exempt from many of the harsh rules that were imposed on women of other social strata.

The plight of women in the Choson era helped to lay the foundation of women's movements in Korea during the late nineteenth and early twentieth century. As in China during this time period, women's status was seen by some progressive reformers as indicative of Korea's overall backwardness. While Confucianism was seen as the culprit for women's misfortune, education was deemed as their salvation, not so much because it would necessarily bring about gender and social equality but because educated women would be able to better serve the needs of the country. Consequently, the effort at promoting women's education became a major component of more sweeping social and political changes.

Conclusion to Part One

In the premodern era, East Asian cultures took divergent paths. Faced with multiple regions, cultures, and geographies, China oscillated between unification and disunity. Japan established central governments, but those governments operated on top of a highly decentralized clan-based Uji system. In what is now Korea and Vietnam, independent regimes rose but were interrupted by very different Chinese efforts at territorial expansion into their areas.

Despite varied premodern historical experiences, each of these East Asian countries shared certain common political and cultural influences. By examining the Confucian-Mencian system's emphasis on increasing order through learning and inculcating common values of behavior, we can see how the differences between East Asian societies were moderated by some common understandings of family and social relations. Additionally, in these chapters we noted how the Confucian-Mencian system of familial and social relations was mapped onto the tribute system, a system to conduct foreign policy and international relations throughout premodern East Asia. This system understood mutual obligations between nations as part of a system of exchange that ritually bound rulers together as fictive relatives of one another, a system that caused them to incur obligations to one another. Finally, part one described how premodern East Asians shared in common the arrival of Buddhism in the first millennium CE, which changed the East Asian religious landscape, offered new spiritual options, and ultimately also changed the Confucian-Mencian system.

Finally, part one of this book outlined the creation of an East Asian modernity in the early modern period. This is significant insofar as East Asian societies possessed, albeit in very different forms, many of the trappings associated with modernity in Europe. These included a sense of territoriality, centralized bureaucratic administrations, robust and far-reaching domestic and international trade (that resulted in many cases in cosmopolitan trading ports), systems of international relations, and the adaptation of new technologies and weapons systems. These advances, however, produced social and economic changes that presented domestic challenges to East Asian regimes, which were exacerbated by military, social, and economic challenges stemming from interactions with Westerners, as we will see in part two.

PART TWO

Early Modern Contact with the West

Introduction to Part Two

Contact with Western countries was nothing new to East Asians. Regular contacts between Asians and Europeans can be dated to at least the inception of Silk Road trading routes well before the beginning of the Common Era. However, by the sixteenth and seventeenth centuries, East Asians experienced new patterns of trade and interaction with Westerners. Missionaries arrived in greater numbers, eager to convert East Asians to Christianity. With the advent of ships—both East Asian and Western—which could sail long distances across wide expanses of the globe, new patterns of trade emerged with European nations, starting with Spain and Portugal, with the Netherlands and Great Britain following close behind.

East Asians were active participants, and not merely passive responders, in shaping these changes in the global economics and cultures of the early modern era. However, different areas approached these changes differently. By the nineteenth century, the Chinese proved themselves unsuccessful at adapting to changes in global political and economic trends that would keep their governing systems intact. Japan, on the other hand, adapted to these changes in the nineteenth century by essentially coopting Western military, political, and economic forms, while Korea and Vietnam experienced a mix of strategies of resistance and reform.

This section of East Asia and the West demonstrates that, by the nineteenth century, three trends shaped the development of modernity in East Asia. The first was a slow economic transition toward the development of manufacturing and trading economies and away from economies focused mainly on agriculture, which in turn altered the relationship between states and their populations. The second was a slow political transition occasioned in part by the economic changes; in areas in which political changes were made more slowly, such as China, economic progress was impeded. The third was a cultural shift in the perception of the world outside East Asia, which contributed to the rise of nationalism across East Asian polities by the nineteenth century.

Chapter 3

Adjusting to the West

Trade, Technology, and Christianity

By the middle of the eighteenth century, the Western maritime powers had made their presence felt throughout East Asia. The Europeans rushed to East Asia with a spirit of adventure, fueled primarily by the search for lucrative trading opportunities. To a lesser extent, they were also motivated by the evangelical zeal to spread Christianity to the "heathen" world.[1] Thus, Western nationals often used Christianity to cover their true intention of commercial profit. Because of its complexity and international dimension, the European commercial and evangelical pursuit became an ultimate political test for all the East Asian countries. D. E. Mungello points out "during the period 1500–1800, the flow of influence between East and West was not constant. Rather, it ebbed and flowed."[2]

In its initial thrust into the region, the primary focus of the West was on China, a Confucian and agrarian kingdom with largely untapped natural resources. The Europeans projected the country of over three hundred million potential consumers to become the largest market for their industrial products. In addition, European traders were aware of the fact that China was the world's premier producer of popular trade items such as tea, jewelry, silk, and ceramic wares, which were much desired by their affluent clients. At that time, the Ming (1368–1644) was merely an old dynasty undergoing a rapid decline. Overconfident and patient with its periodic invaders, the Ming were at the same time too disorganized to fend off a determined West. Although China made some tentative attempts at adopting Western ideas and practices, there was no serious interest in moving toward any major institutional reform or reorganization at that time. This failure proved to be tragic for China in a subsequent dynasty, and one that provided a learning lesson for Japan in the second half of the nineteenth century.

Out of the diversity, some East Asian responses to European trade and the introduction of Christianity proved successful. In Japan, the ruling class adopted a much more pragmatic and effective approach to the challenge than the isolationism in East Asia. Both Vietnam and Korea had a mixed experience. In these two cases, leaders oscillated between cooperation and confrontation with European trade, Christianity, and Western technology.

---

1 Immanuel C. Y. Hsu, *The Rise of Modern China*, 6th ed. (Oxford, UK: Oxford University Press, 2000), 122.

2 D. E. Mungello, *The Great Encounter of China and the West, 1500–1800*, 4th ed. (Lanham, MD: Rowman & Littlefield, 2013), 9.

The chapter examines three key factors that had transformed Eastern Asian economy from an agrarian economy to a manufacturing one and from a traditional state to a modern nation. First, our analysis focuses on social elements, including human resources available for economic transformation, social values and relations affected each state as an institution, and public interests and concerns in political reforms. The East Asian governments were firmly entrenched in their tradition and social structure. It takes time for major transition and significant changes to be made manifest.

The second element leading East Asian countries toward modernity was the impediments to economic and social reform in the context of backward technology, poor living standards, lack of education, and authoritarian centralized governments. Social problems and other domestic difficulties slowed China's and Korea's participation in the early modern global political economy. In Japan, however, decentralized feudalist system and Meiji Restoration in the late nineteenth century had provided favorable social and political circumstances for industrialization and Westernization. Japanese civil war of 1866–1868 and resistances like the 1877 Satsuma Rebellion destroyed the traditional forces and clean the way for Meiji's wholesale reforms. There were no such drastic internal violence in Korea or Vietnam as a political preparation for major phenomenal transformation. As a result, merchants and intellectuals in these countries became much more acquainted with people from the wider world, including Europeans, in the early modern era.

The third is the way in which each state compromised with various social groups in making difficult changes. These compromises and the varying levels of willingness to make changes shaped new East Asian attitudes as well as international views toward each country. The evolution of East Asian efforts at modernization shows that the conventional Western view of East Asia as reactive, anxious, and insure during the seventeenth and eighteenth centuries is misleading. Xiaobing Li explains in his previous work,

> To some extent, Western expansionism and imperialism, including Russian and American expansion, helped engender various forms of reform movements and nationalism in East Asian countries. Contact with the West caused East Asian leaders to question their inherited values, leading some to advocate a rapid modernization. However, stories of emperors and reformers who found themselves swept away by Western learning and a hegemonic "nationalist discourse," as described in conventional accounts of East Asia's modernization reforms, were gravely exaggerated.[3]

As it turned out, leaders in East Asia did not feel compelled to make an either/or choice between "traditional" Eastern ideas and "modern" Western ones.

All three of these trends—the cultivation of domestic resources for reform, impediments to social reform, and pragmatic compromises that reformist leaders made with social groups—describe the defining characteristics of East Asian modernization. Failures of governments to protect their countries' resources promoted people to question and challenge their authorities. Social instability made it difficult, if not impossible, for China, Japan, Vietnam, and Korea to avoid a major confrontation with Western interests and influence.

Europeans Arrive in China (1500s–1800s)

That the Western powers' arrival at the Chinese shores coincided with the Ming dynasty's fatal

---

3   Xiaobing Li, "From Peasants to Professional Soldiers: Social Transition and Military Modernization in China," *The Journal of Comparative Asian Development* (2006), 2–3.

decline was history's worst irony. In spite of its long and enduring cultural heritage, the Ming in the end failed to escape in time from its own entangled and outmoded political system. When the Europeans arrived demanding open relations, the Central Kingdom was not only unprepared for the encroachment of the "barbarian" Westerners but was unable to fully comprehend the gravity of the development. The Ming government had yet to realize the fact that the intruders were decades, if not a century, ahead of China in science and technology.

The Western intrusion into China was spearheaded by Portugal, a major maritime power of the time; in 1535 it extracted from the Ming court a legal sanction to reside and trade in Macao. Spain quickly emulated the Portuguese venture in 1575 by winning a Ming concession to trade along the southern Chinese coast. Shortly afterwards other European powers followed suit. The Dutch, who established a limited trading operation with Japan in the late sixteenth century, organized a China post by 1656.[4] With its extensive commercial interests in India entrenched in the early seventeenth century, England was the most aggressive European power in Asia during that period. Naturally, it was eager to expand trade with China following other maritime powers' East Asian ventures by establishing a Chinese commercial outpost in 1690. France did the same in 1728. By the first half of the eighteenth century, most major European powers had managed to establish commercial outposts in China. Nevertheless, as Ray Huang concludes, the growth of foreign trade did not promote Ming economy and early industry, since the government opposed such an imbalanced growth among the different

regions in China. Such an imbalance "in turn would threaten the empire's political unity."[5]

Soon after securing the Chinese court's legal sanction to trade, the European powers pursued the systematic exploitation of China by employing their seasoned mercantile techniques. Hardly concealing their imperial ambition from the outset, they took full advantage of the declining empire's political weakness. Since the West's early commercial activities did not overly disturb the giant middle kingdom, the Ming court did not regard the West's token presence on its soil as a major threat. Nevertheless, Ming remained contemptuous of European commercialism, seeing it as merely an unpleasant irritation for the court and the wider society, which still harbored the strong anticommercial sentiment inherent in the Confucian doctrine. The Chinese government was not alarmed, as the Western activities at the time presented only a negligible effect on the giant empire. Nor did the Christianity brought by the Western powers impress the court. As it turned out, Ming's mediocre political leadership and cumbersome bureaucracy proved grossly inadequate in dealing with the West's concerted, exploitative maneuvers.

Soon the European traders realized that their China dream was quite premature. Ming's essentially agrarian, self-sufficient economy was far from reaching a state capable of sustaining consumer markets for European industrial products. The impoverished Chinese farmers could ill-afford high-priced industrial items, which the West was eager to sell. However, in the meantime, China possessed ample nonindustrial commodities highly sought after by wealthy European consumers. Contrary to

---

4   The Dutch in fact had established themselves on Taiwan in 1621 and called the island "Formosa" ("beautiful one"). The Dutch maintained their settlement until 1658 when Ming General Zheng Chenggong (Cheng Ch'eng-kung) landed his troops and drove the Dutch from the island. See Xiaobing Li and Michael Molina, "Taiwan," in *Oil: A Cultural and Geographic Encyclopedia of Black Gold*, eds. Xiaobing Li and Michael Molina (Santa Barbara, CA: ABC-CLIO, 2014), 2: 671.

5   Ray Huang, *1587, A Year of No Significance: The Ming Dynasty in Decline* (New Haven, CT: Yale University Press, 1981), 187–8, 204–6.

the expectations of the European industrialists, it turned out that China was more of an enormously profitable exporter of its own nonindustrial goods than an importer of Europe's sophisticated industrial products. According to Mungello, "mutual influence" or a two-way exchange characterized the general pattern of China-West relations during the period of 1500–1800: "While the influence was never equal in both directions, there was always at least some influence flowing in both directions so that the movement was never entirely one way."[6]

This two-way yet lop-sided trade pattern quickly resulted in a huge trade deficit on the part of the European countries. Chinese teas, for example, became famous throughout the world for their unique color, fragrance, flavor, and finely shaped leaves. In the sixteenth century, the Chinese shipped large quantities of tea abroad. In Europe, the earliest tea drinkers were the British. To secure a continuous supply of tea, the British government ordered its East India Company to control the tea supply. In 1773 the revolutionary Boston Tea Party in North America threw 342 chests of Chinese tea into the Boston Harbor in protest against the tea tax enforced by the British government on its American colonies. By the nineteenth century, China had a total tea export volume of forty million tons to England. Chinese tea was referred to as "green gold."[7] For the Western mercantile powers, such unexpected development became intolerable.

The Western systematic attempt to establish its mercantile presence in China was closely followed by its Christian evangelism. St. Francis Xavier of the Society of Jesus came to China in 1552. However, in a society dominated by long-established Confucian tradition, his efforts quickly fizzled. In spite of the initial setback, other Italian Jesuits came in 1577 to continue Xavier's evangelical work. Their efforts bore fruit slowly as they skillfully avoided conflicts with Chinese sensibilities and customs within the Church's prescribed doctrinal parameter.[8] Matteo Ricci, the prominent Jesuit missionary who established a permanent mission of the Catholic Church in 1601, was well known for his close rapport with the Ming Emperor and his judicious missionary work. His effort apparently paid off for, during the subsequent dynasty, the first emperor of the Qing dynasty (1644–1911) appointed a German Jesuit, Adam Schall von Bell, as director of the Board of Astronomy in 1644. By 1651 their deliberate proselytizing efforts had won 150,000 Chinese converts, a notable though modest achievement in populous China.

After the Ming collapsed in 1644, the Manchus founded the Qing dynasty. Unfortunately, the Qing court inherited some of its predecessor's shortcomings, as its countermeasures to the Western attempts to dominate commerce were equally ineffective. While taking realistic views toward individual missionaries, the Qing adopted more unfriendly attitudes toward Christianity, treating the missionaries more as intellectuals than bearers of a new religious canon. Therefore missionaries were quite well accepted; some even won high government positions. However, the Manchu rulers were noncommittal about Christianity, anticipating that fundamental and irreconcilable conflicts would eventually develop between the Confucian doctrines and monotheistic Christianity, and remaining skeptical of the constructive role of Christianity in Confucian China. In spite of its willingness to maintain contacts with some missionaries, the court was vigilant about Christian evangelical work.[9]

---

6   Mungello, *The Great Encounter of China and the West*, 9.

7   Li, *Modern China*, 332–3.

8   Jonathan D. Spence, *The Search for Modern China*, 3rd ed. (New York: Norton, 2013), 69.

9   Frederic Wakeman, Jr., *The Fall of Imperial China* (New York: The Free Press, 1975), 96.

On the other hand, contrary to the conventional view of Chinese ignorance of Western science and technology prior to the Opium War, the Qing court continued to show a high level of interest in the Western scientific knowledge and technologies brought by the missionaries and sought the latter's cooperation. As a result, many missionaries became the Qing government's window to the West in terms of its scientific and technological curiosities. With more general rather than specific knowledge, the Jesuit missionaries' contributions, though notable in some technical areas such as canon casting, calendar making, and cartography, were far from being the catalysts for the modernization of Qing China.

The Qing rulers' moderate tolerance of Christianity might have led to a more constructive relationship with the West if the Europeans had not exacerbated their communal exploitation of China around 1770. This prompted the Chinese government to take an antagonistic approach in dealing with the West in general by enforcing its anti-Christianity laws more stringently. Interestingly and perhaps ironically, despite the growing European commercial and political clout in China, fledgling Chinese Catholicism actually experienced a major setback from which it did not recover until the nineteenth century.

By the mid-nineteenth century, Western European countries had become industrialized and aggressively sought for overseas markets for their manufactured goods in Asia in general and China in particular. Since the Manchu emperors continued their isolationist policy against European trade, Europeans, especially British, found it impossible to make any kind of trade agreement with the Qing government. The struggle over the traditional tributary system eventually led to the First Opium War between Great Britain and China in 1839–1841.

The British force defeated the Qing army, and opened China's market after they signed the Treaty of Nanjing of 1842. Hans van de Ven suggests that "the Qing was ill-prepared to deal with Britain's naval challenge not because it was a backward country or a Confucian society with little regard for the military, but because it had faced different sorts of military challenges and followed a different path of military development than Britain."[10] After the First Opium War ended in 1842, the confrontation between the Qing regime and European countries continued and led to the Second Opium War in 1857–1858. The British and French forces defeated the Chinese army again, and the Qing government had to open up more Chinese cities for European trade after they signed the Treaty of Tianjin of 1858.

After the Opium War, the peasants were subject to both domestic crisis between the Manchus and Chinese and Western influence. Between 1841 and 1850, more than 100 peasant uprisings were recorded by the Qing government. In 1851, the largest peasant uprising in Chinese history took place in Guangdong province as the Taiping Rebellion led by Hong Xiuquan (1814–1864). After failed his civil service examination three times, Hong was frustrated and disappointed by the Qing education and political systems. He became a Christian and organized a secret bible study group, the "Society of God Worshippers" (*Bai Shangdi Hui*), in 1843 at his hometown of Jintian. Among its first members were his schoolmate Feng Yunshan and his cousin Hong Rengan. Hong Xiuquan told his followers, he met the God in his dream, and the God told him he was the younger brother of Jesus Christ. In 1844, Hong wrote the *Doctrines on Salvation* (1844), proposing "all people belong to one family and should share and enjoy the universal peace."[11] Gradually, he cultivated the thought of revolt.

---

10   Hans van de Ven, "Military Mobilization in China, 1840–1949," in Jeremy Black ed., *War in the Modern World since 1815* (London: Routledge, 2003), 37.

11   Hsu, *The Rise of Modern China*, 227–8.

In January 1851, Hong called for an armed uprising against the Qing regime. He adopted Christian ideas of peace and equality, and offered equality to all people, regardless of their political, economic, gender, or ethnic status. His ideology attracted millions of the poverty-stricken peasants in South China to join his army and the new kingdom, named as the "*Taiping Tianguo*" (Heavenly Kingdom of Great Peace). In the summer, his force, or the "Taiping Army," launched offensive campaigns against the Qing army in Guangdong and Hunan provinces in the south. Some of the local warlords also joined the Hong's Army against the Qing, which they had been fighting for years. In the spring of 1852, the Taiping Army achieved victory of the decisive battle at Yong'an, and expanded into central and eastern China with more than 500,000 troops. In early 1853, Hong's army advanced into the Yangzi River Delta, the rice bowl of China. In March, Hong ordered the attack on Nanjing, a major city in Southeast China. After captured the city, Hong renamed it "Tianjing," or "Heavenly Capital," for the new Taiping regime. In 1854, with more than one million troops, Hong began his northern expedition toward Beijing, the capital of the Qing government. By 1856, the Taiping Uprising reached its highest point.

In 1858, however, the Taiping leaders began to struggle openly with one another, resulting in the killing of the outstanding military leader Yang Xiuqing (d. 1856) and more than twenty thousand of his followers.[12] The fortune of the Heavenly Kingdom deteriorated fast because of the internal struggle among its leaders. Moreover, Hong's expectation of European support of his regime failed. In 1856–1858, Hong sent his representatives to contact Christian missionaries, Western merchants, and European diplomats in Shanghai and other cities. He was surprisingly shocked when all the Christian churches in China refuse to recognize and support his course. Instead, many Westerners organized their military groups to support the Qing and fight against the Taiping Army. F. T. Ward, for example, an American in Shanghai, organized the "Foreign Rifle Corps" in 1860. The Qing army seized the opportunity and surrounded Nanjing on all sides.

To turn the tables on the enemy, Hong Xiuquan promoted some young generals in charge of military command. In 1858, the Taiping Army was able to defeat the Qing Army and remove the threat to Tianjing. To win battles against the Taiping, the Qing government allowed the local officials to organize their own forces in their provinces in the late 1850s. Among the others were the Hunan Army (*Xiangjun*) under the command of Zeng Guofan (1811–1872) proved the strongest provincial army of Qing against the Taiping. Zeng's strategy was to rely on local gentries to raise a new type of military organization from those provinces directly threatened by the Taiping rebels. Zeng Guofan led his army along the Yangzi River eastward toward Tianjing in 1860. The Hunan Army attacked Anqing in 1861, one of the Taiping strongholds in Anhui province. After conquered Anqing, Zeng reached Tianjing in 1863. During the siege of Tianjing, Hong Xiuquan died of illness in June 1864. Soon the capital of the Taiping Kingdom fell in July. The larges peasant movement in Chinese history came to an end.

The Taiping Uprising lasted altogether 14 years. The Taiping Army captured more than 60 cities and extended their influence to 18 provinces. However, the rebellion claimed at least 25 million Chinese lives in 1851–1864. It also revealed the expediency and hypocrisy of the Western powers, which refused to come to Hong's rescue despite his

---

12 Among the major internal struggles was the Wei military coup in September 1856. Wei Changhui, one of Hong's five kings and an ambitious man, killed the outstanding military leader Yang Xiuqing and more than twenty thousand of his followers. For more details, see Wakeman, *The Fall of Imperial China*, 147–4; Hsu, *The Rise of Modern China*, 242–3.

proclaimed belief in Christianity. After all, it was far easier for them to exact more concessions from a much-weakened Manchu dynasty than deal with an unknown new leader, Christian or not. In the end, their commercial interest in China trumped their religious concerns. Nevertheless, Qing military power weakened thereafter and, faced with massive rebellions and defeat in wars, the Qing dynasty continued to decline through the second half of the nineteenth century.

Firearms in Japan (1500s–1700s)

Japan remained more of a vacillating amalgamation of small feuding military states than a unified country until 1603, when the Tokugawa shogunate emerged as the central authority. The rule of the Tokugawa shogunate lasted for over 250 years until the imperial authority was restored in 1868. During this period, Japan's feudal culture smacked of aggressive and venturesome nationalism, a unique characteristic that set Japan apart from its more literati-oriented neighbors like China and Korea. Like its continental neighbors, Japan operated as a "rice economy" at the outset of the Tokugawa period.[13] Although farming remained profoundly important to feudal rulers, farmers themselves were not highly regarded as much as in China and Korea.

Unlike its two neighbors where a literati class dominated national politics, Japan was ruled by powerful warlords, shoguns or daimyos, and their followers, the samurai. As a learned and highly motivated group, the samurai played a crucial role not only during the warring period, but also in more peaceful times, remaining the cornerstone of Japan's strong military apparatus.[14] The samurai institution, a Japanese invention, sustained its political advantage until the late Tokugawa period when the shoguns became increasingly interested in European firearms and modern army. Even though samurai as a social class eventually disappeared as a victim of Japan's modernization, they had made a significant contribution to the birth of modern Japan.

After European merchants arrived in Japan during the early sixteenth century, local shoguns and daimyos benefitted from the trade by importing Western medicine and firearms. After all, it was the introduction of European gun technology to Japan in the mid-sixteenth century that gave the victory to the Tokugawa family over its rivals. As a warrior class, samurai also showed much keener appreciation of the superior military power of the West than did the Chinese civil bureaucrats. With the passage of time, some became more curious about the outside world and interested in opening up their country. A relatively light external impetus could set Japan in motion in a way that much heavier blows could not in a far more stable China ruled by Confucian elites. As a result, Japan adjusted to the early modern global climate more quickly than China, and this in turn gave it a decisive advantage during the following century.

One crucial factor in this difference between Japanese and Chinese reactions to the outside world lay in the samurai attitude toward military technology and gunpowder. In 1543 a Portuguese trader sailed to Tanegashima, an island off the west coast of Japan, seeking food and water after being driven off course by a storm. He carried with him a matchlock gun and demonstrated it for Shogun Tokitaka who, without ever having set his sight on a gun before, nonetheless instantly recognized its value as a weapon. The Shogun tried to purchase the weapon; however, the trader refused to sell it, claiming he needed the weapon to supply his crew with food. The Shogun persisted in making all sorts of offers. Finally, the trader gave in and also provided instructions on how to make barrels

---

13   James L. McClain, *Japan: A Modern History* (New York: Norton, 2002), 41–3.

14   Michael S. Neiberg, *Warfare in World History* (London: Routledge, 2001), 25.

and gunpowder. Immediately the Tanegashima shogun set up a factory for the production of guns leading to Tanegashima-tsutsu (tsutsu meaning a barrel or teppo), from the location of the factory. Because the Japanese were superb craftsmen, the copying of the locks presented minimal problems. Puzzled by the steel-coiled spring, they substituted it with the folded brass spring, a common characteristic of these weapons. Portuguese adventurer Mendes Pinto, in recording his experiences in Japan, reported that within several years, the Japanese were effectively manufacturing guns and, by 1556 they had produced more than three hundred thousand weapons.[15]

Guns, though accepted as a necessary weapon, were never considered sporting and did not replace the sword as samurai's principal fighting weapon until the Meiji Restoration in the late nineteenth century. During the epochal *Sengoku Jidai* war, the use of firearms was comparatively limited. Michael S. Neiberg points out that, "Japanese samurai proved to be more successful in resisting guns than their western European counterparts."[16] Nonetheless, the Japanese showed remarkable curiosity about gun making. At first the manufacturing of guns was limited to the island of Kyushu, but within a decade, blacksmiths from across Japan were traveling to Kyushu to study the methods of manufacturing firearms. The more famous gunsmiths founded schools, and the students trained in firearms manufacturing were soon opening shops across the vast reaches of the country. When an artisan gained reputation for superior craftsmanship, apprentices would gather to study his methods. The more capable apprentices were adopted into the family of the master and gained the privilege of practicing the art under the master's name, which became known as the *ryu*, or school. Many types of matchlocks were developed, all individually handcrafted. Nearly all models were decorated with brass inlay on the stocks, reminiscent of the Near-East Arabian guns. From the very beginning, both shogun and samurai, who dominated the Japanese social landscape, had a positive attitude toward Western military technology.

Western influences on Japanese artillery also date back to the early 1600s. The British navigator and trader William Adams is known to have provided Tokugawa Ieyasu with eighteen guns and ammunition for his use in the battle of Sekigahara.[17] This exchange marked the beginning of Western influence on the Japanese use of artillery. The establishment of the Dutch factory in Hirado in 1609, subsequently moved to Nagasaki in 1641, laid the foundation for the evolution of Japanese incorporation of guns into their military model.[18] In 1634 the chief of the Dutch factory, Nicholas Koeckebacker, joined the shogunate army and organized an artillery group of eighty men who participated in a bombardment lasting sixteen days. This same group, then comprised entirely of Japanese troops, would later be commanded by Japanese Yakushiji Kyuzaemon Tanehiro. Just five years later, mortars were manufactured in Hirado under the guidance of another Westerner, German Wolfgang Brawn.[19] Mortars, then favored by the Shogunate, would continue to be manufactured in Hirado.

The next step in the evolution of Japanese adoption of Western artillery occurred in 1649, with

---

15 Delmer M. Brown, "The Impact of Firearms on Japanese Warfare, 1543–1598," *Far Eastern Quarterly* 7, no. 3 (May 1948): 236–7.

16 Neiberg, *Warfare in World History*, 41.

17 Seiho Arima, "The Western Influence on Japanese Military Science, Shipbuilding, and Navigation", *Monumenta Nipponica* 19, no. 3–4 (1964): 353.

18 Ibid., 354.

19 Ibid., 355.

the arrival of a Dutch delegation at Nagasaki. The significance of the visit was twofold. First, among the delegates were four mortar technicians, adding to the already established mortar capabilities of the Japanese. Second, and perhaps more significant for future Japanese development, were the two forty-pound cannons presented to Tatsuke Shirobei Kagetoshi at Osaka. Guns of this size, while beyond contemporary Japanese manufacturing capacities, were nevertheless capable of siege operations, and were thus of interest to the Japanese Shogunate. This interest sparked the beginning of a tradition of Japanese writing on artillery technology and tactics. Among the earliest of these texts is that of Hojo Ujinaga, a Bakufu military instructor who had worked closely with members of the Dutch delegation to learn about Western siege warfare. His work, *Yuriyamu kojoden*, or "Report on Juli-aen's Siege Warfare," outlined this knowledge for Japanese dissemination.

Firearms of domestic manufacture were far from perfect, as their efficiency and accuracy could not compare with weapons produced outside the islands. The shoguns and daimyo still purchased many weapons from abroad, particularly from the Dutch. Before the Meiji era, most imported long arms were patterned after Dutch Models 1830 and 1845, and were commonly known to the Japanese as Geweghr muskets. Not long after these Geweghr muskets were imported, shoguns began reproducing imitations in their own gunsmith shops. Within a short period, the armies of these shoguns were well equipped with copies of the Dutch musket.[20] Some samurais also studied Western medicine, European languages, and modern industries, all of which were known as "Dutch Learning."[21] Subsequently, the Bakufu employed French officers, who were instrumental in the adoption of the Minie type rifle, to train Japanese soldiers at a newly established military academy. The samurai officers quickly recognized the improved accuracy of the new rifles over the Dutch muskets and sought to upgrade their weapons. During the Meiji era, the Tokyo Arsenal was established to manufacture small arms as part of the military modernization, one of the hallmarks of the Meiji Transformation.

Clearly, when the Europeans and Americans arrived in Japan, the reform-minded political leaders and samurais sought to discard their feudal past and replace it with modern Western technology and new institutions. Witnessing the partition of China and the rest of East Asia amongst the Europeans and driven by fear of foreign domination, a fear constantly voiced by prominent individuals in order to motivate the Japanese populace, Japan began to create its new modern army as part of its overall plan for industrialization and modernization. Rather than harboring a strong sense of cultural superiority as the Chinese did, the Japanese rulers were seized by a fear of inferiority. This compelled them to undertake drastic measures to transform their country—a clear difference that lay at the heart of the worldview of Japan and China. As pointed out by Fairbank, Reischauer, and Craig, "Thus, when menaced by the West, they did not react with disdain but rather with that combination of fear, resentment, and narrow pride that one associates with nationalism. In fact, their reaction proved extremely nationalistic."[22]

Trade and Christianity in Two Vietnams (1600s–1700s)

As with several other parts of East Asia, the early modern era in Vietnam was marked by the

---

20   Charles H. Yust, "Japanese Ling Guns, 1539–1905," *Gun Digest*, 11th annual edition, ed. John T. Amber (Chicago: Gun Digest Company, 1957), 85.

21   For more on "Dutch Learning," see Fairbank, Reischauer, and Craig, *East Asian*, 486.

22   Ibid., 490–1.

FIGURE 3.1 Vietnam

development of expanded global trade networks and with the introduction of new social and cultural elements, including Christianity. By the seventeenth century, Vietnamese people had expanded into formerly Cham and Khmer lands to the south and had developed into two separate polities: Tonkin in the north and Cochinchina in the south. Catholicism and global trade fundamentally altered the social, cultural, and economic milieu of both polities. However, the Catholic presence was more profound in Tonkin, while global trade was more robust in Cochinchina.

The origins of Catholicism in Vietnam are associated with the missionary work of the French Jesuit Alexandre de Rhodes (1593–1660). De Rhodes spread the Catholic faith in both Tonkin and Cochinchina. He was in Cochinchina from 1624–1626 and 1640–1645 and was in Tonkin from 1627–1630. De Rhodes's first trip to Cochinchina was essentially unsuccessful. Catholics collaborating with de Rhodes successfully converted Nguyen Hoang's last living concubine, Minh Duc, in 1625. However, Nguyen Hoang's son, Lord Nguyen Phuc Nguyen, was disappointed that the arrival of missionaries did not coincide with Portuguese trade, and was wary of the missionaries because their doctrine might prevent the continuation of the practice of ancestor veneration. However, de Rhodes and his colleagues succeeded in convincing the Lord not to ban Christianity or missionaries; de Rhodes took the opportunity to go to Tonkin by 1627.[23]

In Tonkin, de Rhodes and his colleagues were able to effect a much broader Catholic conversion. They arrived in the environs of the modern-day city of Thanh Hoa in north-central Vietnam. There, Lord Trinh Trang, who was on the way to the front for an attack against Cochinchina, witnessed the missionaries erecting a cross on a high peak. Encouraged by the possibility that this might be a sign that Portuguese commerce might be coming to Tonkin, but wary of the possibility that the Europeans there might be spies for Cochinchina, he asked de Rhodes and his missionaries to remain in the area. There they were given generous lodging and were allowed to construct a church, and upon Trinh Trang's return, they were invited to the capital at Thang Long (modern-day Hanoi).

Eventually, opposition from a variety of social groups who felt threatened by the missionary presence, including Buddhists, practitioners of traditional medicine, and court eunuchs, forced Trinh Trang to order the missionaries to leave in 1629. However, before they left, they trained a number of Vietnamese catechists to continue the faith in their absence. Whereas by the count of the missionaries there were 5,602 Christians by the time of their departure, by 1641, due to the work of the catechists, there were 108,000 Christians and 235 churches. Other missionaries arriving later in the seventeenth century, including Girolamo Maiorica (1589–1656), the "man who probably had the greatest long-term impact on Vietnamese Christianity", supplemented these efforts.[24] Maiorica was so influential because, with the help of Vietnamese catechists, he authored translations of major Christian texts, from the lives of saints to catechisms to biblical stories to practical morality, into demotic Vietnamese characters (*chu nom*). This effort not only advanced Catholicism, which may have reached 250,000 followers in Tonkin by the mid-1650s, but also advanced the *chu nom* script and influenced the development of modern genres of Vietnamese literature.[25]

Scholars offer various explanations for the expansion of Catholicism in Vietnam, especially in Tonkin. Christian conversion may have offered a modicum of community, stability, and hope in the context of demographic and economic change caused by *nam tien*, the political instability of the Trinh-Nguyen wars, and repeated crop failures in early seventeenth century Tonkin. For this reason, Christianity may be associated with a general rise in new religious movements, including a revival of Buddhism and spirit cults. Additionally, prior to the revival of the Confucian scholar-elite in the late seventeenth-century, the intellectual and scholarly orientation of the Jesuits who dominated early

---

23 Peter C. Phan, *Mission and Catechesis: Alexandre de Rhodes & Enculturation in Seventeenth-Century Vietnam* (Maryknoll, NY: Orbis Books, 1998), 47–8.

24 Taylor, *History of the Vietnamese*, 288.

25 Brian E. Ostrowski, "The Rise of Christian Nôm Literature in Seventeenth-Century Vietnam: Fusing European Content and Local Expression," in *Vietnam and the West: New Approaches*, ed. Wynn Wilcox (Ithaca, NY: Cornell University Southeast Asia Program Publications, 2010), 19–40; Brian Eugene Ostrowski, "The Nôm Works of Geronimo Maiorica, S.J. (1589–1656) and their Christology," (PhD Dissertation, Cornell University, 2006); Taylor, *History of the Vietnamese*, 288–9.

conversion efforts may have helped gain conversions of the intellectual class. De Rhodes and his colleagues came armed with the scientific knowledge of the enlightenment, and gave Trinh Trang an hourglass and a mechanical clock as gifts, which apparently impressed him.

On the other hand, the reasons why Catholicism did not continue to expand at the same rate after the mid-seventeenth century, and the reasons why it did not achieve the same level of foothold in Cochinchina, are clearer. In Tonkin the departure of key missionaries also coincided with the literati revival. In Cochinchina, new evidence indicates that at least in the Nguyen royal family, Christianity made more inroads in the seventeenth century than previously thought; Christians may even have constituted a "faction" at the Nguyen court in the late seventieth century.[26] Additionally, even Nguyen lords who were not interested in becoming Catholics were more than willing to employ Jesuit missionaries in scientific or technical positions, much like the Qing emperors to their north.[27] However, two factors constrained the expansion of Catholicism in Cochinchina: the influence of Buddhism in Nguyen state ideology and the competition between different Portuguese and French-based Catholic orders. These factors combined to influence a decision to ban Christianity in 1690.[28] While this ban did not last, it set a pattern of infighting among Catholics and periodic Nguyen prohibitions on Christianity that would characterize the next hundred years in Cochinchina.

Whereas conversion to Catholicism was more prevalent in Tonkin, international trade was of greater importance in Cochinchina. Promoting international trade was an intentional policy priority of the Nguyen. By the time he definitively broke with the Trinh in 1600, Nguyen Hoang actively attempted to court international trade as a means to gain the resources to withstand Trinh attacks. Early in the seventeenth century, the most important of these conduits for commerce were the "Red Seal" ships from Japan, which were named after the official stamp that they were required to have from the Tokugawa shogunate in order to operate. Cochinchina dominated trade with Japan in the early seventeenth century, to the detriment of Siamese, Tonkinese, Cambodian, and Cham competitors, due to its ability to supply large quantities of high-quality raw silk.

After the Japanese market was closed in 1639, the Nguyen commercial center at Hoi An continued to welcome Portuguese, English, and Chinese ships, as well as commerce from other Southeast Asian countries. These merchants found at Hoi An a well-regulated and organized port with relatively low duties that attracted their commerce. Trade in sugar, pepper and other spices, and timber and rare woods expanded. The expansion of this commerce produced wealth that appears to have benefited not only the Nguyen Lords or the merchants but ordinary people as well. By the mid-seventeenth century, Buddhist pagodas in Cochinchina were on average eight times larger than their counterparts in Tonkin.[29]

This prosperity was undone by a fiscal crisis in the eighteenth century. The Nguyen lord cast zinc coins between 1746 and 1748, rather than using copper,

---

26   Brian A. Zottoli, "Reconceptualizing Southern Vietnamese History from the 15th to 18th Centuries: Competition along the Coasts from Guangdong to Cambodia," (PhD Dissertation, University of Michigan, 2011), 278–80.

27   Li Tana, *Nguyen Cochinchina*, 72–3.

28   Nola Cooke, "Strange Brew: Global, Local, and Regional Factors behind the 1690 Prohibition of Christian Practice in Nguyen Cochinchina," *Journal of Southeast Asian Studies* 39, no. 3 (October 2008): 383–8; Catherine Marin, *Le role des missionaires français en Cochinchine aux XVIIe & XVIIIe siècles* (Paris: Églises d'Asie, 1999), 52.

29   Li Tana, *Nguyen Cochinchina*, 84–5.

which was in short supply. While previously the economy could handle these kinds of changes, by the mid-eighteenth century changes in the global economy meant that the global trade could not absorb this increase in the money supply, and the infusion of zinc coins led to dangerous inflation and economic instability. In the late eighteenth century, Nguyen officials were forced to increase taxes to try to make up for the economic downturn that came from this inflation, a move that led directly to the beginning of the Tay Son rebellion in 1773.[30]

International trade changed Tonkin as well, even if on a lesser scale. Trade with Westerners in seventeenth-century Tonkin focused on the Dutch East India Company (VOC), and to a lesser extent on the English. In 1638, in search of a better price for silk to sell to Japan, the Dutch began to focus their trade on Tonkin, where they would experience less competition. For their part, the Trinh lords saw in the Dutch a potential ally in their war against Cochinchina, given that the Portuguese were viewed as commercial if not political allies of the Nguyen, and the Trinh viewed the Dutch, as Protestants, as natural rivals of the Catholic Portuguese.[31] In contrast to the English attempts to trade in Tonkin, which were entirely unsuccessful, the Tonkin trade successfully served for the Dutch as a substitute to their China trade, which had been carried out in Taiwan and had been destroyed by a famous Chinese pirate in the early 1660s. However, a combination of factors destroyed this profitable trade by the late 1660s. The final attempts of the Trinh to defeat the Nguyen in the south deprived the Dutch

of available labor—a depression caused by the lack of copper cash and the devaluation of silver, both of which caused losses for the company's operations.[32] The failure of international trade contributed to a deep and profound economic crisis in Tonkin in the eighteenth century, whose most salient feature was prolonged and repeated famines. These economic crises weakened the Trinh clan and made them vulnerable to the Tay Son rebellion, just as the Nguyen were in the 1770s.

Catholicism in Korea (1700s–1800s)

While China and India were the focal points of European attention, other East Asian countries such as Japan, Vietnam, and Korea attracted only secondary interest. The "Hermit Kingdom of Choson" stayed, for a long while, out of the customary Western commercial curiosity.[33] Its remote location and Chinese-oriented foreign relations had effectively deterred the small kingdom from establishing contacts with nations beyond its immediate neighbors. There had been no direct trade or diplomatic relations between Korea and Western nations prior to the dawn of the nineteenth century. Choson Korea, still known in the West as a Chinese dependency, remained hidden from the views of the European powers even when the latter made serious encroachment into the East Asian continent.[34]

As the Westerners made their presence in China more strongly felt, the Choson court had become aware, although only vaguely, of the highly advanced Western world. The knowledge brought home

---

30   Ibid., 94–8.

31   Olga Dror and Keith Weller Taylor, "Introduction," in *Views of Seventeenth-Century Vietnam: Christoforo Borri on Cochinchina & Samuel Baron on Tonkin* (Ithaca, NY: Cornell University Southeast Asia Program, 2006), 21.

32   Hoang Anh Tuan, "Tonkin Rear for China Front: The Dutch East India Company's Strategy for the North-Eastern Vietnamese Ports in the 1660s," in *Pirates, Ports, and Coasts in Asia: Historical and Contemporary Perspectives,* ed. John Kleinen and Manon Osseweijer (Singapore: Institute for Southeast Asian Studies, 2010), 64–71.

33   Seth, *A Concise History of Korea,* 211.

34   Geoff Simons, *Korea: The Search for Sovereignty* (New York: St. Martin's Press, 1995), 109.

by Korean officials who came into contact with European missionaries in Beijing included some fragmentary information about Western science and the world outside of East Asia. Although far from comprehensive, this trickling of information was enough to shake some officials from their long-standing conviction that the Central Kingdom was the only civilized society in the world. Christianity aroused the interest of Korean officials as the appropriate messenger of Western culture, which the traditional Choson society could accept or even embrace. Unfortunately, the Choson court had been receiving only unfavorable reports on the West from its trusted neighbor, the Qing rulers in China, whose troubled encounters with the Western powers effectively precluded the Choson court from viewing Christianity objectively.

In 1627 several Dutch sailors ended up staying in Korea and made guns for the locals after their ship was destroyed by a storm. In 1653 thirty-six more Dutch sailors joined them and worked for the Korean military for the same reason. Michael J. Seth states, "Few Koreans seemed to take the Europeans very seriously as bearers of a great tradition, rather seeing them as just clever barbarians."[35] Officially, Christianity landed in Korea in 1784; however, some publications of Matteo Ricci, the leading missionary during the late Ming dynasty, were introduced into Korea in the early seventeenth century. Unlike the Chinese, the Koreans had to import the new religion piece-by-piece from the Chinese and recreate it through a long self-study process. As reflected in the time-consuming process that went on undetected for a long time, the Choson court was little concerned with Christianity during its infancy.

Nevertheless, the Korean rulers did not imitate the Manchus in their overwhelming suspicion of the Western religion, nor did the Qing rulers advise the Koreans against Catholicism. In spite of its close alliance with China, the Choson remained independent in the making of its own policy in both domestic and foreign affairs. Its rulers paid close attention to the Western encroachment in China, which later became the foremost reference in Choson's anti-Christian policies.

The early couriers of Korean Catholicism were a few low-level officials whose visits to Beijing led to initial contacts with the Western religion. Even with the limited introduction, the new Western idea of philanthropism and salvation found receptive converts in Korea, mostly among commoners and the oppressed. As the unequal social system and unstable social order were worsening during the latter part of the eighteenth century, economic hardship provided fertile soil for the seeds of Christianity. By 1794 its Korean followers reached ten thousand, a significant accomplishment in a land that was entrenched in Confucian and Buddhist traditions.

A growing number of Christian coverts, who later included some intellectuals of the gentry class, eventually alarmed the reticent Choson rulers. Catholicism not only contradicted the rituals of Confucian doctrines, which were practiced and protected in Korea even more zealously than in China, but also threatened the very foundation of the country's spiritual tradition. To restrain the spread of the scarcely known foreign religion, the court decreed in 1785 a prohibition against the "wrong religion and wrong doctrine." This was followed by the first crackdown against the Korean Catholic church; in 1791 the court inflicted upon the church its first serious setback with the persecution of some three hundred Korean converts. The government's oppression forced the germinating Korean Catholic community to go underground temporarily, thus halting the church's energetic expansion.

The Korean rulers' anti-Catholic stand remained firm, but the enforcement of the prohibition was often inconsistent due to fluctuating political circumstances. Repression slackened when the court

---

35   Seth, *A Concise History of Korea*, 218.

was plunged into another round of factional power struggles during the early 1800s, thus allowing for the growth of the Korean Catholic community. The Seoul diocese was separated from the Beijing diocese in 1831, signifying the Vatican's recognition of the strength of the Korea Catholic community, which had grown to some nine thousand members when Father Pierre Philibert Maubant managed to enter Korea covertly to assume the post of Bishop of Seoul in 1836.

Chapter 4

Fending Off the West

In the early nineteenth century, China, Japan, Vietnam, and Korea adjusted to shifts in the global economy, the rise of industrialization, and the increasing dominance of British and French commercial, political, and military actors, who were gradually occluding the older Spanish, Portuguese, and Dutch Empires. Unlike earlier commercial empires, which had colonized part of Southeast Asia but left East Asian polities reasonably intact, the British and French were much more aggressive in enforcing their vision of East Asian trade by making use of their military superiority.

These global shifts coincided with efforts at reform and social change in East Asian societies. Because the origins of many of these trends toward modernization can be found in indigenous intellectual movements in East Asian countries prior to their military confrontations with British and French powers in the nineteenth century, they are not a matter of East Asians "responding" to the West. However, the urgency of the military and commercial problems wrought by France and Britain greatly accelerated East Asian efforts at military, economic, and political reform. In the nineteenth century, East Asian polities sought to build railroads and telegraph lines and to import new weapons. Given the economic conditions, merchants and other commercial interests

acquired more authority, as the scholar-elites slowly declined.

With the erosion of scholarly influence came a shift in intellectual mentality. Through institutions such as the civil service examination system (in China, Korea, and Vietnam) and the samurai institution (in Japan), East Asian elites relied on universalistic systems of thought. Levels of individual and cultural civilization were contingent upon knowledge of certain canonical texts; for example, whether they could read the works of Confucius or Mencius or key passages from the *Classic of Ritual* in classical Chinese, and whether they could make decisions about present circumstances based on consulting Chinese dynastic histories. One of the advantages of this universalistic thrust was that one did not have to be ethnically Han Chinese to be educated. Indeed, Korean and Vietnamese elites saw the classic texts and histories as very much a part of their own respective civilizations, rather than something "foreign" or "Chinese." Moreover, non-Han peoples, including ethnically Vietnamese subjects of the empire, could pass the exams in China. The flexibility of this system allowed non-Han rulers such as the Qing to adapt to this system. Mark Elliot, for example, describes the Manchu-Han relations during the Qing Dynasty as "ethnic sovereignty," which offered legitimacy for a dynastic central government to run multiple ethnicities in China.[1]

However, with this belief in a universal civilization came a certain chauvinism. Since Europeans did not know the classic texts, they were, by definition, not civilized, and responses to them were therefore to be conditioned on the lessons drawn from dealings with other "barbarians," such as Tanguts or Xiongnu, in the Chinese dynastic histories. Moreover, insofar as this universalistic ideology emerged from the Central Kingdom, Chinese empires could claim a level of superiority that bordered on arrogance. The Chinese emperor believed that he was not an equal of other rulers but a divine appointee with a universal mandate directly from heaven. The Chinese regarded other surrounding kingdoms as tributary states of imperial China because of the presumed cultural superiority of the classics. Traditional Chinese nationalism did not have overtly aggressive forms, because the Chinese assumed that the superiority of classical civilization assured China's cultural and demographic hegemony in Asia.

However, the emergence of the French and British colonial empires in Asia in the nineteenth century brought the universality of East Asian classical civilization into question. East Asians began to see the French and British as possessing a separate civilization, rather than merely being uncivilized. This shift in mentality gave rise to a particularistic point of view, in which Confucianism came to be understood as part of Chinese tradition, and the alternative to Confucianism came to be seen as "Western modernity."

In the particularist worldview, civilizations were associated with specific ethnicities or cultures. By the mid-nineteenth century, this view gave rise to proto-nationalistic discourses throughout East Asia. Liu concludes that "Such an ethnic essence of Chinese nationalism would become further solidified in China's domestic ethno-politics and foreign crises in the years to come."[2] In Korea, the fiery anti-Western disposition that Taewongoon, a regent, maintained throughout his rule originated from his intense seclusion policy, a deliberate choice to protect the antiquated kingdom and to promote nationalism. His view of the West was not firmly established when he came to power through the regency. The events that were mostly initiated by the Western powers from his very first year of rule, however, gradually drove him to extreme anti-Western seclusion. Contrary to the general characterization that he was a natural anti-Western, nationalist leader, to a great extent he was forced to take such an extreme foreign policy in order to safeguard the kingdom. For a man of profound nationalistic pride but of little practical knowledge of the non-Chinese world, the hostile and shortsighted reaction to Western incursion was even predictable under the confusing circumstances of the time.

The isolationist policy, however, failed to stop, or even to slow down, Western expansion in East Asia through the nineteenth century, when European trade, Christian missionaries, new technologies, and intellectual exchanges that had been unfolding for two centuries undermined the Eastern monarchical authorities and made the Westerners the major players in East Asia. The Eastern tradition underwent dramatic transformations, underscored by defeats in the hands of European powers, intellectual soul-searching, and efforts at modernization through combining Eastern ethics and Western science. This was especially true in the great Chinese empire, which had slipped into the downward phase

---

1   See Mark C. Elliot, *The Manchu Way: The Eight Banners and Ethnic Identity in Late Imperial China* (Stanford, CA: Stanford University Press, 2001).

2   Liu, "From Five 'Imperial Domains' to a 'Chinese Nation'," in *Ethnic China: Identity, Assimilation, and Resistance*, eds. Xiaobing Li and Patrick Fuliang Shan (Lanham, MD: Lexington Books, 2015), 31.

of a dynastic cycle just as the Western powers began to beat upon its gates.

By contrast, in less than half a century, the Meiji leaders achieved their goals, creating a relatively sound and modernized economy that enabled Japan to achieve relative equal footing with the West, evinced in its military victories against China and Russia at the end of the nineteenth and early twentieth century. China, on the other hand, was not as successful in its modernization efforts as was Japan.

Qing's Isolationism and Canton System (1800–1864)

By the eighteenth-nineteenth centuries, many Western European countries became industrialized. They actively looked for new overseas opportunities for their manufactured goods. These included Britain, France, and the United States, which energetically expanded their overseas markets. In terms of commercial plundering and colonial expansion, none was more ambitious than Britain. After the founding of the East India Company, the British established in Guangzhou (Canton) a trading company (then called "factory"), which brought the influence of the East India Company to China. In 1793 a British special envoy, Lord George Macartney, arrived in China, requesting the privilege of trading in Zhoushan Island and Ningbo in east China, Tianjin in the north, and some other places. Emperor Qianlong denied the request. At that time, the Qing government, wishing to maintain total control, adopted a closed-door policy regarding foreign trade.

During the long reign of Qianlong, China experienced a population growth from 163 million in 1741 to 200 million in 1762. Historical records show agricultural improvements and the introduction of irrigation technology. One of Emperor Qianlong's most impressive accomplishments was the incorporation of frontier territories into China, including Tibet, which came under military control in 1751, bringing China to its greatest territorial expanse.

Qianlong held the religious figures of Tibetan Buddhism in high esteem, and arranged many favors for the Dalai Lama, whom he attempted to establish as a vassal ruler for all of Tibet. In 1756–1757, Qing armies swept into Central Asia, and Xinjiang (meaning "the New Territories") was incorporated in China. Those conquests doubled the size of China. By the middle of the eighteenth century, Qianlong's government was able to resume the tributary system in Asia with a Chinese dominance and accepted by surrounding countries, including Korea, Nepal, Burma (now Myanmar), Thailand, Vietnam, and the Philippines.

With a self-sufficient economy and China-centered regional trade, the Qing government in the 1790s was uninterested in new European trade, which seemed neither needed nor attractive to the Manchu and Chinese merchants. Furthermore, Western industrial technology and new laborsaving machines also seemed unnecessary in China, which had the largest labor force in the world. In addition, the sale price of the popular trading items like tea and silk was almost the same at both domestic and foreign markets, so there was no incentive to increase profits through European trade. China had developed its own maritime trade with Southeast Asian countries such as Burma, Malaya (now Malaysia), Thailand, Vietnam, and the Philippines through its trading communities overseas. In other words, the Qing Empire already had long-standing outlets for international trade that presented fewer risks to its sovereignty than European trade. A Maritime China along the coast centered its trade at Xiamen (Amoy), Fujian province.

Nevertheless, the signs of decline appeared during the final years of Qianlong when his physical condition and judgement began to fail. Moreover, most of the newly conquered territories were administered by military governments, which were very expensive undertakings. In 1795 Qianlong abdicated the throne and one of his sons, Jiaqing, became the Qing emperor, ruling China from 1795 to 1820.

In the early eighteenth century, both the Jiaqing and Daoguang (r. 1821–1850) emperors continued Qianlong's closed-door policy and limited China's trade with the West through the *Cohong* (government-sanctioned merchant guilds) at Guangzhou (Canton), the only city open to trade with Europeans. The British sold to the Chinese woolens and spices, while buying from China such items as tea, silk, medicine, and porcelain. Beginning in the second decade of the nineteenth century, cotton textiles became the major item of British export to China. However, owing to the Manchu rulers' aversion to foreign trade, British trade with China was never large, and in fact, British trade with China was not particularly profitable. To reverse the negative balance of trade, the British began to ship large quantities of opium from India to China.

The Qing tolerated only a token presence of the Western commercial interests until the middle of the nineteenth century. After the collapse of the British East India Company's trade monopoly in East Asia in the 1820s, London sent government officials to Guangzhou in 1834 to oversee the British commercial activities and improve its China trade. Emperor Daoguang's closed-door policy rendered it difficult for Chinese officials to be proactive. As a result, some profit-driven British and Chinese merchants began to smuggle and trade outside of Guangzhou.

In China, domestic and foreign troubles came hand-in-hand, as the nineteenth century advanced, with each abetting the other. Emperor Xianfeng's reign from 1851–1863 saw the Qing dynasty in serious decline as the dynasty's reluctance to enact meaningful changes compelled it to fall back on Confucian values in a futile attempt to maintain power. Fairbank points out that "the reasons why the late Qing achieved so little industrialization despite its enormous material growth were not only economic but also social, political, and cultural."[3]

Faced with the missionary presence after the first Opium War, the Xianfeng emperor was wary of Christianity and placed Catholicism under tight control, despite the West's persistent pressure, until the ban was lifted in 1844. Initial Western attempts to establish bilateral relationships with China received mostly unfavorable responses from the Qing court, which did not see merit in establishing formal relations with the "barbarian" world. Nevertheless, Qing China was merely an old dynasty undergoing a rapid decline of power. Regardless of its traditional overconfidence and patience with its periodic invaders, Qing was too outdated and disorganized to defeat the determined West. Moreover, it was Emperor Xianfeng's misfortune to simultaneously deal with internal turmoil generated by the Taiping, Nian, Muslin, and Tungan revolts as well as the West. Mao Zedong, cofounder of the Chinese Communist armed forces, had learned a great deal of historical lessons from both the success and failure of the peasant rebellions. He concluded: "The scale of peasant uprisings and peasant wars in Chinese history has no parallel anywhere else. The class struggles of the peasants, the peasant uprisings and peasant wars constituted the real motive force of historical development in Chinese society."[4] He believed that "the poor peasants in China, together with the farm labors, form about 70 percent of the rural population. They are the broad peasant masses with no land or insufficient land, the semi-proletariat of the countryside, the biggest motive force of the Chinese revolution, the natural and most reliable ally of the proletariat and main contingent of China's revolutionary forces."[5] After Xianfeng's regime,

---

3   Ibid., 164–5.

4   Mao Zedong, "Chinese Revolution and Chinese Communist Party," in *Selected Works of Mao Zedong* (Beijing: Foreign Languages Press, 1977), 2: 308.

5   Ibid., 2: 324.

Tongzhi became the emperor from 1862 to 1874, and followed by Guangxu (r. 1875–1908).

The Closing of Japan (1600s–1800s)

Unlike China where a literati class dominated national politics, Japan was ruled by powerful warlords and their followers, the samurai, or warrior class. Samurai, who played a crucial role not only in the warring period but also in peaceful times remained the cornerstone of Japan's strong military character. The samurai institution, a Japanese invention, had sustained its political advantage until the late Tokugawa period when the shogun showed declining interest in samurai-oriented armies owing to the long peace. Patricia Ebrey and Anne Walthall point out that "the military regime established by the Tokugawa shoguns was designed to preserve order and enhance stability. ... The shoguns balanced the need for effective local administration with their fear of treachery by forcing the daimyo to divide their time between their domains and the shogun's capital at Edo where they had to leave hostages as a pledge of good behavior."[6]

In the early seventeenth century, Tokugawa was by far the most powerful shogunate. When Tokugawa Ieyasu took over the control in 1603, he had a domain of thrity-eight vassals of daimyo, totaling five thousand samurai. The daimyo domains became efficient units of local control in Japan, building a uniform and solid national political structure premised on a semicentralized feudalist structure, in contrast to Europe's monarchical centralization. The pattern of social organization and political rule established in this period continued with only minor modifications until Tokugawa Ieshige, who was in power from 1858 to 1866. As a result, Japan was able to maintain most of its unique insular culture in spite of the strong cultural influences of both China and Korea.

In the Tokugawa system, the relationship between the samurai and their shoguns changed from the single lord-vassal band to a multiple lord-vassal groups. While the samurai still lived in their *sho-an* (castle) headquarters, the peasants were organized into semiautonomous tax-paying villages ruled directly by the lords (shoguns or daimyos), who "resisted change, tried to control and freeze society in a number of ways, and suppressed many of the creative tendencies in the land." As articulated by Milton W. Meyer: "In these goals they were successful, for Japan was to enjoy two-and-a-half centuries of social tranquility and domestic seclusion."[7] After two centuries of warfare and long disunity in Japan, the Tokugawa brought political unity, peace, and stability, the impact of which was felt perhaps most strongly by the samurai class itself.

The Tokugawa feudalism was an extraordinarily stable political system, which served the country well without major military conflict or social change for two hundred years. The unique characteristic of this pattern was a considerable reduction in social change and conflict in Japan in this period. The long peace from 1700 to 1850 reduced the traditional warrior functions of samurai, who sought for other opportunities in temple schools, firearm workshops, and manufacturing factories in urban areas. The samurai value system, which had been a natural outgrowth of a feudal warrior society, gradually became transformed into a self-conscious philosophy. As the samurai turned increasingly into a hereditary civil bureaucracy, Confucianism began to take on a new meaning with increased appeal. The Japanese of the Tokugawa period developed an extremely strong sense of honor, duty, and obligation, which gradually spread from the samurai to

---

6 Patricia Ebrey and Anne Walthall, *Modern East Asia: From 1600; A Cultural, Social, and Political History*, 3rd ed. (Boston, MA: Wadsworth, 2014), 302.

7 Milton W. Meyer, *Japan: A Concise History*, 4th ed. (Lanham, MD: Rowman & Littlefield, 2013), 103.

other classes. The combination of feudalism and Confucian values survived the Tokugawa period and became part of Japanese nationalistic consciousness in the modern age.

This long success of political stability was perhaps made possible because the relative remoteness of the islands permitted Japan to isolate itself from Western pressures. Similar to the Chinese emperors, Tokugawa Hidetada, who ruled from 1605 to 1622 after Ieyasu, viewed European trade and Christianity as essentially subversive. He made a new policy of closely regulating foreign trade as part of the Tokugawa governing system. For example, in 1616, European ships were limited to only two ports. In 1622 fifty-five Christians were executed by the shogunate at Nagasaki, followed by anti-Christian decrees issued by Iemitsu, who stayed in power from 1623–1650. Suspected of involvement in illegal missionary activities, some Spanish were expelled from the country in 1624. Throughout the 1630s, more than four thousand Catholic priests and their followers were killed during the attacks on the Catholic Peril. McClain states that in the late 1630s, "Christianity survived only in isolated rural hamlets on Kyushu, far from the zealous eyes of shogun officials."[8] Moreover, in 1635, all Japanese were prohibited from going abroad or from returning home if already overseas. To help enforce this ban, a prohibition was placed on the building of ships of more than 500 *koku* (about 75 tons; 1 *koku* equals 150 kg). Meyer concludes: "In its aim of securing national political stability, the isolationist policy of the Tokugawa proved successful. For two centuries or more, no major revolution, strife, serious disturbances, or grave incidents threatened their rule. Japan slumbered fitfully on in its ocean-protected, semi-isolated cocoon."[9]

Although Japan was isolated from European trade, the Tokugawa period from Ietsuma (1651–1679) to Ienari (1787–1836) experienced an almost explosive expansion of commerce marked by rapid growth of cities and towns throughout Japan. Samurai, about 6 percent of the total population, lived in castle towns and cities where merchants and artisans were required to reside in comparable number to meet the needs of an enlarging rank of social elites. As a result, Japan now became a land of many large and small towns. Edo (later named Tokyo at the onset of the Meiji era) had a total population of one million and was possibly the largest city in the world at that time, while Osaka and Kyoto each had a population of four hundred thousand people. McClain concludes: "For most Japanese, lifestyles and standards of living improved significantly between 1600 and 1850. Indeed, living conditions for most Japanese families in the middle of the nineteenth century probably were comparable to those in England and the United States on the eve of their Industrial Revolutions."[10] Arguably, the remarkable degree of urbanization and commercialization and the resultant internal changes, much to the chagrin of the shogunate in late Tokugawa, went a long way in helping Japan confront the challenges from Western powers during the second half of the nineteenth century.

The Tay Son Uprising in Vietnam (1771–1802)

By the 1770s, Vietnamese peoples faced declining economic conditions and decreasing faith in the leadership of the Trinh and Nguyen clans. These conditions would eventually destroy the relative peace and prosperity created in the two separate Vietnams—Tonkin and Cochinchina—that

---

8   McClain, *Japan*, 44.

9   Meyer, *Japan*, 109.

10   McClain, *Japan*, 74–5.

had coexisted peacefully for more than a century. The Tay Son Uprising emerged out of these factors. By the 1750s, the prosperity that had been built by the Nguyen lords in Cochinchina in previous times had already been compromised by fiscal crises related to coinage. Beginning in 1765, Nguyen governance became increasingly unpopular during the rule of the regent Truong Phuc Loan.

The Tay Son uprising also arose from increasing regional instability around the Gulf of Thailand. Under Truong Phuc Loan's leadership, in 1769, the Nguyen fought and lost a war with Siam over which power would exercise de facto control over Cambodian territory. This war proved to be too great a burden for the Nguyen treasury to bear and also set off a series of conditions that would lead to a regional war through the 1770s, which included not just Cochinchina but also Siam, Cambodia, the Lao regimes, and an ethnic Chinese principality at Ha Tien, on the modern-day border between Vietnam and Cambodia. Under Truong Phuc Loan, the Nguyen responded by moving to aggressively collect tax revenues to make up the deficit.[11] They also attempted to streamline and reform their bureaucracy. To accomplish this, they removed many scholar-officials from power, increasing discontentment with their rule.

In mountains to the west of the city of Qui Nhon, tax responsibility fell to Nguyen Nhac, a young tax collector from Tay Son village, quite near the former Cham polity of Vijaya. Kinh (ethnically Vietnamese) peoples did not dominate this region. Many Chams lived in the area, which was also on a major trade route into Cambodia. They fled west as a result of the Vietnamese political expansion to the south under the *nam tien*. Instead of enforcing Truong Phuc Loan's policies and collecting taxes from the Chams, Nguyen Nhac instead emerged with the regalia of the Cham king. Whether these regalia had been taken from Cham people or actually given to Nguyen Nhac, the local population would perceive Nguyen Nhac as operating with the imprimatur of Cham royalty.[12]

In 1773 forces led by Nguyen Nhac captured Qui Nhon, a major city on Vietnam's south central coast. Nguyen Nhac garnered the support of a coalition of Chinese merchants and peasants upset at the Nguyen fiscal policies, Chams, and a few discontented scholar officials. The Tay Son uprising began to take shape. From his base in Qui Nhon, Nguyen Nhac then used Chinese mercenaries to block commerce from the main Nguyen port at Hoi An, then marched north to capture Phu Xuan (modern-day Hue) from the Nguyen lords. The Nguyen family had no choice but to flee southwards.

In the late 1770s and early 1780s, Tay Son forces struggled to wrest Saigon, a formerly Khmer area that was still far to the southern frontier, from the remaining Nguyen forces. These forces had rallied under the leadership of a young Nguyen prince named Nguyen Anh, who formerly declared himself Lord in 1780. After years of back-and-forth battles, Tay Son forces took and held Saigon in 1783, forcing Nguyen Anh's forces to flee. The remains of the house of Nguyen went first to Phu Quoc Island near the Cambodian coast, and finally to Bangkok by 1785. Nguyen Anh and his entourage would remain in exile until his forces retook Saigon in 1788.

Prior to his leaving for Bangkok, Nguyen Anh entered into an alliance with a Catholic Bishop named Pierre Pigneaux de Béhaine (1741–1799). As an ally of the ethnically Chinese Prince of Ha Tien, Pigneaux had been an important figure in the complicated politics of the region at the time. As an affiliate with the Foreign Mission Society of Paris (MEP), he also operated during a period

---

11   George Dutton, *The Tay Son Uprising: Society and Rebellion in Eighteenth-Century Vietnam* (Honolulu: University of Hawai'i Press, 2006), 34–5.

12   On the cham regalia, see Li Tana, *Nguyễn Cochinchina*, 151.

of competition between the MEP and primarily Spanish or Portuguese Jesuits, Franciscans, and Dominicans for the hearts of Southeast Asian Catholics. When Nguyen Anh asked Pigneaux to seek assistance from European powers for his fight against the Tay Son, Pigneaux took the opportunity. As a guarantee of his sincerity, Nguyen Anh entrusted Pigneaux with his son Prince Canh, who would accompany him on his journey to Europe. Pigneaux petitioned Portuguese officials in Goa and French officials in Pondichery for support, but when it was not forthcoming, the Bishop and the young Crown Prince headed for Paris.[13] By the end of 1787, Pigneaux had negotiated a treaty with the French King, Louis XVI, on Nguyen Anh's behalf. This treaty called for French troops in Pondichery to come to Nguyen Anh's aid, in exchange for the cession of territory and trading preferences for France.

However, this treaty was never executed. The governor of Pondichery, a French colony in India, declined to make troops available. Undaunted, Bishop Pigneaux recruited a number of mercenaries and engineers on his own accord. Together they returned to Saigon in 1789. Though only a handful of these mercenaries stayed in Saigon for more than a few years, they had a substantial impact. Two engineers, Victor Olivier and Théodore Le Brun, were responsible for constructing a European-style citadel in Saigon. Olivier later constructed a similar citadel in Nha Trang. Jean-Marie Dayot (1760–1809) and Laurent Barizy (1769–1802), purchased weapons, ammunition, uniforms, and material to make weapons, chiefly from British and Portuguese proprietors. Several of these mercenaries, including Oliver, Dayot, Philippe Vannier (1762–1842),

and Jean-Baptiste Chaigneau (1769–1832), commanded European-style battleships for the Nguyen during the course of their later operations alongside Vietnamese commanders and Siamese and Cambodian mercenaries.

While the Tay Son brothers slowly lost control of southern Cochinchina in the 1780s, they continued to become stronger in Tonkin. While the Tay Son negotiated a brief alliance with the Trinh lords in the 1770s, the Trinh lords were reeling from years of famine and a messy succession crisis in 1782. At that time, Nguyen Nhac, the eldest of the Tay Son brothers, ruled from his capital at Cha Ban near the city of Qui Nhon. He ordered Nguyen Hue, the middle of the three brothers, to march north and take the former Nguyen capital at Phu Xuan (Hue). However, going considerably beyond his orders, Nguyen Hue continued marching into Tonkin. Trinh resistance collapsed and the Trinh Lord fled.

Initially, the Le dynasty, under the leadership of Emperor Canh Hung (r. 1740–1786), made an alliance with the Tay Son. However, he died soon thereafter, and when a series of internecine conflicts forced the Tay Son to reinvade in 1787, the new Emperor Le Chieu Thong (r. 1787–1789) fled to China and requested assistance from the Qing dynasty. The Chinese emperor Qianlong sent a force of as many as two hundred thousand men and occupied modern-day Hanoi in late 1788. Nguyen Hue, who in the meantime had crowned himself the Emperor Quang Trung, caught the Chinese troops by surprise by attacking during the celebrations of the 1789 Lunar New Year and easily defeated the Qing army.[14]

---

13 Nguyen Anh also separately negotiated an agreement with the Portuguese with the help of merchant Antonio Vicente Rosa in 1786. This tentative agreement was to give Portuguese land and trading concessions in exchange for Portuguese military assistance, but never resulted in a formal treaty. Pierre-Yves Manguin, *Les Nguyen, le Macao et le Portugal: Aspects politiques et commerciaux d'une relation privilège en mer de Chine, 1773–1802* (Paris: École Française d'Extrême-Orient, 1984), 61–7.

14 Dutton, *The Tay Son Uprising*, 47–9.

From 1789 the Tay Son movement gradually lost momentum. Two major factors weakened the Tay Son: their own internal disputes and the untimely deaths of the Tay Son brothers. The youngest brother, Nguyen Lu, who ruled from Saigon, was the first to die in 1787, immediately upon returning to the Qui Nhon area after Tay Son forces were defeated by Nguyen Anh in Saigon. After Nguyen Lu's death, the two remaining brothers competed with each other as rivals for power. They both proclaimed themselves emperors, with Nguyen Nhac ruling as the Thai Duc Emperor and Nguyen Hue as the Quang Trung Emperor, and they cultivated separate power bases in Cha Ban/Qui Nhon and Phu Xuan/Hue respectively.[15] However, this rivalry would not last, as Nguyen Hue would die in 1792 and Nguyen Nhac in 1793.

Though Nguyen Hue's son Nguyen Quang Toan (1783–1802) would become the new ruler of a purportedly unified Tay Son movement, he was a child who was subject to the manipulations of Tay Son officials vying for power. This instability allowed Nguyen Anh's forces to make slow and steady progress in seasonal campaigns against the Tay Son in the 1790s, until Nguyen Anh was able to finally defeat the Tay Son in 1802. Subsequently, he declared himself the Gia Long Emperor and declared the founding of the last Imperial dynasty of Vietnam, the Nguyen (1802–1945).

The Nguyen Dynasty and the Vicissitudes of Vietnamese Attitudes toward Europeans (1802-1841)

Upon taking the throne in Hue, Nguyen Anh, now known as the Gia Long Emperor (r. 1802–1820), was faced with satisfying two very different political groups. The first group consisted of a motley crew of ethnically Vietnamese, Chinese, Khmer, or Siamese military officers, mercenaries, and former pirates that had accompanied Nguyen Anh when he fled Saigon in the early 1780s. John Whitmore has called these men the "Bangkok honor roll" because many of them were present with Nguyen Anh when he was in Siam in the mid-1780s.[16] Though this was a diverse group of individuals, they shared common characteristics. Most had not passed a Confucian-style civil service examination and had only a rudimentary knowledge of the classics. Nevertheless, they were worldly individuals with connections to the Europeans; many of them had been friendly with Bishop Pigneaux and several of the European mercenaries who had fought by their side. One might say that the Bangkok honor roll shared a vision for the Nguyen dynasty that was broadly in concert with the governance of the Nguyen lords, one in which commerce was emphasized and a certain level of diversity appreciated.

The second constituency that the Gia Long Emperor had to satisfy was the intellectual class, especially those from Tonkin. Many of these intellectuals were reluctant to serve the Nguyen dynasty. Those who had remained loyal to the Le dynasty were upset that Gia Long had not restored the Le, and many others were concerned about the lack of education of the Bangkok honor roll and with the Nguyen dynasty's southern roots.

To placate the Bangkok honor roll and ensure stability, Gia Long gave his two most prominent generals, Nguyen Van Thanh (1758–1817) and Le Van Duyet (1763–1832) positions as the "military protectors" of the Hanoi and Saigon respectively, thus keeping Hanoi and Saigon under quasi-autonomous military rule. He also ensured that key contributors to the defeat of the Tay Son were given promotions and honorary titles. To placate the intellectual class, Gia Long sought and received recognition from the Qing dynasty in China, slowly

---

15   Nguyen Hue began construction of a new capital in Nghe An province, but this was never completed.

16   John K. Whitmore, "An Outline of Vietnamese History before French Conquest," *Vietnam Forum* 8 (Summer-Fall 1986), 7.

reinstituted a Confucian civil service system, and made active attempts to recruit officials from prominent families to Hue.

Eventually, however, these groups would come into open conflict. The most prominent of these conflicts occurred in the 1815–1816 period, during which time the Gia Long emperor was choosing a new crown prince who would serve as his successor. Previously, Gia Long's heir apparent had been Prince Canh, the child who accompanied Bishop Pigneaux to France to seek a treaty with King Louis XVI. But Prince Canh had died of smallpox in 1801. Members of the Bangkok honor roll rallied to the support Prince Canh's eldest son My Duong for crown prince. My Duong had a strong case under Nguyen primogeniture law, and had been the presumptive heir apparent.[17] Nevertheless, by 1816, Gia Long chose Prince Dam, the future Minh Mang Emperor (r. 1820–1841), as his successor. This was a choice that was favorable to the intellectuals. In the meantime, after members of the Bangkok honor roll such as Nguyen Van Thanh voiced their concerns, Gia Long took the opportunity to eliminate his position as military protector of the North. Under the pretext of a treasonous poem written by Nguyen Van Thanh's son, the great military hero of the Tay Son wars was forced to commit suicide by drinking poison in 1817. The succession conflict did not end upon the death of the Gia Long Emperor and the coronation of the Ming Mang Emperor. Rather, a shadow campaign for a palace coup resurfaced during the first years of Minh Mang's reign, leading to the stripping of royal titles from My Duong in 1824.

The Nguyen dynasty's hostility to Christianity is rooted in these succession disputes. As Prince Canh had been baptized a Christian, My Duong was seen as sympathetic to Christians, at the very least. For that reason, Christians, Europeans at the court, and mercenaries tended to support My Duong, along with the old guard of the Bangkok honor roll. Probably not coincidentally, 1824 marked a year in which Minh Mang attempted to outlaw the arrival of new Christian missionaries, though no thorough persecution of Christians would begin until 1832.

In the 1830s, two events occurred that tied European missionaries and Vietnamese Christians with rebellions against Nguyen authority. The first was a dispute between two villages known as the Duong Son incident. Duong Son, a predominantly Christian village near Hue, became embroiled in a bitter controversy over land with Co Lao, a neighboring village, which escalated when the Christians armed themselves to protect their land. This resulted in the Ming Mang Emperor's exiling of more than seventy of the villagers to Cambodia and a death sentence for a prominent missionary, Father François Jaccard (1799–1838), though that death sentence was temporarily commuted.[18] Though on its surface this was a minor incident, the spectre of Vietnamese Christians taking up arms against non-Christian communities was sufficient for the Minh Mang Emperor to call for the arrest of the local bishop and to order all ships entering Saigon harbor to be searched for missionaries.

The second incident, the Le Van Khoi rebellion, was much wider in scope. The Gia Long Emperor appointed Le Van Duyet, a hero of the Tay Son wars, the Military Protector of Saigon in 1812. This position gave him de facto quasi-independent authority over all of the Mekong delta and suzerain authority over Cambodia, and he held it, with a

---

17 Agathe Larcher-Goscha, "Prince Cuong De and Franco–Vietnamese Competition for the Heritage of Gia Long," in *Viet Nam Exposé*, ed. Gisèle Luce Bousquet and Pierre Brocheux (Ann Arbor, MI: University of Michigan Press, 2002), 204; Tran My-Van, *A Vietnamese Royal Exile in Japan: Prince Cuong De, 1882–1951* (New York: Routledge, 2005), 21.

18 Jacob Ramsay, *Mandarins and Martyrs: The Church and the Nguyen Dynasty in Early Nineteenth Century Vietnam* (Stanford, CA: Stanford University Press, 2008), 42–3.

brief break in the late 1810s when he was assigned to pacify the north, until his death in 1832. Seeing an opportunity to assert central control over the south, Minh Mang acted, abolishing the position of Military Protector, reorganizing the southern provinces, increasing surveillance of ethnic Chinese who had been privileged under Le Van Duyet's rule, issuing further prohibitions on Christianity, and posthumously declaring Le Van Duyet a traitor.[19]

As a result, Saigon forces loyal to Le Van Duyet's more autonomous vision of Vietnamese governance rebelled under the banner of Le Van Khoi, the "adopted son" of Le Van Duyet. From 1833–1835, loyal officials of Le Van Duyet, Christians, ethnically Chinese merchants, and other ethnic minorities defended the citadel of Saigon. Le Van Khoi rejected Minh Mang's authority and declared My Duong to be the legitimate heir to the throne.[20] Though officially Catholic missionaries remained neutral, among the supporters of the rebellion found in the Saigon citadel when it fell at the end of the rebellion was an MEP missionary, Father Joseph Marchand, along with a very considerable number of Vietnamese Catholics. Marchand was subsequently executed, leading to a hardening of existing anti-Christian policies at Minh Mang's court.[21]

From these anti-Catholic actions, Minh Mang developed a reputation as being a European-hating xenophobe whose brutal and repressive anti-Western policies paved the way for French intervention in Indochina.[22] However, the reality is more complex. Starting in 1816, Western Missionaries and Vietnamese Christians were players in a factional battle at the Nguyen court. They were perceived as taking sides with the Bangkok honor roll, and

with favoring the legitimacy of an alternative line of royal succession emerging from the descendants of Prince Canh. This line would make claims to the throne that would attract the loyalty of some Vietnamese until the death of Prince Cuong De in 1951. Because they took the side of Prince Canh's sons, Minh Mang perceived Vietnamese Christians and Western missionaries as potentially disloyal at best. In turn, Minh Mang's suspicion of the loyalty of Christians became a self-fulfilling prophecy. His suspicion of them led to increasing proscriptions of Christianity, which made Christians even more likely to support movements against him. These politics are more complicated than the interpretation of Minh Mang's *a priori* resistance to Westerners would suggest.

On the other hand, Minh Mang had a keen knowledge of and an active interest in European affairs. In the 1820s, he employed missionaries at the capital as translators. Though this was certainly a way of monitoring missionary activities, it was also a function of Minh Mang's curiosity about European events and the sheer volume of Europeans seeking to trade with the Nguyen. He encouraged Vietnamese delegations to visit British, Portuguese, and Dutch colonial cities for trade and development purposes. He was enthusiastic about developing new technology, such as steamboats, and even attempted a commercial mission to Paris.

Western Gunboat Policy toward Korea (1800s)

Western powers began to reach Korea in the early nineteenth century, evidenced by British

---

19 Taylor, *History of the Vietnamese*, 419–20.

20 Mark W. McLeod, *The Vietnamese Response to French Intervention, 1862–1874* (New York: Praeger, 1991), 30.

21 Choi Byung Wook, *Southern Vietnam under the Reign of Minh Mạng: Central Policies and Local Response.* (Ithaca, NY: Cornell Southeast Asia Publications, 2004), 95.

22 On Ming Mang's purported hatred of Europeans, Missionaries, and Christians, see Trương Vĩnh Ký, *Cours d'histoire Annamite* (Saigon: Imprimerie du Gouvernement, 1875), 268.

ships appearing off the coast of the peninsula in 1832, French warships arriving in 1846, and Russian gunboats clashing with Koreans in 1854. The Choson court's shift to a closed-door policy was greatly influenced by the Sino-British Opium War in 1839–1842. The Korean court received detailed information about the West's opium trade that had triggered extensive socioeconomic calamity in China. The Koreans also knew about the crushing military defeat the Qing dynasty suffered when it resisted the British in the First Opium War. The Qing's Western-caused predicament convinced the Choson court that Western powers' eagerness to open the region was no more than destructive economic exploitation. Korea became even more guarded against the West. One of the major reasons behind the Choson's aversion to Western influence, as James Palais explains, was that "the Korean ideal was a self-contained, self-sufficient agrarian society led by enlightened Confucian scholar-bureaucrats."[23]

Having observed the West's injurious business practices in China, the Choson court was compelled to take all precautions necessary to frustrate Western cultural, religious, and military advances in Korea. The court was convinced that the Western missionaries were merely playing a lead in the profound Western conspiracy to exploit the kingdom—hence its determination to fend off Western encroachment and stave off the same predicament facing its Chinese counterpart. Whatever the true intentions of the Western powers might have been, the developments in China provided Koreans with a clear warning that the West had less than noble intentions in the region. Key-Hiuk Kim uses the term "exclusionism" to describe Korean isolationism, suggesting a protective policy different from that in China and in Japan. Bruce Cumings comments: "Exclusionism was especially strong in the

nineteenth century, since Koreans were not unaware of the increasing Western presence in East Asia, but it was a relatively recent phenomenon in Korea's long history."[24]

Although the Choson court continued its isolationist policy under the rule of the Andong Kim family in the first half of the nineteenth century, the Catholic Church in Korea grew steadily, leading to intensified enforcement of the prohibition edict. Amid the renewed government crackdowns, a small episode was to have a profound implication for Korea's foreign relations for years to follow. The incident was initiated by the authority's discovery of a letter (the "silk letter"), written by a Korean convert, requesting the French mission in Beijing to arrange a French naval intervention. The letter served as timely and justifiable evidence for the suspicious court to intensify its anti-Catholic campaign, culminating in the persecution of more than seventy Korean converts and three French missionaries in 1839.[25] The move marked a drastic departure from the Choson court's heretofore relatively tolerant attitude toward the West. The court, which had until then shown unusual goodwill and cooperation toward the Westerners, mostly shipwreck victims, had begun to single out the Catholic Church as a dire national threat. It decided to apply the most extreme measures in dealing with Christianity and the Western powers in general.

In 1846 France dispatched three warships to Korea and demanded an explanation for the court's persecution of three French missionaries. The Choson court was at a loss in dealing with this scarcely known foreign power, because it had no relevant prior experience. The court adopted a nonresponsive stand. Such an unorthodox policy, adopted not out of deliberate defiance but rather for lack of alternatives, was nevertheless effective;

23   Palais, *Confucian Statecraft and Korean Institutions*.

24   Bruce Cumings, *Korea's Place in the Sun: A Modern History* (New York: Norton, 1997), 89.

25   Seth, *A Concise History of Korea*, 220.

the French gunboats shortly withdrew. Despite this failure, France again sent two warships to Korea on the same mission the next year. In spite of the French naval intimidation, the Choson court continued its passive resistance. France did not resort to the use of military means against the determined Korean court, and the incident was resolved without resorting to actual hostility.

The French conduct greatly intensified the Choson court's suspicion about missionaries and the intentions of the Western powers in general. As unfortunate as the persecution of the three French missionaries was, it should be noted that they entered Korea and worked on their religious mission against the Korean government's royal decree. By threatening the use of military force against the Hermit Kingdom, France failed to acknowledge the fact that Korea was a sovereign independent nation, thus leading to further distrust of Christianity and the West as a whole among the Koreans. The fact that the French naval power did not bear down on Korea probably had more to do with the timing than the lack of will. As Charles K. Armstrong points out, "despite the overwhelming military might of the Western countries—Korea was simply not a prize worthy of much sacrifice, as far as most Europeans and Americans were concerned."[26]

France's gunboat diplomacy, a poorly conceived move for the self-proclaimed protector of the Church, was an inauspicious omen for Korea. While demonstrating French determination to support Korea's Catholic converts and spread Christianity, gunboat diplomacy also created social unrest for the conflict-averse kingdom. The direct consequence of French gunboat diplomacy was not the Choson court's submission but its initiation of another round of harsh Catholic persecution, including the persecution of Kim Tae-gon (Andrew Kim), the first ordained Korean priest, and other lay converts in

1846. Seth also points out, "this persecution became entangled in factional disputes," as "religion became enmeshed with factional politics."[27] The successive persecutions, however, did not muffle the growing popularity of the Christianity in Korea. On the contrary, the church experienced another period of robust growth when the court was preoccupied with its recurring political infighting after the death of King Choljong in 1864. The lack of strict enforcement of the prohibition rule encouraged more French missionaries to enter the country clandestinely and allowed the Korean Catholic community to continue a slow but steady growth. Under the pastorship of twelve French missionaries, the number of Korean Catholics increased from around eleven thousand in 1850 to some twenty-three thousand in 1865. The Church had taken full advantage of the relaxation of political suppression.

After the French episode, the Taewongoon regime had every reason to avoid similar encounters with others. Nevertheless, the West, especially the United States, was hardly in a mood to grant the befuddled Choson court the tranquility it so eagerly sought. Having succeeded in coercing Japan to accept the Kanagawa Treaty in 1854, America once again applied the "Perry approach," the gunboat demonstration, to Korea. In May 1871, America's first Korean expedition force, which was comprised of five warships carrying eighty-five pieces of artillery and 1,230 marines and sailors, arrived at the Korean peninsula and demanded a resolution over a previous case of an American schooner *General Sherman*.

The USS *General Sherman* entered Korean water on August 16, 1866, allegedly to exchange goods. This first Western commercial venture proceeded to Pyongyang along the west coast of Korea despite the Choson court's strict seclusion policy. The Korean authorities had made repeated attempts to turn back the ship as the nation's isolationist policy dictated.

---

26 Armstrong, *The Koreas*, 8.

27 Seth, *A Concise History of Korea*, 220.

The Choson court's official position was that the *General Sherman* was on a mission of piracy punishable by law. Rebuffing the governor of Pyongyang's demands to withdraw, the crew on the ship reportedly fired into a local crowd determined to repel the intruder. Subsequently, upon the disappearance of the merchant ship, the United States first attempted through its Chinese contacts to extract an explanation of its fate. To the American inquiry, the Choson court conveyed a largely vague and defensive response, which may have been all the court could afford due to the lack of more detailed information. Failing to get a satisfactory reply, they applied the "Perry approach," the gunboat demonstration. Even under the threat of a naval squadron that was significantly more powerful than the French expedition, the Korean government did not its once-successful, no-negotiation doctrine. Buoyed by its earlier success in turning back the French, the court undertook measures to strengthen its defenses around Kanghwa Island and brought a formal charge against the American illegal intrusion into Korean waters. The court took the same uncompromising stand with which it succeeded in turning back the French force, willing to endure another military confrontation unless the American force withdrew.

The American intentions were not much different from those of the French except that they were fully authorized by their government. Encountering the Korean court's outright rejection, the American expedition realized that its objectives were obtainable only through a successful demonstration of its military might. The standoff led to a military confrontation in which the modern American military inflicted a severe blow to the Korean defenders. Having overcome the initial setbacks, the Korean troops again persisted against the well-equipped invaders. The ensuing stalemate eventually left the American expedition with two equally painful alternatives: the voluntary termination of its gunboat demonstration, or escalation of the standoff with active military engagement. Remarkably, the United States chose a peaceful solution, and shortly the naval force left the area, aborting America's "little war" on Korea. America's impulsive mission gave the Hermit Kingdom its second victory against the Western powers, however insignificant and deceptive that may have been. The successful repulsion of the American expedition was the crown of the Taewongoon regency's isolationist doctrine. On the other hand, such a victory deluded the Choson government into believing in the deceptive effectiveness of its seclusion policy. As a result, Korea missed an opportunity to open itself to Western trade in exchange for Washington's relatively modest demands.

Conclusion to Part Two

This section of *East Asia and the West* has focused on the extraordinary economic, cultural, and social changes wrought by the globalization of the early modern era. During the sixteen and seventeenth centuries, East Asians were confronted with new economic and political realities stemming from changes in shipping technology and the European colonization of the New World and of portions of South and Southeast Asia. This section has shown how East Asians encountered Christian missionaries and increasing European demands for silks, tea, and other goods from Asian areas. In this section, we have seen that East Asians adapted to new global changes by promulgating political, technical, and religious reforms, all of which influenced the development of East Asian versions of modernity.

The developments led East Asian countries to change their economic structures and to develop policies to cope with the influx of new currencies. By the nineteenth century, East Asian countries were shifting from agricultural to manufacturing economies. By the middle of the nineteenth century, East Asian countries were experiencing the rise of new forms of nationalism and were adjusting to military confrontations with the West, as we shall see in part three.

PART THREE

Confrontation and Westernization

Introduction to Part Three

In part two of this book, we explored the new economic, political, and social conditions under which East Asians formed new relations with Western individuals, institutions, and states. By the middle of the nineteenth century, East Asian countries more frequently found themselves in military confrontations with the West and worked to modernize their military technology to catch up with European and American advancements in weapons and ships. To acquire expertise in new technology, East Asian countries sent their best and brightest to study in Europe and the United States. This development, in turn, led to pressure for political changes, as these intellectuals were exposed to university educations that naturally went beyond technical questions. In turn, the clashes with the West fortified a sense of the particularity of the Japanese, Chinese, Korean, or Vietnamese experience. As a result, by the nineteenth century all of these areas saw the rise of new kinds of nationalism.

Another major theme of this section is the role of imperialism in shaping East Asian modernity. In the late nineteenth century, these forms of nationalism and modernity developed in the context of direct clashes with imperial powers. By the end of the century, the Vietnamese had succumbed to French control and Korea was under the thumb of an increasingly bellicose Japanese Empire. Through the course of two direct conflicts with Britain and countless more negotiations under threat of force, China saw its territory slowly carved into "treaty ports," in which foreign powers enjoyed quasi-sovereign rights given to them through extraterritoriality provisions in unequal treaties that they forced the Qing dynasty to sign. The eventual result was a semi-colonized China that was carved into European, American, and Japanese spheres of influence.

Chapter 5

Opium Wars, Boxers, and Revolutions

China fought five foreign wars from 1839 to 1900 against the European powers, the United States, and Japan over trade, opium trafficking, and foreign intervention in neighboring countries Korea and Vietnam. The Qing government lost all of these wars and signed several treaties that opened China to Western trade. China's defeat by Britain in the First Opium War in 1842, and the resultant unequal Treaty of Nanjing, led R. Keith Schoppa to conclude that "the Opium War was the opening salvo of a century of aggression by Western nations against China, a century of conflict between very different cultures with sharply differing values; yet each clash would have its own particulars and realities."[1] The Qing Empire began to lose the central position and powerful status that had been established and developed by its earlier emperors, such as Kangxi and Qianlong. The Qing's defeat ended the five hundred-year-old tributary system, which centered on neighboring states' recognition of Chinese superiority and dominance in exchange for goods and assistance in times of rebellion.

However, as Harold M. Tanner states, "Neither the Daoguang emperor nor his officials saw the Opium War as the beginning of a new era."[2] In 1857–1858, joint British and French forces in the Second Opium War defeated the Qing military again. The Manchu rulers signed the Treaty of Tianjin in 1858, forcing China to allow Western commercial influence and European imperialist exploitation. Other powers followed suit and forced Qing to sign similar treaties with them. A series of external conflicts deprived the Qing rulers of the capacity to focus on the economic, military, and technological reforms necessary to rejuvenate the country. Consequently, as Tanner observes, "Qing officials still knew almost nothing about the West, its languages, governments, technology, or culture. Westerners were simply another variety of uncivilized barbarian. As such, they were one of many problems."[3]

After the two Opium Wars, the Qing army fought against the French army and navy both in China and in Vietnam in 1884–1885. Defeated, China signed another Treaty of

---

1   R. Keith Schoppa, *Revolution and Its Past: Identities and Change in Modern Chinese History*, 3rd ed. (New York: Prentice Hall, 2011), 54.

2   Harold M. Tanner, *China: A History: From the Great Qing Empire through the People's Republic of China* (Indianapolis, IN: Hackett, 2010), 79.

3   Ibid.

Tianjin with France, recognizing French control of Vietnam and conceding French control in Indochina. In 1894–1895, the Qing navy fought against Japanese forces over Korea. After the Japanese navy defeated the Chinese fleet, the Japanese army invaded China by occupying Manchuria and landing at Shandong province. The subsequent Treaty of Shimonoseki that concluded the Sino-Japanese War in 1895 stipulated Korea's "independence," and ceded Taiwan, Penghu Islands, and Liaodong Peninsula to Japan. Meanwhile, amidst domestic upheavals that went hand in hand with foreign wars, two major uprisings—the Taiping Rebellion (1851–1864) and Boxer Rebellion (1900)—wrought the most havoc on hinese society. During the Boxer Rebellion, eight foreign powers joined forces in a military coalition to defeat the Boxers in Beijing and Tianjin and forced the Boxer Protocol upon the Qing government, stipulating the latter's payment of a large indemnity of 450 million taels of silver payable in thirty-nine years. The Qing dynasty in the late nineteenth century was what William T. Rowe describes as "a constantly moving target," before eventually collapsing in 1912 following the Republic Revolution.[4]

The First Opium War and the Treaty of Nanjing

Until the mid-eighteenth century, China had enjoyed a surplus through European trade, in which the Western merchants purchased tea, silk, spices, and other agricultural items from China. In the meantime, the Europeans did not find a sizable market for their manufactured goods, including shoes, cloth, firearms, and machines. To balance

the trade, some British merchants began to smuggle opium from India to China in the early eighteenth century. They did not introduce opium smoking to the Chinese, who started the habit in the seventeenth century when tobacco was brought to China from Latin America. The opium sale in China skyrocketed in the late eighteenth and early nineteenth centuries. Soon the balance of the European trade was reversed and China had a trade deficit by the 1820s. the opium smuggling did not only cause financial problems of the Qing government, but also resulted in corrupted politics, crimes, and huge health issues. The Qing court tried to deal with the opium problem.

Emperor Daoguang (r. 1821–1850) decided to put the opium trade to an end by appointing Governor Lin Zexu as a special commissioner to Guangzhou, the only seaport open for the foreign trade.[5] After his arrival on March 10, 1839, Commissioner Lin launched an aggressive campaign against opium smuggling and detained about 350 European merchants on March 24, forcing them to surrender their opium supplies.[6] These Western merchants spent six weeks in detention until May 18, when they delivered 21,306 chests of their opium stocks. In June Lin publicly destroyed all the British opium at Humen, a waterfront town outside Guangzhou. In August he ordered the expulsion of all British residents from Macao.[7]

Deeming Lin's campaign as an affront to British national pride, the British government declared war on China on January 31, 1840, thus beginning the First Opium War.[8] In June the British troops arrived at Guangzhou and noticed that Commissioner Lin and his garrison were well prepared for defense. On June 30, Charles Elliot, Chief Superintendent of

---

4   William T. Rowe, *China's Last Empire: The Great Qing* (Cambridge, MA: Harvard University Press, 2009), 10.

5   Li, *Modern China*, 68–70.

6   Pamela Kyle Crossley, *The Wobbling Pivot; China since 1800: An Interpretive History* (New York: Wiley-Blackwell, 2010), 76.

7   Spence, *The Search for Modern China*, 150–2.

8   Hsu, *The Rise of Modern China*, 184.

British Trade who played an instrumental role in the naval maneuvers during the Opium War, ordered his troops to sail north along the coast and bombard the Qing army's positions at Xiamen in Fujian province. On July 6, the British attacked Dinghai in Zhejiang province, and took over the city. On July 28, eight British warships sailed further north, and on August 9, they arrived at Dagu near Tianjin, less than eighty miles from Beijing.[9] Under the threat of big guns, the Qing government began to waver. It relieved Lin of his duties and ordered him to be investigated and punished. The emperor asked the British army to return to Guangzhou and sent Qishan, a leading advocate for making compromise and concessions to avoid more calamities, to negotiate peace with the British.[10]

In November 1840 the British troops concentrated around the Guangzhou area. To gain a better position in the peace negotiation, they attacked Humen with 1,461 men on January 7, 1841. After several hours of fierce fighting, the Qing army lost two fire positions at Humen and suffered six hundred casualties in its first formal defense. The British had more than one hundred casualties. With the military victory, the British demanded Qishan to sign the draft Convention of Chuanbi in January, whereby China ceded Hong Kong to Britain and opened Guangzhou as a trading port. The Qing government, regarding the cession of territories and the payment of indemnities as an insult to the imperial authority, declared war on Britain on January 27. In February, the Qing army sent eight thousand troops to reinforce Guangzhou. On February 26, the British attacked again and took over Humen. In response, the Qing army launched a counterattack on May 21–22, but the battle destroyed seventy-one Qing vessels and more than sixty heavy artillery pieces. The British attacked Guangzhou on May 24, with 2,754 troops against the Qing garrison of 49,000 men. The British took over the high points of the city that evening, forcing the Qing generals to raise the white flags and surrender the next day.[11]

Upon receiving the draft Convention of Chuanbi, the British government was unhappy with its terms, which it believed were too lenient towards the Chinese. Instead of ratifying the treaty, it ordered Henry Pottinger, who had replaced Elliot in August and commanded twenty-six warships and 3,500 men, to carry on the fighting. The British troops took over Xiamen in August and Dinghai in October. Later that year, China also lost Zhenhai and Ningbo, Zhejiang province. In June 1842 the British attacked Wusong at the mouth of the Yangzi River and then captured Shanghai. Great Britain defeated the Qing army in all the battles. In August British warships appeared on the Yangzi River outside of Nanjing. The Qing court sent an imperial commissioner named Qiying to Nanjing to sign the Sino-British Treaty.

This treaty, signed on August 29, 1842, consisting of thirteen articles, was the first treaty that opened a larger Chinese market, provided special privileges, and paid a huge war indemnity after China lost a war to a foreign power. According to the Treaty of Nanjing, the Qing government ceded Hong Kong, opened five ports for trade, including Guangzhou, Fuzhou, Xiamen, Ningbo, and Shanghai, and paid an indemnity of twenty-one million silver dollars to the British. It also stipulated that the tariff on British goods be subject to negotiations between the two countries. In 1843, the British requested the Qing court to sign two supplementary agreements, including the "General Regulations Governing Anglo-Chinese Trade in the Five Trading Ports of Guangzhou, Xiamen, Fuzhou, Ningbo, and Shanghai," and the Sino-British Treaty of Humen.

---

9   Institute of Chinese History, CASS, *Jianming zhongguo lishi duben* [Concise Text of Chinese History], 440–1.

10   Lucian W. Pye, *China: An Introduction*, 4th ed. (New York: HarperCollins, 1991), 115–16.

11   Bruce A. Elleman, *Modern Chinese Warfare, 1795–1989* (London, UK: Routledge, 2001), 22–4.

Both documents allowed the British to rent land and build houses in the trading ports, leading to the so-called "concessions" in these major cities later. Thereafter, other Western powers such as France, America, Germany, Spain, and Russia followed the British and signed the similar treaties with China. In the Sino-French Treaty of Huangpu in 1844, the Qing court agreed with the French government to allow the Roman Catholic and Protestant missionaries to build their churches and promote their faith in these trading cities. In the Sino-American Treaty of Wangxia in 1844, Americans gained the special right of sending warships to these Chinese ports "for the protection of the commerce of their country."[12]

The First Opium War of 1839–1842 had a long-term traumatic effect on China and changed the nature of its foreign relations for the worse. The war was a humiliating defeat for the Chinese Empire. Hans van de Ven suggests that "the Qing was ill-prepared to deal with Britain's naval challenge not because it was a backward country or a Confucian society with little regard for the military, but because it had faced different sorts of military challenges and followed a different path of military development than Britain."[13] Chipping away at China's national sovereignty, the Treaty of Nanjing and the subsequent unequal treaties imposed by several other European powers marked the beginning of the end for the Qing dynasty.

The Second Opium War, the Sino-French War, and the Self-Strengthening Movement

A decade and half later, China lost the Second Opium War to a relatively small Anglo-French coalition force, numbering twenty-five thousand, that captured the capital Peking (later known as Beijing)

and ransacked the Imperial Summer Palace, thus ending the age-old tribute system with its neighboring countries. According to the Sino-French Treaty of Huangpu in 1844, the Qing court would negotiate a revision of the treaty in twelve years. The Qing government, however, did not have any intention to revise or renew the Sino-French Treaty in 1856. The Chinese officials believed that a new negotiation might bring about more demands by the Western powers. However, by the mid-19th century, the Chinese desire or intention no longer mattered, as the Western powers were determined to expand their influences in China. The British demand that the Qing government open the entire country to British merchants was initially rebuffed. The British government used the Incident of Arrow to launch a new military attack on China. On October 8, 1856, a Chinese merchant vessel, Arrow, was burned by some local people in Guangzhou. The Chinese ship registered by the British and had a British flag on it. The British Navy moved its gunboats in and bombed Guangzhou on October 23, when the Chinese governor refused to apologize. Soon the French forces joined the British and their joint expeditionary force captured the city of Guangzhou next year. It became the Second Opium War between China and Great Britain and France, and also known as the Arrow War of 1857–1858. In May 1858, the joint force took over Tianjin. Without an effective defense, the Qing court lost the capital city Beijing to the British-French forces in October.

The military weakness of government forces was further revealed in their combat against the Taiping troops which, totally nearly one million and launching several northern and western expeditions against the Qing army in the mid-nineteenth century, posed a severe threat to the Manchu dynasty. Without much choice, the Qing government sent

---

12   Cohen, *America's Response to China*, 11–13.

13   de Ven, "Military Mobilization in China, 1840–1949," in *War in the Modern World since 1815*, ed. Jeremy Black (London, UK: Routledge, 2003), 37.

representatives and asked for peace negotiations. Without the help of the Western powers, the government forces would have had a much harder time suppressing the Taipings. In June 1858 the Qing government signed the Treaties of Tianjin with Britain, France, the United States, and Russia at the end of the Second Opium War, opening up more ports to foreign trade as well as the interior of the country to Western missionaries and, ultimately, accepting the opium trade. Any hope for relative peace on the part of the Qing rulers was shattered when they were once again facing the French forces over control of Vietnam.

The war between France and China during August 1884–April 1885, or the Sino-French War, grew out of the Black Flag/Tonkin Wars of 1882–1885. The Black Flag Army, a peasant rebel force under the command of Liu Yongfu, attacked French establishment in the Tonkin Gulf region in 1882–1884. In the summer of 1884, a Chinese general named Feng Zicai joined the Black Flags and defeated the French force at Lang Son near the Chinese-Vietnamese border, a defeat caused the French cabinet to collapse.

In the fall of 1884, France sent naval reinforcement to China under the command of Admiral Amedee Anatole Courbet. The French fleet sailed to the southeastern coast of China, and Courbet launched a surprise attack on the Qing's Fujian Fleet at Mawei, Fuzhou, on August 23. In less than thirty minutes, the French destroyed all the eleven warships of the Fujian Fleet, and sunk nineteenth transit and supply ships. Next day, French warships bombed the Fujian naval base, and destroyed the Mawei Naval Ship Yard. On August 26, the Qing government declared war on France. In September, Courbet began to attack Taiwan. In early October, the French force occupied Keelung and attacked Taipei. Then, in February–March 1885, Courbet began to attack Zhenhai, Zhejiang province,

along the eastern coast of China. The Qing court appointed Li Hongzhang to negotiate with the French in the summer. On June 9, 1885, Li and J. Patenotre, French representative, signed the peace treaty at Tianjin. According to the Treaty of Tianjin, China recognized Vietnam as one of the French protectorates, and opened new ports for trade in the border areas between Vietnam and China. It also compelled the Chinese to hire Frenchmen in railway building. D. R. SarDesai points out, "The treaty marked the extinction of the nearly two-millennia-old subordinate relationship of Vietnam to China."[14] By 1893, when France annexed Laos, the development of French Indochina, with an administrative capital in Hanoi, was complete.

During the period between the 1860s and 1900s, a number of Qing high-ranking officials, including Prince Gong, Yixin, Zeng Guofan, Li Hongzhang, and Zuo Zongtang, began to adopt Western technology and learn European military techniques to build a new Chinese navy and army. They were the first people who built modern industries in China. All these efforts are referred to by Chinese historians as the "Self-Strengthening Movement." The bureaucrats who were active in this reforming movement belonged to the so-called "Westernization group," different from the diehards in the ruling clique who did not want any change or reform at all, which could undermine the Machu regime. But the reformers intended to save the Qing from being weakened by Western imperial aggression and also to embrace appropriate strategies to strengthen the nation.

In the name of "strengthening the military and enriching the country," beginning in the 1860s, the reformers introduced modern military technology and European armament industries. In 1861 Zeng Guofan established a new ammunition factory in Anqing, Anhui province. In 1865 Li Hongzhang founded in Shanghai the Jiangnan Arsenal,

---

14   D. R. SarDesai, *Southeast Asia: Past and Present*, 7th ed. (Boulder, CO: Westview Press, 2013), 120.

specializing in the manufacturing of rifles, artillery pieces, ammunition, and steamships. He also founded the Nanjing Jinling Arsenal in the same year. In 1868 the Jiangnan Arsenal made China's first steel gunboat, which was named *Huiji*. In 1866 Zuo Zongtang set up in Fuzhou the Mawei Shipyard for the construction of more warships. Under pressure from the reforming group, the Qing government established the Tianjin Machinery Factory for the manufacturing of firearms. In addition, there were many ammunitions factories of smaller size across the country.

In 1874 the Qing government began to establish a modern navy with Western technology. From 1868 to 1876, the Jiangnan Arsenal built eleven warships for the new navy. Nevertheless, because of financial difficulties, corruption among officials, and the lack of a compound engine, more warships for the Chinese naval force were still produced in Europe. In the 1880s, Li Hongzhang founded a naval academy in Tianjin, a dockyard at Lushun, and a naval port at Weihaiwei, Shandong. He also bought warships from Germany and artillery pieces from Britain to arm the newly founded Northern Sea Fleet.

From the 1870s to 1900s, while attempting to strengthen the military, the reformers also built some modern industrial enterprises. Among the most important were the Chinese Commercial Steamship Navigation Company in 1872, Kaiping Coal Mine in 1878, Shanghai Cotton Mill in 1890, Hubei Textile Factory in 1892, and the Hanyang Iron Enterprise in 1893. Moreover, in 1880, rail was laid between Tangshan and Xugezhuang for the transport of coal; about six and half miles in length, it was China's first railway. Some of these enterprises were owned and managed by the government; others were run by the merchants under government supervision. They had adopted Western manufacturing systems, hired European engineers, and helped the development of Chinese modern industries and capitalism. Meanwhile, crisis developed in Korea, and the Sino-Japanese War broke out in 1894.

The Sino-Japanese War (1894–1895) and the Boxer Rebellion (1899–1900)

Barely a decade after the Sino-French War, China was once again confronted by another foreign power—Japan. Japan's ambition of occupying Korea and then invading the Manchuria was not new. In early 1592, Japan's overlord Toyotomo Hideyoshi (1536–1598) launched a large-scale landing on southeast Korea with more than 150,000 Japanese troops. It is also known as the Imjin War (1592–1598). Peter Lorge points out Hideyoshi's "invasion of Korea with the avowed intention of then conquering China."[15] The Japanese took the capital, Seoul, in April and captured Pyongyang in May. Korea suffered more than 60,000 military and civilian casualties during their failed defense. In June, Hideyoshi ordered his main strength to advance further north toward the Yalu River and the Korean king took refuge there. In recognition of their binding alliance, Korea requested prompt intervention from China as Korea had long been most faithful in its agreement.

Emperor Wanli sent 45,000 Chinese troops to Korea to attack the invading army and force a Japanese withdrawal. In 1597, Hideyoshi launched new attacks with 140,000 troops. The Ming court sent an expeditionary force of 80,000 Chinese troops to defeat the Japanese forces. Due to lack of supplies, Japan began withdrawal in the spring to southern Korea. Hideyoshi's death in the fall (August-September) eventually led the Japanese court's decision to withdraw all forces from Korea in October. Through the 1592–1598 War, the Ming army suffered 29,000 dead while Korean casualties totaled 18,500 killed and 60,000 captured.

---

15   Peter Lorge, *War, Politics and Society in Early Modern China, 900–1795* (London: Routledge, 2005), 131.

In the spring of 1894, a peasant uprising led by the Tonghak ("Eastern Learning") Society occurred in Korea, and the Korean king requested military assistance from China through the tributary relationship to suppress the uprising and protect the Korean government. Early in June, the Qing court sent 3,500 Chinese troops to Korea. The Japanese, however, considered it as a violation of the Treaty of Tianjin, which limited Qing military deployment by a request that China had to inform the others of any troop movement to Korea. Thereby, Japan sent 8,000 troops of its own to Korea, captured the Korean king, and occupied Seoul. When the both armies clashed in Korea, the Sino-Japanese War broke out on August 1, 1894.

In early August, Japanese ground force began to move northward and attack the Qing troops. In September, after lost Pyongyang, the Chinese troops withdrew back to Manchuria. The Japanese force continued their pursuit, crossing the Yalu River and entering China. On September 18, the Japanese Navy attacked the Beiyang (North Sea) Fleet of the Qing navy. During the Battle of the Yellow Sea, the Chinese fleet lost eight out of ten warships, and withdrew back to its Weihaiwei naval base in Shandong (Shantung) province. In October, Japanese army occupied Dalian and Port Arthur in Liaoning province and threatened Beijing.

In 1895, China and Japan signed the Treaty of Shimonoseki. The treaty provided, among other things, that the Qing government cede to Japan the Liaodong Peninsula and Taiwan together with the adjacent islands and the Penghu Islands. Qing also agreed to pay Japan an indemnity of 200 million taels of silver. Japan was allowed to establish in the trading ports consular offices and factories and to ship to China machinery of all kinds.

The first Sino-Japanese War exposed China's military weakness and severely compromised its national sovereignty. After the signing of the Treaty of Shimonoseki, the ambition of the international powers to expand their influence and interests in China was whipped up. The payment of large indemnities meant that China, from then on, must borrow regularly from foreign countries. Its reliance on the foreign loans became greater, and the burden on the Qing government and people became heavier. Moreover, after Japan had the privilege to open manufacturing factories in China, other industrial countries followed to receive the same right. The Treaty of Shimonoseki was the most damaging to the Chinese sovereignty and interest among all the other treaties after the Treaty of Nanjing. It sped up Qing's downfall.

Meanwhile, deepened foreign domination in China following the end of the Sino-Japanese War triggered another round of serious domestic unrest. It was not accidental that the Boxer Rebellion began in Shandong, which was the province that suffered the most from the Japanese invasion during the Sino-Japanese War in 1894. The "Boxer" (*Yihetuan*) was one of the popular martial arts organizations in North China, offering martial arts classes and training the youth in villages and small towns. Some of the Boxer schools also provided local self-defense and crime watch teams against bandits. In 1896, the Boxers began to organize the peasants for armed struggle against the Qing tax collection and service recruitment in Shandong, Zhili (Hebei), and other provinces. In early 1897, the Boxers called for a rebellion against the Qing government, and the Boxer Rebellion soon became a widespread movement in North and Central China. In that fall, however, the armed Boxers run into a lot troubles with the foreign establishments in Shandon since the Qing government had agreed with Japan's building several factories there, leasing two counties to Britain, and allowing Germany to construct the Jiaozhou-Ji'nan railway across Shandong.

In 1898, the Boxer Rebellion shifted their target from the Qing government to foreign establishments, including European trading posts, railroads, factories, hospitals, schools, and Christian missionaries. The Boxers focused their assaults on missionaries since the Western missionaries, including both the Catholic and Eastern Orthodox churches, had a huge development in China through the late nineteenth century with more than 3,300 churches and 800,000 Chinese converts. In the province of Shandong alone, there were more than 1,000 Christian churches with more than 100,000 converts. It was not surprising that the anti-missionary sentiment became more popular and stronger with the passage of time. In 1899, the Boxer Rebellion exploded in North China. Its members traveled from city to city, burning churches, killing missionaries and their families, and beating up converts. The Boxers continued to punish corrupt Qing officials and local bullies. In that spring, the movement spread to Shanxi, Henan, Inner Mongolia, and other provinces in Central China. Several groups also traveled to Northeast and South China. This anti-Western movement became nationwide. Soon the Boxers marched toward Tianjin and Beijing in the summer.

The Qing court faced a dilemma. At the beginning, it considered the Boxers as an anti-Qing rebellion and sent the troops to Shandong to crush them. Then, the Boxers attacked the Western establishments and chased out the Europeans. The Qing government stopped its suppression when the Boxer strength increased rapidly and moved into Zhili, Henan, Shanxi, and other provinces. The Qing government decided to use the movement's anti-Western policy to seize popular leadership. It, therefore, declared that the movement was legal. Emperor Guangxu ignored the foreigners' cry for help and opened the gates of Beijing, allowing the Boxers to march into the capital city to burn the churches and kill the missionaries and their families in 1899–1900.

The news of chaos and violence against the Christian missionaries in Beijing shocked the West. Eight powers, including Russia, Britain, Germany, France, the United States, Japan, Italy, and Austria, established a military coalition and sent troops to China to fight against the Boxer Rebellion. On June 10, 1900, about 2,000 of the allied forces, led by a British naval commander E. H. Seymour, landed on Dagukou and moved towards Tianjin. More troops were thrown in later that month. The Boxers quickly engaged the allied troops in bloody defense around Tianjin. Without artillery and chain of command, the Boxers lost Tianjin on July 14.

After taking over Tianjin, about 20,000 allied force attacked Beijing on August 4. Qing's imperial troops and more than 50,000 Boxers defended the capital city and suffered heavy casualties. On August 14, the allied force occupied Beijing. Emperor Guangxiu and his mother, Empress Cixi, fled to Xi'an. For several days, the foreign troops pillaged the city. All the treasures, documents, and historical relics in the Imperial Palace and in the Summer Palace were looted or otherwise destroyed. Besides, they raped women and put the whole city to fire and sword.

At Xi'an, the Qing court had no choice but declared that members of the Boxers were "rioters." It expressed "friendship" for the foreign troops and request them to exterminate the "rioters." Attacked by both the Qing army and the allied force, the Boxer Rebellion failed in the end. On September 7, 1901, the Qing government signed a treaty of peace, or the "Boxer Protocol," with the Eight Powers, including Britain, the United States, Russia, Germany, Austria, France, Italy, and Japan, plus Belgium, Spain, and Holland. According to the treaty, China was forced to pay an indemnity of 450 million taels of silver in thirty-nine years. Since the unpaid balance carried an annual interest of 4 percent, total payment amounted to 980 million taels. The treaty designated a "legation quarter" in Beijing, where foreign troops would station to protect foreigners in the capital. It also decided on twelve strategic points between Beijing and Manchuria, where the allied powers could station their troops along the railways. The treaty was the Qing's biggest sellout, politically, militarily, and economically. Soon the anti-Qing movement became one of Chinese nationalism and led directly to the 1911 Revolution to end the Qing dynasty.

Sun Yat-sen and the 1911 Revolution

Modern nationalism did not appear until modern nation-states were established in Western Europe in the eighteenth century, and it was shaped by people's reaction to their own state and the state system. United by the same language, culture, religion, and traditions, those peoples who lived together in a territory began movements to establish an independent and sovereign state to reduce papal power and to abolish feudal privileges of the aristocracy. The Chinese did not accept modern nationalism until the late nineteenth century when Sun Yat-sen, the founding father of the Republic of China (ROC), advocated national independence and the principle of national equality within China. Modern nationalism in China owes its origin to the anti-imperialism campaigns, such as the Boxer Rebellion in 1900.

In 1903–1904, Sun developed a Chinese version of modern nationalism in his "Three Principles of the People" (*anmin zhuyi*). It included "nationalism" (both anti-Manchu and anti-imperialism), "democracy" (a constitution with people's rights), and "people's livelihood" (a classic term for social equality).[16] In 1905 Sun organized the Tongmenghui (the United League) in Japan. The political program of the new organization, as proposed by Sun, had four points: repulsion of the Manchus, restoration of China, establishment of a republic, and equal land-ownership. In August, a meeting in Tokyo marked its formal inauguration, and to this meeting came more than 100 delegates from seventeen of China's twenty-two provinces. The meeting passed its new constitution, elected Sun as its director-general, and decided the leadership structure. After its establishment, secret branches came into being across China and abroad. In less than one year, its membership exceeded 10,000. Its members published more than 100 newspapers and magazines, and its revolutionary ideas spread far and wide.

During the time when the United League was active in staging uprisings, people in various parts of the country launched their own struggles spontaneously. The local uprisings numbered 113 in 1909, and increased to 285 in 1910. However, all the uprisings faced brutal suppressions by the Qing's New Army, which was a newly established Western-style army. The Qing government hired German officers and armed its troops with modern weapons purchased from European countries. The New Army had six divisions and totaled 80,000 men under the command of Marshall Yuan Shikai in 1909.

Soon the revolutionary ideas and anti-Qing activities of the United League became popular in the New Army. By August 1911, about 15,000 men, one-third of the New Army in Hubei province, were either its secret members or had close relations with the league. On the evening of October 10, the armed uprising led by the commanders of the New Army in Wuchang exploded. A fierce battle went on throughout the night; by next morning, the insurgents succeeded in taking over Wuchang, the capital city of Hubei province. (October 10, or "Double Ten," became the National Day for the Republic of China.) After taking over the cities of Hanyang and Hankou, the officers declared the independence of Hubei province from the Qing regime. The Wuchang armed uprising and Hubei's independence like a wild fire swept the country. Fifteen provinces followed the Wuchang Rebellion by launching their armed uprisings and declaring their independence within two months.

In December 1911, Sun Yat-sen returned to China from abroad. Towards the end of the month, delegates from these independent provinces gathered in Nanjing to organize a provisional central government and elected Sun as the provisional president. On New Year's Day, 1912, Sun Yat-sen was sworn in, and the establishment of the Republic of

---

16   Harold R. Isaacs, *The Tragedy of the Chinese Revolution*, 2nd ed. (Stanford, CA: Stanford University Press, 1961), 56–7, 90, 148.

China (ROC) was formally announced. In March, Sun promulgated the Provisional Constitution of the ROC, and a provisional national assembly also came into being.

The victory of the Wuchang Uprising dealt a severe blow to the Qing court. Then, the military power of the Qing was in the hands of Marshal Yuan Shikai, commander in chief of the New Army. While ordering him to suppress the uprisings, the Manchu rulers also offered Yuan prime minister post in the government if he remained under the Qing. To avoid a civil war, Sun Yat-sen sent his representatives to negotiate with Yuan by offering him the presidency of the new republic. Yuan Shikai took Sun's offer and joined the anti-Qing revolutionary forces. On February 12, 1912, when Yuan forced the last emperor abdicated in Beijing, the Qing dynasty ended. Then, Sun resigned in Nanjing. On February 14, Yuan Shikai became the president of the Republic of China.

Yuan Shikai was never a revolutionary and not interested in Sun's "Three Principles of the People." From 1912 to 1916, he used his presidency to develop his own military power and became the "Father of Chinese Warlords." He even tried to reinstall the monarchy. To continue the republican revolution, Sun reorganized the United League from a secret society into a national political party, the Chinese Nationalist Party (Guomindang, GMD; or Kuomintang, KMT) in August 1912. Sun and his party controlled the Parliament of the ROC and fought against Yuan's dictatorship until he died in 1916.

After Yuan's death, state power remained in the hands of the military leaders, or other warlords, from 1916 to 1927. The 1911 Revolution was incomplete because Sun Yat-sen failed to create a democratic constitutional republic. In 1916, after the warlord president abolished both the provisional constitution and the parliament, Sun left Nanjing and returned to his hometown Guangzhou. Although he continued his struggle against military government for the protection of the constitution until his death in 1925, he failed to mobilize the Chinese masses, especially the peasants. The revolutionary leaders lacked an agrarian program that truly reflected the interest of peasants who constituted the sheer majority of the Chinese populace.

The Warlords (1916–1927) and the Republican Period (1927–1937)

China entered the Warlord Period in 1916–1927. Among the warlords, seven or eight of them exercised autonomous political power by virtue of their personal control of their military force. They fought against each other for the control of the central government in Beijing. Edward A. McCord points out that "by the end of this decade of civil war, the possession of armed force had become an essential determinant of political power."[17]

During the Warlord Period (1916–1927), two major wars occurred between two groups of warlords over the control of the central government: the Fengtian clique and Zhili clique. The Fengtian clique under the command of Marshal Zhang Zuolin controlled Northeast China, or Manchuria, outside the Great Wall, including Liaoning, Jilin, and Heilongjiang provinces. The Zhili clique under the command of Marshal Wu Peifu and Cao Kun controlled North China inside the Great Wall, including Hebei, Inner Mongolia, and Henan provinces. The two groups had been engaged in some conflicts over the areas along the Great Wall in the early 1920s. After the first Zhili-Fengtian War, the Zhili clique intended to unite China by force with the support of the central government. In order to save the Fengtian, Zhang Zuolin negotiated with other warlords such as Duan Qirui from

---

17   Edward A. McCord, *The Power of the Gun: The Emergence of Modern Chinese Warlordism* (Berkeley: University of California Press, 1993), 1.

the southeastern Anhui clique to form a new military coalition against the Zhili clique. In addition, Zheng's faction gained the support of some Western countries that did not want to see the reunification of China. The Fengtian won the second Zhili-Fengtian War. In 1924, Zhang Zuolin, along with Feng Yuxiang created a new provisional government in Beijing.[18] Duan Qirui, from the Anhui clique, was selected as a figurehead to balance the interests of Zhang and Feng. Finally, the national power fell into the hands of the Fengtian clique.

During the Warlord Period, Sun Yat-sen moved his political center from Nanjing to Guangzhou and continued the Republican revolution by fighting against the warlords. In 1924 Sun established a political alliance with the Soviet Union and Chinese Communist Party (CCP), called the First United Front (1924–1927). Thereafter, the GMD began to receive military and economic help and advice from Moscow.[19] In May 1924, Sun founded the Whampoa (*Huangpu*) Military Academy (the "West Point of China") with the assistance of the Soviet Union. The first commandant was Jiang Jieshi (Chiang Kai-shek) and the GMD representative was Liao Zhongkai. In November, Sun was ill and left Guangzhou for Beijing. Jiang Jieshi began to build the GMD military force in Guangzhou.

On March 12, 1925, Sun died of cancer in Beijing. In July, Jiang Jieshi organized the Nationalist Government at Guangzhou and served as its president. In August, President Jiang established the National Revolutionary Army (*Guomin Gemingjun*), including five infantry armies and totaling 90,000 troops, with himself as its commander in chief. In July 1926 Jiang launched the military campaign, or the Northern Expedition, against the major warlords. His main targets were Wu Peifu in Hunan,

Hubei, and Henan; Sun Chuanfang in Jiangsu, Anhui, Zhejiang, Fujian, and Jiangxi; and Zhang Zuolin, the overlord of the northeastern provinces plus Beijing and Tianjin.

The main battlefields of the Northern Expedition were Hunan and Hubei. The National Revolutionary Army quickly took Changsha and Yuezhou. Several warlord commanders began feuding amongst themselves, and one Hunan commander began to express sympathy for the Northern Expedition. This commander agreed to integrate his troops into the Guomindang army, and Jiang Jieshi decided that the time was ripe to begin the attack. The mobilization order was given on July 1, 1926, and the Nationalist troops began to head out. The troops under Jiang pressed forward from Guangzhou, with the Hunan troops fighting through Changsha, the capital city of Hunan Province. By the end of August, Nationalist forces seized many bridgeheads that guarded the approaches to Wuhan and more warlord forces began joining Jiang's army. On the approach to Wuchang, the warlord who controlled the city put up strong resistance. Attempting to hold out against the Nationalists, the warlord instituted severe punishment of those he deemed sympathetic to the enemy. After rounding up the suspects, he began beheading them and displayed the severed heads in the surrounding lake cities of Jiujiang and Nanchang in Jiangxi Province. After a prolonged siege however, the populace was on the brink of starvation. The warlord finally relented on October 10, and allowed Nationalist troops to take the city.[20]

By late 1926, GMD and Communist forces consolidated their control over Wuhan and began to turn their attention towards Jiangxi. The Nationalist armies proved equally as successful in these future attacks, and by December of 1926 they

---

18 Tanner, *China*, 121–2.

19 Yi Sun and Xiaobing Li, "Mao Zedong and the CCP: Adaptation, Centralization, and Succession," in *Evolution of Power: China's Struggle, Survival, and Success*, eds., Xiaobing Li and Xiansheng Tian (Lanham, MD: Lexington Books, 2014), 31.

20 Isaacs, *The Tragedy of the Chinese Revolution*, 99, 104, 111–29.

controlled Guangdong, Hunan, Hubei, Jiangxi, Fujian, Guangxi, and Guizhou. The successes of the Northern Expedition led to diplomatic recognition of the Guomindang government by the British, who sent a minister to China to hold talks with the Nationalist foreign minister.

The Nationalist forces next began to turn their attention towards Shanghai. In the beginning of 1927 arguments broke out between the various commanders on how to approach the city. Labor unions that were led by the CCP had made strong headway in Shanghai during this time, which antagonized the local warlord. In February 1927 these labor unions organized a general strike to support the Nationalist forces, but were put down by warlord forces who beheaded the leaders and disrupted their meetings. This produced a backlash, with many Shanghai city leaders meeting in secret with Jiang Jieshi and offering him their support. On March 21, 1927, workers once again launched a strike and began an armed insurrection against the local warlord. With strict orders not to harm foreigners, Nationalist troops marched into the city and took control of it.

In April 1927, Jiang reestablished the national government of the Republic of China and carried out a purge of Communists from his Nationalist forces, massacring several thousand Communists in the process. This action caused a rift between the GMD and CCP. The leftist leaders in Wuhan maintained their loyalty to the CCP and condemned the actions of the GMD.[21] Soon afterwards, the Communists were forced to leave Shanghai and other urban areas where the GMD forces were strong and went into hiding in the remote rural areas.

Taking advantage of China's disunity, Japan began its military aggression against China in 1931 by taking over all of Manchuria and transforming it into a puppet state. After World War I, Japan had replaced Germany in Shandong and intended to expand its influence in China. Then, Japanese army attacked the Chinese forces in Shenyang (Mukden) on September 18, 1931, and occupied the entire Manchuria in northeast China. The Manchurian Incident was also known as the September 18 (9-18) Incident. Within a few months, Japanese armed forces occupied the entirety of Manchuria, including Liaoning, Jilin, and Heilongjiang Provinces.[22] This aggression was later considered the first step on the path to the Japanese invasion of the Republic of China in 1937–1945. The impact of this event was far-reaching. Japanese de facto seizure of Manchuria exposed a constant threat to China. In fact, with the outbreak of the Manchurian Crisis, the Japanese unleashed military and political forces, which led ultimately to the full invasion of China on July 7, 1937. It was not until August 1945, at the end of WWII in the Pacific following the American use of two atomic bombs on Hiroshima and Nagasaki, and with the help of Soviet Union, that the Chinese regained their control over Manchuria.

---

21 Crossley, *The Wobbling Pivot*, 181–2.

22 Elleman, *Modern Chinese Warfare*, 196.

Chapter 6

Japan's Meiji Transformation

The success story of Meiji Japan from 1868 to 1912 only highlighted China's contemporaneous failure. Both countries had been confronted with the unequal treaties that impaired their sovereignty and threatened their economic independence. Japan undertook speedy and comprehensive reforms, leading to its successful military defeat of Russia, one of the major world powers, in the beginning of the twentieth century. In a short span of thirty-five years, Japan transformed itself from a feudal society into a major, growing power in East Asia. More than anything, Japan was blessed with many far-sighted and brave political leaders during this critical period, which was perhaps the most profound difference that set the country apart from its less fortunate neighbors like China, Vietnam, and Korea. The progressive leadership and the national unity only an insular Japan could have mustered contributed to this outstanding accomplishment. One reason for Japan's achievement was its capacity to act as a nation and unleash patriotic mobilization.

Barely a year after the onset of the Meiji era, the whole country came under the control of the military and reform-minded leaders, who wanted to transform Japan into a modern country with a strong military that would be capable of not only resisting but also competing with the West. Without any experience in operating a national regime, they established a centralized government, which lasted until the end of WWII. In a remarkably short period, Japan became a worthy rival of the industrialized and imperialistic West. By 1894 it had successfully implemented a national reorganization; its feudal system was dismantled and new government structures were in place despite some early difficulties. Industry and commerce were in a state of vigorous growth, benefitting from an ever-expanding commercial respectability and expanding communication and transportation systems. Western-style educational systems were established, and systematic efforts to acquire advanced knowledge and technology from the West were launched. More importantly, the "land of the rising sun" developed an army and navy modeled after the best of the West. Japan's rapid modernization in the late nineteenth century produced closer parallels to the West than those to be found in China, Korea, or anywhere else in Asia.

The sudden rise of Japan as a military and naval power contrasted with the final collapse of the Qing tribute system and the vulnerability of Britain's informal commercial empire based on the unequal treaty system. Japan was not only ready to claim its newly earned international prestige but also anxious to play the territorial games the West had monopolized.

The island nation had become confident enough to challenge the Middle Kingdom, an ancient but continental power, for the leadership of the Asian-Pacific region. With the unexpected and unparalleled transformation of Japan, international relations in East Asia entered into a half-century of instability.

Perry's Treaty and the Fall of the Shogunate (1853–1868)

Since the eighteenth century, the West expressed interests in opening Japan to commercial ventures under various pretexts. Like its two neighbors, Japan was not interested in a trade relationship with Western countries and refused the requests made by both Russia and England. The United States made more resolute attempts to force its will on Japan, as it needed a coaling station in Japan to develop a direct sea line with China.

When it became apparent that the Japanese would not consent to the request peacefully, Washington dispatched a naval squadron. The expedition force, commanded by Commodore Matthew Perry, entered Yokohama Bay in July 1853 and demanded of the Tokugawa government an immediate acceptance of its "open-door" request. Under the imposing naval intimidation, even though the Shogunate did not immediately agree with America's request, the Edo government was ready to enter a treaty relationship. When Perry returned the following February, the Tokugawa leaders signed the so-called Kanagawa Treaty of Friendship on March 31, 1854. Under the treaty, Japan granted the United States two open ports, the right to appoint a consul, the protection of shipwrecked sailors, and the most-favored-nation (MFN) treatment.[1] Other Western powers quickly took advantage of the success of Perry's mission and extracted similar concessions

from Japan: England in 1854, Russia in 1855, and the Netherlands in 1857.

The American consul, Townsend Harris, arrived in Edo in 1856. Two years later, he succeeded in negotiating a new treaty in July 1858, one that was a lot more damaging than Perry's. Not only was Japan forced to open six additional ports to American traders, but more importantly Japan had to surrender its sovereign right to regulate tariffs on American imports and to confer extraterritoriality on American diplomatic posts. A weakened Tokugawa found it difficult to mount any effective resistance against the "gunboat diplomacy"; it had no choice but to capitulate to the American demands in the end.

The opening of its doors to the Western powers accentuated Japan's internal turmoil. Powerful feudal lords began to defy the Tokugawa shogunate rule when the signing of treaties with the West shattered the country's existing order. Overlooked was the fact that the Tokugawa government was realistic enough to decide to accommodate Western demands upon realizing that it could not mount an effective military defense in the case of an American invasion. In any event, with the signing of the Townsend Harris Treaty, the Tokugawa shogunate unintentionally relinquished its 250-year-old political domination.

When Tokugawa rulers extended these treaties from Edo to all of the daimyo, they brought strong criticism, leading to a rapid erosion of Tokugawa authority. The leaders of Choshu and Satsuma challenged the Tokugawa shogunate. The whole shogun system had depended on mutual antagonism among the domains; however, now many daimyo realized that alliance with one another under the emperor in Kyoto would be a better system than strengthening the Tokugawa control. In 1864 the civil war broke out when the Choshu daimyos and samurais

---

1   Andressen, *A Short History of Japan*, 75.

attacked Kyoto and occupied it.[2] The revolting daimyos and reforming samurais chanted the slogan "honor the Emperor" and insisted on returning the power to Emperor Komei (r. 1831–1866). In the meantime, Komei established his own army, the "imperial troops" in Kyoto, and joined forces with the samurais from Choshu and Satsuma. In January 1868 the shogunate forces made the last attempt to attack Kyoto, but they were defeated by the imperial forces south of the capital.[3] Later that year, the imperial army marched on Edo and crushed the shogunate troops in November. The civil war was over with a victory of the Meiji Emperor.

Meiji, the Constitutional Monarchy (1868–1912)

After Komei died during the civil war, his son, Mutsuhito, then only fourteen years old, succeeded to the throne in 1868. He adopted the title of Meiji, meaning "Enlightened Rule," and soon became the purported leader of Japan's modernization. In fact, a group of reform-minded samurai, who were the ones primarily responsible for overthrowing the Tokugawa government, would subsequently engineer the national transformation in the name of the emperor. They helped the imperial court to quickly consolidate its central authority in firm control. The era of the remarkable Meiji Restoration thus began.

On April 8, 1868, Emperor Meiji issued the Charter Oath (or the Charter Oath of Five Articles) to abolish all the feudal domains, privileges, and titles. It removed feudal social limitation by ending class restrictions on professional fields of activity in 1869.[4] Most of the samurai disappeared as a class. The abolition of the feudal system was problematic even for the highly motivated post-Tokugawa regime. In order to reinstate imperial

authority, it was most urgent to neutralize the feudal authority throughout the country. In the meantime, the imperial capital moved from Kyoto to Edo, renamed as Tokyo (Eastern Capital). In May 1869 many and daimyo began to return their domains to the emperor. By 1870, the new regime obtained major clan members' consent for total abolition of the feudal system. Even with effective persuasions and generous offers, the undertaking caused some serious after-effects. By August 29, 1871, all the 260–270 domains were returned.

The end of feudalism was an auspicious beginning for the new central government, which established three metropolitan prefectures (*fu*) and seventy-two other prefectures (*ken*). The central governing council was divided into three chambers in charge of legislative, administrative, and judicial functions, respectively. In 1872, the Meiji government established the army and navy departments. During the following years, it issued the conscription law, by which all men, regardless of social background, were made liable for three years of active military service. It was a revolutionary step that made the commoners the foundation of a centralized and modernized military institution. For centuries commoners had been denied the right to even possess swords. The whole feudal system had depended on the functional division between the commoners and samurai and the deeply entrenched social stratification. After the domains were abolished, samurai lost their professional and social status. The Japanese military was turned from a closed, class profession into a mass, conscript system. In 1878 Yamagata Aritomo, Minister of Internal Affairs, adopted the German general staff system. He then established the principle that the chiefs of staff in matters of military command should be independent of the army minister and entire civil

---

2   Mikiso Hane and Louis G. Perez, *Modern Japan: A Historical Survey*, 4th ed. (Boulder, CO: Westview, 2009), 75.

3   Henshall, *A History of Japan*, 69.

4   Hane and Perez, *Modern Japan*, 85–6.

government, a principle that was included in the Meiji Constitution.

In the late 1870s, Emperor Meiji appointed Ito Hirobumi, Minister of Finance, to prepare a national assembly and draft a constitution. In 1882 Ito led a group to visit European capitals to study Western political systems. After his return in the following year, Ito chaired a special commission to draft the constitution. Six years later, on February 11, 1889, the Meiji government promulgated a new constitution that embraced a mixture of restoration concepts and feudal ideas.[5]

Under its provisions, the emperor was both the sole source and dispenser of all power. Ito and his commission made sure that the emperor remain in the political center controlling the entire governing apparatus. The Constitution also made clear that "the supreme command" of the army and navy was in the hands of the emperor. The Meiji leaders had safeguarded the monarchal system by protecting the imperial power. The Constitution also made the individual ministers directly responsible to the emperor rather than collectively responsible as an administration or cabinet. Nonetheless, the national political power was to be exercised through governmental bodies such as the Council of Ministers. The judiciary was modeled upon that of France and Prussia. Japan's new Western-style government was fully operational in 1890 with the convocation of its first national assembly, the Diet.

According to the Meiji Constitution, the first national election was held in July 1890 to create the Diet. Then, the first Diet convened that November. It was a bicameral parliament, including an upper house, or the House of Peers, and a lower house, or the House of Representatives. The first Diet had most of its peers from the higher ranks of the nobility. The representatives were elected by adult males twenty-five years of age or older and paying an annual tax of fifteen yen or more. There were only 450,000 persons, or about 5 percent of the adult male population, who were eligible to vote in the first election on July 1, 1890. Nevertheless, the Diet was given some real power, including the right to authorize the annual budget, formulate foreign policy, make permanent laws, and appoint the prime minister.[6] The Constitution also promised a whole series of civil rights, including freedom of religion, freedom of speech and publications, and freedom of public meetings, among others.

The Meiji leaders were able to create representative political bodies, a practice that departed from East Asian traditions. They assumed that there was something in constitutions and representative institutions that produced the progress and strength of the Western powers. They expected no foreign aid, and their low expectations allowed more pragmatic, careful approach to the problems. A large number of Japanese students were sent to America and Europe to study Western ideas, practices, and institutions in various fields. The nation actively but selectively experimented with Western ideas and practices. The governmental reforms assured internal stability and created a political mechanism for developing a "rich country with a strong military."

Economic Reforms and Industrialization

Meiji Japan accomplished a truly remarkable feat in laying down a sound foundation for a modern nation. However, its chief achievement was not the extensiveness of its reform but the rapidity of its implementation. Discarding a feudal isolationist policy, it aggressively sought Western ideas and practices for its own benefit. Its priority was to revamp entirely the old-fashioned governing structure.

---

5   Andressen, *A Short History of Japan*, 87.

6   W. G. Beasley, *The Rise of Modern Japan*, 2nd ed. (New York: St. Martin's, 1995), 78.

Equally systematic efforts were directed to economic development. The Meiji court's priority went to building the nation's commercial infrastructure; railroads and improved roads in which the reform-minded government had heavily invested became responsible for the early blossoming of commerce. Moreover, by emphasizing the respectability of entrepreneurship, the government encouraged the samurai and other former ruling elites to use their energies in commercial and industrial undertakings. In most areas, Japan was actively seeking a radical departure from the Confucian culture by adapting itself to the Western industrial-commercial culture.

The Meiji government played an important role in Japan's economic development during the late nineteenth and early twentieth centuries. It provided a favorable business environment for industrial growth by removing feudal restrictions and isolationist policy on trade. Some of the political leaders even played a dual role in politics and business. A number of Western nationals were hired into government service as advisers, engineers, and military instructors until the foreign-trained Japanese experts were able to replace them. For example, the Bureau of Mines hired thirty-four foreign engineers in 1873. The government was particularly interested in developing the strategic industries, such as steel and iron manufacturing, railway construction, export-oriented industries, and defense industry.

In 1871 the government began its financial reform by establishing a national banking system under the newly founded Bank of Japan, following the model of the American banking system. It helped assemble the needed capital, forced weak companies to merge into stronger corporations, and provided the private sector with financial aid and privileges. In 1873 a new land tax system was introduced, replacing the agricultural tax, which depended on individual farmer's annual yields or income, and changing from an unpredictable and uncontrollable tax revenue to a fixed one, based on land size and values.[7] The land tax set the rate at 3 percent of the assessed land value in 1873, and the rate was reduced to 2.5 percent three years later. Soon the land tax became the chief source of the government's revenues. By the end of the 1870s, the Meiji government finance had developed a sound foundation for the new industries.

In the 1880s the Japanese steel and iron making engineers had managed to incorporate Western manufacturing techniques. Their steel and iron industry developed several major production bases. In 1882, for example, a reverbertory furnace of the type used in Europe went into production in Osaka, allowing engineers trained abroad to incorporate their knowledge of European steel making into the manufacturing processes. Throughout the remainder of the 1880s, the Osaka steel and iron industry achieved ever-increasing levels of steel manufacturing. When new concerns regarding material availability and quality arose, the government began an aggressive exploration of iron ore overseas. Less durable metals such as bronze and copper, which had been used previously, were eliminated by 1890 in favor of cast iron and steel components. By this time, the Tsukiji factory in Osaka was capable of producing "Western" steel using Krupp-type equipment, allowing Japan's steel and iron products to approach Western standards. In the meantime, the government created a steady market for the products of Japan's heavy industries when they were not yet competitive with those of the West.

The government started new manufacturing fields and sponsored the development of risky industries. For instance, railway construction in Japan was considered a risky investment since rail transportation in its initial development was losing money. It cost as much as to move the goods onto the island as it did to produce them. Coastal offshore shipping had been the main means of transportation for Japan

---

7   Beasley, *The Rise of Modern Japan*, 61.

until 1880, when the Meiji government began to invest in railroad construction and built 181 miles of track in three years, while the private sector had only completed 63 miles. After the rail network developed and brought in revenues, the government passed on the rail construction and transportation to the private companies. In 1890 the private sector built more than 900 miles of railways out of a total of 1,400 miles. From 1887 to the 1930s, the government investment in the economy averaged 40 percent of the country's total investment.

At the beginning of the 1870s, the textile industry was small in Japan since the country did not have the needed access to cotton or the applicable technology for the processing of raw materials. It had to import textile products such as uniforms from Europe, and these textiles amounted to half of Japan's total annual imports. In 1872 the government began to play a significant role in promoting and financing the textile industry by building new factories and importing new machines from European countries. By the end of the 1870s, Japan had produced more cotton yarn and goods than it needed. In the early 1880s it became the largest exporter of textile goods in Asia. A decade later its foreign trade began to show a favorable balance.

Japan's economy began a boom in 1905 in the wake of its victory in the Russo-Japanese War. The military triumph over the Russians, and the peace treaty thereafter, expanded Japan's colonial empire and made more raw materials, larger international markets, and overseas investment opportunities available. After Meiji died in 1912, the new emperor Taisho (r. 1912–1926) continued Meiji's reform policy. He did not intend to deal with the political, economic, and social problems left behind by the Meiji government. One of the major issues was the emergence of giant financial and industrial trusts, or *zaibatsu*, namely. They were owned by family groups and dominated manufacturing, investment, shipping, and markets through monopoly.[8] The Taisho government encouraged the growth of these industrial giants instead of curbing the concentration of wealth and economic powers. In the 1920s, the top four companies—Mitsui, Mitsubishi, Sumitomo, and Yasuda—not only dominated the domestic economy but also controlled the politics. In 1941 Mitsui itself had seventy corporations hiring more than one million employees in Japan, and another million in its East Asian empire and beyond. The economic domination and wealth concentration became an obstacle to the development of a democratic society and a healthy middle class.

Demographic Change and Education Reform

At the beginning of the twentieth century, Japan experienced tremendous demographic changes. Its population increased from 42 million in 1895 to 70 million in 1930, and to 73.1 million in 1940, which coordinated with an accelerated pace of urbanization and industrialization. In 1895 the number of urban residents who lived in the cities of more than 10,000 people consisted of only 12 percent of the total population. By 1930, however, more than 45 percent of the 70 million Japanese lived in large cities with 100,000 residents.[9] By 1940 Tokyo had a total of 6.7 million residents, rivaling New York City and London, while many other cities also hosted large populations, such as Osaka, Kyoto, Nagoya, Kobe, and Yokohama.

With more and more Japanese moving into cities as the result of industrialization, urban areas developed more rapidly than rural areas. The gap between the city and countryside was widening in terms of economy, living standard, culture, and social values. Such an urban-rural divide, and its accompanying

---

8   Ibid., 117.

9   Henshall, *A History of Japan*, 111.

problems, begged for a strong political leadership. However, the second and third generations of leaders in the 1920s and 1940s, including Emperor Hirohito (r. 1926–1989), were the heirs of the Imperial Restoration trying to carry on the Meiji legacy rather than enact any major changes.[10]

Japan's educational development during the Restoration period was successful, as the Meiji leaders considered an organized system of education fundamental and necessary for a modern society. The reforms put into practice Western concepts of a uniform, government-operated educational system. At the same time, mindful of the pitfalls of excessive Western learning, the Meiji government conducted selective reforms by adopting the American system for the primary and secondary education, the French system for universities, and the German system for vocational education, all within the confines of a centralized mechanism.

From the very beginning, public education received particular attention. In 1871 the Ministry of Education was established to develop a public education to replace the non-Western aspects of the curriculum.[11] In the 1880s, the Ministry made education compulsory for children of both sexes for four years, and it extended the requirement to six years in the early twentieth century. The rise of cultural nationalism was evident in the fact that, in 1890, the Meiji government issued an Imperial Rescript in an effort to create a more centralized and nationalistic education system. It emphasized ideological indoctrination, curricular standardization, and increased government control over private institutions, especially at the lower education levels. The compulsory education system was responsible for the dramatic increase of the literacy rate of the Japanese. In 1886 only 46 percent of school-age children enrolled in schools; the number increased to 95 percent twenty years later. Above the elementary level, there were five-year academic middle schools for boys, various technical schools, and girls' high schools. Above those were three-year higher academic schools and technical schools. At the top of the pyramid were the three-year universities, which produced the elite leadership for the country. Tokyo University (formerly the Confucian University in Edo until 1877) became the training center for future government officials.[12] The successful transformation of the entire society, which was selectively modeled after Western practices, gave the Japanese a new sense of national pride and confidence.

Military Development and Imperialism

Along with its wholesale structural transformation in the civilian sector, Japan also rebuilt its retrograde military. It was natural for the nation with a long military tradition to emphasize strong armed forces. The importation of Western military hardware was not new for Japan; it had obtained some advanced firearms from the Dutch as early as the sixteenth century and used them with devastating impact against the Koreans during Hideyoshi's Korean invasion. This time Japan also adopted the Western military system, departing from its clan-oriented feudal tradition. Its first national army was organized under a system of universal service in 1873. The new military was not only armed with modern weapons but also trained in Western tactics. More importantly, Japan rebuilt its navy, still a vastly inferior force to that of the West, with the help of England, the world's mightiest naval power at the time. By adopting Western practices and weaponry,

---

10   Ibid., 110.

11   Hane and Perez, *Modern Japan*, 100.

12   Beasley, *The Rise of Modern Japan*, 95.

Japan was rapidly establishing itself as the premier military power of the region.[13]

The rise of modernized armed forces caused the birth of powerful military bureaucrats who came to wield increasing leverage over domestic as well as foreign policies. Hard-liners both in and out of the government advocated early on for the nation's territorial expansion onto the continent of Asia; they insisted on occupying Korea, Manchuria, a large portion of China, and Siberia.[14] For a while, the reemerging imperialism was blocked by the nation's more conservative faction, the civil bureaucrats, who, though endorsing the imperial expansion, insisted that any campaign not be launched until the completion of national reorganization. It is worth noting that both ends of Japan's political spectrum were in agreement over territorial expansion and differed only in time and method. As imperial sentiment rose high among military bureaucrats and former samurai, Japan was becoming the region's first imperial power.

While the Japanese leadership was decisively shifting toward a militant approach in its Korean policy, the Choson court remained largely ignorant of these critical political developments in Japan. Not only did its inability to sense the gravity of the shifting regional geopolitics persist, but its knowledge of the rapidly modernizing Japan and its expansionist intentions remained paltry. Contrary to the obtuse Choson court, Meiji Japan was gathering accurate information on the nature of Korea's political instability. Sensing the arrival of an opportune moment, the Meiji government formally endorsed a militant Korean policy long advocated by the nation's hard-liners and expansion-oriented military bureaucrats. As a result, in 1875, Japan dispatched armed vessels to Korea's coastal waters on the pretext of surveying the area, concealing its real purpose of provoking the Choson court into a military confrontation. When the armed conflict occurred, Korean troops failed to stop the Japanese intrusion. In 1876 Korea and Japan signed the Treaty of Kanghwa, the first international treaty that officially ended Korea's anachronistic policy of isolation and opened its doors to Japan, and one that challenged its traditional tributary relations with China.[15]

Japan's imperialist aggressions in Korea, followed by its annexation of the Ryukyu Island in 1879, alarmed China. When the Choson court requested that Beijing send troops to subdue a domestic revolt in 1893 in accordance with the traditional practices stipulated by the tribute system, the Qing government felt ready to confront the Japanese garrison in Korea in the hope of resuming its extraordinary political-military influence over Korea. Japan again chose military confrontation against China in 1894. The Sino-Japanese War was a contest between Japan's thoroughly reorganized and modernized forces and the Qing's numerically superior but poorly trained and equipped forces. As detailed in the previous chapter, the Qing troops were defeated both on land and sea by the highly motivated Japanese forces. In 1895 the belligerents agreed to terminate the war by signing the Treaty of Shimonoseki. The defeat for China was costly: in addition to its painful concessions in Korea, China had to make other humiliating accommodations to the victor. It was forced to cede part of the Liaodong Peninsular, Formosa (Taiwan), and the Pescadores to Japan.[16]

---

13 Andressen, *A Short History of Japan*, 91.

14 As early as 1871, the militant faction of the Japanese government pushed for an expedition to both Formosa and Korea. The idea was blocked by the opposition.

15 Hane and Perez, *Modern Japan*, 163.

16 Ibid., 166.

The Russo-Japanese War (1904–1905) and WWI in East Asia

In 1895, Russia, as a continental power in Asia, had its own plans for the region and convinced France and Germany to apply diplomatic pressure to Japan, forcing it to turn over the control of Port Arthur, a city on the Liaodong peninsula between Korea and China, back to the Chinese. Russia then in turn leased the port from China and maintained control over the surrounding area. During the Boxer Rebellion of 1900, European powers, including Russia, intervened and stationed troops in China. Russia subsequently placed a military force in Manchuria and began to eye further expansion in the surrounding area, including Korea. Japan saw its sphere of influence threatened, as it maintained considerable influence over Korea and considered Russian expansionistic aims to be dangerous to its goals.

On February 9, 1904, Japan's navy attacked the forces of the Russian navy at Port Arthur. A declaration of war had been sent to the Russian Government, but it was delivered three hours after the attack. Tsar Nicholas II did not believe the Japanese would attack, and the Russian forces were taken completely off guard by the maneuver. Japan commenced a blockade of Port Arthur and turned back attempts by the Russians to break out. Russian Far East general Aleksey Kuropatkin wanted to stall the Japanese advancement into Manchuria in order to have reinforcements arrive via the Trans-Siberian Railway. On May 1, 1904, the Japanese army crossed the Yalu River and assaulted the entrenched Russians. The Japanese suffered heavy losses, but with support from other troops landing in Manchuria, they were able to drive the Russians further back.

In December 1904 Japan took a strategic hill near Port Arthur and began to shell the Russian fleet. This had a devastating effect as all the Russian ships were either destroyed or forced to scuttle. Major General Anatoly Stessel, commander of the garrison at Port Arthur, became dismayed after the loss of the Russian fleet and surrendered to the Japanese on January 2, 1905.[17]

In February 1905 Japan threatened Russian forces near Mukden, the largest city in what is now Liaoning province in northeastern China. The Russian general, Aleksey Kuropatkin, put up a defense of the area utilizing artillery. The Japanese pressed on, and the two forces engaged in fierce and bloody fighting. The Battle of Mukden was one of the largest land battles waged prior to World War I, and it lasted from February 20 to March 10, 1905. The Russian army had over two hundred thousand men, with the Japanese army boasting a similar number.[18] The Japanese troops were under the command of Prince Ōyama Iwao, a field marshal in the army. The superior Japanese tactics allowed them to encircle the Russian forces, and General Kuropatkin finally issued the call to retreat. The Russian forces suffered roughly ninety thousand casualties, with the Japanese suffering seventy thousand. Although the cost was high for the Japanese, the battle proved to be a resounding success for them, as they had successfully smashed the major Russian army in the region. No further significant land battles would take place for the rest of the war.

The Russian Empire mobilized elements of its Baltic Fleet to sail around the world to confront the Japanese navy. This battle group, renamed the Second Pacific Fleet and under the command of Admiral Zinovy Petrovich Rozhestvensky, consisted of eight battleships and several other smaller cruisers and destroyers. The fleet set out for the Pacific coast in October 1904. Unable to use the Suez Canal controlled by the British who had entered an alliance with Japan in 1902, the Russian fleet had to detour through the Indian Ocean.

---

17   Henshall, *A History of Japan*, 94.

18   Hane and Perez, *Modern Japan*, 183.

The Russian fleet finally arrived in late May 1905. It attempted to sneak undetected into the port at Vladivostok through the strait between Korea and Japan known as Tsushima Strait. The fleet was sighted by the Japanese navy and battle commenced from May 27 to 28. The Japanese fleet consisted of four battleships, but they outnumbered the Russians in destroyers and cruisers and possessed a significant number of torpedo boats. The Russian fleet was almost completely destroyed, losing all eight of its battleships in addition to some other smaller vessels, and over five thousand men. The Japanese by comparison lost only several torpedo boats and a little over one hundred men. Japanese forces then occupied the Sakhalin Islands and forced the Russians to sue for peace.

American President Theodore Roosevelt stepped in as a mediator between the two sides and helped them negotiate peace terms. The Treaty of Portsmouth was eventually signed by Japan and Russia at the Portsmouth Naval Shipyard near Portsmouth, New Hampshire in the United States on September 5, 1905, putting an end to the Russo-Japanese War. The treaty gave Manchuria back to China and allowed Japan to keep half of Sakhalin that it had captured. According to a prior treaty negotiated earlier in the year, the Japanese were also able to have total control of Korea. By the end of the war, the Japanese were seen as a new global power in the world, having successfully taken on a Western power and won, and having been able to project its imperialist domination to other regions.

Although the Russo-Japanese War promoted many industries in Japan, World War I of 1914–1918 was described as the "best" war in Japan's history in terms of international trade and national economy. During WWI, Japan's military participation was minimal, but it gained maximum benefits from the war in East Asia. W. G. Beasley points out that "during the war years, Japan had used her status as an 'ally' to secure a position of dominance" in East Asia."[19] After 1914 there was a vast increase in demand for Japan's manufacturing goods in Asia since European supply had been cut off. Between the 1910s and 1930s, Japan's production of raw materials more than tripled, and its output of manufacturing goods increased over twelvefold. From the 1900s to the late 1930s, Japan's export trade surged almost twentyfold, more than 60 percent of which was made up of manufactured goods. Moreover, WWI destroyed European shipping to the Asian-Pacific region, and the Japanese merchant marine replaced the Europeans. After the war, Japanese shipping doubled in size and increased its net income about ten times. Thus, a new demand for international trade and shipping security requested a rapid build-up of military might to protect Japanese resources and markets overseas. Japan then inevitably involved itself in imperialist competitions against other colonial powers in Asia. Curtis Andressen concludes, "The changes also unleashed a fierce nationalism, which in turn fed the fires of imperialism. Ultimately, this led to war—with China, Russia and eventually the Western Allies. From the end of isolation to consolidation as a world power took less than 70 years."[20]

---

19 Beasley, *The Rise of Modern Japan*, 153.

20 Andressen, *A Short History of Japan*, 78.

Chapter 7

French Colonial Rule in Vietnam

In 1857 a joint expedition of French and Spanish forces attacked Vietnam with the blessing of the Vatican. Spanish-led forces concentrated their attack in the northern part of the country, while French-led forces, after an unsuccessful attempt to attack the capital at Hue, began an offensive against the southern part of the country. The French had considerably more success. Failing to dislodge French forces, the Nguyen dynasty agreed to the terms of the Treaty of Saigon in 1862, which among other terms ceded directly to the French three provinces in the south, including the city of Saigon. The French declared a protectorate over the Cambodian king in 1863 and seized another three provinces in 1867 under the pretext that the Nguyen had violated the Treaty of Saigon.

In 1883 the French took advantage of instability at the court in Hue following the death of an emperor to force treaties on the Nguyen establishing a protectorate over central and northern Vietnam, a process concluded after the French defeated an effort by the Qing dynasty to come to the aid of the Nguyen in 1884–1885. Finally, responding to Siamese aggression, the French established a protectorate over the Lao monarch in Luang Prabang in 1893. At this point, the French established control over the five regions making up French Indochina: Laos, Cambodia, Tonkin in northern Vietnam, Annam in central Vietnam, and Cochinchina in southern Vietnam. They also established Hanoi as the capital of French Indochina. Four of these five regions were controlled as protectorates, which meant that many of the domestic laws of the Lao, Cambodian, and Vietnamese monarchs still technically applied. Significantly, one region—Cochinchina, which included Saigon—had been ceded directly to the French and was not under Nguyen imperial authority.

The French decision to colonize Indochina had three main motivations. The first, and initially the most salient, was to protect French missionaries and Vietnamese Catholics. The second and third aims, which became more important as French colonial control solidified nearing the end of the nineteenth century, were to establish a firm foothold in Asia to compete with British imperial possessions and to exploit natural resources and waterways in Vietnam for the economic and material advantage of French merchants and the French state.

Vietnamese subjects had various responses to French imperialism. Some continued to serve the Nguyen dynasty faithfully even as it became controlled by French officials, and still others became employed by French companies or the French administration. Those who rejected French imperialism, however, did so in three phases. The first phase began with the Treaty of Saigon in 1862 and ended in 1897 when the French Governor Paul Doumer eliminated the Nguyen viceroy in Hanoi, effectively cutting off all residual Nguyen authority in Tonkin. This phase focused on restoring Nguyen power. When Vietnamese intellectuals realized that a restoration of the *status quo ante* would be impossible, the second phase of resistance (1897–1925) began. This phase focused on developing new ideas from Japan, India, and Europe, and in promoting language reform by touting the Romanization of the Vietnamese language. However, it was largely promoted by a generation of scholars who had been educated in the Chinese classics and had taken the civil service examinations, and were therefore still imbued with the assumptions of those texts. This is in contrast to those involved in the third phase of resistance (1925–1939), who were educated from their youth in French or Romanized Vietnamese and espoused localized Vietnamese versions of radical or liberal ideologies from Europe.

Prelude: The Thieu Tri Era and the Tu Duc Succession Crisis (1841-1851)

When the Minh Mang Emperor died early in 1841, Vietnamese Catholics and European missionaries alike saw an opportunity. However, they would be disappointed. The new emperor, Minh Mang's son Thieu Tri, had a reputation of being more tolerant of Christians and foreigners than his father. But upon taking the throne, Thieu Tri allowed the prohibition on the practice of Christianity that had been adopted in Minh Mang's later years to stay in place. Thieu Tri was, however, less inclined to kill Christians. Though missionaries were condemned to death under his reign, none of them were actually executed. This may have been because Thieu Tri was occupied by increasing Vietnamese clashes with Siam over Cambodia.

In contrast, by the 1840s, the Catholic French population's attention was captured by stories of Catholic martyrs in Asia. The 1830s and 1840s saw the rise of such publications as the *Annales de la propagation de la foi (Annals of the Propagation of the Faith)*. This journal "produced 150,000 copies of its journal six times a year in seven languages" by 1842. Journals such as these gave Catholic missionaries in Asia and Vietnamese Catholics a forum to explore shared values, investigate geographical and cultural differences, and build widespread sympathy for those martyred for the faith.[1] Despite the general indifference to Catholic interests of King Louis Philippe, "a virtual Voltarian who attended Mass," he did authorize the French navy to defend French missionaries in East Asian waters in 1843. He did this perhaps not only because of pressure from prominent Catholics and Catholic publications, but also because of the need to establish a foothold in East Asia to counterbalance British dominance in China in the aftermath of the First Opium War (1839–1842).[2] French naval officers were inclined to intervene in cases of the persecution of French missionaries in Asia. In chapter three, for example, we discussed French gunboat diplomacy in response to the persecution of Catholic missionaries in Korea in 1846.

In the Vietnamese case, there were several instances in the 1840s in which French ships

---

1 Nola Cooke, "Early Nineteenth-Century Vietnamese Catholics and Others in the Pages of 'Annales de la propagation de la Foi,'" *Journal of Southeast Asian Studies* 35, no. 2 (June 2004): 268–9.

2 Joseph F. Byrnes, *Catholic and French Forever: Religious and National Identity in Modern France* (State College: Pennsylvania State University Press, 2005), 87; McLeod, *The Vietnamese Response*, 35; Charles Keith, *Catholic Vietnam: A Church from Empire to Nation* (Berkeley: University of California Press, 2012), 37. On the French desire to counteract British expansion in China, see Ernest P. Young, *Ecclesiastical Colony: China's Catholic Church and the French Religious Protectorate* (New York: Oxford, 2013), 24–5.

attempted to intervene on behalf of missionaries. In February 1843 Captain Favin Léveque of the French ship *Héroine* presented a letter to French officials demanding the release of five missionaries that had been imprisoned by the court.[3] This mission was successful, and it made Thieu Tri's court, already wary from the events of the Opium War, even more suspicious of foreign missionaries. On two occasions, in 1845 and 1847, the French navy was involved in efforts to secure the release of an imprisoned French bishop, Dominique Lefèbvre (1810–1865). In the first instance, the French acted after Captain John Percival of the United States Navy failed to gain Lefèbvre's release earlier in the year. The French were successful where the Americans were not, but Lefèbvre reentered Vietnam and was arrested again in 1846.

Lefèbvre set the conditions for the first naval battle between the French and the Nguyen. In 1847 two French warships arrived at Da Nang harbor and demanded the release of Lefèbvre and another missionary and religious freedom for Catholics.[4] Ironically, unbeknownst to the two captains, Lefèbvre had already been released and left for Singapore. A naval battle ensued in which forty Vietnamese were killed, and the French ships left without their demands being met.[5]

The Thieu Tri Emperor died in October 1847, just a few months after the French bombardment of Da Nang. His death came immediately after an unsuccessful British mission directed by Sir John Davis, the governor of Hong Kong, to extract special trading privileges from the Vietnamese.[6] The influx of Western demands left Thieu Tri so enraged that he may have died from apoplexy.[7] A complicated imperial succession heightened the intensity of Nguyen confrontations with Westerners.

In the spring of 1848, the Tu Duc Emperor (r. 1848–1883) succeeded Thieu Tri, but not without controversy. Thieu Tri's eldest son, Hong Bao, was Thieu Tri's choice of heir. However, he was passed over for the throne in favor of Tu Duc. Truong Dang Que (1793–1865) was the most powerful official at court at the time and was the architect of many of Thieu Tri's policies. Because he was concerned that Hong Bao would be too headstrong to be controlled, he favored Tu Duc. Although Tu Duc possessed a keen intellect and vast knowledge, he was both physically weaker (he had been rendered impotent by smallpox in 1845) and constitutionally less inclined to challenge existing authority.[8]

European missionaries approached the situation with the new emperor with a sense of hope. They reported that in the first months of his reign in 1848, persecutions were on the decline. In fact, rumors spread that Tu Duc had issued a secret order not to persecute missionaries. However, their hopes were dashed when in August 1848, Tu Duc entirely

---

3   Phan Phat Huon, *Viet-nam giao su* [Vietnamese Religious History] (Saigon: Cuu The Tùng Thu, 1965), 272–3.

4   Georges Taboulet, *La geste française en Indochine: histoire par les textes de la France en Indochine des origines à 1914* (Paris: Adrien-Maisonneuve, 1955–1956), 362–5.

5   McLeod, *The Vietnamese Response*, 36–7.

6   Nicholas Tarling, "British Relations with Vietnam, 1822–1858," *Journal of the Malaysian Branch of the Royal Asiatic Society* 39, no. 1 (July 1966): 33–5; Alastair Lamb, *The Mandarin Road to Old Hué* (Hamden, CT: Archon Books, 1970), 296–304.

7   Taylor, *History of the Vietnamese*, 435.

8   C. Michele Thompson, *Vietnamese Traditional Medicine: A Social History* (Singapore: NUS Press, 2015), 60; Nguyen Q. Thang and Nguyen Ba The, *Tu dien nhan vat lich su Viet nam* [Dictionary of Vietnamese Historical Figures] (Hanoi: Khoa hoc xa hoi, 1991), 584–5.

prohibited "foreign religions."[9] Subsequently, French missionaries looked for clandestine ways to support Hong Bao as an alternative. When Hong Bao launched an unsuccessful rebellion that was put down in 1851, Tu Duc suspected that Catholics had supported Hong Bao's revolt.[10] In this context, Father Augustin Schoeffler, a French missionary, was arrested and put to death for illegally preaching Christianity and "seducing and fooling the people."[11]

The execution of Schoeffler further increased the tension on both sides. After Schoeffler's execution, Nguyen authorities became acutely aware of how many non-Christian Vietnamese were eager to take his hair and blood as relics, believing them to have magical power.[12] Moreover, given that there was no evidence linking Schoeffler to Hong Bao, his execution was controversial. Influential scholars such as Nguyen Dang Giai (d. 1854) protected Christians from increasing officially sanctioned harassment, though this was perhaps because Nguyen Dang Giai may have been partisan of Hong Bao, only increasing Tu Duc's perception that Catholics were associated with efforts to dethrone him.[13]

The Franco-Spanish Invasion and the Treaty of Saigon

When Schoeffler's execution was followed by Tu Duc's decision to kill another French missionary, Jean-Louis Bonnard, in 1852, the French government had "the pretext it needed for the launching of the 1858 invasion."[14] Political events in France also helped to spur on French military action against Vietnam. Louis-Napoleon, the nephew and heir to Napoleon I, had been elected president of France in 1848 after the July Monarchy of Louis Philippe had been overthrown. In 1852, after he was blocked for running for a second term as president of the French Second Republic, he staged a military coup and proclaimed himself Emperor Napoleon III (1852–1870). The Second Empire, which Napoleon III founded, was heavily dependent on Catholic support. This was on his mind in 1852 when eight French bishops located in Asia wrote to him to demand intervention on their behalf. Intervention was delayed, however, because of the outbreak of the Crimean War (1853–1856) and the continued havoc being created by the Taiping Rebellion in China.[15]

In January 1857 the French began a diplomatic effort to gain concessions in Southeast Asia, including Vietnam, under the leadership of Former French consul to Shanghai Charles de Montigny (1805–1868). As a response to being beaten out by both the English and the Americans in winning diplomatic concessions from the Siamese, the French quickly responded by entering their own negotiations in Bangkok and by trying to open negotiations with the Vietnamese court in Hue. After completing a treaty in Bangkok on August 15, 1856, de Montigny sent a letter to the Vietnamese court via the French ship *Catinat* demanding religious freedom and favorable trading policies for the French in Vietnam.[16] Unfortunately, the commandant of that vessel, Captain Le Lieur, grew impatient with officials in Danang

---

9 Etienne Vo Duc Hanh, *La place du catholicisme dans les relations entre la France et le Viet-Nam de 1851 à 1870.* (Leiden: Brill, 1969), 294–5.

10 McLeod, *The Vietnamese Response*, 39.

11 Adrien Launay, *Les cinquante-deux serviteurs de Dieu*, vol. 2. (Paris: Téqui, 1893), 136.

12 Cooke, "Vietnamese Catholics," 280.

13 Ibid., 282; Yoshiharu Tsuboi, *L'empire Vietnamese face à la France et à la Chine* (Paris: L'Harmattan, 1987), 134–5.

14 McLeod, *Vietnamese Response*, 40.

15 Tarling, "British Relations with Vietnam," 47.

16 Etienne Vo Duc Hanh, *La place du catholicisme*, 98–103.

who refused to deliver the letter. In response, on September 16, 1856, he ordered the bombing of the Nguyen dynasty's gun emplacements at Danang before leaving angrily for Macao.[17] By the time de Montigny himself arrived in Vietnam in January 1857, no further negotiations were possible. In fact, they led to even more severe persecutions and to the death of a Spanish Bishop, José María Díaz Sanjurjo, on July 20, 1857.

By this time, personal appeals to Napoleon III from prominent Catholics, in particular the missionary Abbé Évariste Régis Huc (1813–1860) and the bishop of North Cochinchina, François Pellerin (1813–1862), along with an aggressive public relations campaign in pro-Catholic newspapers, persuaded the emperor that a major military expedition was in order. A Franco-Spanish joint force under the command of Charles Rigault de Genouilly (1807–1873) attacked Da Nang harbor, swiftly destroyed Vietnamese defenses, and took a small strip of land. However, they had insufficient supplies to pursue further operations, and the Franco-Spanish invasion stalled. Genouilly then took a contingent of troops to occupy Saigon, which he did successfully by February 1859. His aim was to force the Vietnamese to negotiate a satisfactory agreement that would guarantee freedom for Christians to worship and missionaries to work, as well as trading privileges at key ports. Genouilly believed that occupying Saigon would weaken the Nguyen by depriving them of a key source of rice.[18]

Though this strategy would take some time to bear fruit, the Nguyen eventually agreed to the Treaty of Saigon on June 5, 1862. Meanwhile, due to changes of governments in Spain and French machinations, the Spanish were virtually excluded from the provisions of the treaty. The treaty ceded three provinces in the South, including the city of Saigon, to the French. This area would become French Cochinchina. It also guaranteed religious freedom for Catholics and the free movement and exercise of religion for missionaries throughout Nguyen territory.[19] It also forced the Nguyen to pay an indemnity to the French.

Under the leadership of the governor of Cochinchina, Admiral Pierre-Paul de La Grandière (1807–1876), the French expanded their commercial and political interests in Southeast Asia from their base in Saigon. They established a protectorate over Cambodia in 1863 and sent an expedition up the Mekong to explore potential commercial routes. In 1867 they took the remaining three provinces of southern Vietnam (Vinh Long, An Giang, and Ha Tien) to protect their newly gained interests in Cambodia.[20]

The Francis Garnier Affair and the Birth of French Indochina (1873–1885)

The Vietnamese response to this aggression was to attempt to negotiate with the French to seek the retrocession of the territory under French control. The Tu Duc Emperor was open to the possibility of negotiating with the French. He was concerned about the severity of other threats to his throne. One of these threats was the rebellion of Pierre Le Duy Phung (d. 1865), a Vietnamese Catholic convert and pretender to the throne who wished to restore the Le dynasty. Another threat was from the independent mercenary armies that roamed the border regions with China. The Black Flags, mostly ethnically Zhuang mercenaries from the border regions between China, Laos, and Vietnam who were forced to flee into Vietnam and Laos when the

---

17   Henri Cordier, *La France et la Cochinchine, 1852–1858: La mission du Catinat a Tourane (1856)* (Leiden: EJ Brill, 1906), 17–18.

18   Thompson, "Diplomacy of Imperialism," 336–8.

19   Keith, *Catholic Vietnam*, 40.

20   Le Thanh Khoi, *Le Viet-Nam: Histoire et Civilisation* (Paris: Éditions de Minuit, 1955), 370–1.

Qing government put down the Taiping Rebellion, were willing to work with the Nguyen dynasty as mercenaries. They were led by Liu Yongfu, a charismatic ethnically Hakka man from Guangdong, who was discussed in chapter four. The Black Flags came to serve the Nguyen forces as a mercenary army that could be used to help defeat other brigand armies such as the White Flags or Yellow Flags. The Black Flags were also eventually useful against the French. However, the Nguyen were also acutely aware that relying on the Black Flags was problematic to a Nguyen state that was "increasingly concerned with defending its monopoly on force in northern Dai Nam."[21]

Both Le restorationists and the Black Flags would find themselves thrust into history by the acts of a French naval officer. This officer went well beyond his instructions by starting an insurrection in the north in 1873. His name was Francis Garnier (1839–1873). He was sent up the Red River to negotiate the release of Jean Dupuis, a French merchant who had gotten into a diplomatic dispute with the powerful official Nguyen Tri Phuong (1800–1873) over his shipments of weapons up the Red River into China.[22] Francis Garnier believed that his unofficial mission was to secure the Red River for French commercial interests.[23] When negotiations with Nguyen Tri Phuong were not fruitful, Garnier used the forces at his disposal to take the citadel at Hanoi. He then promptly secured the four provinces in the Red River delta on behalf of France. He was aided in this effort by members of the Yellow Flag Army, by partisans of the Le dynasty who were interested in another restorationist effort similar to the one carried out by Pierre Le Duy Phung in the previous decade, and by Christians in Tonkin, including the French missionaries who had been inciting Garnier.

The Nguyen dynasty responded by appealing to the assistance of Liu Yongfu and his Black Flag Army, which had helped them in previous fights against a White Flag group. On December 21, 1873, the Black Flags successfully ambushed Francis Garnier in the citadel at Hanoi and killed him. In the meantime, the news of Garnier's extralegal actions received a mixed reaction back in Paris. Napoleon III had been forced into exile in 1870, and the new Third French Republic was not as uniformly enthusiastic about French imperial designs in Indochina and was not as sympathetic to missionary interests. As a result, in 1874, the French signed the Philastre Treaty, reaffirming the pre-Garnier *status quo ante* and ceding back the four northern provinces that Garnier had seized.[24]

The retrocession hardly strengthened the hand of the Tu Duc Emperor. Northern officials who were upset at Catholic participation in the Garnier affair wanted to seek reprisals. Thus, Tu Duc increasingly faced pressure from those who felt his government was too soft on Catholics. As bands of vigilantes rose up in the North to seek retribution for Catholic actions against the Nguyen, Tu Duc was forced to act to calm the storm.[25] But when he did, as in an October 1876 edict prohibiting the interference of

---

21   Bradley Camp Davis, *States of Banditry: The Nguyen Government, Bandit Rule, and the Culture of Power in the post-Taiping China-Vietnam Borderlands* (PhD Dissertation, University of Washington, 2008), 90.

22   Henri Cordier, *A Summary of Recent Events in Tong-King* (Shanghai: American Presbyterian Mission Press, 1875), 34–40.

23   Davis, *States of Banditry*, 171.

24   Patrick J. N. Tuck, *French Catholic Missionaries and the Politics of Imperialism in Vietnam, 1857–1914* (Liverpool: Liverpool University Press, 1987), 168–9.

25   Nguyễn Phan Quang and Võ Xuân Đàn, *Lịch sử Việt nam từ nguồn gốc đến năm 1884* [History of Vietnam from its foundations to 1884] (Hồ Chí Minh: NXB Tổng Hợp, 2011), 421.

missionaries in the trials of Vietnamese Christians, he would face equal pressure from the French side.[26]

In the meantime, the French naval officer Henri Rivière, again exceeding his authority just as Francis Garnier had done, briefly took the citadel in Hanoi again in 1882. Rivière captured the citadel of Nam Dinh in March 1883. Tu Duc again pressed Liu Yongfu and the Black Flag army into his service. Rivière was killed outside Hanoi in May 1883. The precarious situation remained until the Tu Duc Emperor, the last independent monarch in Vietnamese history, died in July of 1883.

Tu Duc's death precipitated a series of factional conflicts at the Nguyen court. Officials were divided between those who wished to take a stand against the continued French military and commercial presence in the North and those who wished to continue to seek peaceful solutions. This conflict resulted in the deposing of Tu Duc's successor, Duc Duc (1852–1883) after a reign of only three days. Two powerful officials with ties to Liu Yongfu engineered the rise of Emperor Hiep Hoa (1847–1883), with the hope that he would pursue an aggressive anti-French policy.[27] The French responded in kind with the backing of Paris. At that time, the French prime minister, Jules Ferry (1832–1893), was a strong supporter of colonial expansion. In August 1883 the French laid siege on the capital of Hue by taking control of the nearby port of Thuan An, forcing the Vietnamese into negotiations.[28] As a result, Hiep Hoa was forced to agree to the Harmand Treaty, which ensured that the French would establish a "protectorate" over the North.

However, the Harmand Treaty was never ratified. Anti-French officials at the Nguyen court retaliated by deposing Hiep Hoa, stripping those who had supported negotiations with the French of their titles, and calling for Chinese assistance. As we discussed in chapter four, the Black Flag Army, the Nguyen Army, and the Qing Army, under the command of the notable reformer Li Hongzhang, fought the French in the North, but they were unsuccessful. Although the Qing continued to fight the French in the northern borderlands until 1885, the Nguyen had been forced to reaffirm the protectorate under the terms of the Patenôtre Treaty of July 1884. This new treaty kept the Nguyen monarchy in place but severely limited its ability to rule independently. French Indochina was born, though it was only to be fully completed with the establishment of a protectorate over Laos in 1893.

The First Phase of Resistance (1862–1897)

Resistance to French rule began as soon as Franco-Spanish troops seized the citadel at Saigon. From that time until the elimination of the Nguyen viceroy in Hanoi in 1897, resistance was mostly under royal auspices. Most anticolonial resisters in this period envisioned their resistance as a means to restore power to the Nguyen monarchy and had not yet lost faith in Nguyen institutions or in the possibility of their restoration.

An early example of this first phase of resistance was the rebellion of Truong Dinh (1820–1864). Between the French occupation of the Saigon citadel in 1859 and his suicide in 1864, Truong Dinh led a protracted resistance against the French. As the leader of a military plantation, he had five hundred men and weapons at his disposal at Thuan Kieu, near Saigon. By 1861 he had moved his forces southeast, further from Saigon, and had incorporated former Nguyen soldiers and their weapons into his

---

26   Tuck, *French Catholic Missionaries*, 188–9.

27   Nguyen The Anh, *Monarchie et fait colonial au Viêt-Nam (1875–1925): le crepuscule d'un ordre traditionnel* (Paris: L'harmattan, 1992), 59–62.

28   Davis, *States of Banditry*, 270–1.

ranks.[29] From this strategic geographic position, Truong Dinh's forces proved difficult to dislodge. After the Treaty of Saigon was signed in 1862, Truong Dinh refused to surrender, despite being ordered to do so. Scholars disagree on why this was the case, with some arguing that continuing the fight was a form of loyalty (despite explicit orders from the emperor to the contrary), and others arguing that Truong Dinh had secret orders to continue resistance.[30] By 1864 French operations against Truong Dinh's army became more effective, and he committed suicide during an ambush.

A second episode of resistance in this model of restoring dynastic power was the Aid the King (*can vuong*) movement. In the summer of 1884, the Kien Phuc Emperor died, only months after taking the throne. Anti-French forces in the palace put on the throne the Ham Nghi Emperor (1872–1943, r. 1884–1885), whom they believed to be pliable toward their interest in resisting the French. Key scholar-officials then stockpiled weapons and cash and waited for a convenient time to engage in resistance. They found that point on July 5, 1885, when anti-French officials attacked the French garrison in Hue and then forced the emperor and his entourage out of the palace and into a remote mountainous area near the Lao border. By this time, many members of the Nguyen Royal Family, led by the Nguyen matriarch, Tu Duc's mother Pham Thi Hang (1810–1902), had decided to return to Hue and submit to the French, who promptly placed Ham Nghi's half-brother Dong Khanh (r. 1885–1889) on the throne.[31]

Despite these setbacks, the Aid the King movement managed to capture the imagination of scholar-officials bent on resistance. Ham Nghi wrote an edict larded with references to the Chinese classics on July 13, 1885, calling for resistance to the French. However, Ham Nghi was betrayed by one of his guards and captured in 1888, at which time the French sent him to a life of exile in Algeria. The Aid the King movement, however, had become sufficiently institutionalized that it was able to continue in the mountains of north-central Vietnam for a number of years more under the leadership of Phan Dinh Phung (1847–1896), until he was surrounded and died of dysentery early in 1896.[32]

The man responsible for Phan Dinh Phung's encirclement was the viceroy of Tonkin, Hoang Cao Khai (1850–1933), who was from Phan Dinh Phung's own village, and was related to him by marriage.[33] As viceroy, he was the representative of the emperor for Tonkin and was responsible for conveying Imperial policy to French officials in Hanoi. In the next year, 1897, the French eliminated the position of viceroy. Instead, the French resident

---

29   Mark W. McLeod, "Truong Dinh and Vietnamese Anti-Colonialism, 1859–1864: A Reappraisal," *Journal of Southeast Asian Studies* 24, no. 1 (March 1993): 93–4; David G. Marr, *Vietnamese Anticolonialism, 1885–1925* (Berkeley: University of California Press, 1971), 31.

30   McLeod, "Truong Dinh and Vietnamese Anti-Colonialism," 94–5; Milton Osborne, *The French Presence in Cochin China and Cambodia: Rule and Response (1859–1905)* (Ithaca, NY: Cornell University Press, 1969), 60. One point in favor of Osborne's interpretations—that French suspicions that Truong Dinh's movement was secretly supported by the court—can be found in the fact that Nguyen Huu Lap, in his top-ranking answer on the policy question of the 1862 Confucian civil service examination, advocated that the court at a minimum look the other way in response to Truong Dinh's actions. See *Quoc Trieu Dinh Đoi Sach Van*. Archival Manuscript V. Hv. 318/2. Vien Hán Nôm, Hanoi, Vietnam, 34.

31   Marr, *Vietnamese Anticolonialism*, 47–9; Taylor, *History of the Vietnamese*, 476.

32   Marr, *Vietnamese Anticolonialism*, 66–7; Hue-Tam Ho Tai, *Radicalism and the Origins of the Vietnamese Revolution* (Cambridge: Harvard University Press, 1992), 16–17.

33   Hue-Tam Ho Tai, *Radicalism*, 16.

superior of Tonkin was made the emperor's official delegate to the French government.[34]

The elimination of the viceroy was part of Governor-General Paul Doumer's (1857–1932) scheme to establish a strong administrative structure for French Indochina. Doumer asserted authority over all five parts of Indochina, despite efforts of the French in Cochinchina to govern themselves independently. He also created a unified budget and embarked on ambitious infrastructure projects.[35] For enterprising Vietnamese willing to work with the French administration, these projects could prove lucrative, as they brought new economic prosperity over time, especially to urban centers in Vietnam.

For Vietnamese scholar-officials, the combination of the collapse of the Aid the King movement, the slow decline of the Nguyen dynasty's independent control of their own financial matters, and the elimination of the viceroy's position meant the virtual extinction of the Nguyen dynasty's independence.[36] Elites who would previously have taken the examinations to start official careers were, after 1897, much more inclined to find different routes to success.

The Second Phase of Resistance (1897–1925)

For those continuing to resist French imperial control, 1897 would mark a turning point. After this time, it became increasingly difficult to imagine a path to rid Vietnam of colonial rule by restoring power to the Nguyen, though there continued to be efforts to do just that—most notably with the uprising spearheaded in the name of Emperor Duy Tan by the scholar-official Tran Cao Van (1866–1916). This uprising was cut short before it began in 1916 by French authorities who had discovered the plot; they promptly arrested Duy Tan, whom they sent to exile at Réunion Island in the Indian Ocean. They also executed Tran Cao Van. These, however, would not be the main lines of resistance. Most of this younger generation of scholars understood that restoring independence to Vietnam would only be possible with a significant modernization of institutions. Because of this assumption, they tended to look outside Vietnam—to Japan, to India, or to France, among other options—to seek inspiration for anticolonial action. This second phase of resistance was led by scholars whose formative years were spent studying the Chinese classics, and whose worldview always contained elements of the classics, but who looked to transcend the education of their youth and embrace new possibilities for modernizing Vietnam.

Two anticolonial figures in particular stand out in this second phase of resistance: Phan Boi Chau (1867–1940) and Phan Chu Trinh (1872–1926). Phan Boi Chau was born in Nghe An province into a family of local scholar-officials, his father having been awarded a licentiate or *tu tai* degree on the regional examination.[37] Phan Boi Chau followed in his father's footsteps in pursuing success on the civil service examinations. After several failures, he passed the regional examinations in 1900. However, he never advanced beyond this stage. He failed in

---

34 Truong Buu Lam, *Colonialism Experienced: Vietnamese Writings on Colonialism, 1900–1931* (Ann Arbor: University of Michigan Press, 2000), 157.

35 Taylor, *History of the Vietnamese*, 482.

36 A thorough discussion of these developments can be found in Nguyen The Anh, *Monarchie et fait colonial*, 173–82.

37 For a description of this and other Vietnamese examination degrees, see Alexander Woodside, *Vietnam and the Chinese Model* (Cambridge, MA: Harvard University Council on East Asian Studies, 1971), 172.

his one attempt to pass the palace examination, the highest level of the civil service examinations.[38]

Even while working to pass the examinations, Phan Boi Chau became involved in anticolonial activity. As a young man, he became involved in efforts to support the Aid the King movement. Around the turn of the century, he began to organize anticolonial efforts with three main aims: first, to locate and support remnants of the Aid the King movements in the mountains and countryside and attempt to give them aid; second, to find a suitable member of the royal family to serve as a focus of resistance; and third, to send anticolonial activists out of Indochina to seek foreign assistance against the French.[39]

Over the course of the first several years of the twentieth century, he set out to do exactly these things. He established the *Duy Tan Hoi*, or Renovation Society. To develop this organization, Phan Boi Chau found veterans of the Aid the King movement, recruited a direct descendant of Prince Canh, Prince Cuong De (1882–1951), and sought to travel to countries that would help Vietnam modernize and expel the French. As many Vietnamese intellectuals of his era were, Phan Boi Chau was inspired by the success of Japan's modernization. Therefore, he traveled to Japan. There he was able to meet with the great Chinese reformer Liang Qichao (1873–1929), who had a reputation as a leader of reform throughout East Asia, including Vietnam. Prince Cuong De followed thereafter.

Once settled in Japan, Phan Boi Chau wrote inflammatory anti-French pamphlets for the purpose of encouraging young students to travel to Japan to study. This began the *Dong Du*, or Eastern Travel, movement. By the end of 1907, more than one hundred young men, the majority of whom were wealthy sons of landowners from Cochinchina, came to Japan at Phan Boi Chau's urging. Their Japanese, Chinese, and Vietnamese teachers gave these students a modern educational curriculum and helped them prepare strategies against the French. These students also studied military tactics.[40] However, under pressure from the French, Qing, and British authorities, the Japanese closed down the schools and societies providing these educational opportunities.[41]

By this time, however, Phan Boi Chau had made an impact on many more than just the students who came to Japan. His anticolonial writings found their way into circulation in China and Vietnam and proved to be influential. Moreover, for those in Cochinchina who had never accepted the authority of the ancestral line of Nguyen emperors leading back to Minh Mang, Prince Cuong De provided an alternate leader that inspired anticolonial movements until his death in 1951.

Intellectuals in Tonkin were less likely to support Phan Boi Chau's efforts. They were considerably less inclined toward the use of violence. Moreover, many of them were wary of using foreign assistance to modernize Vietnam and rid Indochina of the French. Instead, they rallied around Phan Chu Trinh, who argued that "to depend on foreign help is foolish and to resort to violence is self-destructive."[42]

---

38 Vinh Sinh and Nicholas Wickenden, "Introduction," in *Overturned Chariot: The Autobiography of Phan Boi Chau* (Honolulu: University of Hawaii Press, 1999), 4–6; Marr, *Vietnamese Anticolonialism*, 83–6. While Vinh Sinh and Wickenden indicate that Phan Boi Chau failed the palace examination in 1903, this would be impossible as no palace examination was held in that year. It is more likely that Phan Boi Chau failed this examination in 1904.

39 Marr, *Vietnamese Anticolonialism*, 101.

40 Ibid., 139.

41 Ibid., 149.

42 Vinh Sinh, "Introduction," in *Phan Châu Trinh and His Political Writings*, ed. Vinh Sinh (Ithaca, NY: Cornell Southeast Asia Publications, 2009), 1.

Phan Chu Trinh can also be distinguished from Phan Boi Chau because of his rejection of monarchism; he would not endorse plans to put Cuong De on the throne. Instead, Phan Chu Trinh believed that what was needed in Vietnam was a fundamental political transformation. Vietnamese needed a shift in their intellectual mentality, a change in their fundamental value systems.

Phan Chu Trinh was from a village in Quang Nam province, about one hundred kilometers south of Da Nang, where the fighting of the Franco-Spanish invasion began some fifteen years before he was born. His parents hailed from scholarly families, and his mother was able to give him a classical education, but she died while he was young. His father was a part of the Aid the King movement. In 1887 his father was probably unjustly suspected of being a traitor to the movement and was murdered, leaving Phan Chu Trinh an orphan at fifteen. He was also gifted with a keen intellect and developed a fondness in particular for the writings of Mencius.[43]

Phan Chu Trinh quickly passed the civil service examinations and earned a *Pho Bang* (subordinate list or second-class doctorate) degree on the Palace Examination in 1901. In 1903 he accepted a low-level position as a secretary at the Nguyen Ministry of Rites in Hue. While in the Nguyen administration, he was able to meet with many of the leading scholar-officials at the time and join them in reading the reformist and revolutionary texts emerging from Chinese intellectuals such as Kang Youwei, Liang Qichao, and Sun Yat-sen, among others. Inspired by their ideas, in 1905 he joined two fellow examination graduates on a tour of Cochinchina to raise objections and critiques of the Confucian education

system in Vietnam. Famously, they disguised themselves as candidates for a regional examination that was being held in Binh Dinh province and wrote answers mocking the rigidity of the examination system.[44] In a way, the antiexamination stance of these men was ironic, not only because they themselves were graduates of the 1901 and 1904 examinations but also because the examination system had by that time become quite willing to grapple with Western ideas.[45]

Nevertheless, this intellectual stunt gave Phan Chu Trinh a reputation as an educational reformer. After visits to China and Japan in which he met an aged Liu Yongfu, Phan Boi Chau, and probably Liang Qichao, he came to the conclusion that "modernization was necessary before one could even contemplate independence."[46] Returning to Vietnam in the middle of the first decade of the twentieth century, Phan Chu Trinh set out to modernize Vietnam by promoting changes in Vietnamese commerce, culture, and education. To accomplish the first goal, he founded and supported businesses to promote the self-sufficient production of handicrafts and textiles that could be produced locally without French help. In culture and customs, he urged Vietnamese men to cut their hair very short, abandoning a traditional Confucian custom of not cutting one's hair as part of a respect for hair as a gift from one's parents. And in education, he favored modern schools that would teach about new technology rather than merely teach the classics.[47]

In connection with that final activity, Phan Chu Trinh came to be associated with the Tonkin Free School movement. In a narrow sense, the Tonkin

---

43 Ibid., 12.

44 Ibid., 14.

45 See Wynn Gadkar-Wilcox, "French Imperialism and the Vietnamese Civil Service Examinations, 1862–1919," *Journal of American-East Asian Relations* 21 (2014): 373–93.

46 Vinh Sinh, "Introduction," 18.

47 Ibid., 20–1.

Free School (*Dong Kinh Nghia Thuc*) was a short-lived private school that taught Vietnamese youth from the fall of 1907 to very early in 1908. This school sought to provide students with a more modern educational experience through criticizing the examination system, placing an emphasis on teaching science and technology, adopting a heavily nationalist interpretation of Vietnamese history, and endorsing the use of *quoc ngu* (Romanized Vietnamese) and French in addition to instruction in classical Chinese, which was the *lingua franca* for scholarly activity in Vietnam at the time. Although the school was run by another scholar and included the participation of many other famous thinkers in Vietnam, Phan Chu Trinh was the school's "most popular speaker." Students remembered his rousing and persuasive speeches on the need for modernization and in favor of the adoption of the Romanized script for writing Vietnamese.[48]

The fervor created by Phan Boi Chau's Duy Tan society and the Tonkin Free School movement had an immediate impact. In 1908 there were a series of disturbances inspired by these movements. A mutiny of the French army on behalf of Hoang Hoa Tham (1858–1913), the last holdout of the Aid the King Movement, was one example. There was also a tax revolt that was especially strong in central Vietnam. This revolt was blamed on Phan Chu Trinh, who was subsequently arrested and sentenced to life imprisonment on Con Son Island off of the coast of Indochina.[49] However, in the summer of 1910, French admirers of his interceded. He was released and allowed to depart for France.[50] While in Paris, Phan Chu Trinh was able to mentor another young anticolonial revolutionary, who called himself Nguyen Ai Quoc. By the 1940s, the world would come to know this man as Ho Chi Minh (1890–1969).

The Third Phase of Resistance (1925–1939)

By the mid-1920s, a new generation of Vietnamese young people opposed the French. Unlike those leading the second phase of resistance, they had not been educated in the Chinese classics. Rather, they benefited from a transition that had occurred in 1917. That year, in the wake of the failed Duy Tan uprising, the French governor-general Albert Sarraut (1872–1962), forced the new Nguyen emperor Khai Dinh (r. 1916–1925) to abolish the examination system. The last examination was held in Hue in 1919. In its stead, Sarraut endorsed a liberal and modern curriculum of study in Franco-Vietnamese schools. These schools emphasized European ideas but also taught aspects of Vietnamese history and culture that seemed unthreatening to French rule, such as the national literary classic *The Tale of Kieu* and Confucian texts on obedience such as the *Classic of Filial Piety*. Significantly, these schools abandoned teaching classical Chinese in favor of *quoc ngu* and French. Sarraut's position ironically put the French colonial authorities in the same position as Vietnamese anticolonialists. Both sides believed that the use of *quoc ngu* would increase literacy, and both thought that this would benefit their cause.

The promotion and distribution of literature in *quoc ngu* would fundamentally transform Vietnamese thought and society. By the mid-1920s, especially in Cochinchina but also in Annam and Tonkin, young Vietnamese journalists and writers had founded an astounding array of magazines, journals, and book series. The existence of this substantial new body of literature had a number of significant impacts. First, anticolonial agitators could disseminate new ideas much more quickly and completely than they could before. Moreover, their ideas increasingly were founded on concepts derived from

---

48 Marr, *Vietnamese Anticolonialism*, 169.

49 Vinh Sinh, "Bibliographical Chronology," in *Phan Châu Trinh*, xv.

50 Ibid.

European modernist discourse directly, whereas in the second phase of resistance these discourses arrived after having been mediated through the works of Chinese reformers. Second, they brought new genres of literature, such as modern theatre, investigative reporting, and the serialized novel, into popularity in Vietnam. Third, with these new genres came a diverse array of political and social ideas. By the early 1930s, articles and journals arose focusing on women's rights, criticizing Confucian culture and traditional medicinal practices, critiquing social problems such as prostitution and venereal disease, supporting religious sects and new religious movements, and advocating for a variety of political positions, among them anarchism, constitutionalism, Trotskyism, socialism, and communism.[51] Political debates over the status of women, in particular, occupied an important space in the changing social scene of the 1920s and 1930s, so much so that they were featured in the popular serial *Phu Nu Tan Van* (Women's News), which aired grievances about the traditional position of women in Vietnamese society. This publication, which advocated for reforms in marriage and divorce practices and in the economic situation of women, became increasingly radical by the mid-1930s.[52] Literature reflected these changes as well. Literature in the 1920s and 1930s increasingly championed resistance to arranged marriages and grappled with the increasing Westernization of urban society in Vietnam.[53]

In addition to the rise of this new literature, two political events galvanized young anticolonialists in Vietnam toward these new political ideas. First, in 1925, Phan Boi Chau was arrested by the French colonial regime. He was accused of having been involved in a plot to assassinate a French official years before. The newly invigorated *quoc ngu* press covered this trial extensively. Phan Boi Chau took the opportunity to defend himself by putting French rule itself on trial. He questioned the legitimacy and justice of French rule itself. Vietnamese youth were galvanized by this event. They read Phan's statements and testimony in these papers. They became angry when Phan Boi Chau was convicted and sentenced to death, though the sentence was eventually commuted to house arrest.

The second event that galvanized young intellectuals was the death of Phan Chu Trinh in 1926. Phan Chu Trinh was allowed back to Vietnam from France a year earlier when it became clear that he was ill. He continued to publish influential tracts even while ill in Saigon. After he passed away, his funeral became a moment of national commemoration and political protest against the French. Spurred on by the new *quoc ngu* newspapers, sixty thousand people attended in Saigon and processed with the body from downtown Saigon to his gravesite near Saigon's airport. Sixteen other places in Indochina, including Phnom Penh, held similar remembrances.[54]

Phan Boi Chau's trial and Phan Chu Trinh's funeral further galvanized the modernist and anticolonial forces that had already been put in place through the educational reforms brought about by both Sarraut and anticolonial activities such as the Tonkin Free School. In this period, movements inspired by these events proliferated. One of these

---

51 See Shawn McHale, *Print and Power: Confucianism, Communism, and Buddhism in the Making of Modern Vietnam* (Honolulu: University of Hawaii Press, 2008).

52 David Marr, *Vietnamese Tradition on Trial, 1925–1945* (Berkeley: University of California Press, 1981), 223–7; Micheline Lessard, "Women's Suffrage in Viêt nam," in Louise Edwards and Mina Roces, *Women's Suffrage in Asia: Gender, nationalism, and democracy.*

53 Cao Thi Nhu-Quynh and John C. Schafer, "From Verse Narrative to Novel: The Development of Prose Fiction in Vietnam," *Journal of Asian Studies* 87:4 (1988): 756–77.

54 Marr, *Vietnamese Tradition on Trial*, 21.

was the Vietnamese communist movement. In the mid-1920s, Vietnamese communists were led by the man who would later be known as Ho Chi Minh. A decade before his death, Phan Chu Trinh had taken Ho Chi Minh under his wing in Paris. In 1919 Ho Chi Minh famously attempted to present a petition to United States president Woodrow Wilson during the negotiations for the Treaty of Versailles. This petition called for political autonomy and basic rights for the Vietnamese.[55] He also became a member of the French Communist Party. He was present at the founding of the party during the national congress of the French Socialist Party in 1920.[56] In the subsequent years, the French secret police targeted him. Ho Chi Minh fled to Moscow in 1923. At that time, the Comintern, the organization tasked with aiding international communism, was making plans to assist with anticolonial efforts around the world.[57]

After being educated in Moscow, Ho Chi Minh was sent to Canton in late 1924 to work with Comintern agents there. Ho Chi Minh, with the help of the Comintern agents and members of the Chinese Communist Party, would develop Vietnamese communism and Vietnamese resistance against the French.[58] In 1925 he took two steps toward this end. First, he converted former members of an anarchist-oriented *Tam Tam Xa* (Society of Like Hearts) into a new frontist organization called the Revolutionary Youth League (*Thanh Nien*).[59] Though the Revolutionary Youth League was not explicitly communist, it was carefully organized along lines recommended by the Comintern. Moreover, within the Revolutionary Youth League was a communist youth group that was "designed to be the nucleus of a future communist party."[60] Second, Ho Chi Minh authored a text called *The Revolutionary Path* (*Duong Kach Menh*), which was designed to introduce communist youth to Leninism.[61]

Over the course of the next several years, the Revolutionary Youth League fractured amidst disagreement. Relations between Ho Chi Minh, Comintern representatives, and authorities in Moscow became tenser. Under the leadership of Joseph Stalin (1878–1953), the Soviet Union shifted its priorities away from international revolution and toward building socialism domestically. In addition, the political climate in China at the end of the First United Front between the Guomindang and the Chinese Communist Party forced Ho Chi Minh back to Russia. From there he continued to Europe, then to Thailand. During the latter half of this trip, he was so sick from tuberculosis that he reported to a colleague that he was unable to participate in organizing activities.[62]

The combination of these events pushed Ho Chi Minh into obscurity, which was exacerbated when he was arrested by British authorities in Hong Kong in 1931. A persistent rumor spread that Ho Chi Minh had, in fact, died of tuberculosis in 1932.[63]

---

55   William Duiker, *Ho Chi Minh: A Life* (New York: Hyperion, 2000), 58–60.

56   Ibid., 71–3.

57   Sophie Quinn-Judge, *Ho Chi Minh: The Missing Years* (Berkeley, CA: University of California Press, 2003), 40.

58   Ibid., 69.

59   On the *Tam Tam Xa*, see Hue-Tam Ho Tai, *Radicalism*, 64. On the foundation of *Thanh Nien*, see Quinn-Judge, *Ho Chi Minh*, 78–81.

60   Marr, *Vietnamese Anticolonialism*, 374.

61   William Duiker, "What is to be done? Ho Chi Minh's *Duong Kach Menh*," in K.W. Taylor and John K. Whitmore, *Essays into Vietnamese Pasts* (Ithaca, NY: Cornell Southeast Asia Program Publications, 1995), 207–20.

62   Quinn-Judge, *Ho Chi Minh*, 129.

63   Duiker, *Ho Chi Minh: A Life*, 209.

After briefly directing an effort to unite factions of Vietnamese communists in early 1930, he became an obscure figure. Throughout the 1930s, Ho Chi Minh did not hold an official post in either the Comintern or the Indochinese Communist Party.[64]

In the meantime, with only minimal participation from Ho Chi Minh, newer and younger leaders of the communist movement took the lead in reorganizing themselves into the Indochinese Communist Party (ICP), which was founded in October 1930. Ho Chi Minh attempted to develop a patriotic front in unity with noncommunists. In contrast, these new leaders focused on class struggle and revolution.[65] The result was the Nghe-Tinh Soviet movement of 1930–1931.

The Nghe-Tinh Soviet movement started as a series of peaceful antitax demonstrations in Nghe An and Ha Tinh provinces. However, by the late summer of 1930, the demonstrations escalated. Communist cadres urged the peasants to burn down government buildings and assassinate officials. By the fall of 1930, under communist leadership, peasants in the rural parts of these provinces were expropriating land from landlords and officials. Villagers created "soviets" or "red villages" with the support of the ICP.[66] By 1931 French forces counterattacked mercilessly, capturing or killing hundreds of ICP members and their supporters. In response, the ICP endorsed a campaign of violence against local landlords and officials, and turned against more moderate ICP members that objected to the violence.[67] As a result, by 1932 the ICP was in total disarray. Many of its members and nearly all of its leadership had been captured or killed in the wake of the Nghe-Tinh Soviet movement. Those that survived would spend most of the next years in prison.

The ICP was not the only anticolonial movement in Indochina. Equally significant was the Vietnamese Nationalist Party, or *Viet Nam Quoc Dan Dang* (VNQDD), which was founded in 1927 by the nationalist intellectual Nguyen Thai Hoc (1902–1930). This was an anticolonial party loosely based on the Chinese Guomindang, from which it borrowed its name. Nguyen Thai Hoc envisioned a three-stage rebellion leading to the establishment of a democratic republic.[68] In 1927–1928, the Vietnamese Nationalist Party gained in popularity and insurgents. When a member of the party assassinated a French recruiter without authorization, the French attacked the nationalists.

Facing increasing pressure, Nguyen Thai Hoc concluded that an immediate insurrection was necessary. On February 10, 1930, members of the Vietnamese Nationalist Party, supported by approximately sixty Vietnamese troops in the French Colonial Army rose up against their French officers in Yen Bay, about two hundred kilometers to the northwest of Hanoi. The Yen Bay mutiny failed, however, when the other Vietnamese troops refused to join.[69] French troops quickly rounded up the leaders of the mutiny. Several months later, the "martyrs of Yen Bay," including Nguyen Thai Hoc, were executed by the guillotine. Though this crippled the Vietnamese Nationalist Party, the leaders of the mutiny would become heroes in popular culture. Due to the notoriety of this movement, the Vietnamese Nationalist Party would again rise to relevance.

---

64   Huynh Kim Khanh, *Vietnamese Communism, 1925–1945* (Ithaca, NY: Cornell University Press, 1982), 181.

65   Huynh Kim Khanh, *Vietnamese Communism*, 161.

66   Ibid., 154.

67   Ibid., 158–9.

68   Hue-Tam Ho Tai, *Radicalism*, 184.

69   Tobias Rettig, "French Military Policies in the aftermath of the Yên Bay Mutiny," *South East Asia Research* 10, no. 3 (November 2002): 310.

Other important noncommunist political movements included constitutionalism, anarchism, and Trotskyism. The Vietnamese Constitutionalist Party was a political movement in Cochinchina. It was supported by wealthy Vietnamese landowners, as well as elites in Saigon. The constitutionalists attempted to "use constitutional methods to try to force the colonial government to live up to its expressed ideals."[70] The fact that this movement occurred in Cochinchina was significant. It made progress within the French colonial system possible. Cochinchina was directly ruled by the French, so the Vietnamese could enjoy more political rights—and considerably more if they became French citizens. Bui Quang Chieu (1872–1945) led the constitutionalist movement. He was an urbane man who had acquired French citizenship. He had attended schools in France and was employed in the French civil service as an agricultural engineer.[71] Under his leadership, the constitutionalists advocated for additional Vietnamese seats on the elected Cochinchinese colonial council. They also supported candidates for election and led a boycott of Chinese goods in Saigon.[72]

Anarchism also played an important role in anticolonial movements. Certain strands of Phan Boi Chau's thinking during his time in Japan had anarchist elements, and the Society of Like Hearts (*Tam Tam Xa*), the organization that was co-opted by Ho Chi Minh in Canton in 1925, had anarchist tendencies.[73] In Cochinchina, anarchism was influential. It was central to the writings of Nguyen An Ninh (1900–1943), who published the influential

French-language journal *The Cracked Bell* (*La Cloche Fêlée*). Nguyen An Ninh lived in France in the early 1920s and was influenced by concepts in French anarchism and by the ideas of Friedrich Nietzsche. Nguyen An Ninh presented a moral argument against both the traditionalist Confucianism of the Nguyen bureaucracy and Vietnamese cultural conservatives and the civilizing mission of the French.[74] Nguyen An Ninh found himself subjected to the repression of the French colonial government, however. French authorities shut down his journal and arrested him multiple times. He died in prison.[75]

Similarly, Trotskyism had a strong popular following in Vietnam. Based on the ideas of Leon Trotsky, Trotskyism supported an international revolution of workers and opposed the Stalinist state-centered development of socialism. Among its leaders were Ta Thu Thau (1906–1945), a man from a poor family in the Mekong delta who was radicalized during university study in France. Under his leadership, Trotskyists participated in—and sometimes won—elections to the Saigon colonial council and participated with other communists in the publication of *La Lutte*, a radical French-language newspaper published in Saigon.[76]

The final anticolonial movements were associated with religious groups. Cao Dai was a new religious movement. It was founded by Ngo Van Chieu (1878–1932), a Vietnamese man who worked for the French colonial administration. Ngo Van Chieu developed a fascination with spirit mediums and believed he received a message from God in the form of a divine eye. As the religion grew, Caodaists

70 R. B. Smith, "Bui Quang Chiêu and the Colonialist Party in French Cochinchina, 1917–30," *Modern Asian Studies* 3, no. 2 (1969): 132.

71 Ibid., 133.

72 Ibid., 135–6.

73 Hue-Tam Ho Tai, *Radicalism*, 58–65.

74 Ibid., 73–7.

75 Nguyen Q. Thang and Nguyen Ba The, *Tu dien nhan vat lich su*, 476–7.

76 Hue-Tam Ho Tai, *Radicalism*, 239.

believed that they had developed the ability to communicate through spirit mediums to a variety of "Saints," including Victor Hugo, Joan of Arc, Confucius, Gautama Buddha, and the famous intellectual and savant, "the Vietnamese Nostradamus" Nguyen Binh Khiem (1491–1585). These spirits were said to often reveal messages critiquing the French colonial administration and predicting their demise. Deceased colonial administrators would sometimes reveal themselves to Caodaists and apologize for their actions.[77]

The Hoa Hao were a millenarian Buddhist sect founded in 1939 by Huynh Phu So (1919–1947), a Buddhist mystic who in that year cured himself of persistent illness, claimed to be a *bodhisattva* with special healing powers, and preached that a true king would reappear and save the Vietnamese from French colonial rule. Though the French confined Huynh Phu So to a psychiatric hospital, his Buddhist movement would become very important in the 1940s and 1950s.

Finally, and most significantly, Vietnamese Catholics became increasingly important nationalists in the 1930s. Though the French justified their attack on Vietnam as an attempt to shield Vietnamese Catholics from persecution, some Vietnamese Catholics opposed French colonial rule from the start.[78] Moreover, Catholics became more ambivalent about colonial rule by the late nineteenth century, as French Indochina came to be dominated by business-oriented colonial officials. Some of these officials were quite hostile to Catholics.[79] By the early twentieth century, the Vatican became concerned that Catholicism should not be too closely tied to colonial rule. As a consequence, it began advocating for an expanded role for indigenous Catholics throughout the colonized world.

In Vietnam the result was "the emergence of a national Church in Vietnam." The Church began to appoint indigenous Vietnamese bishops. Vietnamese Catholics adopted ambivalent or even hostile views toward French colonial authorities.[80] A leading family in this effort was the Ngo clan of Quang Binh province in north-central Vietnam. The patriarch of the clan was Ngo Dinh Kha (1850–1923), who served as Minister of Rites and Grand Chamberlain for the Nguyen dynasty during a long career.[81] His eldest son, Ngo Dinh Khoi (1885–1945), became a prominent anti-French official with the Nguyen dynasty. His second son, Ngo Dinh Thuc (1897–1984), was among the most influential Catholic intellectuals; in 1938, he became only the third Vietnamese to be consecrated as a bishop.

The most important of all was his third son Ngo Dinh Diem (1901–1963). Diem rose to prominence in 1933, shortly after the Emperor Bao Dai (r. 1932–1945) had come back to Vietnam from France to begin his actual reign. In 1933, with the help of Catholic officials at Hue, Ngo Dinh Diem was appointed the Interior Minister in Bao Dai's cabinet. But several months later, Ngo Dinh Diem resigned in protest of the lack of de facto

77   On Caodaism, see Janet Hoskins, *The Divine Eye and the Diaspora: Vietnamese Syncretism becomes Transpacific Caodaism* (Honolulu: University of Hawaii Press, 2015), and Jayne Werner, *Peasant Politics and Religious Sectarianism: Peasant and Priest in the Cao Dai in Viet Nam* (New Haven, CT: Yale Southeast Asia Studies, 1981).

78   For one interesting case, see Wynn Wilcox, "Dang Duc Tuan and the Complexities of nineteenth-Century Vietnamese Christian Identity," in *Vietnam and the West: New Approaches*, ed. Wynn Wilcox (Ithaca, NY: Cornell Southeast Asia Program Publications 2010): 71–90.

79   J. P. Daughton, *An Empire Divided: Religion, Republicanism, and the Making of French Colonialism, 1880–1914* (New York: Oxford University Press, 2006), 85–120.

80   Keith, *Catholic Vietnam*, 89.

81   Ibid., 98.

Nguyen sovereignty and French control over the court.[82] This would give him a reputation as an uncompromising nationalist.

By the late 1930s, these seemingly inchoate groups of nationalist youth competed for the loyalty of the Vietnamese on the pages of newspapers and magazines throughout Vietnam. The embrace of *quoc ngu*, the educational reforms, the abolition of the Confucian-style civil service examinations, and the increasing number of Vietnamese traveling abroad gave rise to a dizzying array of competing new ideas. Despite their differences, these movements had two positions in common: first, they all had a goal of curtailing or eliminating the French presence in Indochina; and second, they all sought to forge a path for a more modern contemporary Vietnam. The story of Vietnamese history for the rest of the twentieth century is about the competition between these fundamentally different views of Vietnamese modernity.

---

82 Edward Miller, *Misalliance: Ngo Dinh Diem, the United States, and the Fate of South Vietnam* (Cambridge, MA: Harvard University Press, 2013), 26.

Conclusion to Part Three

This section of *East Asia and the West* revealed what on the surface appears to be three very different experiences of modernization in the context of a direct military threat by Western powers. In the Chinese case, the late nineteenth century saw the Qing dynasty, who was twice defeated at the hands of British troops, descend into a semicolonial situation in which Europeans dominated a seemingly ever-expanding list of treaty ports. In Japan, the threat of American interference was one factor prompting a wholesale political change that precipitated the fall of the shogunate and the reforms of the Meiji restoration. The Meiji policies transformed Japan into an industrial and military power, and this in turn led to major shifts in Japanese culture and an embrace of modernization. In Vietnam, conflict with European missionaries, coupled with domestic unrest and uncertainty over royal succession, created an unstable situation. This led to the French taking advantage of this situation and gradually establishing colonial control over Vietnam, in addition to Cambodia and Laos, and establishing French Indochina. This section, therefore, showed us three different outcomes to direct conflict with Western powers: direct colonialism (Vietnam), informal colonialism (China), and a reform movement that prevented colonization (Japan).

Despite these different outcomes, these three case studies of East Asian countries in conflict with the West also have considerable similarities. In all three cases, the nineteenth century saw attempts at technological reform and modernization. This led, in all three countries, to movements for cultural and intellectual reform and to an infusion of new ideas, many but not all of which came from Europe. Finally, in all three cases, these confrontations led to the development of new forms of nationalism that would have profound consequences for the development of East Asia in the twentieth century, as we shall see in part four of this book.

PART FOUR

Wars and Revolutions

Introduction to Part Four

Part three demonstrated how in the nineteenth and early twentieth centuries East Asians altered their economies, technologies, and cultures in tandem with the major global developments of colonization and modernization. Two important, and related, consequences of those shifts were the transformation of East Asian nationalisms and the introduction of new ideas, many of which originated in the West.

What part four will show is how those new nationalisms that emerged out of new ways of understanding the world led to a series of revolutions—political, cultural, and social—in Japan, Korea, China, and Vietnam. In all four countries, the shock waves initiated by intellectual changes and the rise of nationalism led to armed conflicts. In the early twentieth century, an increasingly bellicose Japan, seeking to gain raw materials and prove its mettle as an imperialist power on par with those from Europe, colonized Korea, invaded Manchuria, and eventually became involved in an all-out war with China. By the late 1930s, Japan's gambit for East Asian supremacy became the focus of the Pacific theater of war in World War II. After the United States dropped atomic bombs on two Japanese cities, however, Japan surrendered, and endured several years of US occupation. By this period (the late 1940s), East Asia became one of the key theaters of the Cold War, a complex battle of will fought between capitalist and communist forces for world supremacy. The Chinese Civil War, the Korean War, and the First Indochina War were all early tests of the military and ideological strength of each side in this larger battle. Finally, in 1949, mainland China fell under communist control. The leaders of the new People's Republic of China, chief among them Chairman Mao Zedong, attempted to carry out fundamental transformations of agricultural and industrial economies and ways of life in China. By the 1960s, these transformations would eventually lead to a rift with the Soviet Union, and surprisingly, by the 1970s to a détente with the United States.

Chapter 8

Japan as Occupier and as Occupied

After World War I (1914–1918), Japan quickened its pace of industrialization and replaced China as the dominant power in East Asia. A Japan-centered economy, supported by colonized Korea and Taiwan, experienced a golden age from the late 1900s to the 1920s. Rapid technological progress continued; the military continued to expand; and the infrastructure and the institutions of government continued to modernize. In the 1920s, however, Japan suffered a serious depression. The boom produced by WWI ended by 1921, resulting in substantial labor unrest in the industrial sector. Protectionist policies and tariffs introduced by the United States to protect its own industry placed high barriers on Japanese trade. High unemployment, overpopulation, and acute shortages of raw materials all plagued the Japanese economy. The disparity between the rich, especially those who had profited from the war, and the poor caused popular resentment. The Rice Riots broke out in 1918, in which tens of thousands of people angry at the rising price of rice attacked government offices and police stations across the country. Then, in 1923, the Great Kanto earthquake destroyed Yokohama and half of Tokyo, killing more than one hundred thousand people. Finally, in 1927, the banking crisis bankrupted 25 percent of banks in Japan.

Economic problems were not the only ones that plagued Japan during the Taisho period. When the death of Emperor Meiji in 1912 seemed conveniently to bracket the end of an era known for its swift and effective modernization, it also left a paradoxical legacy. Rapid industrialization generated a great deal of social anxiety which, although suppressed during the Sino-Japanese War and Russo-Japanese War in the name of nationalism, was nonetheless finding an outlet during the Taisho years. The drain on economic resources, especially because of the Russo-Japanese War, made it imperative for the country to rebuild, a task that continued well into the Taisho era. Moreover, the influx of various western ideologies into Japan in the wake of WWI, including liberalism, socialism, communism, and feminism, among others, further contributed to the sense of social change and discord. The prevalence of labor strikes unnerved many conservative politicians. The emergence of the "new women" who asserted their brand of feminism through progressive magazines such as Bluestocking to advocate for women's suffrage and gender equality, and who boldly embraced western fashions and the concept of romance, was perceived to be disruptive to the much-prized social harmony.

To make matters more complicated, the process of political democratization during the Taisho period proved to be problematic. While the development of a functional party system was a welcomed departure from the Meiji oligarchical rule, the two major parties—Seiyukai (Friends of the Constitutional Government Party) and Minseito (Democratic Party)—failed to attract widespread public support due to their elitist nature. The parties' close affinity to the zaibatsu further compromised their integrity and weakened their appeal to the masses.[1] Under these circumstances, all it took was an economic disaster that would give the military leadership within the Taisho government a pretext to attack the party system and tighten its grip over the country. As it turned out, the Great Depression provided precisely that opportunity. With its economy heavily dependent on foreign trade, especially with the United States, the Great Depression hit Japan hard. Massive unemployment, which happened seemingly overnight, wreaked havoc on an already jittery society.

In order to solve the economic and political problems, voices for a campaign to win new colonies abroad grew in popularity in Japan. Supporters included political rightists and the leadership of the Japanese Army in particular. As a counterweight to the modernization of Japan, the military, the repository of conservative influence, had now gained popular support and political influence inside and outside of the government. At that moment, the Japanese people needed a stronger government, which could protect their achievement of modernization and save their livelihood. Moreover, the Great Depression called into question the European-centered economic order. This in turn sped up Japan's expansions on the Asian continent and Pacific islands. In 1931 Japan invaded Manchuria. In 1937 the Japanese forces launched a total war in China. In 1941 Japan attacked Vietnam.

The Colonization of Korea (1905-1945)

Japan's expansionist impulse did not begin in the late 1920s; in fact, fueled simultaneously by a sense of insecurity and superiority, Japan had always harbored a strong desire to exercise greater influence over Korea. Just as the European powers did in their Asian colonies, Japan advanced a greatly exaggerated notion that Korea was a backward kingdom that existed outside of the civilized world. Anxious to establish its dominant role in Korea, and After defeating its two regional rivals, China in 1894–1895 and Russia in 1904–1905, Japan concentrated on extracting international recognition for its dominant position in Korea. According to the Protectorate of Treaty of 1905, the Russian government accepted Japan's dominance of Korea after its navy and army lost the war to Japanese force. The treaty, which was under the mediation of U.S. President Theodore Roosevelt (1858–1919) and signed in Portsmouth, New Hampshire, also recognized Japan's control of Korea's foreign relations and later its military.

In early 1906, Ito Hirobumi, the leading Japanese elder statesman, arrived in Seoul to assume the office of the resident-general, thus initiating Japan's notorious rule in Korea, and culminating in its full annexation of the country in 1910. The beginning of Japanese overlordship meant the end of the independent Korean state; shortly thereafter, all of the foreign legations except the Japanese had deserted Seoul. The West had given its formal approval for Japanese takeover of Korea. Ito's primary task at this time was to lay down a foundation for a permanent Japanese colonial administration. He carried out the task of dissolving the Korean government with ruthless suppression and unabashed intervention over Korea's political process. Ito proved to be an aggressive political operative, a man of merciless drive destroying weaker competition.

---

1 For a more comprehensive coverage of the party system during the Taisho era, see Kenneth B. Pyle's *The Making of Modern Japan* (Lexington, MA: D.C. Heath and Company, 1996).

During its Korean colonization, the Japanese government encouraged its citizens to move to Korea to alleviate overcrowding in its home island. This open attempt to colonize must have caught the fancy of many Japanese citizens, as indicated by an explosive increase at that time in the number of Japanese residents in Korea. The Japanese population in Korea, which was only 20,000 in 1897, increased to more than 170,000 by 1910. Japanese who chose to move from their overcrowded homeland to Korea included all strata of society, including a large number of unemployed people. Korea had become Japan's new frontier, greatly exciting both Tokyo's government as well as the claustrophobic public.

The Koreans mounted fierce resistance to Japan's colonial intrusion, from King Kojong at the top, to guerrilla armies at the bottom. A young Korean patriot named Ahn Joong-Geun assassinated Ito, the first Japanese resident-general and the foremost architect of the Japanese takeover of Korea, in Manchuria. As the formal annexation of Korea approached, Japan's oppression intensified, forcing a large number of the Korean resistance groups to flee abroad. The bordering states of Chinese Manchuria and Russian Siberia provided easy sanctuaries for most Korean refugees.[2] Some continued their anti-Japanese activities and military campaigns, and some joined Chinese forces.

Japan's formal annexation of Korea followed when it realized that the Koreans would never accept nominal sovereignty with actual Japanese control. In 1910 Tokyo forced the new Korean king to abdicate and turn over the throne to his young son. Then, the Japanese filled most official posts, and the Korean army was disbanded. On August 22, 1910, the rubber-stamp Korean government was forced to sign the Japan-Korea Annexation Draft in a ceremony guarded by Japanese military forces. Korea was officially annexed to Japan as the "Province of Choson," and became part of the Empire of the Rising Sun. From the beginning, Japan's colonial administration in Korea was sustained by its large-scale military and police forces. Imperial Japan intended to use this force to check the Korean independence fighters in Manchuria and Siberia, to apply military pressure to Chinese Manchuria, and to provide support to the colonial administration in Seoul. The Japanese military police had become the most dreaded enforcers of the colonial directives, and their brutal oppression gave rise to deep-seated resentment and nationalistic resistance among Koreans against the Japanese colonial rule.

From 1910 there had been open rebellions in Korea, met by brutal Japanese suppressions, in which an estimated twenty thousand "rebels" were killed. In 1919 these measures, along with the general demand for national self-determination following the Paris Peace Conference officially ending WWI, led to what is known as the March First Movement. During the movement, millions of Koreans participated in the political rallies, protesting parades, and signing petitions to the international Peace Conference at Paris. The European powers, however, including the United States, did not provide any solution for the colonization and exploitation in Korea. As one of the Allied powers, Japan continued its colonial policy and suppressed the Korean nationalist movement. In April 1919 a Korean Provisional Government (KPG) in exile was established in Shanghai. During the early 1920s, after the Bolshevik Revolution (1917), some radical Koreans formed communist parties in the Soviet Union.[3]

From the beginning, Japan was attempting to extort not only political but total control of Korea.

---

2   The total of Korean residents in Manchuria reached ninety-two thousand in 1910.

3   See Patricia Ebrey and Anne Walthall, *East Asia: A Cultural, Social and Political History* (Cengage Learning, 2013). Ebrey and Walthall point out that "a number of Koreas living across Russia formed communist parties … divided geographically between groups in Moscow, Siberia, Manchuria, Shanghai, and Korea proper." 409.

Along with political colonization, Japan appropriated a variety of economic interests with no less passion. Japanese capital entered Korea, overwhelming the backward Korean economy. As a result, the majority of large firms in Korea were owned and operated by the Japanese. Many of Japan's major banks, utility companies, and industrial giants established Korean operations, securely protected by the colonial administration. Japanese filled most nonmenial jobs, including machine operators and engine drivers, while Koreans labored as near-slaves. Even though the Japanese built manufacturing factories, modern mines, railways, and postal service for the first time, most of the Korean coal, iron, and food crops (including over half of the rice) were shipped to Japan.

To imperial Japan, the public education system in Korea was no more than another colonial tool devised to teach Japanese values and mores—another step toward molding the children into the emperor's subjects. By 1929 only Japanese textbooks and the Japanese language could be used in schools. By 1932 Koreans were obliged to take Japanese names. The Japanese claimed that they and the Koreans had the same origins and that the takeover by Japan was thus a natural development. By 1945 when the Japanese colonization was over, there were too few Koreans with the education or administrative experience to form a viable government.

The lives of Korean women were further impacted by Japan's colonization that lasted for thirty-five years from 1910 to 1945. To add insult to injury, the Japanese military institutionalized sexual slavery by forcing tens of thousands of Korean women to become the so-called "comfort women" serving Japanese soldiers during WWII. Drafted to the "comfort stations" across Asia through deception and coercion, a minimum of twenty thousand young Korean women, the majority of whom were virgins, were subject to horrendous sexual abuse in the hands of Japanese officers and soldiers. The brutalization of the "comfort women" went hand in hand with the Japanese military's desire to subdue the Korean national spirit, because violating Korean women was believed to be tantamount to conquering their country.

The progress in Korean women's lives in the early decades of the twentieth century was compromised by the fact that Korea remained under Japanese colonial rule. Japan's colonization became increasingly harsh and brutal as Japan intensified its militaristic expansion in China and the Pacific throughout the 1930s, leading to its eventual collision with the United States and culminating with the Pacific War in the early 1940s. Once again, Korean women's lives became submerged in the broader national struggle for survival. Throughout the harsh colonial rule, Koreans jealously guarded their heritage and resisted "Japanization" with their lives. They effectively frustrated Japan's concerted attempts for cultural assimilation.

Meanwhile, since the status of women became associated with the hallmarks of a civilized society, child marriages were abolished, as was the rule against widowed women remarrying.[4] Notably, these social reforms also took place under religious influences.[5] Women's education, first and foremost, was advocated by American missionaries, and several prominent early feminists in Korea were closely associated with the religious efforts. For example, Kim Hwal-lan, a female pioneer for women's education, attended missionary schools and subsequently went to the United States to pursue more advanced education.[6] Other "educated Korean Protestants

4 Ibid., 286–7.

5 Kenneth M. Wells, "The Price of Legitimacy: Women and the Kunuhoe Movement, 1927–1931" in *Colonial Modernity in Korea*, eds. Gi-Wook Shin and Michael Robinson (Cambridge, MA: Harvard University Press), 193.

6 Seth, *A History of Korea*, 184.

in particular strongly promoted reform of social practice and thought regarding women, partially for moralistic reasons but also as part of a campaign to 'strengthen the nation.'"[7] By enduring long and cruel mistreatment, Koreans rejected Japan's overtures to make them second-class citizens. They remained resolutely nationalistic until the end of the ordeal.

Invasion of Manchuria and the Total War with China (1931–1945)

After colonizing Korea, Japan's next target was Manchuria in northeastern China. With its rich minerals, fertile soil and nearly two hundred thousand square kilometers of land, Manchuria was a much-coveted site for Japanese expansion. An unknown explosion on a section of the Japanese-held rail line at Shenyang (Mukden) gave the Japanese army the pretext that it sought to charge the local Chinese with sabotage and to launch an attack on Manchuria. This was the Mukden Incident, also known as the September 18 (9–18) Incident, in commemoration of the date of its occurrence. Within a few months, the Japanese armed forces occupied the entirety of Manchuria, including Liaoning, Jilin, and Heilongjiang provinces and created the puppet state of Manchukuo under the leadership of Pu Yi, the last Qing Emperor who was dethroned in 1912. The occupation of Manchuria was a precursor to Japanese's subsequent aggression into other parts of China.

The impact of this event was far reaching. The de facto Japanese seizure of Manchuria exposed the Japanese state as an existential threat to China. In fact, with the outbreak of the Manchurian crisis, the Japanese unleashed military and political forces, which led ultimately to the full invasion of China on July 7, 1937. The objectives of the Japanese leaders who began the war in China were to maintain Japan's position in Manchuria and establish a new East Asian empire, a so-called "Greater East Asia Co-Prosperity Sphere."

On July 7, when Japanese troops clashed with Jiang Jieshi (Chiang Kai-shek)'s troops at the Lugouqiao or Marco Polo Bridge outside Beijing, a total war started between the two countries. In less than one month, Jiang lost first Beijing and then Tianjin. On August 13, Japanese troops attacked Shanghai and threatened Nanjing, capital city of the Jiang's government. He organized a defense with nearly 700,000 troops in the Nanjing-Shanghai region. The Chinese defense, however, failed. In November, Japan occupied Shanghai. In December, it captured Nanjing. Iris Chang pointed out in her book, *The Rape of Nanking; The Forgotten Holocaust of WWII*, that after the Japanese troops entered the capital city, they killed 90,000 POWs and 260,000 civilians, while raping approximately 30,000 women, hence the infamous Rape of Nanking.[8]

Jiang's army continued its ineffective defense from 1938 to 1941, despite a few victories in the Battle of Taierzhuang and Battle of Wanjialing. In October 1938, Japan captured Guangzhou and Wuhan, two major cities in South China. Jiang had to remove the seat of his government from Nanjing to Chongqing, Sichuan province. He also moved its forces to China's southwest and northwest to conserve their strength, avoiding the total lost. From July 1937 to November 1938, he had lost one million troops to the Japanese Imperial Army. Wherever the Japanese invading troops went, they burned, killed, and pillaged. Countless villages, towns, and cities were reduced to ashes, and millions of civilians were killed. In the meantime, Japanese forces slowed down their southward advance, stopping short at China's southwestern region. The Chinese war of resistance entered a protracted phase of six years.

On September 1, 1939, the German army invaded Poland, sparking WWII in the European theater

---

7   Kenneth M. Wells, "The Price of Legitimacy," 194.

8   Iris Chang, *The Rape of Nanking; The Forgotten Holocaust of World War II* (New York: Basic Books, 1997), 4.

between the Axis powers, including Germany, Italy, and Japan on one side, and an Anglo-French coalition on the other. However, the conflict eventually widened to include most of the nations in the world. As the war continued, the Allied powers expanded to include the United States, China, and Korea. Anti-Japanese independence movements, such as the Viet Minh Front in Indochina, also joined the Allied war effort. By 1940 the GMD army had lost the coastal and other port cities that once had been their bases of power.[9]

It is worth noting that by the time that WWII broke out in Europe, a full-blown Sino-Japanese War had been going on for over two years. Japan's aggression in China since the Manchurian (Mukden) Incident in 1931 further complicated the power struggle between the Nationalists and the Communists. Under immense pressure to adopt a strong anti-Japanese stand, Jiang Jieshi's initial policy in favor of eliminating the Communists before tackling Japan cost him a great deal of public support. After the Xi'an Incident in late 1936 in which Jiang was kidnapped by his own generals in an effort to force him into an anti-Japanese alliance with the Chinese Communists, Jiang reluctantly entered the second United Front with the communists.

According to the agreement between the GMD and CCP, the Communist forces were reorganized into the Eighth Route Army, totaling 30,000 troops under the command of Zhu De and Peng Dehuai, in the north and the New Fourth Army, totaling 10,300 troops under the command of Ye Ting and Xiang Ying in the South. Thus, an anti-Japanese partnership formally came into existence.[10] This front is often called the Second United Front (1937–1945) to distinguish it from the First United Front of GMD-CCP cooperation (1924–1927). Moscow firmly supported the CCP-GMD coalition through the war. In August 1937, the Eighth Route Army left Shaanxi, crossed the Yellow River, and moved into Taihang Mountain. In September, its 115th Division attacked the Japanese troops at Pingxingguan, Shanxi province. In its major engagement, the Eighth Route Army annihilated more than 2,000 enemy troops. Later, all its divisions marched to the enemy-occupied territories where they carried out guerrilla warfare and developed anti-Japanese bases in North China.

From 1938 to 1945, there were three separate regions established in wartime China. First, the GMD-controlled region with Chongqing as its wartime capital in Southwest China. Secondly, the CCP-controlled region behind the enemy line in North and East China. Thirdly, the Japanese-occupied region in Northeast, Central, and Southeast China. The GMD Army under the Jiang's government continued the frontal resistance and suffered very heavy casualties. The CCP guerrilla tactics and "people's war" strategy worked through its land reform and peasant mobilization. The Eighth Route Army, for example, had a large recruitment and increased from 46,000 in 1937 to a half million men in 1940. Nevertheless, the CCP-GMD conflict continued, even though both tried to maintain the united front throughout the war. The major incidents included the South Anhui (Wannan) Incident of January 1941, between the CCP's New Fourth Army and the GMD armies. The New Fourth Army suffered heavy casualties, including 2,000 prisoners.

Japan's attack on Pearl Harbor also refueled public enthusiasm in China. After four years of ineffective resistance against Japanese invaders, a frustrated Jiang Jieshi and exhausted Chinese forces became suddenly encouraged and extremely motivated by seeing that the United States was now fighting on their side against Imperial Japan in the Pacific. Such enthusiasm was buoyed by the Nationalists' success in obtaining American aid through

---

9   Edward L. Dreyer, *China at War, 1901–1949* (New York: Longman, 1995), 7.

10   Elleman, *Modern Chinese Warfare*, 205–6.

diplomatic efforts, many of which were carried out by Song Meiling, wife of the Generalissimo Jiang. The Chinese government thereafter enjoyed unprecedented activism in Allied diplomacy through the war for international support in general, and US aid in particular. The new vigor of nationalism revealed a profound change taking place in China partly because of "China's own tenacious resistance against Japan and partly from Washington's promotion."[11] While Jiang and his government attempted to improve the ROC's international status in Cairo and Moscow, where he attended the Allied summits as one of the international leaders, his efforts actually strengthened the nationalist leadership at home in a way Jiang had never before enjoyed. Important internal reasons also drove this crucial turn for the GMD government.

Pearl Harbor, the Pacific War, and the Atomic Bombs (1941–1945)

Japan's imperialist expansion, fueled by the invasion of China in 1937, did not achieve the objectives of the Japanese leaders in Tokyo. They had expected economic returns, in the form of fuels and raw materials, to at least cover the cost of the war. What made it even worse was that "the American government answered each Japanese move," beginning with a trade embargo on Japan by banning the sale of airplanes in July 1938; then, extending the embargo to oil and petroleum products in December 1939; and to scrap iron, munitions, and other implements of war in July 1940.[12] The US government refused to recognize Japan's military occupations of the Indochinese countries and demanded an immediate withdrawal of all Japanese troops from China. After the trade negotiations failed between Tokyo and Washington in the spring of 1941, the US

government froze Japanese financial assets in July and signed agreements with the Dutch and British to end their oil exports to Japan also.

The road to Pearl Harbor was a long one. Deeply resentful about the US economic sanctions and its tacit aid to China, and running out of strategic resources in a protracted war, Japan in early July 1941 proposed at an imperial conference a southward drive led by the navy into Southeast Asia, where crude oil, rubber, coal, and other natural resources were accessible for Japan's needs to continue the war. However, the United States had significant military strength in the Pacific, which would be an obstacle to Japan's ocean-going expansion into the western Pacific. In September Admiral Yamamoto Isoroku planned a surprise attack on Pearl Harbor to cripple the US Pacific Fleet there. In October Army general Tojo Hideki became prime minister and decided to put the war plan into action. On November 1, Yamamoto issued the orders for an attack on Pearl Harbor. On the 26th, the Pearl Harbor Striking Force, including six aircraft carriers, two battleships, three cruisers, and nine destroyers, left Etorufu in the Kuriles. In the meantime, an American decoding project named *Magic* had been successful in breaking the Japanese diplomatic code, and it provided information leading to the conclusion that Japan would launch military operations in Southeast Asia, but it was uncertain about target and timing.

On December 7, 1941, the Japanese Strike Force launched a surprise attack on the US military bases at Pearl Harbor in Hawaii. Nearly 200 Japanese aircraft attacked the US Pacific Fleet, sinking four of the fleet's battleships and damaging four more. Another 200 aircraft smashed the US Army and Navy airfields and destroyed about 350 aircraft. The raid lasted less than two hours, killing more than

---

11 Xiaoyuan Liu, *A Partnership for Disorder: China, the United States, and their Policies for the Postwar Disposition of the Japanese Empire, 1941–1945* (Cambridge, UK: Cambridge University Press, 1996), 3.

12 McClain, *Japan*, 473.

2,400 Americans, and almost crippling US defenses in the Pacific. For Japan, however, the attack was only temporarily successful, since its pilots failed to destroy oil storage facilities at Pearl Harbor, and the three aircraft carriers of the US Pacific Fleet were not at Pearl Harbor that day. After the US Congress endorsed President Franklin D. Roosevelt's call for a declaration of war on December 8, the US Navy was able to rebuild its huge naval power in the Pacific over the next year. On December 11, both Hitler and Mussolini declared war against the United States, bringing the United States into all-out war with the Axis powers in both East Asia and Europe.

After Pearl Harbor, Japan continued its attacks on Southeast Asia and occupied the Philippines, Malaya, Singapore, Thailand, and Burma. In June 1942 Japanese armed forces conquered the Dutch East Indies and began to invade Australia and New Zealand. By that summer, Japan possessed a vast oceanic and continental empire stretching four thousand miles from the Western Aleutian Islands south almost to Australia, and six thousand miles from Burma in the west to the Gilberts in the east. In November 1942 the Japanese government established the Ministry of Great East Asia in Tokyo to handle the national puppet governments to develop an economic empire to meet the needs of its war in the occupied regions. Because of the war situation and strong resistance, Tokyo was unable to create the "Great East Asia Co-Prosperity Sphere" as a self-sustaining economic community in the territories overrun by Japan. Japan found it difficult to achieve such a goal due to the strong resistance in its occupied areas as well as the military counter offensives from the United States and other Allied powers.

At home, the Tojo cabinet (1941–1944) mobilized the entire country for Japan's war effort.

For instance, the manufacturing of aircraft had increased from 1,080 fighters in 1941 to 2,935 in 1942; to 7,147 in 1943; and to 13,811 in 1944, while bombers had increased from 1,461 in 1941 to 2,433 in 1942; to 4,189 in 1943; and to 5,100 in 1944. Japan also built five aircraft carriers in 1941, six in 1942, three in 1943, and four in 1944, while it also built nine destroyers in 1941, nine in 1942, fifteen in 1943, and thirty-one in 1944.[13] Nonetheless, it was a war of attrition, in which Japanese war-fighting capability was ground down by a steady growth of American industrial-military power. Already drained out by the war with China in more than five years, soon the Japanese economy could not match the American capacity for rapid expansion of industrial-military power.

Even though the Allied counterattack in East Asia was slowed by the Allied decision to defeat Germany first, the tide turned in the Pacific during the summer of 1942. In May the American fleet defeated a Japanese armada in the Coral Sea north of Australia. Then, in the Battle of Midway on June 3–6, American planes sank four Japanese aircraft carriers, and Japan lost its Strike Force. Thereafter, the Japanese had to defend many islands and places they had occupied. The island-hopping campaign began in August 1942, when US Marines landed on Guadalcanal in the southern Pacific. Savage battles raged for control of the strategic islands in the Pacific. In 1943 American and British forces, along with Indian and Chinese allies, launched an offensive against Japanese outposts in Southern Asia. In mid-1943 Allied forces launched offensives in New Guinea and the Solomon Islands that eventually led to control of the South Pacific. While the island-hopping campaign kept pressure on Japanese forces, the Allies landed in the Philippines in the fall of 1944. After the American fleet crushed the Japanese armada in one of the greatest naval

---

13   Jerome B. Cohen, *Japan's Economy in War and Reconstruction* (Minneapolis: University of Minnesota Press, 1949), 211, 237, 262.

battles in world history, the Allied forces liberated Manila, the capital city of the Philippines, in February 1945. In the meantime, American forces also captured Iwo Jima, a crucial island group in the Pacific.

In early 1945 the Allies began large-scale bombing of Japan. In one raid in March, Allied planes dropped bombs across Tokyo, unleashing a firestorm in which more than 100,000 people died. In April, US general Douglas MacArthur, commander in chief of Allied Forces in the Pacific, ordered the invasion of Okinawa. To defend the Japanese island, thousands of suicide pilots, known as kamikaze, crashed their bomb-laden planes into American ships. During the landing, Allied forces suffered 49,100 casualties, while thirty-four warships were sank. MacArthur estimated a total of 350,000 American casualties for the landing campaign on Japan's major islands, which became one of the most important factors in the Truman administration's decision to drop atomic bombs on Japan to end the war.

President Franklin D. Roosevelt established a government-sponsored atomic research project in May 1943—the so-called "Manhattan Project." After Roosevelt's death in April 1945, Harry S. Truman became the president and continued the nuclear bomb development in Hanford, Washington, Oak Ridge, Tennessee, and Los Alamos, New Mexico, trying to beat Germany to the new technology. On July 16, the first successful atomic bomb was successfully detonated at Alamogordo in the New Mexico desert. President Truman saw no reason not to use the atomic bomb against Japan to save American lives and to end the war. After the Japanese failed to respond to the Allied ultimatum for an "unconditional surrender," Truman issued the order to drop the bombs. On August 6, the first bomb was dropped on the city of Hiroshima, incinerating about one hundred thousand people and destroying nearly 96 percent of buildings. Three days later, after the Japanese government still refused to surrender,

the second atomic bomb was dropped at Nagasaki, killing about ninety thousand people. There have been ongoing debates concerning the need for the atomic bombs to end the war. Some scholars maintain that Truman's decision was based on military necessity and was made to save American lives, as a prolonged war would have certainly resulted in more casualties. Others attribute the decision to strategic calculations to intimidate the Soviet Union in an emerging Cold War.

Even after these catastrophes, the Japanese military remained unmoved. At an imperial conference on August 14, the cabinet split 3:3, and Emperor Hirohito gave his support to the group favoring surrender. When the emperor's surrender speech was broadcast, the civilian populace had been prepared for a final "battle of Japan." On August 15, 1945, Hirohito made a public speech on radio asking all Japanese to lay down their arms and wait for repatriation. On September 2, the instrument of surrender was signed by MacArthur and the Japanese government on the US battleship *Missouri*, in Tokyo Bay. Japan was defeated in the war, which started in 1937. Over the eight years, 3.1 million Japanese had lost their lives, including 2.3 million military deaths and 800,000 civilian deaths.

The American Occupation of Japan (1945–1952)

According to the agreement, the occupation of Japan after its surrender was international. It was to be administered by a four-power Allied Council for Japan in Tokyo under General MacArthur, supreme commander for the Allied powers (SCAP). In fact, the occupation was carried out almost entirely by MacArthur, his staff, and the American troops under his command. The first decade after the war set the pattern for Japan's future. The first segment of the decade, the American Occupation, succeeded because it built on earlier trends, yet also broke with the prewar system in revolutionary ways.

The American Occupation began with the liquidation of the apparatus of Japanese militarism. The empire was dismembered and all Japanese abroad, soldiers and civilians, were returned to Japan. The police were decentralized and the imperial leadership removed. In 1946 Hirohito was forced to publicly renounce his divinity. The Military Tribunal for the Far East was held in Tokyo between 1946 and 1948. Twenty-five of the top leaders were brought to trial for having begun the war; seven of them, including Tojo, were hanged in December 1948. Of approximately 6,000 people charged with war crimes, 920 were executed. The SCAP also purged about 200,000 former politicians and military officers. Wartime political prisoners were released from jail, and Shinto was disestablished. The targets of the Occupation were the *zaibatsu*; the first wave of reforms dissolved 83 *zaibatsu* holding companies. In December 1947 the SCAP issued a new act to further deconcentrate about 1,200 companies.

The most significant reform was the promulgation of the 1947 Constitution, drafted by SCAP's staff, that gave sovereignty to the people and stipulated a democratic system with three branches of government—legislative, executive and judicial. Under the new constitution, the emperor became the symbol of the state with no governing power. According to the new Constitution, all men and women over the age of twenty had political rights. In the first post-WWII election held in 1949, forty-two million Japanese, out of a total population of seventy-eight million, voted. Along with the reforms, the Occupation helped the women's movement and labor unions. Workers were given the rights to organize, engage in collective bargaining, and go on strikes.

Among other important constitutional provisions, Article 9 stands out for its stipulation that Japan "forever renounce war as a sovereign right of nation" while giving up "land, sea, and air forces" or "other war potential."[14] After the Korean War broke out in June 1950, the National Police Reserve was organized for national security. It was renamed the National Safety Force in 1952, and the Self Defense Forces in 1954.

Fundamental changes unfolded in Japan under the Allied Occupation; however, they would not have been possible without the support and cooperation of the Japanese politicians and the general public. Meyer emphasizes, "in contrast to their record in Germany, the U.S. administrators in Japan utilized the Japanese as much as possible inasmuch as there was a dearth of Japanese-speaking Americans."[15] Soon, Yoshida Shigeru became a Japanese hero. One of the few politicians who had opposed Japan's war with the United States, he served as Japan's foreign minister after WWII, then as president of the Liberal Democratic Party (LDP) and prime minister in 1947.

Yoshida emphasized economic recovery in a political context, which provided Japan a well-balanced position in the early Cold War years, especially during the Korean War of 1950–1953. The danger Japan faced in the early 1950s was possible involvement in the US-Soviet Cold War, which would have led to massive military spending, something Japan tried very hard to avoid. In Yoshida refused the demand made by John Foster Dulles, who would later become the American secretary of state during the Eisenhower administration, to rearm Japan to participate in the Korean War. Meanwhile, Yoshida maintained a close relationship with the United States, which in turn enabled Japan to receive four-billion dollars' worth of American military orders during the Korean War. He called the war "a

---

14   Article 9 in the Constitution is quoted from Fairbank, Reischauer, and Craig, *East Asian*, 826.

15   Meyer, *Japan*, 222.

gift from the gods."[16] By 1955 Japan's manufacturing capacity had returned to the prewar level.

On September 8, 1951, the United States and forty-seven other nations signed a peace treaty with Japan in San Francisco. On the same day, Japan also signed a mutual security treaty with the United States, which committed US armed forces, including a "nuclear umbrella," to the safety and security of Japan in the Cold War. The US protection of Japan thereafter held the cost of Japanese defense at minimum; it cost about one percent of GDP through the 1990s. Overall, Japan's Cold War alliance with the United States, the rejuvenating economic impact of the Korean War, and pragmatic domestic policies, as well as an educated work force, combined to propel the Japanese postwar economic transformation. By 1955, Japan had not only recovered from the devastation of WWII but also become more prosperous than other Asian nations. In the late 1960s Japan reached an economic level comparable to that of Europe.

---

16   Andressen, *A Short History of Japan*, 125.

Chapter 9

Divided Loyalties

The Cold War in East Asia

The Cold War started when Soviet and American interests clashed in Eastern Europe after World War II ended in 1945. Under the leadership of Joseph Stalin, the Soviets installed communist governments in several Eastern European countries such as Poland, Bulgaria, Romania, Albania, and later Czechoslovakia and Hungary by denying them general elections. In 1946 propaganda war escalated between Moscow and Washington. In March US president Harry Truman (1884–1972) accompanied former British prime minister Winston Churchill (1874–1965) to Fulton, Missouri, where Churchill made his famous "iron curtain" speech to denounce Soviet intention to divide Europe by a communist expansion. Stalin condemned Churchill's speech as "a call to war against the USSR".[1] In 1947 Truman began to implement his containment policy, the Truman Doctrine, to stop the Russian-sponsored communist expansion in the world. In 1948, for instance, US Congress approved an economic recovery program proposed by Secretary of State George C. Marshall, known as the Marshall Plan, which appropriated $13 billion (about $180 billion in 2015) for the purpose of rebuilding the post-war European economy. The Plan was designed to strengthen the collective economic power of American allies in Europe in order to fend off Soviet influence. In 1949 the United States established the North Atlantic Treaty Organization (NATO) as a military pact to protect Western Europe from a possible Russian invasion.[2]

Although the Cold War was characterized by the confrontation between the United States and the Soviet Union, East Asia's position in the Cold War was not peripheral; in fact, it was central in many ways. Scholars in the West recognize the importance of East Asia's role in the Cold War in their recent studies.[3] The alliance between Beijing and Moscow after the founding of the People's Republic of China was

---

1   Jeremy Black, *The Cold War: A Military History* (London, UK: Bloomsbury Academic, 2015), 42.

2   For more details on the NATO member countries, see John Lewis Gaddis, *The Cold War: A New History* (New York: Penguin Books, 2005), 96–7.

3   For the publications on this topic in the recent years, see Leslie James and Elisabeth Leake, eds., *Decolonization and the Cold War: Negotiating Independence* (London, UK: Bloomsbury Academic, 2015); Tsuyoshi Hasegawa, ed., *East Asia and the Cold War: 1945–1991* (Stanford, CA: Stanford University Press, 2011); Odd Arne Westad, *The Global Cold War: Third World Interventions and the Making of Our Times* (New York: Cambridge University Press, 2005); Gaddis, *We Know Now: Rethinking Cold War History* (New York: Oxford University

the cornerstone of the Communist International alliance system in the 1950s.[4] Communist documents that have become available in the past ten to fifteen years after the collapse of the Soviet Union have provided historians with more opportunities and resources for research.

With the Chinese Communists' victory against the Nationalists in 1949 and the Korean War in 1950, East Asia became a focal point of the global Cold War. The Korean War and the subsequent Vietnam War from the 1960s to the 1970s were the only two "hot wars" that the United States fought during the Cold War—both happened in East Asia. Chen and Li state, "But the active role that China played in East Asia also turned this main Cold War battlefield into a strange 'buffer' between Washington and Moscow. With China and East Asia standing in the middle, it was less likely that the United States and Soviet Union would become involved in a direct military confrontation."[5]

On the other hand, East Asia itself experienced some "hot" episodes during the Cold War. The Communist invasions by North Korea and Vietnam against their southern counterparts from the 1950s to the 1970s also helped to continuously marginalize the "Japan question" in East Asian international politics. Compared with the "German question,"

which had occupied a central position in defining the agenda of big power politics in Europe throughout most of the twentieth century, including a large part of the Cold War period, the Japan question did not have such a troublesome long history and overwhelming influence. However, as mentioned in the previous chapter, the origins, as well as the actual historical path leading to the Second World War in Asia and the Pacific, were closely related to the complex Japan question. Thus, the great powers paid adequate attention to the Japan question during the early postwar period. Throughout the Cold War period, settling the Japan question never occupied a central position in the making of Washington and Moscow's grand strategy toward East Asia. In the early 1970s, China's normalization with Japan following the "Nixon Shock" further sidelined Japan in the overall agenda of big-power politics in East Asia.[6]

The Chinese Civil War (1946–1949)

In August 1945, when Japan surrendered, Chinese people expected independence, prosperity, and peace after eight years of Anti-Japanese War. Both Nationalist and Communist Parties approached post-war issues from an exclusive, China-centered,

---

Press, 1997); Vladislav Zubok and Constantine Pleshakov, *Inside the Kremlin's Cold War: From Stalin to Khrushchev* (Cambridge, MA: Harvard University Press, 1996).

4   For the importance of the Sino-Soviet alliance, see Lorenz M. Luthi, *The Sino-Soviet Split: Cold War in the Communist World* (Princeton, NJ: Princeton University Press, 2008); Robert S. Ross and Jiang Changbin, eds., *Re-examining the Cold War: U.S.-China Diplomacy, 1954–1973* (Cambridge, MA: Harvard University Press, 2001); Westad, ed., *Brothers in Arms: The Rise and Fall of the Sino-Soviet Alliance, 1945–1963* (Washington, DC and Stanford, CA: Woodrow Wilson Center Press and Stanford University Press, 1998); Michael M. Sheng, *Battling Western Imperialism: Mao, Stalin, and the United States* (Princeton, NJ: Princeton University Press, 1997); Michael H. Hunt, *The Genesis of Chinese Communist Foreign Policy* (New York: Columbia University Press, 1996); Gordon H. Chang, *Friends and Enemies: The United States, China, and the Soviet Union* (Stanford, CA: Stanford University Press, 1990).

5   Chen Jian and Xiaobing Li, "China and the End of the Global Cold War," in *The Cold War: From Détente to the Soviet Collapse*, ed. Malcolm Muir, Jr. (Lexington: Virginia Military Institute Press, 2006), 121.

6   Ibid., 123.

absolute nationalist calculation for an "independent and strong China."[7] They did not expect U.S. or Soviet hegemony, nor restoration of pre-war European colonial powers in China. General Jiang Weiguo (Chiang Wei-kuo), former secretary general of the ROC's Council of National Security and ROC President Jiang Jieshi's son, said that his father was convinced that the Roosevelt administration did not have a strategic plan for postwar China, nor did it consider China as a new power that would replace Japan in the position of dominance in East Asia after the war.[8] The US government hoped the GMD and CCP would maintain their 1937–1945 united front after the war. However, both parties had different visions for post-war China and could not continue their political and military coalition. Jiang Jieshi, president of the ROC, found himself having 4.3 million troops, controlling three quarts of the country with three quarters of the population, more than 300 million, and receiving a strong international support, especially that from the US. Jiang believed the ROC government should bring the Chinese Communists to the GMD terms. The CCP and Mao Zedong, however, enjoyed an unprecedented development of the Communist movement in the country through the war. By the end of the war, Mao had 1.2 million regular troops, plus 2.4 million militias with a control of the population nearly 100 million. Mao refused to accept Jiang's political demands and challenged the GMD post-war proposal by mobilizing the urban population. Jiang's earlier strategic blunders in delaying resistance against Japan, inflation, and economic hardships in the GMD-controlled areas had cost

him crucial public support and gravely weakened the Nationalists' position in an impending Civil War.

In August, the Truman administration instructed Ambassador Patrick Hurley to mediate a peace talk between the GMD and CCP.[9] Hurley traveled to Yan'an, wartime capital of the CCP, and convinced Mao to go with him to Chongqing for negotiations with Jiang. Mao argued the principle of peaceful construction of the country based on peace, democracy, and sollidarity, and establishment of an independent, free, and prosperous China. Jiang agreed to end the despotism, to guarantee democracy, freedom, and the equal status of all political parties. After forty-three days of negotiations between Mao and Jiang, an agreement was signed on October 10, 1945. Although both sides agreed that civil war must be avoided at all costs and a free and strong new China be created, neither Jiang nor Mao intended to give up their political agenda without a fight. After his efforts failed, Hurley resigned in November as the US Ambassador to China. Even though the United States and the ROC fought as allies during the war, the leaders of the two countries found it extremely difficult to establish a partnership for a postwar order due to conflicting backgrounds and beliefs and incompatible visions for the future of East Asia.

Then, President Truman appointed the Secretary of State George C. Marshall, former chair of the Joint Chiefs of Staff (JCS), as his envoy to China in December for continuing mediation effort. Marshall used US aid as a negotiating tool to push Jiang to accept terms that Mao could also accept. The secretary of state thought even a threat of a reduction of US aid to the ROC could bring Jiang around.

---

7   Lanxin Xiang, *Recasting the Imperial Far East: Britain and America in China, 1945–1950* (Armonk, NY: M. E. Sharpe, 1995), 30–31.

8   General Jiang Weiguo (Chiang Wei-kuo) (GMD Army, ret.), son of Jiang Jieshi, and adoptive brother of Jiang Jingguo (Jiang Ching-kuo), president of the ROC from 1978–1988, interview by the author at Rongzong [Glory's General] Hospital in Taipei, Taiwan, on May 25–27, 1994.

9   "Aide Memoirs," September 25, 1944, and Hurley's letter to President Roosevelt accompanying the memoirs, September 25, 1944, *Hurley Papers*, University of Oklahoma Library, Norman, Oklahoma.

Nevertheless, Jiang believed a strong support to his regime in and outside the US government as long as he fought against the Chinese Communists in the Cold War. While the Communist forces made full preparations for fighting a new war against the GMD. Although both parties signed a truce agreement on January 10, 1946, it was just as symbolic as the "Double Ten Agreement" of 1945. Marshall was so disappointed when he found out neither Jiang nor Mao would compromise. He returned to the US in January 1947 after an announcement that his mission failed in China.

In June 1946, a full-scale civil war began between the GMD and CCP armies in Manchuria, or Northeast China. After the Soviet Red Army withdrew from Manchuria, the CCP had sent more than a hundred of thousands troops and tens of thousands of party cadres there to receive Japanese and Russian weapons and equipment. Moreover, with its rich coal, crude oil, natural gas and other mineral resources, Manchuria has been the heavy base for steel and iron, automobile manufacturing, mechanics, and petro-chemical industries. It is not only one of the key region of China's economic lifeline, but also one of the population centers with total of 100 million people, including Han Chinese, Manchus, Mongols, Hui, Koreans, and others. After the Pacific War was over, Manchuria became the first major battleground in the Chinese Civil War between the CCP and GMD. In 1946, Jiang sent a large number of his troops into Manchuria along the four major railroad lines and tried to push the People's Liberation Army (PLA, the CCP forces) out of Manchuria. Harold M. Tanner points out in his book, *The Battle for Manchuria and Fate of China*, the PLA's victory over the GMD Army in Manchuria set the stage for a Communist victory in the Chinese Civil War.[10]

At the beginning of the civil war, the GMD government had an obvious military superiority, and controlled the large cities and most lines of communication and transportation. The PLA, on the other hand, was a peasant army, or a force equipped with "millet plus rifles," as Mao described.[11] With a different strength like this, Jiang launched an all-out offensive campaign against the CCP-occupied areas from June 1946 to March 1947 to squeeze the PLA out of their bases. Facing the general attack by Jiang's superior forces, Mao decided to avoid any major battle or an urban defense, but to move his troops into deep country and continue the united front among the people against the Jiang's regime and the US policy of supporting Jiang. Although the PLA lost some of its bases in the first phase of the civil war, the CCP army increased in number and popularity by the spring of 1947. Odd Arne Westad points out that the key to the CCP's success in mobilizing the Chinese masses was their ability to manipulate local politics. Moreover, the party cadres made their own decisions and practiced their skills without "undue interference" from the central authority.[12]

In March 1947, Jiang shifted his war strategy from the all-front offensives to focused attacks on two targets: the CCP-held Shandong region in East China, and Yan'an, CCP capital since 1935 in Shaanxi province in Northwest China. Jiang concentrated thirty-four brigades, totaling 250,000 troops, to surround the CCP base region in Shaanxi. In mid-March, Jiang ordered General Hu Zongnan, commander of the GMD forces in Shaanxi, to launch a large-scale attack on Yan'an

---

10   Harold M. Tanner, *The Battle for Manchuria and Fate of China* (Bloomington: Indiana University Press, 2013), 2–3.

11   Mao Zedong, "The Situation and Our Policy after the Victory in the War of Resistance against Japan," in *Selected Works of Mao Tse-tung*, 4: 15–16.

12   Odd Arne Westad, *Decisive Encounters: The Chinese Civil War, 1946–1950* (Stanford, CA: Stanford University Press, 2003), 107.

with fifteen brigades, totaling 140,000 troops and more than seventy aircraft.[13] With only 20,000 troops at Yan'an, Mao could not successfully defend Yan'an against a superior GMD attacking force. Mao instructed Peng Dehuai, later the commander in chief of the Chinese forces in the Korean War, to cover a general retreat of the CCP Party Center on March 16–18. General Hu continued to chase Mao in Shaanxi and tried to annihilate Peng's force. To limit Hu's air and artillery firepower, Peng designed small-scale defenses using local topography as a natural barrier wherever possible to slow down Hu's pursuit and protect the Party Center and his main force. Cliffs and hills provided obstacles for Hu's troops, and Peng was quick to capitalize and increase his defensive capacity and using hills to better ambushing the attackers. Pro-CCP peasants also took up arms to defend themselves. Locals formed CCP-backed militias geared toward fighting off the invading troops. There were also instances of guerrilla warfare, which significantly weakened the fighting power, logistical support, and morale of Hu's troops. The longer the distance that Hu's army had to march, the more susceptible it was to guerrilla attacks; the deeper the GMD army was into CCP territory, the more damaging each of those guerrilla attacks might potentially be. CCP military and civilians ensured that there was no weak link in their defense, which Hu could exploit. Peng's defense allowed Mao and his Party Center moved around among the mountains and stayed in Shaanxi during the second phase of the war. From March to April, Peng destroyed nearly 20,000 Hu's troops in forty-five days.[14] During the second phase of the civil war from March 1947 to August 1948, Mao engaged the PLA in mobile warfare as a smaller and weaker army against a stronger and superior attacking force. His defensive strategy worked by trading base areas for time and opportunity to launch counter-attacks against the invading GMD army.

By the fall of 1948, the strength of the two sides in the war had changed with the PLA increasing to 2.8 million troops and the occupied areas expanding rapidly. Jiang's army began its defense across the country. In the third phase of the Chinese Civil War, from September 12, 1948 to January 31, 1949, the CCP launched three major offensive campaigns of Liaoxi-Shenyang (or the Liao-Shen Campaign in Manchuria), Beiping-Tianjin (or the Ping-Jin Campaign in North China), and Huai River-Hai Zhou (or the Huai-Hai Campaign in East China). The PLA's three campaigns destroyed the main forces of the GMD Army, and took over most of North China. In terms of scale, or the number of GMD troops were annihilated (about 1.5 million), the three offensive campaigns were unprecedented in the war annals of China and seldom known in those of the world. After January 1949, Jiang deployed his troops on the south bank of the Yangzi River, which was a natural barrier for his defense of South China.

Jiang Jieshi issued a declaration for ceasefire talks in January 1949. In his response on January 14, Mao proposed eight conditions for securing peace, including punishment of war criminals, and Jiang was the first one on the list. Frustrated and faced tremendous pressure from his own party, Jiang announced "retirement" from his presidency on January 21. With the CCP's eight conditions as the basis, the GMD government under new leadership of Li Zongren held peace talks in Beijing on April 1. Delegates of the two sides drew up the final revised version of an "Agreement on Domestic

---

13   Military History Research Division, PLA-AMS, *Zhongguo renmin jiefangjun de 70 nian* [The Seventy Years of the PLA], 286–87.

14   Peng Dehuai, "Report on the Battles in North Shaanxi during the Past Nine Months," in *Peng Dehuai junshi wenxuan* [Selected Military Papers of Peng Dehuai] (Beijing: Zhongyang wenxian chubanshe [CCP Central Archival and Manuscript Press], 1988), 233–35. Hereafter cited as *Selected Military Papers of Peng*.

Peace" on April 15. For political reasons, President Li Zongren did not sign the document.

On April 21, 1949, the PLA high command launched the Crossing River Campaign with one million troops against the GMD defense. On April 23, the PLA crossed the Yangzi River and captured Nanjing, the capital of the ROC, thus ending the GMD rule on the mainland. President Li Zongren and Jiang Jieshi removed the seat of their government from Nanjing to Taiwan with one million GMD troops and government officials. In the summer, the PLA advanced into Southeast and Southwest China, and continued to destroy the remnants of the GMD troops on the mainland. By September, the CCP controlled the Chinese mainland except Tibet and Taiwan.

There were many political, economic, military, and international factors behind the CCP's victory over the GMD in the Chinese Civil War. One of them appears more likely that it was Jiang's failure of the takeover and economic reconstruction after WWII cost the GMD state its "legitimacy"—if indeed the "loss of legitimacy" is the best way to interpret the GMD defeat. Corruption of the GMD played an important role in promoting the anti-GMD movement in China and became one of the major grievances of the forces of undermining the GMD regime in China.

The Guomindang as a party was seriously weakened by the Japanese invasion and occupation for eight years. Because of the war, Jiang was pre-occupied by the warfighting and had less time for the party and its organization in 1937–1945. The attempts a forming the GMD into an elite party with a strictly hierarchical organization were dropped, and the party's policies suffered under the thousands of big and small compromises it had to strike with local power-holders, including warlords and CCP guerrilla forces. It became the GMD culture to use public resources to cater to particularistic loyalty, even if the same activities would be perceived as corrupt in the West. In particular, the norm of reciprocity embedded in GMD political culture socialized people to treat corrupt exchanges as neutral and acceptable.

The GMD had a chance to promote major changes short of revolution. Jiang Jieshi, however, did not launch a much-needed political reform to clean the GMD party by stopping corruption and mismanagement. A political reform could weaken or even collapse the party during the Civil War. Corruption continued to be rampant in the GMD-held regions in the last year of the Chinese Civil War. The corrupt system was made possible by a broad network of personal network and patron-client relationships whose focal point was, naturally, the presidency. Many top governmental appointments were distributed to Jiang's followers, while the bulk of the provincial administration was filled by family and friends of the senior officials. Chinese people's trust in the GMD government through the war against Japan's invasion had been eroding rapidly. The decline in institutional trust partially resulted from failed anti-corruption policy and corruption tolerance in and outside the government. The institutional trust is a key linkage between a government and society and a foundation for democracy. In other words, tolerance for corruption undermines people's trust in government and interests in participating in politics, and slows down, if not totally stops, democratization.

The People's Republic of China (1949–1954)

Mao Zedong, CCP Chairman, proclaimed the founding of the People's Republic of China (PRC) in Beijing on October 1, 1949. China became the largest communist state in the world in term of the population. The West and America were shocked by another communist taking-over in East Asia after it happened in North Vietnam in 1945 and in North Korea in 1948. Some Republican Senators and Representatives blamed the Truman administration "lost China" since the president did not provide full support to the GMD government in the Chinese Civil War. The State Department issued a 1,000-page *China White Paper* in 1950 and tried to "white wash" the problems of the US policy toward postwar China by explaining that the situation of the Chinese Civil War was out of America's control.

Before the founding of the PRC, Mao had issued the "lean-to-one-side" policy in the summer of 1949. New China had chosen the side of the Soviet Union in the global Cold War by joining the communist/socialist camp against the United States and the free world. In December, Mao paid a state visit to Moscow in an attempt to gain for China desperately needed economic aid and military alliance with the Soviet Union. During his long stay in Moscow, a total of sixty-five days, Mao gained a better understanding of Stalin's intentions. Among other things, the Soviet leader wanted to convince Mao that the Soviet Union had its own difficulties, and that there would be no free ride for China.[15] Through their negotiations, the PRC and USSR (Union of Soviet Socialist Republics) signed the Sino-Soviet Treaty of Friendship, Alliance, and Mutual Assistance with Stalin on February 14 in Moscow.[16]

Soon Mao established a party-state after the Soviet totalitarian model. The Central Committee of the CCP, composed of approximately three hundred members, did not have legislative power; however, it had constitutional power since the most important and high-ranking officials of the Chinese government were all members of the Central Committee. The Politburo, lodged within the Central Committee, consisted of twenty-five people who controlled the CCP. Theoretically, members of the Central Committee elected the Politburo. Politburo members held offices in China's national government and regional offices concurrently to strengthen the CCP's power in government and provincial affairs.[17]

As for the ideological platform, Mao made it clear that the new government was a democratic coalition under CCP's leadership, or a "people's democratic dictatorship" (sometimes called a "proletarian democratic dictatorship"), to unify possible support for the regime against its enemies.[18] Using Marxist-Leninist theories, the CCP emphasized the class-based nature of the society and its legal system. In contrast to the old system, which favored the rich and wealthy, the new government would protect the poor against the former ruling classes, which were now enemies of the state. The Communist government, drawing a line between enemies and allies, identified supporters of the new regime and sought to destroy the old social order by targeting the wealthy gentry, landlords and social elites, who, as leaders of the "old China," could potentially lead resistance against the new state, its new government, and the Communist Party.

During the 1950s, Mao launched one political movement after another to engage the masses in a class struggle and to eliminate those labeled as established or potential counterrevolutionaries through initiatives such as land reform, the Three-anti campaign, the Five-anti campaign, and the

---

15 During their second meeting on December 24, for example, "Stalin did not mention the treaty at all," but, instead, mainly discussed with Mao "the activities of the Communist Parties in Asian countries...." The quotation is from Pei Jianzhang, *Zhonghua renmin gongheguo waijiaoshi, 1949–1956* [Diplomatic History of the PRC, 1949–1956] (Beijing: Shijie zhishi chubanshe [World Knowledge Publishing], 1994), 18.

16 Zhou Enlai Military Record Compilation Team, *Zhou Enlai junshi huodong jishi* [Zhou Enlai Military Affairs Record] (Beijing: Zhongyang wenxian chubanshe [CCP Central Archival and Manuscript Press], 2000), 2:117–18.

17 Xiaobing Li, "Chinese Communist Party," in *China at War*, ed. Xiaobing Li (Santa Barbara, CA: ABC-CLIO, 2012), 58–63.

18 Mao Zedong, "on the People's Democratic Dictatorship," commemoration of the twenty-eighth anniversary of the CCP on June 30, 1949 in *Selected Works of Mao*, vol. 4: 411–24.

anti-Rightist movement—all of which turned into violent reactions against millions of people. During the 1950s, the CCP believed that it needed charismatic authority and absolute power to achieve its idealistic goals. The Communists' successful military struggle against the GMD had convinced the leaders that violent means were necessary not only for establishing national power, but also for continuing their Communist revolution after the founding of the PRC. The ideology, experience, and nature of this transformation left little room for civil liberties of Chinese citizens.[19]

The movement to suppress counterrevolutionaries in the early 1950s became a brutal struggle against former officials and supporters of the GMD government. The Common Program stipulated in Article 75: "By law, the trials in the People's Court shall be conducted through the people's assessors system."[20] Many of the accused, however, did not have a lawyer, a hearing, or even a trial before they were sentenced or executed.

To meet the drastic war needs, the CCP had to strengthen its economic and financial control more than ever. The government launched the Three-antis and Five-antis movements from 1951–1954 to target the private manufacturing, commerce, trade, financial, and real estate sectors in urban areas. The Party Center mobilized and encouraged manufacturing workers, company employees, and bank clerks to report their employers' wrongdoing and the companies' illegal activities. Most private entrepreneurs were found guilty in one way or another, and almost all of their businesses, properties, and even homes were confiscated by the government. The criteria for punishable crimes and the accompanying sentences became noticeably

harsher against business owners, and more than two hundred thousand of these individuals and their families died during these two campaigns, resulting in the virtual elimination of the bourgeoisie as a class.[21] These movements made China a Soviet-style state, in which the government owned 98 percent of all industry, commerce, finance, and trade. The Chinese leaders had constructed a communist institution that put severe limits on individual freedoms, such as movement, employment, and economic activities.[22]

On September 20, 1954, the First National People's Congress (NPC) passed the first formal constitution by secret ballot and promulgated the Chinese Constitution. This document included a preamble and was divided into 106 articles in four chapters, much like the Soviet Union's Constitution of 1936, which can be regarded as a civil law system. Parts of the Soviet legal code were directly translated into Chinese, and Russian legal experts assisted in rewriting the code to better fit the conditions in China. The 1954 Constitution stipulated the president as chief executive, the NPC as the main legislative body (a unicameral parliament), the state council as the executive body, and the courts and procurates as the judicial branch. According to the Constitution, the NPC exercised most of its power on a day-to-day basis through the Standing Committee in Beijing. Due to its overwhelming majority in the Congress, the CCP had total control over the composition of this committee. Until the late 1980s, the NPC and its Standing Committee played only a symbolic role as a powerless rubber-stamping legislature. They followed the Party Center's instructions and made sure to pass all the party's decisions at the congressional meetings. All

---

19 Xiaobing Li, *Civil Liberties in China* (Santa Barbara, CA: ABC-CLIO, 2010), 4–6.

20 In fact, the People's Assessors System did not formalize in the new republic until September 1951 when the "provisional Regulations for the Structure of People's Court Organization" was stipulated.

21 Sun and Li, "Mao Zedong and the CCP: Adaptation, Centralization, and Succession," 39.

22 Li, *Civil Liberties in China*, 5–7.

local governments at the provincial, district, county, city, and town levels served as agents of the central government in Beijing.

The Korean War (1950–1953)

The origin of the Korean War still remains controversial to the present day. Yet most available records conclusively indicate that North Korea initiated the so-called "liberation war." Moreover, it appears that North Korea began the war with no direct prodding from either of its Communist backers. It is equally evident that both the Soviet Union and the People's Republic of China willingly cooperated with North Korea once Kim Il-sung's (1912–1994) invasion scheme was presented to them. Korea soon became the battleground for the first "hot war" in the Cold War; the United States and other nations sent armed forces under the UN flag to stop Communist aggression on the Korean Peninsula from 1950 to 1953.

The causes for the Korean War were rooted in the division of the Korean Peninsula into two separate entities at the end of the Pacific War. After Japan surrendered in August 1945, American troops arrived in South Korea and set up a military government. Meanwhile, the Soviet troops occupied the North. From 1945 to 1950, the United States did not have a firm policy toward Korea. In September 1947, for example, the Joint Chiefs stated that Korea was not essential for the security of the United States. In the North, however, the Soviets had a clear vision and solid plan for a nationwide "Korean revolution." Unlike the Americans, who governed southern part of the Korean peninsula with direct military control, the Soviets maintained indirect control by delegating governing power to the North Korean Communists. In September 1948, the Korean Communists founded the Democratic People's Republic of Korea (DPRK, North

Korea) under the leadership of Kim Il-sung with his capital at Pyongyang. Kim served as a major in the Soviet Army during WWII and returned with the Soviet Red Army after the war. Thereafter, Washington abandoned its goal of a unified Korea in favor of an independent South Korea with its capital in Seoul. With US support, South Korea National Assembly was elected on May 10, 1948, followed by the promulgation of a new constitution. Syngman Rhee, a politician with strong American support, became the president of the Republic of Korea (ROK) in July.[23] After the new government was officially proclaimed on August 15, North Korea denounced the ROK and threatened to unify the peninsula by force.

Thereafter, President Rhee faced serious problems from organized guerrilla activities in the South. Washington's policy remained fluid, and the Truman administration regarded the security of the ROK as the UN's responsibility. In 1949, after the Soviet Union withdrew the Red Army from the North, the US troops withdrew from South Korea. Regardless of its true intentions, Washington's lukewarm support of South Korea projected a strong impression that the United States would not rush to save South Korea even if a hostile attempt was launched by North Korea. Furthermore, US secretary of the state Dean Acheson publicly declared, in his Asian policy speech on January 12, 1950, that the American defense perimeter in the Pacific ran from the Aleutians to the Philippines, enclosing Japan. By deliberate omission, he managed to leave a strong impression that South Korea was excluded from America's critical defense perimeter.

On June 25, 1950, North Korea launched a surprise attack on South Korea, which signaled the beginning of the Korean War as a civil war. The invading divisions of the North Korean People's Army (NKPA) equipped with Russian-made tanks and heavy artilleries quickly threw the South into

---

23 Cummings, *Korea's Place in the Sun*, 211–12.

chaotic confusion. The northern Communist troops captured Seoul in four days, forcing the Rhee government to flee the capital city. The Security Council of the United Nations held an emergency meeting later on June 25, denouncing North Korea's invasion of the South and passing a resolution to demand an immediate withdrawal of the invading forces. Nonetheless, the military situation deteriorated daily as the invasion columns encountered only token resistance. It was evident that the South possessed neither manpower nor equipment to stop the invaders. Two days later, the UN Assembly adopted the resolution on using all possible means to aid the Republic of Korea against the northern Communist invasion. The Truman administration authorized General MacArthur to employ US air and naval forces to assist ROK defense of Pusan. On June 30, with President Truman's approval, MacArthur began to send US ground troops to Korea. On July 7, the UN officially intervened in Korea by establishing the United Nations Force and its Command for the Korean War. It had a rescue mission by stopping North Korea's invasion and saving the South Korean government. Seventeen nations responded to the UN's call and participated in the UNF, including the United States, Britain, Canada, Australia, France, Turkey, Belgium, Netherlands, Greece, Colombia, the Philippines, Thailand, and other nations. Since the US armed forces consisted of more than 90 percent of the UNF, Washington demanded a US commander. President Truman appointed MacArthur as Commander in Chief of UNF on July 10.

MacArthur planned a large-scale landing campaign behind the line in central Korea. Although the JCS questioned about the risk, the general did it anyway on September 15 by landing UN/US troops in Inchon. The Inchon Landing collapsed the northern invasion by cutting off the transportation and communication line of the NKPA. Then, the UNF retook Seoul, the capital of South Korea in late September. Kim Il-sung was not prepared for any effective defense when the UNF crossed the thirty-eight parallel and advanced into North Korea on October 1. Stalin declined Kim's request for Soviet direct intervention. Instead, in his telegram to Mao Zedong on October 1, Stalin asked China to send troops to North Korea to save the Kim regime.[24]

By that moment, Mao had made up his mind to send Chinese troops to Korea, even though other Chinese leaders were not sure about fighting the most powerful militaries in the world only one year after the founding of the PRC. Mao chaired a Politburo meeting on October 2 after he received Stalin's telegram requesting Chinese intervention in the Korean War. All of the Politburo members, however, opposed Mao's idea of sending Chinese troops to Korea. The military leaders did not see any possible victory against the UNF. Mao argued that China should help the communist neighbor when it faced a foreign invasion as he had promised Stalin during his visit in Moscow.[25] Through an active defense by sending troops to Korea, China would also safeguard its own territory and sovereignty

---

24 Stalin's telegram quoted in Shen Zhihua, "China Sends Troops to Korea: Beijing's Policy-making Process," in *China and the United States: A New Cold War History*, eds. Xiaobing Li and Hongshan Li (New York: University Press of America, 1998), 28.

25 For more detailed discussions on the Soviet factors in the recent works, see Tao Wenzhao, *Zhongmei guanxishi, 1949–1972* [PRC-US Relations, 1949–1972] (Shanghai: Shanghai renmin chubanshe [Shanghai People's Press], 1999), 24–25; Qi Dexue, "Several Issues on the War of Resisting the U.S. and Aiding Korea," in *Zhonggong dangshi yanjiu* [CCP Party History Research] 1 (1998): 75–6; Andrew Scobell, *China's Use of Military Force: Beyond the Great Wall and the Long March* (Cambridge, UK: Cambridge University Press, 2003), 82–9.

by preventing a perceived US invasion of China. [26] Without support from the Politburo, Mao called for an enlarged meeting to include more political and military leaders from outside Beijing. Among the others was Peng Dehuai, chief of the Northwestern Military Command, from Xi'an, Shaanxi province.

On October 4–5, Mao chaired the enlarged meeting of the Politburo and made the same argument that China had to secure its Manchuria by sending troops to Korea to stop a UNF invasion. Peng Dehuai supported Mao's idea and convinced the participants that, if there would be a war between China and America, the sooner China fought it, the better it would be for the country's economic recovery. By the afternoon of the 5th, Mao's decision to send troops to Korea was finally passed at the meeting. Mao ordered the PLA high command to reorganize its Northeastern Border Defense Army (NEBDA)

into the Chinese People's Volunteer Force (CPVF) on October 8 and appointed Peng Dehuai as its commander in chief and political commissar. [27] The CPVF had five infantry armies and three artillery divisions, totaling 260,000 troops. In mid-October, another army joined the CPVF in Manchuria. [28]

Chinese Intervention and Truce Negotiations (1951–1953)

On October 19, 1950, the CPVF troops began to cross the Yalu River and enter Korea. By the end of November, the CPVF had thirty-three divisions in Korea, about 450,000 troops. [29] China's military intervention in the Korean War of 1950–1953 can be divided into three phases. The first phase of the Chinese operation focused on offensive campaigns through mobile warfare in order to drive the UNF

---

26 The PRC and the Soviet Union signed the Sino-Soviet alliance treaty on February 14, 1950, at Moscow. The treaty stated that if one side was attacked by a third country the other side "must go all out to provide military and other assistance." Mao, "Telegram to Liu Shaoqi, January 25, 1950," in *Jianguo yilai Mao Zedong wengao* [Mao Zedong's Manuscripts since the Founding of the State] (Beijing: Zhongyang wenxian chubanshe [CCP Central Archival and Manuscript Press], 1993), vol. 1: 251–2. Hereafter cited as *Mao's Manuscripts since 1949*. See also Shuguang Zhang and Chen Jian, eds., *Chinese Communist Foreign Policy and the Cold War in Asia: New Documentary Evidence, 1944–1950* (Chicago: Imprint Publications, 1996), 140–1.

27 Mao, "CMC Order to Establish the Chinese People's Volunteer Force," in *Mao Zedong junshi wenji* [Collected Military Papers of Mao Zedong] (Beijing: Junshi kexue chubanshe [Military Science Press], 1993), vol. 6: 117; *Mao Zedong wenji* [A Collection of Mao Zedong's Works] [Beijing: Renmin chubanshe, 1999], vol. 6: 100–101; Zhang and Chen, eds., *Chinese Communist Foreign Policy and the Cold War in Asia*, 164–5.

28 The CMC document, "The Central Military Commission's Circular on the Combat Characteristics of South Korean Troops, October 30, 1950," drafted by Mao, in *Mao's Manuscripts since 1949*, trans. and eds. Xiaobing Li and Glenn Tracy, "Mao's Telegrams during the Korean War, October–December 1950," *Chinese Historians* 5, no. 2 (Fall 1992), 66–7.

29 Peng concentrated a superior force so as to outnumber the enemy wherever the situation permitted in order to eliminate entire enemy battalions, regiments, or divisions, rather than to simply repel the enemy from the peninsular. Peng Dehuai Biography Compilation Team, *Yige zhanzheng de ren: Peng Dehuai* [A Real Man: Peng Dehuai] (Beijing: Renmin chubanshe [People's Press], 1994), 178; Peng, "My Story of the Korean War," in Li, Millett, and Yu, eds., *Mao's Generals Remember Korea*, 32–3; Military History Research Division, China Academy of Military Science (CAMS), *Zhongguo renmin zhiyuanjun kangmei yuanchao zhanshi* [Combat Experience of the CPVF in the War of Resisting the U.S. and Aiding Korea] (Beijing: Junshi kexue chubanshe [Military Science Press], 1990), 11; Feng Xianzhi and Li Jie, *Mao Zedong yu kangmei yuanchao* [Mao Zedong and the War of Resisting the U.S. and Aiding Korea] (Beijing: Zhongyang wenxian chubanshe [CCP Central Archival and Manuscript Press], 2000), 30.

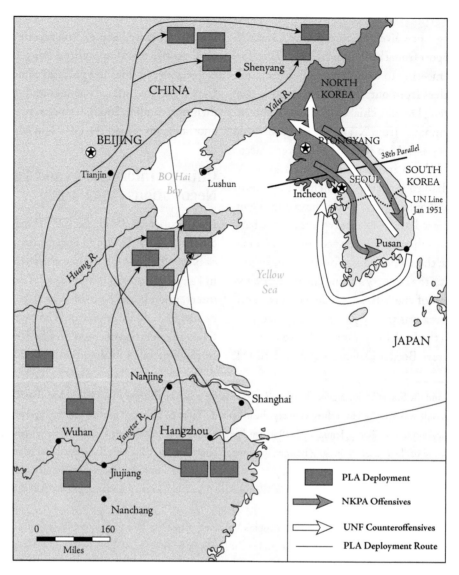

FIGURE 9.1 The Korean War

out of the Korean Peninsula from October 1950 to June 1951. The second phase of the CPVF engagements were mainly in defense along the thirty-eighth parallel through trench warfare after July 1951 when the truce negotiation began until September 1952. The third phase of the CPVF operations were described as key counteroffensives with selected targets for military and political reasons from October 1952 to July 1953 when the Armistice was signed.

From October 1950 to May 1951, Peng Dehuai, commander in chief of the CPVF, launched five offensive campaigns against the UNF in Korea. The first campaign lasted from October 25 to November 5, when the vanguards of the CPVF run into the ROK divisions in the area north of the Chinchon River. Peng concentrated 150,000 Chinese troops to attack 50,000 UN troops, including three ROK divisions and units of the First US Cavalry Division, with surprised attack and outnumbering the enemy force by 3:1. After the battle was over, Peng reported to Mao that the CPVF annihilated six to seven ROK battalions and a small unit of the First Cavalry

Division. Mao agreed with Peng that the first campaign was a victory for the Chinese army, even though the CPVF suffered 10,000 casualties.[30] The first campaign enabled the CPVF establish a firm base in North Korea. Shuguang Zhang points out that the first campaign had convinced the Chinese commanders that "they had accomplished a great deal: the troops had settled in North Korea and experienced their first combat."[31]

During the First Campaign, it became obvious that MacArthur did not expect or prepare for any large-scale Chinese intervention in November 1950. Peng took the advantage of UNF misinformation and planned his second offensive campaign immediately. He employed deception by luring the enemy forces in deep north and attacked the UNF on both western and eastern fronts. His commanders were confident of such an all-out attack since they gained some battleground experience through the first campaign and received the second wave of 150,000 fresh troops in mid-November.[32] They had built the forward base in the north of the Chongchon River, which served as a hub of logistics and a point of consolidation for fresh troops embarking on the Second Offensive Campaign.[33] When their base was self-sufficient, it would serve as a line of departure for the CPVF preparing to attack and advance into the south.

From November 25 to December 24, the CPVF launched its second campaign against General MacArthur's "home-by-Christmas" offensive toward the north. While 240,000 Chinese troops attacked the U.S. Eighth Army on the west, the CPVF Ninth Army Group, totaling 150,000 men, attacked the U.S. X Corps, including the First Marine and Seventh Divisions, at the Chosin Reservoir in the east on November 27.[34] Peng Dehuai believed that "This crucial campaign will determine the war situation in Korea."[35]

At the Chosin area, the Chinese attacked from the surrounding hills and often established roadblocks to cut off the retreating American troops. The First Marine put up a strong defense. This fierce fighting, combined with the bitter cold, made Chosin one of the worst battles of the Korean War for both sides.

---

30 The CPVF claimed to have eliminated fifteen thousand enemy troops during the "first campaign." For more details, see Military History Research Division, CAMS, *Zhongguo renmin zhiyuanjun kangmei yuanchao zhanshi* [Combat Experience of the CPVF in the War of Resisting the U.S. and Aiding Korea], 27; Xu Yan, *Diyici jiaoliang: kangmei yuanchao zhanzheng de lishi huigu yu fansi* [The First Encounter: A Historical Retrospective of the War of Resisting the U.S. and Aiding Korea] (Beijing: Zhongguo guangbo dianshi chubanshe [China's Radio and Television Press], 1990), 47.

31 Shu Guang Zhang, *Mao's Military Romanticism; China and the Korean War, 1950–1953* (Lawrence: University Press of Kansas, 1995), 106.

32 This statement explains the CPVF commanders' perception of the US forces. The Chinese believed, for example, that the US mechanized units had tremendous firepower and mobility but depended considerably on roads, bridges, air cover, and uninterrupted fuel supplies. Therefore the US troops tended to stay near the roads and had no flexibility to occupy advantageous terrain, thus providing the CPVF opportunities to cut them into pieces. See Military History Research Division, CAMS, *Zhongguo renmin zhiyuanjun kangmei yuanchao zhanshi* [Combat Experience of the CPVF in the War of Resisting the U.S. and Aiding Korea], 28.

33 Xiaobing Li, "Kim Il-sung," in John Powell, ed., *MaGill's Guide to Military History* (Pasadena, CA: Salem Press, 2001), 952.

34 Hong Xuezhi, *Kangmei yuanchao zhanzheng huiyi* [Recollections of the War of Resisting the U.S. and Aiding Korea]. Beijing: Jiefangjun wenyi chubanshe [PLA Literature Press], 1990), 90–1.

35 Peng Dehuai's telegram to the CPVF armies at 1:00 pm on November 28, 1950, in *Peng Dehuai junshi wenxuan* [Selected Military Papers of Peng Dehuai] (Beijing: Zhongyang wenxian chubanshe [CCP Central Archival and Manuscript Press], 1988), 348. Hereafter cited as *Selected Military Papers of Peng.*

On November 29, MacArthur warned the Chiefs of Staff at Washington, "We face an entirely new war," while he planned a general withdrawal for the UNF troops facing an all-out Chinese attack in North Korea.[36] The marines retreated southward, fighting through Chinese roadblocks. Major General Oliver P. Smith, Commander of the First Marine Division, gave his well-known explanation of the retreat, in response to a reporter's question—"Retreat, hell—we're attacking in another direction"—made headlines in the United States and has been forever associated with the marines at the Chosin Reservoir.[37] General Matthew B. Ridgway, then commander of the U.S. Eighth Army and later the commander of the UNF after MacArthur's dismissal, complained in his memoir about the misleading reports on the UNF retreat. "When actually they had performed a magnificent withdrawal in the face of unremitting attacks by overwhelmingly superior forces—and thanks to some extremely gallant fighting, particularly by the 1st Marine Division and the U.S. 2nd Division, had kept their losses to a minimum."[38]

When the Second Offensive Campaign was over by mid-December 1950, both the CPVF and the Ninth Army Group claimed victory at Chosin. Beijing was also pleased with the campaign's outcome. Mao Zedong cabled Peng Dehuai on December 17 that "This campaign operated by the Ninth Army Group under extremely difficult conditions on the eastern front has accomplished a great strategic task."[39] The First Marine's retreat has become a part of Marine lore, but it was still a retreat, not a victory. Marshal Peng states later in his writing "the Second Campaign was a big victory."[40] General Hong Xuezhi, CPVF Deputy Commander, points out in his memoir that, after "the First Campaign stabilized the frontline, the Second Campaign turned the war situation around in Korea. We fought so well and the campaign was very successful."[41] Strategic analyst Bin Yu points out that the Second Offensive Campaign "represented the peak of CPVF performance in the Korean War."[42] Within less than three weeks, the CPVF pushed the battle line back to the 38th Parallel, recaptured Pyongyang, capital city of North Korea, and inflicted 36,000 UNF casualties, including 24,000 Americans, according to the Chinese field reports.[43]

Meanwhile, the CPVF suffered heavy casualties, 80,000 men in less than three weeks. Mao Anying,

---

36 General Douglas MacArthur, *Reminiscences* (New York: McGraw-Hill, 1964), 375.

37 Major General Smith also said, "There can be no retreat when there's no rear. You can't retreat, or even withdraw, when you're surrounded. The only thing you can do is break out, and in order to do that you have to attack, and that is what we're about to do." Quoted in Martin Russ, *Breakout: The Chosin Reservoir Campaign, Korea, 1950* (New York: Penguin Books, 1999), 355.

38 General Matthew B. Ridgway, *The Korean War* (Garden City, NY: Doubleday, 1967), 73.

39 Mao Zedong's telegram to Peng, passed on to Gao Gang, Song Shilun, and Tao Yong, on December 17, 1950, in *Jianguo yilai Mao Zedong junshi wengao* [Mao Zedong's Military Manuscripts since the Founding of the PRC] (Beijing: Junshi kexue chubanshe [Military Science Press] and Zhongyang wenxian chubanshe [CCP Central Archival and Manuscript Press], 2010), 1: 410–11. Hereafter cited as *Mao's Military Manuscripts since 1949*.

40 Marshal Peng Dehuai, "My Story of the Korean War," in Li, Millett, and Yu, *Mao's Generals Remember Korea*, 33.

41 General Hong Xuezhi, *Hong Xuezhi Huiyilu* [Memoirs of Hong Xuezhi] (Beijing: Jiefangjun chubanshe [PLA Press], 2007), 429.

42 Bin Yu, "What China Learned from Its 'Foreign War' in Korea," in Li, Millett, and Yu, *Mao's Generals Remember Korea*, 17.

43 The CPVF claimed that the UNF had total casualties of 36,000 men, including 24,000 American troops. See Hong, *Hong Xuezhi Huiyilu* [Memoirs of Hong Xuezhi], 429; Du, *Zai zhiyuanjun zongbu* [At the CPVF General HQ], 125; National

one of Mao Zedong's sons, was killed on November 25 in a U.S. air raid against CPVF headquarters.[44] The Chinese attacks at Chosin failed to achieve their campaign objectives of destroying the First Marine and Seventh Divisions. During their attacks, the CPVF Ninth Army Group lost 40,000 men, and was forced to abolish three infantry divisions because of their heavy losses. Some of the Chinese commanders were punished after the Battle of Chosin. On December 17, the badly depleted army group was recalled to China. One of MacArthur's objectives was to stop the Chinese in the North. He might have missed an opportunity to lure the CPVF into the South and destroy its main strength by further exploiting the Chinese problems such as transportation, communication, supply, and air protection. Nevertheless, the battle had changed the American attitude toward the Chinese army from dismissing and ignoring it to taking the Chinese intervention in the Korean War seriously, since "the UN command in the last week of 1950 found itself in full retreat before this 'bunch of Chinese laundrymen.'"[45]

Almost every Communist leader, including Mao Zedong in Beijing, Kim Il-sung in Korea, and Josef Stalin to some extent in Moscow, was feeling it

was only a matter of time before the UN/U.S. forces were driven out to sea. From December 31, 1950 to January 8, 1951, the CPVF launched its Third Offensive Campaign against a strong UNF defense along the 38th Parallel. In the afternoon of January 4, the CPVF Thirty-ninth Army and NKPA I Corps entered Seoul. The next day, the Fiftieth Army and two divisions of the NKPA I Corps crossed the Han River.[46] On January 7, the Fiftieth Army took over Kimpo (Keumpo), and the NKPA I Corps occupied Inchon. In the meantime, the Forty-second and Sixty-sixth Armies continued their drives, shifting their thrust to central South Korea.[47] Since the mechanized UNF withdrew faster than the Chinese could advance, Peng ended the CPVF Third Offensive Campaign on January 8.

After the Third Offensive Campaign ended, the CPVF Command required a more cautious strategy. By this time, the American and UN forces had brought to bear superior firepower on the ground and in the air, inflicting heavy casualties and serious damage on CPVF troop movements and lines of supply and communication. However, Russian advisors in Beijing questioned the CPVF Command

---

Defense University (NDU)'s War History Series Compilation Team, *Zhongguo renmin zhiyuanjun zhanshi jianbian* [A Concise History of the CPVF War-Fighting] (Beijing: Jiefangjun chubanshe [PLA Press], 1992), 43. The Chinese figures, however, did not coincide with the UNF Command's own casualty accounting. The U.S. Eighth Army exceeded 10,000 casualties by December 3, 1950, see Millett, *The War for Korea, 1950–1951*, 347. X Corps had 8,735 battle casualties between November 27 and December 10, see Mossman, *U.S. Army in the Korean War*, 147. In addition, the Marines had suffered 4,418 battle and 7,313 non-battle casualties, see Hastings, *The Korean War*, 164.

44 Mao Anying was Peng's Russian interpreter and secretary at the CPVF General HQ. For more information on his death, see General Hong Xuezhi, "The CPVF's Combat and Logistics," in *Mao's Generals Remember Korea*, trans. and ed. Xiaobing Li, Allan R. Millett, and Bin Yu (Lawrence: University Press of Kansas, 2001), 118–21; Lieutenant General Du Ping, *Zai zhiyuanjun zongbu: Du Ping huiyilu* [At the CPVF General HQ: Memoirs of Du Ping] (Beijing: Jiefangjun chubanshe [PLA Press], 1989), 94–98; Senior Colonel Yang Di, *Zai zhiyuanjun silingbu de suiyueli; xianwei renzhi de zhenshi qingkuang* [My Years at the CPVF General HQ: Untold True Stories] (Beijing: Jiefangjun chubanshe [PLA Press], 1998), 292–95.

45 Stanley Sandler, *The Korean War: No Victors, No Vanquished* (Lexington: University Press of Kentucky, 1999), 127.

46 Peng's telegram to all the CPVF armies and CMC, January 4, 1951, in *Selected Military Papers of Peng*, 360–63.

47 Brian Catchpole, *The Korean War, 1950–1953* (New York: Carroll & Graf, 2000), 101–102; Millett, *The War for Korea*, 384–87; Mossman, *U.S. Army in the Korean War*, 201–202.

why they did not follow up their victory and pursue the UNF farther into South Korea. Pressure was mounting to press another attack. Stalin and Kim pressured the CPVF to launch a new offensive immediately and to drive the UNF out of Korea. Mao also cabled Peng at the end of January and urged organization of the CPVF's Fourth Offensive Campaign to drive the UNF farther south. Under tremendous pressure from the political leaders of all three Communist countries (China, the Soviet Union, and North Korea) for a quick victory, the CPVF Command recognized the growing gap between political goals and strategic realities.[48] As the CPVF struck farther south, its tactics, such as surprise attack, flanking operation, and encirclement and annihilation, began losing effectiveness. In the meantime, the UNF had recovered from its early surprise and launched a counterattack on January 25. General Hong Xuezhi later recalled, "We were compelled to fight the Fourth Campaign."[49] From January 25 until April 21, the CPVF engaged in its Fourth Campaign. Instead of a mass offensive, it became a series of back-and-forth mobile battles.

Of all these campaigns the Chinese Fifth Offensive, or the Spring Offensive Campaign, proved the most decisive. Lasting from April 22 through June 2, 1951, it was the largest and longest Communist military operation of the war, as well as the largest battle since WWII. The CPVF-NKPA Joint Command deployed more than 700,000 men, including 600,000 CPVF troops, against 340,000 UNF troops. As Peng Dehuai anticipated, "this is the battle [that] will determine the fate of the Korean War."[50] However, he did not expect that the CPVF Spring Offensive would fail. Peng's sudden change, moving up the offensive starting date by almost an entire month, threw entire second echelon forces, including the Third and Nineteenth Army Groups, into action without necessary preparations. Most of the divisions were not combat ready, and some had not received much needed food and ammunition. The UNF put up a strong defense, drove the Chinese forces back north of the 38th Parallel and inflicted 105,000 casualties. After the Chinese failure in this one-million-men battle, the war settled into a stalemate and a more conventional pattern of trench warfare along the 38th Parallel.

After the Chinese forces lost their Spring Offensive Campaign, the Communists never again came so close to Seoul, nor mounted another major southward incursion of such magnitude. Their defeat forced Mao to reconsider both his political and military aims. Realizing the huge gap between Chinese capabilities and the ambitious aim of driving the UNF from the peninsula, the Chinese leadership became willing to accept a settlement without total victory. The Chinese Spring Offensive Campaign was the turning point that not only shaped the rest of the war, but also led to truce negotiations in July 1951.

The Korean War entered its second phase in July 1951 when the truce negotiations began. During the cease-fire talks, the war continued. This phase, lasting from July 1951 to September 1952, was a stalemate and described as trench warfare while both sides held their positions along the thirty-eighth parallel. Nevertheless, about 45 percent of all UN/US casualties occurred after truce talks started. By 1952, Mao Zedong had committed 1.45 million Chinese troops to the defense of North Korea. Although the bloody fighting continued through this phase, the front lines remained unchanged.

To improve their negotiating positions at Panmunjom, the CPVF launched piece-meal attacks on

48 Xiaobing Li, "Chinese Army in the Korean War, 1950–53," *The New England Journal of History* 60 (nos. 1–3, 2003–4): 282.

49 Hong, *Kangmei yuanchao zhanzheng huiyi* [Recollections of WRUSAK], 90–91.

50 Peng's telegram to all the CPVF army commanders and the CMC at 5:00 pm on March 14, 1951, in *Selected Military Papers of Peng*, 379.

the UNF defensive positions from October 1952, and started the last phase of the war with selected attacking targets. From October 13 to November 8, 1952, for example, the Chinese troops attacked the UNF positions in the Iron Triangle, known as "Shangganling" in Chinese. Lt. General James Van Fleet launched counterattacks as Operation Showdown, a limited assault to take Chinese positions at Triangle Hill. The Battle of Triangle Hill soon became one of the bloodiest of the war. The largest offensive campaign the CPVF launched during the third phase took place two weeks before the Armistice was signed. More than 240,000 Chinese troops with 1,100 artillery pieces attacked the UNF positions at Kumsong. During the ten-day offensive, the Chinese concentrated their attacks on the ROK divisions along the front line and forced the South Koreans to fall back. Finally, the cease-fire became effective on July 27, 1953.

China sent 2.3 million troops to the Korean War between October 1950 and July 1953. The Chinese forces suffered heavy casualties due to US firepower, including 183,108 dead, 383,218 wounded, 455,199 hospitalized, 21,400 prisoners of war, and 4,221 missing in action, totaling 1,047,146 casualties.[51] About 14,200 Chinese POWs did not return to China, but went to Taiwan after the Armistice was signed.[52] Nevertheless, Mao judged China's intervention a victory because it saved North Korea's

Communist regime, shaped China's relations with the Soviet Union, and secured China's northeastern border by preventing North Korea from being conquered or controlled by a Western power like America. The military intervention in Korea had maintained China's brooding influence in East Asia permanently. Chinese military involvements in Korea had promoted the CCP international status and projected a powerful image of China as the vanguard of the communist countries against the United States.[53] Then, China's increasing political ambition and rising international position demanded a strong, modern military to enhance "China's prestige and influence in the international arena."[54]

From 1953–1959, the PLA launched a reform movement to continue its modernization that began during the Korean War. The 1950s reforms aimed to transform the PLA from a peasant army to a modern professional force with new capacities. The reform programs, following the Soviet model, included major institutional changes, a centralized command system, technological improvement, advanced training and educational programs, reorganization of defense industries, establishment of a strategic missile force, and a nuclear weapon research and development program. At all PLA academies, Russian advisors worked in the academy at all the administrative positions, and made many

51   Chen Hui, "Tracing the 180,000 Martyrs of WRUSAK," in Zhang ed., *Kangmei yuanchao* [The WRUSAK], 127; Xu, "Chinese Forces and Their Casualties in the Korean War," 56–57; Li, *Zhiyuanjun yuanchao jishi* [The CPVF Records of Aiding Korea], 13; Shuang, *Kaiguo diyi zhan* [The First War since the Founding of the State], 2: 836–37. The UNF intelligence statisticians put Chinese losses for higher: 1.5 million casualties in all categories including killed, in action, died or wounds, and disease, missing in action, and wounded in action. For example, see Walter G. Hermes, *Truce Tent and Fighting Front, U.S. Army in the Korean War* (Washington, DC: Office of the Chief of Military History and U.S. Government Printing Office, 1966, reprinted in 1988), 477–78.

52   Xu, *Diyici jiaoliang* [The First Encounter], 308–10.

53   For example, Mao's conclusion at the Second Plenary Session of the CCP Seventh Central Committee, March 13, 1949, and Mao's speech, "Address to the Preparatory Meeting of the New Political Consultative Conference," *Selected Works of Mao*, 4: 1464, 1470.

54   Ellis Joffe, *The Chinese Army after Mao* (Cambridge, MA: Harvard University Press, 1987), 1.

executive decisions, hired the instructors, supervised the academic affairs, and managed the facilities, labs, classrooms, and equipment. It was not until 1957 when the Chinese administrators, instructors, and technicians began to manage the academy and carry on the curriculum.[55]

After the Chinese-American confrontation in Korea, China and East Asia became a focal point of the global Cold War. Although the global Cold War was characterized by the confrontation between the United States and the Soviet Union and the two contending camps headed by the two superpowers, China's position in the Cold War after Korea played a new role by turning East Asia into a "buffer" region between Washington and Moscow. It was unlikely that the United States and the Soviet Union would engage in a direct military confrontation with China and East Asia standing in the middle. China's intervention in the Korean War created a new international condition for the Cold War to remain cold in the West.

The Slow Rise of Vietnamese Communism (1932–1945)

To examine Vietnam's place in Cold War East Asia, it is appropriate to start with a movement that was to be the focus of battles between Communist and non-Communist forces: the Vietnamese Communist movement. As we shall see, however, the appearance of Vietnamese Communism as a central issue in the Cold War was far from inevitable. In fact, two circumstances make this eventuality seem extraordinary. First, in the early 1930s, the communist movement in French Indochina was in disarray. Second, the rise of the Vietnamese communists came in the 1940s when they were leading

an anti-Japanese frontist organization, much of whose support came from the United States.

In the wake of the failure of the Nghe-Tinh uprisings to trigger a widespread anti-French rebellion, those leaders of the Indochinese Communist Party who had not been killed in the repression of the uprising had been sent to prison. Many of them were sent as political prisoners to remote Poulo Condore (Con Son) Island off the coast of southern Vietnam, where they lingered for many years. In the meantime, as was articulated in chapter six, other anticolonial political and religious groups rose to the forefront.

An important development in the reversal of communist fortunes in French Indochina was the election of a coalition of left-wing parties—a coalition that included the French Communist Party—in France in 1936. The anticolonial sympathies of these parties raised false hope among Vietnamese that the new government of this coalition, which was known as the Popular Front, would liquidate France's colonial empire. In reality, however, the Popular Front struggled to retain power and became fixated on the economic problems in France that stemmed from the great depression and on the nearby Spanish Civil War. They did, however, make one political decision of consequence to the communist movement in Vietnam: they ordered the mass release of political prisoners in French Indochina, including members of the ICP.[56] Moreover, the Communists were also able to recruit other convicts while in prison, though scholars have suggested that the Communist Party may have exaggerated the import of these conversions.

In the meantime, the man who after 1945 would come to be known as Ho Chi Minh continued to toil in obscurity. In the early 1930s, Ho Chi Minh

---

55   Xia Guang, 'From Naval School to Naval Academy', in PLA Navy History Compilation Committee (ed., Classified Documents), *Haijun: huiyi shiliao* [The Navy: Memoirs and History Records] (Beijing: Haichao chubanshe [Ocean Wave Publishing], 1994), 2: 631–32.

56   R. B. Smith, *Communist Indochina* (New York: Routledge, 2012), 75.

had been eclipsed by ICP figures that were willing to support more immediate revolutionary efforts. While they organized the Nghe-Tinh uprisings, he remained north of the border in China. In 1931, under pressure from French authorities, he was arrested in Hong Kong. In 1932 persistent and false rumors circulated that Ho Chi Minh had died while in prison. In the meantime, his case became entangled with larger issues of British diplomatic relations with France, as orders for Ho Chi Minh's extradition to French authorities remained locked in political and legal wrangling. Finally, early in 1933, the governor of Hong Kong, William Peel, decided to quietly release Ho Chi Minh. The future father of the Vietnamese revolution was escorted to Shantou, a city on the coast of Guangdong province on the Chinese mainland.[57] From there, Ho Chi Minh made his way through several Chinese cities to the Soviet Union, where he arrived in 1934.[58]

Ho Chi Minh eventually arrived in Moscow, and remained in the Soviet Union until 1938. For most of this period, he remained an obscure castoff on the fringe of the Comintern. The ICP leadership declared that his "nationalist tendencies" were out of step with Soviet policies at the time, which emphasized class struggle over finding common cause with non-Communists in fighting imperialism.[59] However, by 1937 Ho Chi Minh was able to benefit from a change in Soviet policy. With the increasingly bellicose policies of Nazi Germany and the rapid expansion of Japan into Chinese territory, the Comintern's policy shifted toward making alliances with antifascist, non-Communist forces. This shift coincided with the advent of the Second United Front in China (1937–1945), and it favored the production of such frontist policies among Vietnamese nationalists.

Ho Chi Minh returned to China in 1938 and reached southern China by February 1939 after spending a month in the CCP headquarters in Yan'an. He spent the next two years organizing and gathering loyal associates around him. In the meanwhile, world events continued to be favorable for his coalition-building leadership style. The German defeat of France in June 1940, followed by the Japanese invasion of French Indochina in September 1940, further lent international support for the organization of an anti-Japanese, antifascist coalition for Indochina. In October 1940 Ho Chi Minh and his supporters established a base at Guilin and began to call themselves the League for Vietnamese Independence (Viet Nam Doc Lap Dong Minh Hoi), or Viet Minh for short.[60] At the Eighth Plenum of the Indochinese Communist Party in 1940, which had to be held in a cave at Pac Bo in Vietnam's Cao Bang province near the Chinese border, the ICP's change in attitude toward the Viet Minh Front was formalized. Ho Chi Minh was the chairman of the Plenum, thus completing his rehabilitation; and the Plenum declared that henceforth, their focus would not be on an "anti-feudal" class revolution but instead on a "revolution of national liberation."[61]

In the next two years, the Ho Chi Minh-led Viet Minh government struggled unsuccessfully to gain recognition from the military authorities in the GMD and to compete with another frontist organization. That group was the Vietnamese Revolutionary League, which was led by prominent non-Communists and therefore favored by GMD leaders.[62] Ho Chi Minh was so unsuccessful in

---

57 Quinn-Judge, *Ho Chi Minh*, 194–5; Duiker, *Ho Chi Minh*, 205–9.

58 Brocheux, *Ho Chi Minh*, 56–8.

59 Ibid., 64.

60 Quinn-Judge, *Ho Chi Minh*, 246.

61 Khanh, *Vietnamese Communism*, 256–61; Bradley, *Imagining Vietnam and America*, 110.

62 Bradley, *Imagining Vietnam and America*, 112–14; Taylor, *History of the Vietnamese*, 531.

gaining notice for the group that he was arrested by GMD authorities on suspicion of being a spy in August 1942. He was transferred from prison to prison until September 1943, when he was put under house arrest, not to be formally freed until August 1944.[63] By late in 1943 the fortunes of the Viet Minh were turning for the better. On the Vietnamese side of the border, they had successfully recruited ethnic minority groups to their cause and were beginning to cause the French to take notice, though within Vietnam they were at best a "minor irritant" before the end of 1944.[64] By this time, however, the Viet Minh was cultivating more productive relationships with the GMD and was beginning to attract the positive attention of the United States Office of Strategic Services (OSS), the predecessor to the CIA, for assisting US pilots that were shot down in Japanese-controlled territory in Indochina.[65]

1945 was an extraordinary significant year in world history and in the history of Vietnam. By the spring of 1945, the Japanese military was facing heavy losses to US forces in the Pacific and realized the need to fortify defenses of the Japanese islands for a possible American invasion. In the meanwhile, Allied powers were decisively winning the war in Europe, and Paris had already been liberated from the Nazi occupation. Given this reality, the Japanese saw a need to place a government in control of reliable and loyal Vietnamese. The Japanese already had numerous Vietnamese groups willing to work with them. From 1940, some groups in Indochina, recalling the Japanese role in Phan Boi Chau's anticolonial movements and remembering the anticolonial actions of the exiled Prince Cuong De, who had been in Japan for so many years, were

willing to believe in the Japanese rhetoric of "Asia for the Asiatics" and of providing a "Greater East Asia Co-Prosperity Sphere." Among those supporting Vietnamese independence under Japanese terms were the Hoa Hao and Cao Dai religious sects (whom by 1944 the Japanese actually trained and even armed) and a nationalist party known as the Dai Viet Party.

With these groups as a base of support, in March 1945 the Japanese military rounded up and arrested the French authorities in nominal charge of Indochina. They turned the country over to a new government, the Empire of Vietnam, which would bear the trappings, if not the reality, of independence from the Japanese under the leadership of the Bao Dai Emperor (r. 1932–1945). Initially, Bao Dai chose Ngo Dinh Diem, who had been his interior minister in 1933, to be the prime minister of the new Empire of Vietnam, but Diem refused, either as a tactic to gain concessions or because of his concern that the Empire of Vietnam would continue to be dominated by the Japanese. In his stead, Bao Dai chose a mild-mannered but respected historian, Tran Trong Kim (1883–1953), to be prime minister.

The Empire of Vietnam worked hard to establish the symbols of independence. They replaced French place names with Vietnamese ones, established a national flag and national anthem, organized national holidays, and aroused young people to support them through their energetic and popular youth minister Phan Anh (1912–1990), who was also tasked with chairing a committee to prepare a constitution.[66] However, none of this allowed the Empire of Vietnam to function effectively across Vietnam. The Japanese military retained de facto control over key areas. Moreover, the Empire of

---

63   Brocheux, *Ho Chi Minh: A Biography*, 79.

64   David Marr, *Vietnam 1945: The Quest for Power* (Berkeley, CA: University of California Press, 1995), 193–4.

65   Bradley, *Imagining Vietnam and America*, 122–3.

66   Taylor, *History of the Vietnamese*, 533–4; Stein Tønneson, *The Vietnamese Revolution of 1945: Roosevelt, Ho Chi Minh, and De Gaulle in a World at War* (Oslo: International Peace Institute, 1991), 289.

Vietnam found itself powerless to manage the great crisis of its young existence: a massive famine in northern Vietnam that possibly took the lives of as many as two million Vietnamese, who could not open rice stocks that were being guarded by the Japanese.[67]

Meanwhile, in the spring of 1945, the Viet Minh were in an excellent position to take advantage of these political changes. They were buoyed by a strong relationship to Americans due to their assistance with recovering downed American pilots. Ho Chi Minh developed a strong personal relationship with OSS captain Archimedes Patti (1913–1998), who was sent to develop connections with the Viet Minh to secure intelligence on the Japanese; Ho Chi Minh came to be known as "OSS Agent 19" with the code name "Lucius."[68] Additionally, Viet Minh in northern Vietnam achieved success and popularity by breaking into granaries and distributing food to the victims of the 1945 famine.[69]

Upon the surrender of Japanese forces in August 1945, the Viet Minh were in an excellent strategic position to take advantage of the passivity of Japanese troops and the lack of action from the government in Hue. As various nationalist groups acted to assert authority over various regions, the Viet Minh benefited from a better organizational structure, the support of northern peasants, and better information. They also carried out a highly effective campaign of political assassinations, conveniently eliminating many of the most experienced rival Vietnamese leaders by simply killing them. Those killed in the Viet Minh's August Revolution

included the Trotskyist leader, Ta Thu Thau; the Constitutionalist leaders, Pham Quynh and Bui Quang Chieu; and the Catholic Leader, Ngo Dinh Khoi, who was Ngo Dinh Diem's elder brother.

By September 2, 1945, the August Revolution had resulted in de facto Viet Minh control of the major cities of Vietnam. The Bao Dai Emperor, whom the Viet Minh had forced to abdicate the throne with the famous statement that he would rather be "a citizen of a free country than a king of a slave state."[70] On that day, Ho Chi Minh and other Viet Minh leaders were able to ascend onto a platform at Ba Dinh Square, where Ho Chi Minh's mausoleum is today, and use the words of the United States Declaration of Independence and the French Declaration of the Rights of Man and Citizen to declare Vietnam independent.[71]

The First Indochina War (1946-1954)

In the wake of the August Revolution of 1945, the Viet Minh sought to accomplish two goals. Domestically, their aim was to consolidate their hold on the major cities of Vietnam and to be in a position to retain that hold in the face of the two military forces of the Allies—the British in the southern part of Vietnam and the GMD in the North—who were tasked with securing the surrender of Japanese troops. Internationally, their goal was to gain diplomatic recognition that would ensure their continued ability to govern even in the face of British and GMD occupations. Of particular importance was to secure diplomatic recognition from the

---

67 Huynh Kim Khanh, *Vietnamese Communism*, 301; Vu Ngu Chieu, "The Other Side of the 1945 Vietnamese Revolution: The Empire of Viet-Nam (March-August 1945), *Journal of Asian Studies* 45, no. 2 (February 1986): 298; Geoffrey Gunn, "The Great Vietnamese Famine of 1945 Revised," *Asia-Pacific Journal* 9, no. 5 (January 2011): 4.

68 Marr, *Vietnam 1945*, 283; Bradley, *Imagining Vietnam and America*, 123.

69 Huynh Kim Khanh, *Vietnamese Communism*, 313.

70 Bui Diem with David Chanoff, *In the Jaws of History* (Bloomington, IN: Indiana University Press, 1987), 42.

71 David Marr, "Ho Chi Minh's Independence Declaration," in *Essays into Vietnamese Pasts*, eds. K. W. Taylor and John K. Whitmore (Ithaca, NY: Cornell Southeast Asia Program, 1995): 220–3; Marr, *Vietnam 1945*, 531–5.

United States, which the good relationship fostered between the Viet Minh and the OSS in the spring and summer of 1945 made seem possible. In reality, the Viet Minh were unsuccessful at these two goals, though they did benefit from GMD delays in handing power in northern Vietnam back to the French. This led Ho Chi Minh to adopt a conciliatory posture toward the French in 1946, and led to nearly a year of diplomatic negotiations. However, these negotiations ultimately failed, leading to a French takeover of Hanoi in December 1946. The Viet Minh were forced to flee into the "resistance zone" in the countryside, and the First Indochina War began.

At the Potsdam Conference in July 1945, the Allies had agreed on dividing Vietnam at the sixteenth parallel, just above Da Nang and below Hue, and to have British forces take a Japanese surrender below this line and GMD forces take the surrender above this line. In the South, the British forces were under the leadership of General Douglas Gracey (1894–1964). Within two weeks of Gracey's landing in Saigon on September 13, 1945, he had evicted the Viet Minh from the former governor-general's palace, turned major ammunition depots and other key infrastructure points over to a small French unit, declared martial law and enforced it with the help of the Japanese troops he was charged with disarming, and armed former French prisoners of war.[72] By early October 1945, Saigon was back in French hands.

The situation in the north was more complicated. When General Lu Han (1895–1974) arrived in Hanoi on September 14, 1945, he promptly kicked out the French representative Jean Sainteny (1907–1978), met with Ho Chi Minh, and made clear that the Viet Minh government was to remain in place so long as it could maintain law and order.[73] At the same time, it became clear by October that the GMD's troops intended to remain in Indochina for some time to come. The GMD's position had two motivations. First, they recognized that the Viet Minh government in Hanoi was entrenched and popular enough that removing them would cause a backlash.[74] Second, allowing the Viet Minh to remain in place would give the GMD diplomatic advantage against the French that they could use to bolster the GMD position in China.[75]

The decision of Lu Han to leave the Viet Minh in place prompted several months of diplomatic negotiation and positioning on both the parts of the Viet Minh and the French. The Viet Minh sought diplomatic recognition, particularly from the United States, and to avoid antagonizing their Chinese nationalist occupiers. To do so, they officially dissolved the Indochinese Communist Party, at least on paper, in November 1945. Bowing to GMD pressure, they guaranteed non-Communist representation in the national assembly by reserving seats for two non-Communist parties. Famously, they appealed for support from the American government and from American industry. Ho Chi Minh wrote several letters to President Truman and to Secretary of State James Byrnes calling for the diplomatic recognition of Vietnam, and through 1946, the Viet Minh made contacts with American oil and insurance companies. The motorcycle manufacturer Harley-Davidson even sent an agent to Hanoi to explore commercial contacts.[76] Ultimately, however, the advent of the Cold

---

72   David Marr, *Vietnam: State, War, and Revolution, 1945–1946* (Berkeley, CA: University of California Press, 2013), 186–7.

73   Ibid., 266.

74   Taylor, *History of the Vietnamese*, 537.

75   Archimedes L. A. Patti, *Why Viet Nam? Prelude to America's Albatross* (Berkeley, CA: University of California Press, 1980), 213.

76   Bradley, *Imagining Vietnam and America*, 126–32.

War and the US desire to maintain good relations with France prevented any decisive action in favor of the Viet Minh.

By early 1946 the Viet Minh were forced into a position of negotiating with the French. In February of that year, the GMD concluded an agreement with the French in which the French gave up territorial claims in China in exchange for GMD recognition of French sovereignty in Indochina.[77] However, Lu Han's troops, not wishing to be caught in the middle of a French-Viet Minh war, pressured Ho Chi Minh and Jean Sainteny to come to an agreement and would not allow French troops to reach Hanoi without it. On March 6, 1946, they agreed that Vietnam would be a "free state" within a loose confederacy of the French Union. In return, fifteen thousand French troops would be allowed into the northern part of Vietnam, and other more difficult problems, such as the status of Cochinchina, would be worked out through a future referendum and further negotiations.[78]

For the rest of 1946, French and Viet Minh authorities attempted without success to iron out details of a comprehensive agreement. In July 1946, negotiations were opened between the French and Viet Minh at Fontainebleau, but these negotiations dragged on through the summer of 1946 without any substantial breakthroughs. The two sides could not agree on whether the Viet Minh would be given control over Cochinchina, particularly given that the French high commissioner in Indochina, the former Catholic monk Georges Thierry d'Argenlieu (1889–1964), continuously attempted to sabotage the negotiations. He had recognized a "Republic of Cochinchina" under right-wing Vietnamese leadership in violation of the March 6 accords.[79] A *modus vivendi* implementing a cease-fire took effect on October 30, but this did not result in any traction toward an agreement of the two sides.[80] With these attempts at peace falling flat, both sides prepared for the eventuality of war. On November 20, 1946, French forces reoccupied Haiphong harbor, and on December 17, they reoccupied Hanoi, forcing the Viet Minh into the countryside and beginning the First Indochina War.

In 1947 and 1948, the First Indochina War quickly ground to a stalemate. Viet Minh forces were not strong enough to remove French troops from major cities or from key transportation routes; French forces were unable to locate and successfully annihilate Viet Minh leadership in the resistance zone. Militarily, this series of inconclusive battles would remain the norm until 1949, when the Viet Minh could take advantage of additional support from the north owing to the CCP's victory over the GMD in the Chinese Civil War. In the meantime, the Viet Minh became a more openly hard-line Communist organization, ejecting non-Communists, from whom it could no longer gain significant political advantage, from its ranks, restricting future Communist party membership to people from proper class backgrounds, and formulating a more radical land policy in occupied areas.[81] By 1951 this process was complete; the ICP created separate Communist parties for Laos and Cambodia and renamed itself the Vietnamese Workers Party in support of a class struggle line and in line with the aspirations of the CCP.

---

77   Stein Tønneson, *Vietnam 1946: How the War Began* (Berkeley, CA: University of California Press, 2010), 41.

78   Mark Atwood Lawrence, *The Vietnam War: A Concise International History* (New York: Oxford University Press, 2008), 32; Tønneson, *Vietnam 1946*, 40.

79   Marr, *Vietnam: State, War and Revolution*, 229–32.

80   Tønneson, *Vietnam 1946*, 94–7.

81   Tuong Vu, "'It's Time for the Indochinese Revolution to Show Its True Colors': The Radical Turn of Vietnamese Politics in 1948," *Journal of Southeast Asian Studies* 40, no. 3 (October 2009): 519–42.

In the meanwhile, the French sought to gain international legitimacy and support for their position in the First Indochina War by creating a plausible but pliable non-Communist government. They turned to the former Emperor Bao Dai. After abdicating the throne during the August Revolution of 1945, the former emperor accepted a role as a political adviser to Ho Chi Minh whose primary responsibility was to give Viet Minh decisions the imprimatur of whatever political authority or legitimacy the ex-emperor could wield.[82] But as negotiations broke down in 1946, Bao Dao found it more advantageous to remain outside of the Viet Minh's orbit; he never returned home from a diplomatic trip to China that Ho Chi Minh had sent him on in the spring of 1946, and instead eventually settled in Hong Kong—though he did not officially break from the Viet Minh until late 1947. At that point, the former emperor slowly became receptive to French plans for him to become involved in a non-Communist government that had been favored by High Commissioner d'Argenlieu since early in 1946 when the Republic of Cochinchina was created with few, if any, areas of authority separate from French rule. In December 1947 Bao Dai met with the new High Commissioner Emile Bollaert in Ha Long Bay off the northern Vietnamese coast.[83] This meeting sparked a series of negotiations for a new state that continued for more than a year. In March 1949 an accord was signed at the Élysée palace in Paris announcing the organization of a new state of Vietnam. The Élysée Accords allowed Bao Dai to create a State of Vietnam with himself as head of state. Bao Dai would have nominal control over all of Vietnam, including Cochinchina,

which had been a major priority for him. This meant that Vietnam was no longer partitioned into three regions—Cochinchina, Annam, and Tonkin—as it had been under French rule, and that all of the areas not under Viet Minh control were in one country. However, the French retained control of foreign affairs, retained extraterritorial rights for French citizens, and specified that for as long as a state of war existed, the Vietnamese army would take orders from a French commander.[84]

In reality, Bao Dai probably lacked sufficient popular support to rally non-Communists to his side, and his efforts at securing major French concessions fell flat. Even Bao Dai's attempts to organize a non-Communist "Unity Congress" in 1953 did not produce the desired result of rallying these groups under a single banner. Other nationalists severely damaged Bao Dai's credibility when the result of these negotiations was a statement rejecting participation in the French Union in favor of "total independence."[85] Still, the State of Vietnam was not inconsequential. Instead, seeing a quasi-legitimate Vietnamese polity come to fruition made it more palatable for the United States to act in Indochina. Still reeling from having "lost China" to the Communists, the United States recognized the State of Vietnam in 1950 and began to direct material support French operations in Indochina shortly thereafter.

However, American support for Bao Dai's State of Vietnam was tentative, and the United States was quite interested in finding reliable "third force" options that would be neither puppets of the Communists or beholden to the French. In the early 1950s, there were a plethora of "third force"

82 Ellen Hammer, *The Struggle for Indochina* (Stanford, CA: Stanford University Press, 1955), 175.

83 Bruce McFarland Lockhart, *The End of the Vietnamese Monarchy* (New Haven, CT: Yale University Southeast Asia Studies, 1993), 170–1.

84 Nguyen Phut Tan, *A Modern History of Viet Nam* (Saigon: Khai Tri, 1964), 567–4.

85 Edward Miller, *Misalliance: Ngo Dinh Diem, the United States, and the Fate of South Vietnam* (Cambridge, MA: Harvard University Press, 2013), 50.

options to choose from, from Hoa Hao Generals to Bay Vien, the leader of the Binh Xuyen organized crime group in the Saigon area, to General Trinh Minh The, a renegade general who split off from the Cao Dai army.[86] In the early 1950s, however, some Americans—as well as French and Belgian Vietnamese expatriates—became intrigued by the possibility of supporting Ngo Dinh Diem. After once again refusing to participate as prime minister of Bao Dai's new State of Vietnam, Diem spent the early 1950s moving from Vietnam to Europe to the United States and back to Vietnam. While in the United States, he spent time at Maryknoll Seminary in New York and met such luminaries as the influential Cardinal Spellman of New York and Senator (and future President) John F. Kennedy. Though these contacts were not a crucial factor in Diem's eventual rise to power, they did assist in his being able to present to other Vietnamese the impression that he had support in American circles.[87]

In the meantime, as the situation for the Viet Minh continued to improve, French forces adopted new tactics.[88] The French sent General Jean de Lattre (1889–1952), a hero from World War II, to take over not only as chief of the Expeditionary Corps but also as high commissioner for Indochina, making him effectively in charge of both the French military and political apparatuses in Indochina. The hope was that de Lattre could eliminate petty disputes and implement a new policy against the Viet Minh.[89] In 1950 and 1951, de Lattre implemented a much more aggressive campaign against the Viet Minh, trying to reduce the effectiveness of their forces by limiting their access to supplies and food through a "scorched earth" campaign that burned crops near areas of concentrated Viet Minh attacks. This policy produced some tactical successes but was a strategic failure, as it deprived not only the Viet Minh but also local villagers of necessary food, supplies, and transportation, and thus only increased the ire of locals against the French.

By May 1953, the French had again gone in a different direction, appointing Henri Navarre as chief of the Expeditionary Corps. French troops then implemented what has come to be known as the Navarre Plan. This plan called for French forces, assisted by Bao Dai's Vietnamese National Army, to use their advantage in technology and force of arms to hold key territory and strategic points along roads between them. The intent of this plan was to force the Viet Minh into a position of negotiation by fighting them into an impasse. Whatever gains the Viet Minh might make in the countryside, Navarre's defenses would prevent the communists from having any reasonable chance at taking cities or holding major roads.[90]

Navarre's plan proved to be a failure at the conclusive and most famous battle of the First Indochina

---

86 For an explanation of these factional groups, see Jessica Chapman, *Cauldron of Resistance: Ngo Dinh Diem, the United States, and 1950s Southern Vietnam* (Ithaca, NY: Cornell University Press, 2013), 40–60.

87 Joseph G. Morgan, *The Vietnam Lobby: The American Friends of Vietnam, 1955–1975* (Chapel Hill: University of North Carolina Press, 1997), 5; Miller, *Misalliance*, 52.

88 In 1951, the Viet Minh front officially ceased to exist as it came to be entirely subsumed into the Lien Viet Front, another umbrella organization of the Vietnamese Communists. Also in 1951, the Vietnamese Communists came to be organized under the title Vietnamese Workers Party, which was designed to reflect their renewed commitment to class struggle. For the purposes of simplicity and reflecting the conventions of English-language sources at the time, until 1954 this book will refer to the forces of the People's Army of Vietnam as the Viet Minh.

89 Fredrik Logevall, *Embers of War: The Fall of an Empire and the Making of America's Vietnam* (New York: Random House, 2014), 260–4.

90 Ibid., 355–6.

War: the Battle of Dien Bien Phu in 1954. Dien Bien Phu is a town along a main route between Hanoi and Vientiane, the capital of Laos. As such, it was a critical military and transportation route, and was heavily fortified by French troops who were supplied by aircraft. Unfortunately for the French, Dien Bien Phu is also ringed by mountains. Under the direction of the famous General Vo Nguyen Giap (1911–2013), Viet Minh forces pushed antiaircraft guns up the peaks and simply shot down French resupply aircrafts, effectively laying siege on French positions at Dien Bien Phu. After months of this siege, the French will to fight the war waned, and the French made the decision to conclude the war in talks at Geneva that were already underway. The resulting Geneva Accords were quite comprehensive, but their most salient effect was the partition of Vietnam at the seventeenth parallel, north of the city of Hue, with the Communist-led Democratic Republic of Vietnam in the north and the non-Communist forces of the State of Vietnam under Bao Dai in the South.

Chapter 10

China's Continuing Revolution (1955-1977)

In the 1950s, Mao Zedong continued his revolutionary movements, which had started during the Korean War. His political approach was a manageable path to achieving his goal. An interaction of China's military and politics bolstered the intuitive governmental policy and propelled the CCP government toward dominance. The wartime bureaucracy benefited all aspects of the administration, from economy to the military to the society. Advances in each sector of the party-state are mutually supporting and create a stronger state, thereby facilitating a more aggressive strategy in the war. Subsequent successes on the battleground in Korea increased state resources, such as land, troops, and weapons, which accelerated state growing control. In other words, the foreign intervention promoted the development of New China.

During the 1950s, the CCP carried out a Soviet style social and economic reform. The Chinese Communist revolution established this new socio-economic system with a mixture of Marxism-Leninism and its Chinese version—Mao's Thoughts. After the founding of the PRC, the CCP developed an integrated plan for the nation's economic recovery. Mao's social reforms, based on Soviet doctrine, modified to the Chinese situation. The Chinese land reform, for example, followed after the Soviet "collective ownership" model. As the result, China emphasized the new state's revolutionary and communist nature. Soviet financial, technological, and educational support aided China's reconstruction and economic growth, marking the "closest collaboration" between China and the Soviet Union.[1] In 1953, Mao called for a national movement to learn from the Soviet Union. The chairman remarked that "we are facing tremendous difficulties because we are building a great country. We do not have enough experience. Thus, we must carefully learn from the Soviet success."[2]

David Shambaugh identifies the CCP's trait of adaptation as a key difference from the Soviet Union. As the leading party of the most populous "third world" country, the CCP's culture of "borrowing" or "copying" from other countries like the former Soviet Union has proven to be conducive to its evolution and recreation. Shambaugh believes that "this is the stage—the transition from being a developing

---

1   Chen Jian, *Mao's China and the Cold War*, 60.

2   Mao's speech at the Fourth Plenary of the First Chinese People's Political Consultative Conference (CPPCC) on February 7, 1953, in *Mao's Manuscript since 1949*, 4: 45–6.

country to a newly industrialized one—that much of China has now entered."[3] The CCP may have learned from its negative lessons, adapted to a new international environment, rebuilt or reformed itself, and sustained its political legitimacy in the near future. In the late 1950s, however, complicated domestic and international factors undermined the Sino-Soviet alliance. The most important of these factors was whether Beijing or Moscow should become the center of the Asian Communist movement. Mao began to criticize Nikita Khrushchev as a "revisionist" who betrayed communism. The hostility between China and the Soviet Union reached a new height in the 1960s, when two bloody clashes occurred on the Sino-Soviet border. All of this paved the way for US President Richard Nixon's visit to China in 1972.

Radical Movements in the Party-State (1954–1962)

According to the PRC Constitution of 1954, the Chinese National People's Congress (NPC) was the highest state body and the only legislative house in China. Until the 1990s its representatives were determined by the CCP, which maintained effective control over the composition of the body at various levels. Each village could elect its own representative, with no restriction on the number of candidates, as the lowest level in the electoral system.[4] Only this representative could enter the next level as a candidate to become the town or city congressional representative. After approval of the Party committee of each town or city, each elected official could then enter the county level election. At this level, the Party exercised additional control over the process by limiting the number of candidates in proportion to the number of seats available. At the election of the county's people's congress (about 2,861 counties and county-level administrations in 2016), a maximum of 130 candidates were allowed per 100 seats. Following the approval of the county's Party committee, each elected representative could serve a five-year term and enter as a candidate in the district election. The next higher up was the provincial election, at which level the ratio was 120 candidates per 100 seats. Delegates who were reelected by the provincial people's congresses could then enter the election for the NPC where, at this highest level, the ratio decreased again to only 110 candidates per 100 seats. This tiered electoral structure made it impossible for a candidate to become a member of a higher legislative body without Party approval. In 2013 about 2,987 delegates attended the Twelfth NPC, the largest parliamentary body in the world.[5]

In this party-state, Party leaders believed the legal system should serve, rather than restrict, the power of the CCP. Checks and balances were nonexistent; the government was not able (nor willing) to correct itself through the system, and the mass media was merely a mouthpiece of the Party Center. None of the liberties in the Constitution were actually implemented. Article 89 of the Constitution theoretically protected individual rights by guaranteeing the freedom of speech, freedom of demonstration, and freedom of religion.[6] These civil and political rights, however, were severely limited in practice or entirely cancelled out by other articles,

---

3 David Shambaugh, *China's Communist Party: Atrophy and Adaptation* (Berkeley: University of California Press, 2008), 7.

4 Li, *Civil Liberties in China*, 8–9.

5 According to governmental records, 2,987 NPC delegates were elected in China by February 27, 2013, and 13 special delegates were from Taiwan, totaling 3,000 delegates.

6 English translations of the 1954 and 1982 Constitutions and their amendments are available in Standing Committee, PRC National People's Congress (NPC), *The Constitution of the People's Republic of China* (Beijing: Renmin Chubanshe [People's Publishing], 2004).

by constitutionally proscribed duties, or by other legislative acts. More and more intellectuals became concerned about the issues and problems inherent in the 1954 Constitution.

The NPC elected Mao Zedong as the PRC's president on September 27, 1954. Mao, who served as the first president of the PRC until his resignation in 1959, established the concept of supreme leader. In contemporary Chinese history, the selection of the paramount leader of the world's most populous country generally takes place after two five-year terms in accordance with the constitution. The supreme leader simultaneously holds these three official titles: general secretary of the CCP as head of the party; president of the PRC as head of state; and chairman of the Central Military Commission (CMC) as commander in chief of the Chinese military.[7] Not all Chinese leaders have held all of these titles at the same time, except Mao and those who came to power after Deng Xiaoping in the late 1990s.

Between 1949 and 1980, the Chinese unitary party-state maintained complete control of all social resources. The Chinese Communist Party Center controlled the government, including courts, law enforcement, and the legal system to serve its communist political agenda as a totalitarian authority. In order to solidify this new establishment, the CCP institutionalized discrimination against tens of millions of people on the basis of their wealth, or "class origin." People regarded as having a "bad class origin" were considered possible threats to the new China. They and their children, and even their grandchildren, were socially stigmatized, treated as political outcasts, discriminated against in education, employment, and daily life, and often viewed as potential criminals who were watched with suspicion. Mao justified the necessity of class struggle and stated that the Chinese people could never have any rights or liberties until they took them away from their social enemies, or counterrevolutionaries. Thus, under the people's democratic dictatorship, class struggle continued year after year through ruthless suppression, antagonistic contradiction, and massive violations of civil and human rights through the 1950s–1970s.

During the 1950s, Mao launched one political movement after another to engage the masses in the class struggle and to eliminate those labeled as potential or active counterrevolutionaries through initiatives such as land reform, the Threed-antis movement, Five-antis movement, and anti-Rightist movement. The Three Antis campaign targeted corruption, waste, and obstructionist bureaucracy, and the Five-antis attacked business men accused of bribery, theft of state property, tax evasion, cheating on government contracts, and theft of state economic information. All of these campaigns turned into violent reactions against millions of Chinese people. During the 1950s the CCP believed they needed a charismatic authority and absolute power to achieve their idealistic goals. Their successful military struggle for power during the Chinese Civil War against the GMD had convinced the leadership that violent means were necessary not only for establishing national power, but also for continuing their Communist revolution after the founding of the PRC. The ideology, experience, and nature of this transformation left little room for the Chinese people's civil liberties.

Between 1954 and 1956, the tension mounted between the intellectuals and the cadres, who were more concerned about communist ideology than the legal system. The legal scholars and experts also questioned the 1936 Soviet Constitution since Joseph Stalin never intended to grant the Russian people freedom, liberties, or fair trials. In 1956 Mao called for the "Blooming of the Hundred Flowers"

---

7   Ralph Folsom, *Law and Politics in the People's Republic of China* (Boulder, CO: Westview, 1992), 76–7; NPC, *The Constitution of the People's Republic of China*.

movement to encourage the Chinese people, especially the intellectuals, to express their grievances on the mistakes, corruption, and mismanagement both in the government and in the Party. When the criticism spread like wildfire across the country, the chairman decided to stop the complaints by launching another political movement, the "anti-Rightist" campaign in 1957.

By the end of the year, over 550,000 intellectuals had been labeled as "rightists" who were therefore enemies of the people. Many of these individuals were purged and denied the right to work, teach, or live with their families. A large number were exiled to labor camps or remote villages for reeducation, and numerous others were jailed or executed. The accused received no respect for their human decency, let alone their rights and liberties. A whole generation of artists, scientists, journalists, educators, and even college and high school students were penalized. Three middle school students who were against a party secretary in their school were shot to death in the presence of ten thousand people, including their teachers and classmates.

In the late 1950s, Mao also launched social and economic campaigns in the country to improve the difficulties in China's socio-economic condition. The Great Forward Leap was Mao's radical economic policy to industrialize the country through labor power and collectivization instead of technology.

In rural areas, most peasants were organized into communes that controlled their productivity and distribution, as private land ownership and independent farming were rendered nonexistent. Every peasant worked with others in a team and through collective production shared the annual yields. Under the People's Commune System, peasants could not leave their units, and if they wanted to travel, permission from village cadres was required. Furthermore, the markets in rural areas were banned as cradles for the petty bourgeois economy.

In the urban areas, residents were similarly denied freedom of movement without permission. Factory workers could not change or quit their jobs and were dependent upon their work unit for everything from food, medical care, and housing, to their children's education. The state controlled all the resources necessary for manufacturing, transportation, trade, banking, education, and social welfare. Traditional craftsmen were all forced to participate in collectivized firms. China had become a state based on the complete control of all resources by the party-run government.

The Great Leap Forward movement became an economic disaster and resulted in the widespread famine for three years (1960–1963), or the "three-year natural disaster" (*sannian ziran zaihai*). In 1959–1962 China experienced a serious economic depression, which claimed more than ten to fifteen million lives due to serious shortages of food, fuel, and other daily needs. The total grain production decreased from 200 million tons in 1958 to 144 million tons in 1960.

In 1960 starvation became a nationwide phenomenon. Some provinces lost 5 percent of their total population. In some areas, animals disappeared, birds were not to be seen in the sky, and even the grass and leaves were gone. The government blamed it on the bad weather and called it a "natural disaster".[8] The Great Leap Forward Movement merged as one of the most controversial events in modern Chinese history. Mao never admitted that his policy led to massive failure and economic disaster, although he stepped down as China's president in 1959.

After Mao's resignation, Liu Shaoqi was elected as the PRC's second president. Liu had been vice chair of the Central People's Government, and he later assumed the title of the first vice chair of the NPC from 1954 to 1959. In April 1959 he succeeded Mao as president of the PRC. Liu's work concentrated on the party's administrative functions and ideological

---

8   For more details on the 1959–1962 "natural disaster," see Spence, *The Search for Modern China*, 552–3.

matters. Liu, a traditional Soviet-style Communist, supported state planning and expansion of heavy industry. He was publicly acknowledged as Mao's chosen successor in 1961.[9] Later, however, Liu fell victim to the Cultural Revolution, the largest and longest mass movement in PRC's history. He was forced from the presidency in spite of the fact that legally he could not be removed from office; thus, the Constitution failed to protect the president of the Republic. Liu died in jail in 1969 after enduring much abuse and indignity at the hands of his political opponents.

The Sino-Soviet Split (the 1960s)

The Sino-Soviet relations began to encounter a serious challenge when Soviet leader Nikita Khrushchev made a "secret report" at the Russian Communist Congress in 1956. The new leader in Moscow criticized Stalin as a dictator, who had made serious mistakes in his late years and risked the Soviet Union with a nuclear war.[10] Khrushchev's report shocked Mao since he had followed Stalin to establish a Stalinist state in China and create his own personality cult. When Mao visited Moscow in 1957 to attend the fortieth anniversary of the Russian October Revolution's celebration,

he opposed Khrushchev's criticism and worldview. Mao spoke to Communist leaders from the world at the meeting, emphasizing that they should not be afraid of a nuclear war, and that it would "bring the imperialist system to its grave."[11] Chen Jian points out that Mao's statement was "a deliberate challenge to Khrushchev's emphasis on the necessity and possibility of 'peaceful coexistence' with Western imperialist countries," and "it inevitably worried Moscow's leaders."[12]

The dramatic Sino-Soviet split shattered the shared perception among Communists and their sympathizers all over the world that communism was a solution to the problems created by the worldwide process of capitalistic modernization. The Sino-Soviet polemic soon undermined their military, economic, and diplomatic relations. Their confrontation also changed the bipolar international system since the end of WWII.[13] China's important role in the Cold War is also clearly indicated in the historical process leading to the end of the Cold War from the late 1960s/early 1970s to the late 1980s. This process began first and foremost with the Sino-Soviet split and the Sino-American rapprochement. The Sino-Soviet split changed the character of the Cold War.

---

9   For a review of Liu Shaoqi, see Lowell Dittmer, *Liu Shao-ch'i and the Chinese Cultural Revolution: The Politics of Mass Criticism* (Berkeley: University of California Press, 1974).

10   For a chronological development of the Sino-Soviet split, see Song Enfan and Li Jiasong, eds., *Zhonghua renmin gongheguo waijiao dashiji, 1957–1964* [Chronicle of the People's Republic of China's Diplomacy, 1957–1964] (Beijing: Shijie zhishi chubanshe [World Knowledge Press], 2001), vol. 2; Yang Kuisong, *Zouxiang polie; Mao Zedong yu Moscow de enen yuanyuan* [Road to the Split; Interests and Conflicts between Mao Zedong and Moscow] (Hong Kong: Sanlian Shudian [Three Alliance Books], 1999), chapters 13–14.

11   Mao, "Speech at the Moscow Conference of Communist and Workers' Parties, November 16, 1957," in *Mao's Manuscript since 1949*, 5: 625–44.

12   Chen Jian, *Mao's China and the Cold War* (Chapel Hill: University of North Carolina Press, 2001), 71.

13   Former Soviet major (Red Army, ret.) and KGB agents, interviews by the co-author in 2004–2009. See also Major T., "Russian Missile Officers in Vietnam" and Russian Agent (KGB), "Russian Spies in Hanoi," in *Voices from the Vietnam War: Stories from American, Asian, and Russian Veterans*, Xiaobing Li (Lexington: University Press of Kentucky, 2010), 65–72, 93–100.

In July 1958, Beijing had prepared a large-scale bombing and shelling campaign against the GMD-held islands in the Taiwan Straits off the coast of Fujian province without informing Moscow or Khrushchev during his visit. In response to the rapidly escalating PLA threat, the Eisenhower administration reinforced US naval forces in East Asia and directed US warships to help the GMD protect the Jinmen supply lines. Khrushchev wrote twice to Mao in October 1958, offering Russian C-75 bombers with surface-to-air (SAM) missiles and Soviet advisors. In his replies, Mao only accepted Russian bombers and SAM missiles but did not want to have any more Soviet advisors. The proposed Russian aid and new technology never came.[14]

Mao criticized Khrushchev as the "new revisionist," "having betrayed international communist movement" with "socialist imperialist" aggressive policy.[15] In 1959, the PLA began to install listening devices on the Russian advisors' telephones in their offices and at their hotel rooms. The monitors recorded the advisors' phone conversations both with Chinese and with the Russians in the Soviet Union. Many Russian advisors also complained that their mail and family letters had been opened and checked.[16] More and more military advisors felt uncomfortable working with the PLA officers. Khrushchev did not expect at all that within less than two years, by 13 August 1960, all 12,000 Soviet "specialists" would have to leave China.[17]

Among the Russian advisors were experts of nuclear and missile technology. Some of them had worked in China for four years to build the Chinese nuclear and missile programs. Without Soviet aid, they believed that China "won't be able to develop its own nuclear weapons within the next twenty years."[18] The Chinese leaders, however, continued their nuclear and missile programs after the end of Soviet aid in technology and materials. The Central Committee of the CCP met on July 18, 1960, and decided to undertake the task of advanced technology themselves. Four years later, China had its first successful nuclear bomb test on October 16, 1964. After its second nuclear test on May 14, 1965, the PLA established its strategic force, officially the Second Artillery Corps, including nuclear weapons, strategic and tactical missiles, and surface-to-air missile troops in 1966. The same year, the PLA began to test rockets carrying warheads. Then, the first Chinese-made hydrogen bomb tested on June 17, 1967. In less than eight years after the Sino-Soviet split, China became a nuclear power.

Through the 1960s, the Sino-Soviet relations became worse. In the spring of 1962, more than sixty-seven thousand Chinese fled Xinjiang to Soviet Kyrgyzstan. Beijing blamed the KGB, claiming that the Soviet security agency was behind the mass flight. The tension between the two communist states led to the Sino-Russian border conflict in 1969.

China and Russia share a long land border about 4,000 miles. According to the Sino-Soviet Friendship and Mutual Assistance Treaty, the two countries accepted the status quo in 1950. However, in the late

---

14   Li, *A History of the Modern Chinese Army*, 188–9.

15   For example, Premier Zhou said on April 29, 1968, that the Soviet Union [like America] was apparently circulating and containing China. Li Danhui, "Conflicts between China and the Soviet Union in Their Efforts to Aid Vietnam and Resist America," in *Lengzhan yu zhongguo* [The Cold War and China], eds. Zhang Baijia and Niu Jun (Beijing: Shijie zhishi chubanshe [World Knowledge Publishing], 2002), 373n1.

16   Shen, *Sulian zhuanjia zai zhongguo, 1948–1960* [Soviet experts in China, 1948–1960], 358–9.

17   Lüthi, Lorenz M., "Sino-Soviet Split," in Li, Xiaobing (ed.), *China at War: An Encyclopedia of Chinese Military History* (Santa Barbara, CA: ABC-CLIO, 2012), 406–9.

18   Zhang Aiping, "Retrospect and Great Hopes," in GAD, *Liangdan yixing* (The Bomb, Missile, and Satellite), 23.

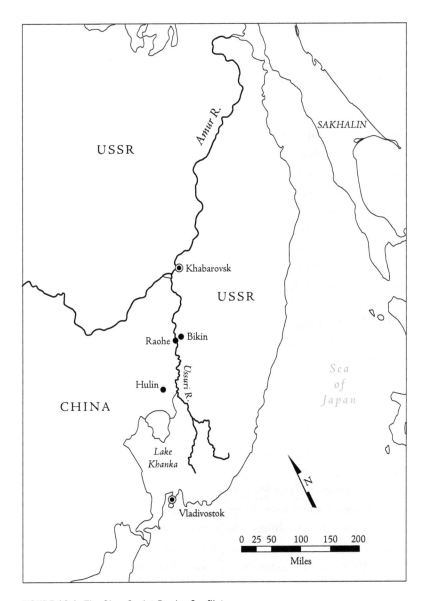

FIGURE 10.1 The Sino-Soviet Border Conflict

1960s when the Sino-Soviet relations became hostile, the territorial issues resurfaced over some disputed border areas. In 1968, both sides reinforced their troops to the border and increased border patrols. On March 2, 1969, the patrol troops from both sides clashed at the Damansky (Zhenbao) Island, a small, uninhabited island in the middle of the Ussuri River in Heilongjiang province. In the battle, the Soviet troops lost more than 30 men. On March 15, hundreds of the Soviet troops with six heavy tanks attacked the Chinese position on the other side of the river. The PLA lost 40 soldiers that day. While the border clash continued in Northeast China, both sides also attacked the other along the Northwestern border in Xinjiang. On July 8, for example, about 300 Soviet troops with 20 tanks and two helicopters attacked the PLA border post at Tieliekti and annihilated all the Chinese troops in the battle.

Between March and August 1969, the Soviet government pursued two very distinct policies of military preparation and escalation and public appeals for an end to the conflict. After several weeks of negotiations, on August 8–9, the Soviet Union and Chinese reached an agreement that improved the shipping situation on the Ussuri-Amur River system.[19] These talks were the fifteenth annual discussion of the topic and took place as part of an already standing agreement, thus, while not signaling any great improvement in relations, at least did not further escalate the situation.[20] Within a day, however, the Soviet government appointed its number two strategic missiles officer to command its Far Eastern forces.[21] This personnel transfer also followed Soviet calls for reconciliation throughout the spring and summer of that year.[22] Concurrently, the U.S.S.R. was allegedly preparing for the most violent confrontation since March in Central Asia.[23] The Sino-Soviet border conflict continued into the 1970s.

The Cultural Revolution (1966-1976)

After the failure of his Great Leap Forward movement in 1958, Mao resigned from the presidency. Liu Shaoqi became the president of the People's Republic in 1959. Liu Shaoqi's disapproval of Mao's policies had given rise to the latter's profound displeasure and distrust. To make the government more competent and dedicated to Communist values, Liu himself presided over the enlarged Politburo meeting that formally started the Cultural Revolution. However, he quickly lost control of the movement while Mao and his political allies tried to use this opportunity to take over the political power and destroy Mao's alleged enemies—Liu and Deng Xiaoping. Liu disappeared from public sight soon after the Cultural Revolution started. With Marshal Lin Biao by his side, Mao began to organize the students and launched the Great Proletarian Cultural Revolution.

On May 16, 1966, Mao drafted the "May Sixteenth Circular," which was passed by the Central Committee's Politburo.[24] It was the beginning of the Chinese Great Proletarian Cultural Revolution. To ensure his total control of the nationwide political movement, Mao organized the Cultural Revolution Leading Group with his wife, Jiang Qing, as its chairperson. The Leading Group replaced the Politburo in 1966–1967 as the top decision-making organ for both the party and the country.[25] Soon Mao and the Leading Group began to organize high school and college students as the Red Guard (*Hongweibing*) against his political rivalries like Liu Shaoqi and Deng Xiaoping.[26]

In the summer of 1966, the Cultural Revolution became a nation-wide political struggle with extensive purges. The students organized the Red Guards as the driving force for the movement. The

---

19   "Russians, Chinese reach Accord Over River Shipping," *The Washington Post*, 9 August 1969, 2.

20   "Soviet-Chinese Talk on Border Rivers Begun in Far East," *The New York Times*, 22 June 1969, 7.

21   "Soviet Picks Missile Expert to Head Force in Far East," *The New York Times*, 8 August 1969, 2.

22   These proposals were often multifaceted, attacking Mao and warning of escalation, while putting forward the possibility of reconciliation. For an example, see Bernard Gwertzman, "Soviet Seeks Conciliation," *The New York Times*, 6 July 1969, 2.

23   Kuisong, "The Sino-Soviet Border Clash of 1969," 34.

24   The quote of the "May 16 Circular" is from Fang Zhu, *Gun Barrel Politics; Party-Army Relations in Mao's China* (Boulder, CO: Westview Press, 1998), 116.

25   CCP Party History Research Division, *Zhongguo gongchandang lishi dashiji, 1919–1987* [Major Historical Events of the CCP, 1919–1987] (Beijing: Renmin chubanshe [People's Press], 1989), 283.

26   Mao's letter is quoted in Deng Rong, *Deng Xiaoping and the Cultural Revolution—A Daughter Recalls the Critical Years*, trans. Sidney Shapiro (Beijing: Foreign Languages Press, 2002), 17.

masses were urged to be guided by Mao's Thought instead of the law. Mao used the Red Guard youth to publicly attack, or "bomb" (*paoda*), the CCP and PRC hierarchy officials. The Red Guards, mostly college, high school, and middle school students, were empowered by Mao and called for "bombing the headquarters," "rebellion is justified," and "learning revolution by making revolution." From June to August 1966, all high schools and colleges dismissed classes and allowed the students to participate in the new revolution. There were three months of the "red terror," or "great chaos under the heaven" (*tianxia daluan*) as Mao said.[27] The Cultural Revolution was contrived from top to bottom. Lin Biao, Jiang Qing, and other leftists grabbed the revolutionary enthusiasm and naiveté of the students, inflaming them with a lot of demagogic flummery. At the same time, the numerous Red Guard organizations became seriously factionalized, constantly arguing and debating heatedly amongst themselves as a result of their differing interpretations of the "supreme instructions." On August 18, Mao showed up at a mass meeting celebrating the "Great Proletarian Cultural Revolution" with one million of the Red Guards at Tiananmen Square. It became the first of eight mass rallies at Tiananmen Square where Mao met 11 million of the Red Guards from all over the country in the fall of 1966. They marched into the center of the capital city Beijing, singing "The Great Helmsman" in praise of Mao and carrying the *Little Red Book* of Mao's quotations.[28] With Mao's support and encouragement, the Red Guards were poised to take over the country. Some members of the Red Guards even traveled to Vietnam with

the desire to join the "anti-American imperialists" movement there.

In October, Liu Shaoqi, president of the PRC, Deng Xiaoping, vice premier, and many high ranking government officials in the State Council, ministries, and offices of the central government in Beijing were publicly criticized and purged. One of the Red Guard groups attacked and looted the Ministry of Public Security (China's FBI) for six times in the fall. Most of the ministers and important government officials were detained by the Red Guards. Some of them were tortured and killed by the Red Guards. From the summer to the fall of 1966, the Chinese students moved into the center of domestic politics during the Cultural Revolution. In 1967, the movement had begun to overthrow provincial, county, and metropolitan governments across the country. By early 1968, Mao had achieved his political objectives. The Red Guards helped Mao's political agenda and defined his legacy for all of modern Chinese history the way that his purges have done for him and the legacy of the Chinese Cultural Revolution.

Meanwhile, Lin Biao, Mao's hand-picked successor, used the Cultural Revolution and the Red Guards to reshape the PLA as radical political and military institutions. Before long, the new high command "subverted the programs of the professional military for ideological and political reasons."[29] The PLA's poor performance in the Vietnam War during 1966–1967 began to show its outdated war-fighting tactics, lack of combat training, and outdated, ineffective weapon system. In December 1966, Grand General Luo Ruiqing, chief of the PLA General

---

27 Mao's quote in Deng Rong, ibid., 20.

28 For more discussions on the Great Cultural Revolution, see Gao Meng and Yan Jiaqi, *Wenhua dageming shi nian shi* [Ten Years of the Cultural Revolution] (Tianjin: Tianjin renmin chubanshe [Tianjin People's Press], 1986); Li Ke and Hao Shengzhang, *Wenhua dageming zhong de renmin jiefangjun* [The PLA during the Cultural Revolution] (Beijing: Zhonggong dangshi ziliao chubanshe [CCP Central Committee's Party Historical Document Press], 1989; Meisner, *Mao's China*, chapters 18–20.

29 Ellis Joffe, *The Chinese Army after Mao* (Cambridge, MA: Harvard University Press, 1987), 2.

Staff and head of China's Vietnam War command, was accused of "conducting anti-party activities" and "planning a plot to take over the power," charges that were often raised against those who had differing opinions from Mao. In October 1968, Liu was relieved of all his posts, and in 1969, his position as the successor of Mao was officially passed on to the defense minister, Marshal Lin Biao. On November 12, 1969, Liu died in prison in Kaifeng, Henan province, of medically neglected diabetes, thus ending an enduring yet tragic political career.

In January 1967, the Red Guard movement began to take over the local governments. The first such "power seizure" took place in Shanghai, when the Red Guards and Workers Revolutionary General Headquarters joined force and forced their way into the city hall. They organized a "revolutionary committee" as the new authority to replace the municipal government and party committee. This "power seizure" was called the "Shanghai Spring" and followed the Red Guards all over the country. They began to seize power of the local governments, including provincial, county, and municipal governments. The Cultural Revolution entered the phase of a "total taking-over" of the authorities. The Red Guards took over the government offices at all the levels, jailed the officials, and administrated provincial and local affairs through their newly established "revolutionary committees."

> In Beijing, some marshals and generals tried to stop the Maoists' attempt to involve the PLA in the Great Cultural Revolution in early 1967. Their efforts failed and they were branded the "February Countercurrent" against the Cultural Revolution. Mao asked them to leave their posts and make self-critiques. In March 1967, Lin mentioned several times the need to identify "a small handful in the army" and burn them to death. Then, the "Cultural Revolution Leading Group" moved into

power, replacing the Politburo. Lin used the Cultural Revolution mass movements to purge the military leaders who did not agree with his strategy and policy. He mobilized PLA soldiers and commanders in Beijing to look for "bourgeoisie agents in the PLA." Then, with Mao's approval, Lin dismissed and jailed many marshals and generals.[30]

Since early 1967, the situation worsened across the country, as the Cultural Revolution entered the phase of a "total taking-over" of the authorities. But different factions within the Red Guards had contradictory political orientations and different plans, leading to violent conflicts within the Red Guards in many places resembling a civil war. The Red Guard movement continued and became more violent, and did greater damage not only to the government and the people, but this time to themselves. In early 1968, the Red Guards began to splinter into zealous factions, based on the schools they had attended, the political status of their families, and the rivalry among Red Guards leaders. Each group claimed to be the "true" representative of the Thought of Mao Zedong. The resulting chaos led to the civil wars between the different Red Guard organizations and anarchy paralyzed the urban economy.

To stop the widespread violence and social disorder, Mao Zedong employed the PLA to control the situation and restore social and political order in 1967. Following Mao's order, the military violently put down the national Red Guard movement in late 1967 and early 1968. Some of the suppressions were often brutal. For example, a radical alliance of Red Guard groups in Hunan, Mao's home province, refused to give up their weapons. When the PLA sent local units (like the National Guards in the U.S.) to the area searching for the illegal weapons, the soldiers were ambushed by the armed Red Guards. Then, the PLA sent in filed army with tanks and heavy artillery pieces to the area to attack the Red Guards. It was reported that more than 8,000

---

30   Mao approved most of Lin's requests. See Mao's instructions and approvals in *Mao's Manuscripts since 1949*, vol. 12 (Beijing: Zhongyang wenxian chubanshe, 1992), 201, 209, 218, 226–68, 380, and 383.

Red Guards were killed during the conflicts. At the same time, in Guangxi province, the PLA carried out mass executions of Red Guards in order to stop their armed clashes against the PLA units.

From 1967 to 1971, the PLA became the dominant political force in the country. When "revolutionary committees" were established as authorities, PLA officers consisted of the majority of civilian government office-holders. For example, by September 1968, each of the twenty-nine provinces across the country had established a provincial revolutionary committee to replace the governor's office, provincial congress, and provincial court. The majority of the provincial committee members were from the military: about 98 percent in Hubei, 97 percent in Yunnan, 95 percent in Shanxi, 84 percent in Liaoning, 81 percent in Guangdong, and 78 percent in Beijing. Lin's power grew to an unprecedented level. At the CCP Ninth Congress in April 1969, the Central Committee and the entire party recognized Lin as Mao's "close comrade in arms and successor."[31]

After the Chinese military moved into the political center in 1967–1969, Lin Biao increased his personal influence and began to question Mao's policy of the Cultural Revolution. Their disagreements burst out at the CCP Central Committee Plenum at Lushan in 1970. In his concluding speech, Mao sternly criticized Lin and the military. Fang Zhu considers the Lushan conference only a prelude of the Mao-Lin showdown a year later. "By disagreeing with Mao during the plenum, for whatever

reason, Lin had provided Mao with hard evidence of his political ambition. The relationship between the two men had deteriorated to the point of open confrontation."[32]

In early 1971, Lin's wife, Ye Quan, and their son, Lin Liguo, realized Mao was going to purge Lin soon. Lin Liguo, Chief of the Operational Division of the PLA Air Force, planned an assassination of Mao by an air strike on Mao's train on his way from Hangzhou to Beijing. Lin's plot failed after Mao changed his travel schedule and returned to Beijing days earlier. Panic and desperate, Ye and Lin Liguo took Lin Biao with them on an airplane on September 13, 1971, and flew north from Shanhaiguan, Hebei province. After the plane crossed the northern border, it crashed in Mongolia that evening for unknown reasons.[33] Lin Biao, his family, and crew members were killed in the crash.

After Lin's death, Mao launched a nationwide movement to "Criticize Lin and Confucius," and labeled Lin as a "closet Confucianist," "Bourgeois careerist," conspirator, and "ultra-rightist." Historians are surprised to see that "These obviously contradictory criticisms were heaped on a man who had been a brilliant general and one of Mao's closest friends." June Grasso, Jay Corrin, and Michael Kort state that "Lin Biao was blamed for nearly everything that went wrong in China during the late 1960s."[34] Since Lin promoted the Mao cult and the Cultural Revolution, his death brought great joy to China's millions. But cool scrutiny also revealed that the Cultural Revolution was open to serious

---

31 Li Zhisui, *The Private Life of Chairman Mao; The Memoirs of Mao's Personal Physician* (New York: Random House, 1994), 512.

32 Zhu, *Gun Barrel Politics*, 181.

33 There have been several speculations about the crash of Lin's plane, including a Chinese missile attack, running out of fuel, or simply an accident. See Gao Wenqian, *Wannian Zhou Enlai* [Zhou Enlai's Later Years] (Hong Kong: Mingjing chubanshe [Bright Mirror Publishing, 2003), 350–5; Huang Yao and Yan Jingtang, *Lin Biao yisheng* [Lin Biao's Life], 490–507; Ye Yonglie, *Gaoceng jiaoliang* [Power Struggle at the Top] (Urumqi: Xinjiang renmin chubanshe [Xinjiang People's Press], 2004), 369–76.

34 June Grasso, Jay Corrin, and Michael Kort, *Modernization and Revolution in China; From the Opium Wars to World Power,* third edition (Armonk, New York: M.E. Sharpe, 2004), 234.

question. It raised doubts about the entire course of action, orientation, and policy followed since the advent of the Cultural Revolution. Mao himself certainly knew better. A person who worked closely beside him later recalled: "After Lin Biao crashed, the Chairman became very ill. Lin's betrayal had a serious effect on his health. We heard him quote the old adage: 'At 73 or 84, if Death doesn't invite you, you should go to its door!' We felt badly. He was very depressed."[35]

The "Gang of Four" and Death of Mao (1976)

After Lin Biao crashed, Mao had been in poorer shape for a number of years before his demise.[36] Due to his illness and age, Mao, aware of his own mortality, started to search with growing anxiety for a successor to maintain and continue his revolution. The "Gang of Four" became Mao's another alternative.

The "Gang of Four" was the name given to a radical leftist political group composed of four CCP bureaucrats led by Mao's wife Jiang Qing, and they became notorious due to the Cultural Revolution. After being condemned by other CCP high-ranking officials for the failure of the Great Leap Forward, Mao turned to Jiang. Powered by her husband, whose support made it possible for Jiang to be assigned the position of deputy director of the Central Cultural Revolution Group, Jiang made the best use of her advantage to carry out the reform of the Chinese theatre. While wiping out Mao's political rivalry, she also recruited radical and loyal Maoists under her leadership. Among these on the top were Wang Hongwen, Zhang Chunqiao, and Yao Wenyuan. Since all of them were from Shanghai, they were also known as the "Gang of Shanghai".

Jiang Qing gained actual power within Chinese politics for the first time and became one of the architects of the Cultural Revolution, during which time she played a progressively vigorous political role, participating in principal CCP and state activities. Her position was cemented by her membership in the all-powerful Politburo in 1969, when she had already created a particularly strong relationship with what was eventually recognized as the Gang of Four. After 1973 these four radicals held unlimited control over all national institutions in practice limited by Mao and to a lesser extent by Zhou Enlai, and occupied influential positions in the Politburo. Among them were Wang Hongwen became vice chairman of the CCP and Zhang Chunqiao was vice premier.

Jiang Qing and Lin Biao worked together at the beginning of the Cultural Revolution, but after Lin's death in 1971, Jiang turned against him publicly in the Condemning Lin and Confucius movement. During the mid-1970s, Jiang Qing directed her crusade against Deng Xiaoping. At that time, the Chinese people became vehemently dissatisfied with her and chose to blame her when the entire Gang of Four was working hard to take advantage of Mao's declining health and power.

Mao's favourite was Wang Hongwen, one of the radicals who seemed poised to become Zhou Enlai's successor, but Mao knew that Wang was not up to the task and feared that the Gang of Four would plunge the country into renewed chaos with their revolutionary zeal. Nearing the end of his life, Mao turned against Jiang Qing and her associates, leading to the rise of Hua Guofeng.

Hua Guofeng (1921–2008) was only a local party chief of the Hunan province during the Cultural Revolution. Hua, however, raised to the national leadership in the mid-1970s. After Lin's death in 1971, Hua chaired a party committee investigating

---

35 Mao's quote in Deng Rong, *Deng Xiaoping and the Cultural Revolution*, 189.

36 Deng, *Deng Xiaoping and the Cultural Revolution*, 189.

the Lin Biao Incident and earned Mao's trust. In 1973, Hua raised to become a member in the Politburo. After Zhou Enlai died in January 1976, Mao appointed Hua as the premier. Eight months later, after Mao died, Hua gained the titles of the chairman of the CCP and the Central Military Commission in charge of the party, government, and military. For the first time, the supreme power of the country peacefully transferred from a paramount leader to an unknown local official in the history of the PRC. A new power struggle soon began between Hua Guofeng and the Gang of Four.

On September 9, 1976, Mao died. Hua Guofeng established a political alliance with the old guard, who had been the victims of the Cultural Revolution. In October, Hua announced the end of the Cultural Revolution. On October 6, 1976, Hua sent his security force to arrest the Gang of Four. The Maoist Gang of Four was defeated by the returning old guard. After getting rid of the radicals, Hua tried to carry out some reforms and abandon some radical policies of the Cultural Revolution-era, but he attempted to extend Mao's policies, asserting the rightness of Maoist ideologies. Thus, Deng Xiaoping, a realistic reformer, together with his supporters, overcame Hua in December 1978, compelling him to retire. Deng thereafter became the paramount leader until his death in 1992. For the second time the supreme power was peacefully transferred from the new CCP and PRC leader to a paramount leader again in just two years. The CCP experience between 1949 and 1979 indicated that the party could learn from both its successes and failures; such an ability provided to be essential in ensuring the party's survival for decades to come.

Conclusion to Part Four

In part four of this book, we have witnessed how technological, cultural, military, and intellectual transformations in East Asian areas manifested themselves in new nationalisms and newfound loyalties to modernist economic systems and ideologies. These new ideologies and nationalisms arose in the context of colonialism and imperialism. Japan became an imperialist power; Korea and China struggled to respond to the challenges of Japanese imperial expansion. In Vietnam, successive generations of leaders crafted new strategies to end the French colonization of Indochina.

The century began with an ascendant Japan, poised to show the world of its equivalence with European powers. Having defeated a European power (Russia) in war in 1904 (as discussed in part three), Japan sought prestige and resources through its colonization of Korea, and later of Manchuria and other parts of northeastern and coastal China. By the late 1930s, Japanese expansion in East Asia became the Pacific Theater of WWII, and the Japanese expanded into Southeast Asian areas and into Vietnam. At the end of the war, an occupation of Japan by the United States transformed Japanese culture and society.

Meanwhile, in the aftermath of World War II, an ideological and sometimes military conflict between communists and non-communists known as the Cold War was on the rise. In the late 1940s and early 1950s, three "hot wars" to control the fate of East Asian countries became embedded in the Cold War. In the late 1940s, nationalists and communists fought to control China in the aftermath of the Japanese defeat, while a communist-led coalition fought against French efforts to maintain colonial control over Indochina. In the early 1950s, a conflict between communist and non-communist forces in Korea drew in other powers, including China and the United States.

Finally, after 1949, the Chinese Communist Party took control of the Chinese mainland and sought to radically remake the Chinese economy and society. Through the transformation of agriculture and industry, and ultimately through efforts to reject traditional culture, they upended Chinese society, which eventually destabilized relations between China and the Soviet Union. By the early 1970s, these developments led to a thawing of relations with the United States and a new path for China toward economic liberalization, as we will see in part five of this book.

PART FIVE

The East Wind Prevails over the West Wind

Introduction to Part Five

As the Cold War raged on, East Asian nations also worked to develop and expand their economies. Japan in particular experienced dramatic economic growth in the 1950s and 1960s and emerged as an economic superpower by the late 1960s and early 1970s, only to suffer from economic crisis by the late 1990s. Korea similarly experienced rapid economic growth from the 1960s to the 1980s, only to be hit hard by the Asian financial crisis of the late 1990s.

The economies of China and Vietnam experienced consistent expansion after those countries implemented economic liberalization. In the Vietnamese case, their new economic vitality only began under the reformation policy enacted in 1986. Before that, however, Vietnam found itself embroiled in the Second Indochina War (1959–1975), which pitted non-Communist forces represented by South Vietnam, with its capitol in Saigon, against Communist forces and their allies, represented in part by North Vietnam, with its capital in Hanoi. This war concluded in 1975 when North Vietnamese troops took Saigon and reunified the country. However, by the late 1970s, the Vietnamese found themselves at war again, this time in a battle with the Khmer Rouge forces of Cambodia and their allies in China, known as the Third Indochina War. The desperate economic conditions of much of Vietnam and the devastation of war demonstrated by the early 1980s the need for the reform that would come. In the Chinese case, reform could come only after the Cultural Revolution had run its course and the leader of that revolution, Mao Zedong, had died.

China and Vietnam both experienced an economic boom with the implementation of liberalizing economic reforms in the 1980s and 1990s. To a greater degree than Korea and Japan, China and Vietnam were able to weather the Asian financial crisis of the late 1990s. They continued to see considerable economic and technological growth into the twenty-first century. However, this growth has not been without its costs. China and Vietnam face challenges related to the environment, the gap between rich and poor as well as urban and rural areas, and maintaining the rule of law, upholding human rights, and reducing corruption.

Chapter 11

New Japan and Two Koreas (1952-2000)

The first decade after the Pacific War set the pattern for Japan's postwar future. The American Occupation from 1945 to 1952 successfully broke with Japan's prewar system and made revolutionary changes in terms of government, economy, society, and military. The United States also provided what Japan wanted most: a long-term guarantee of its security, later referred to as the "nuclear umbrella."[1] On September 8, 1951, the United States and forty-seven other nations signed a peace treaty with Japan in San Francisco, California. The treaty ended the American Occupation and returned independence and sovereignty to Japan on April 28, 1952. On the day that the peace treaty was signed, Japan also signed a mutual security treaty with the Unites States, committing American armed forces to the safety and security of Japan. The United States' protection of Japan thereafter held the cost of Japanese defense at minimum. Some critics later accused Japan of enjoying a "free ride" throughout the Cold War years and beyond. Japan's low annual military budget did allow the government to steer its spending in other sectors, as its small Self Defense

Forces (SDF, including army, naval, and air forces) cost only one percent of Japan's GNP for decades.[2]

The postwar Japanese leaders, nevertheless, successfully avoided entanglement in the Cold War through the 1950s–1980s, especially during the Korean (1950–1953) and Vietnam (1965–1973) wars, two "hot wars" in East Asia, even though Tokyo renewed its mutual defense treaty with Washington. Yoshida Shigeru, Japan's first postwar prime minister, developed an overall foreign policy for new Japan, sometimes called the Yoshida Doctrine, which gave primacy to economic growth and avoided ensnarement in the Cold War.[3] He believed that the danger Japan faced in the postwar world was that it might be drawn into the American-Soviet Cold War and waste its resources on military spending. If that danger could be avoided, Japan might survive. After the Korean War broke out in June 1950, American diplomat John Foster Dulles visited Tokyo and demanded Japan's participation. Yoshida refused the US government's request by citing Article 9 of the new constitution, in which "the Japanese people

---

1   Henshall, *A History of Japan*, 155–6.

2   Glenn D. Hook, Julie Gilson, Christopher W. Hughes, and Hugo Dobson, *Japan's International Relations: Politics, Economics and Security*, 2nd ed. (London, UK: Routledge, 2005), 7, 13, 146–7.

3   James L. Huffman, *Modern Japan: A History in Documents* (New York: Oxford University Press, 2011), 150.

forever renounce war as a sovereign right of nation," and will never maintain "land, sea, and air forces" or "other war potential."[4] In the meantime, Japan took full advantage of the Cold War by maximizing the opportunities and resources that the United States had provided during the Occupation to build a democratic, prosperous, and strong country through the 1950s–1970s. Andrew Gordon states, "In response to these reforms, a virtual fever of 'democratization' swept Japan in the late 1940s and 1950s. Advocates understood democracy and equality in extremely expansive terms; the terms meant far more than voting and land reform. They implied too many— and this was both promise and threat—a remaking of the human soul."[5]

In retrospect, Tokyo's way of handling international relations in the postwar years helped to deflect the international attention to Japan in East Asian geopolitics. While a culprit for many conflicts and several wars in East Asia during the late nineteenth and early decades of the twentieth century that culminated in the Pacific War, Japan was the focal point in the power competition in East Asia. Its postwar polices reoriented the country largely toward domestic affairs. Compared with the Germany, which occupied a central position in defining the agenda of big power politics in Europe during not only the first half of the twentieth century but also the Cold War, Japan did not exercise overwhelming influence on the strategic reconfiguration after the Allied Occupation.[6] After the Sino-American détente in the early 1970s and the end of the Vietnam War, the "Japan question" was further relegated to the strategic periphery of the Washington-Moscow power dynamic in East Asia. On the other hand,

Japan's "economic miracle," partially because of its new international profile, gave rise to its frictions with the United States, at times even threatening to fracture their Cold War alliance. Interestingly if not somewhat ironically, Japan's prolonged economic stagnation since the early 1990s, coupled with the rise of China, has contributed to the reemergence of the "Japan question" as a sensitive geo-political issue in the post-Cold War era in the twenty-first century.

Japan's Economic Growth (1952–1965)

After the American Occupation ended, the years 1952–1965 transformed Japan into a new nation in terms of economy, politics, and society. The first postwar decade became Japan's economic recovery period. First, after SCAP dissolved hundreds of *zaibatsu* headquarters and their holding companies, Prime Minister Yoshida employed the existing pyramidal structure of the centralized administration with SCAP support. The Konoe Fumimaro cabinet had established the political centralization and economic nationalization in 1937–1940 for national mobilization with the support of militarists for war.[7] Although the imperial system under the new constitution was sharply reduced, the Yoshida cabinet was able to employ its mechanism as a centralized government for national economic recovery in 1947–1954.

For example, the government used the Board of Economic Stability, which was established in 1946, and Recovery Financial Public Trust to plan the nation's economic recovery, decide on production and purchases, allocate financial resources for certain industries, control imports and exports, and regulate the minimum wage. SCAP supported

---

4 Dale M. Hellegers, *We, the Japanese People: World War II and the Origins of the Japanese Constitution* (Stanford, CA: Stanford University Press, 2002), 2: 576.

5 Andrew Gordon, "Society and Politics from Trans-war through Post-war Japan," in *Historical Perspectives on Contemporary East Asia*, eds. Merle Goldman and Andrew Gordon (Cambridge, MA: Harvard University Press, 2000), 279.

6 Chen and Li, "China and the End of the Global Cold War," 123.

7 For the domestic policy of the Konoe cabinets (1937–1939, 1940), see previous chapters.

the Yoshida administration's goal of organizing the nation's recovery, involving the government in business, and macromanaging the nation's economy. The Board and Trust had adopted the "focused production methods" in 1948, by which the government concentrated its limited resources to recover certain key industries first.[8] Then, the Ministry of International Trade and Industry (MITI) was established to supervise and coordinate demotics banking, trade, and manufacturing. In the 1950s and early 1960s, MITI played an important role as the economic authority to complete Japan's economic transition from postwar recovery to economic take off. It also provided favorites for Japan's exports and allowed the maintenance of protective tariffs over foreign imports to promote the country's productivity and enhance its labor market. The Ministry also encouraged and supported industrial research and technology development during the critical years of 1952–1965.[9]

Throughout the 1950s, especially with the radical transformation of American fortunes in the Korean War, the Truman administration turned Japan into an economic and military base for the UNF intervention in Korea. Yoshida emphasized economic recovery in a political context, which provided Japan a well-balanced position during the Korean War. Meanwhile, Yoshida had maintained a close relationship with the United States, which enabled Japan to receive American military orders of $4 billion during the war, more than half of the nation's total exports. Yoshida called the war "a gift from the gods."[10] The revenues from manufacturing war supplies increased from $149 million in 1950 to $809 million in 1953. War supply industries also promoted other major industries such as steel, machinery, shipbuilding, textile, and construction.

The war also stimulated the service industry, including vehicle repairs, ship rebuilding, food processing, and medical assistance. By 1954 the nation's industrial production had returned to its prewar level.[11]

After the Korean War, the Japanese government continued its successful postwar policy of central control by introducing a state monopoly of the key industries like steel, iron, coal, electricity, and shipbuilding. Following the Yoshida Doctrine, the Japanese government furthered its pro-business policy by becoming more deeply involved in economic planning, financial support, and trade promotion than any other non-Socialist state. The government made central plans for these industries, provided low interest loans to them, reduced tax rates, controlled imports and exports, improved their infrastructure, and updated the equipment. Since the state monopoly protected them by reducing the competition and guaranteeing their profits, these industries were able to attract more than 40 percent of private investment and continued to enjoy rapid growth after the Korean War in the 1950s. In the meantime, the government established the Bank of Japan, which backed commercial banks in providing capital investment. The Japanese Diet passed resolutions to protect growing industries at home and limit foreign competitions in these fields. The government only welcomed foreign investment that brought in new technologies based on the rationale that it was cheaper and faster to license new technology than to develop it domestically.

During the early 1950s, the industrial priority was the development of heavy industry, especially iron, steel, and products like ships and heavy machinery. By 1954 Japan's manufacturing had returned to the prewar level, while its agricultural output had exceeded the prewar level. By 1955 Japan

---

8   Beasley, *The Rise of Modern Japan*, 245.

9   Hane and Perez, *Modern Japan*, 408.

10 Andressen, *A Short History of Japan*, 125.

11 Walthall, *Japan*, 191.

had recovered from the devastation of war and provided enough rice for the entire population. In that year, Japan's annual GNP totaled $24 billion, and its per capita GNP was $268, exceeding the prewar level. In 1955 Japan's manufacturing capacity had resumed the prewar level. By 1956 the Japanese economy pulled ahead of other Asian countries. Its economic growth continued through the following decade with an average annual economic growth rate of 9 percent, comparted to 4 percent for the United States, with Great Britain at 2.5 percent, France at 4.2 percent, and West Germany at 5.7 percent economic growth.

By the late 1960s, Japan had achieved an economic level comparable to that of Europe.[12] In 1956 private investment in infrastructure and equipment has increased 54.6 percent from the previous year. Thereafter, this increase continued at a rate of more than 70 percent in the steel and iron, machinery, electricity, and chemical industries. These traditional industries also laid a solid foundation for the newly established industries, such as automobile manufacturing, electronics, petrochemicals, and plastic manufacturing.[13] Due to the ready availability of capital, these new industries were able to import new technology, equipment, and even entire manufacturing facilities from Western countries like the United States, West Germany, and France. Japan imported 1,148 foreign technologies between 1950 and 1955; such imports almost doubled during the following decade. In 1956 the Japanese government published its *Economic White Book* that reviewed the country's economic recovery over the previous ten years and announced the end of recovery and beginning of a new era of economic growth.[14]

Japan's domestic factors aside, the international environment also aided in Japanese economic development. First, Washington was more than willing to share American science and technology with Japan. President Dwight Eisenhower (1953–1961) and his administration believed that a strong Japan was important and necessary for the United States to curb Communist expansion and influence in the Asian-Pacific region after the Korean War. The United States did not only make the new technologies available for Japan's industry, but also made its domestic market available for Japanese manufactured items such as toys, shoes, and clothing in the 1960s. The availability of the American market was vital to Japanese products, both because of mass consumption in America, and the introduction of good-quality and low-cost Japanese manufactured items. Soon Japan expanded the exports and moved far beyond cheap manufacturing by including plastic products, polymers, and automobiles. The United States became Japan's single most important trading partner, and Japan became the manufacturing leader of Asia, with its exports increasing dramatically throughout the 1950s.[15]

Tokyo continued its government control of exports and imports during the 1960s, favoring importing new technology and avanced machinery and protecting domestic industry by limiting similar foreign imports. Eventually, in 1960, the Japanese government issued the Free Trade and Exchange Outlines, lifting some of the governmental controls over imports and opening part of the domestic market for foreign goods. Subsequently, Japan joined the GATT (General Agreement on Tariffs and Trade) in 1963 and IMF (International Monetary Funds) in 1964. Its exports increased from

---

12   Mikiso Hane, *Eastern Phoenix: Japan since 1945* (Boulder, CO: Westview, 1996), 100.

13   Edwin Reischauer, *Japan: The Story of a Nation*, 4th ed. (New York: McGraw-Hill, 1990), 229–30.

14   Sachiko Hirakawa, "Japan Living in and with Asia," in *Regional Community Building in East Asia*, eds. Lee Lai To and Zarina Othman (London, UK: Routledge, 2017), chapter 12.

15   Beasley, *The Rise of Modern Japan*, 245–6.

$2 billion in 1955 to $8.45 billion in 1965, with Asia and Europe taking up 28.4 percent and 14.4 percent of Japan's exports, respectively. Between 1956 and 1964, Japan's exports had an average annual growth rate of 13.5 percent, higher than any other Western country.[16]

New Political Culture and Demographic Changes (1950s–1970s)

In 1955 several conservative political parties formed the Liberal Democratic Party (LDP, *Jiyu Minshuto*) to control national politics as the majority party against the left-wing groups. Yoshida was chosen as its first chairman. The LDP was the party in power from the 1950s until the 1990s. It emphasized free enterprise, the expansion of foreign trade, government aid to small business, and close relations with the United States and Europe. Nevertheless, James L. McClain points out that:

> Organizationally the LDP functioned as a party of factions. Throughout its political heyday, a half of a dozen or so major alliances jockeyed with one another for influence. Each faction constituted a separate entity that raised its own campaign funds, promoted the careers of its members, negotiated with other factions for control of high party and cabinet posts, and rotated the office of prime minister among themselves.[17]

Thereafter, the LDP dominated the Diet until 1993. As a conservative party, LDP usually gained two-thirds of the popular vote in the elections from the 1950s to the 1980s. The Japan Socialist Party (JSP, *Shakaito*) emphasized nationalization of major industries and expanded social welfare. The party also favored a policy of neutrality in foreign affairs.

Groups that broke away from those two founded other parties in the 1960s–1970s, following middle-of-the-road policies.[18]

In politics, the country continued to witness one-party domination (the LDP). According to the representation in the Diet, the majority political parties in the 1990s were the LDP, JSP, the Clean Government Party (*Komeito*), the Democratic Socialist Party (DSP), and the Communist Party of Japan (CPJ). According to the 1947 Constitution, the Diet is the supreme organ of government power and sole law-making body of the country. As a bicameral body, it consists of the House of Representatives (lower house) with 480 members and the House of Councilors (upper house) with 242 members. Elected by universal suffrage, the representatives serve for four-year terms, while the upper house members serve for six-year terms. Elections for one-half of the membership are held every three years in Japan. The lower house is the more powerful of the two since it retains control over legislation, dealing with treaties, and the national budget. It can also veto the decisions made by the upper house by a two-thirds majority. In the 1950s, the one-party control, historically referred to as the 1955 System, provided a new political stability in Japan. Hane and Perez conclude, "The LDP's dominance of the political world did not translate into a monopoly of power. Intraparty factionalism kept the LDP from becoming a steamrolling power machine. The presence of major factions made compromises and mutual accommodations necessary."[19]

Economic development and political stability during the two decades after WWII gave the Japanese public renewed confidence and optimism in their country, which was reinforced by Tokyo's successful hosting of the 1964 summer Olympic Games.

---

16 McClain, *Japan*, 572–3.

17 Ibid., 565.

18 Reischauer, *Japan*, 294–6.

19 Hane and Perez, *Modern Japan*, 391.

This was a dramatic juncture for the nation, which had survived almost total destruction at the end of the war in 1945 and an occupation by foreign forces in 1945–1951. It was the first such international recognition for the Rising-sun nation in history. The International Olympic Committee decision galvanized Japan. Tokyo spent billions of dollars to construct ultra-modern Olympic facilities in Tokyo. Being eager to fully exploit the rare opportunity and showcase Japanese ingenuity and accomplishments, Japan poured in resources to make the Olympics a showcase. The 1964 Tokyo Olympics helped elevate the prestige of industrial Japan worldwide. The island nation had staged the games with unparalleled grandeur and professionalism.

Unlike their forbearers in the nineteenth century who procrastinated in opening their country to the outside world, contemporary Japanese leaders were anxious to exhibit their progress and success to the international community. McClain concludes that "most Japanese treasured the Olympic experience as a time of national bonding, a shining moment when the nation came together to affirm its political, economic, and spiritual recovery from the horrors of war and defeat."[20] Remarkably, their fast-paced economic development was accomplished without incurring the social dislocation that often accompanied the process of industrialization in the West.

Japan has also experienced unprecedented demographic changes during its transformation into a modern society. First, the generation from the 1950s to the 1970s witnessed the establishment and growth of a middle class. After twenty years of economic growth, more Japanese citizens have improved their standard of living and moved up to the social middle. The developing middle class included engineers, managers, specialists, professional technicians, legal service staff, business administrators, and private business owners.

Secondly, education has transformed the postwar society by narrowing the gap between the masses and social elite. The number of all school-age children in high schools increased from 43 percent in 1950 to 93 percent in 1975, totaling 4.3 million in that year. In 1950 about eighty-four thousand students enrolled in colleges, only 8 percent of the college-age population. By 1975 about 1.7 million students enrolled in colleges, more than 44 percent of the college-age total. By that time, the social and educational gap between the elite and masses had largely disappeared. Moreover, almost 90 percent of the Japanese people defined themselves as middle class.[21]

Thirdly, Japan became highly urbanized after the war, when more than 50 percent of Japanese citizens lived in the cities. The economic recovery in the 1950s generated a substantial portion of capital for the urbanization. The rapid expansion of manufacturing opened up a large labor market in the 1960s. During that decade, many rural laborers migrated to the cities seeking work. Among the major cities were Tokyo, Yokohama, Osaka, Nagoya, Sapporo, Kobe, Kyoto, and Fukuoka. In 1972 one of every nine Japanese citizens lived in Tokyo, and one out of four lived in the Tokyo-Osaka industrial belt. As the result of the urbanization, the physical setting in rural Japan had begun to change by the 1960s. Factories were built in rural areas to take advantage of cheaper labor costs. Japan's agriculture had lost its workforce, young and new farming laborers, to factory jobs. The number of farm families decreased from 6 million in 1960 to 5.67 million in 1965, and again to 4.95 million in 1975. In the 1970s farming in Japan became an enterprise for profit, not subsistence. As a result, the average annual farm family

---

20 McClain, *Japan*, 564.
21 Reischauer, *Japan*, 233–4.

income increased from $1,143 in 1960 to $11,086 in 1975.[22]

Fourthly, as a social consequence of urbanization, the status of women rose. Nearly all girls received primary education, while most girls went to high school and many to college. The legal rights of women increasingly became accepted. The government passed several major pieces of legislation to protect women's rights and improve their social and economic status. For example, the Diet passed the Equal Employment Opportunities Law (EEOL) in 1986, the Tax Exemption Act for Low-income Females in 1988, and Leave Laws in 1992. The cabinet also created the Gender Equality Council, which oversaw and enforced the regulations and labor standard. In 1993 the first sexual harassment suit was tried in court. By the 1990s, Japanese women occupied more than 50 percent of teaching jobs, 32 percent of government employment, and 16 percent of medical, legal, and engineering occupations. About 14 percent of CEOs, high-ranking managers, and board directors were women, while 9 percent of elected Diet members were women.[23]

Fifthly, a significant social change in postwar Japan that distinguished it from China and most other nations in Asia was the decline in the population growth rate. After 1950 the overall rate of increase in Japan's population had been stabilized, with a total of 72 million people in 1945, 89 million in 1955, 98 million in 1965, 112 million in 1975, and 120 million in 1990. During the same period, China's population had increased from 400 million in 1945 to 800 million in 1965, and to 1,200 million in 1990.[24] Multiple factors contributed to Japan's demographic stability. The improvement of medical care enhanced people's lives and the life expectancy; advancement in education for women led to later marriages and fewer children; and general concerns of the negative impact of overpopulation on economic growth compelled the Japanese population to engage in conscientious family planning.

Economic Superpower (1965–1988)

From 1965 to 1975, Japan experienced rapid economic growth through its export-oriented manufacturing. After the completion of the transitional era, Japan entered a new period of development and growth with many new economic programs of its own. In 1965 Japan's GNP doubled, increasing to $88 billion with per capita GNP of $898. By 1970 Japan more than doubled its annual GNP to $203 billion, and its per capita GNP reached $1,939. By 1975 the Japanese GNP had doubled again to $484 billion with a per capita GNP of $4,320. By the same year, Japan had obtained a productivity level comparable to that of Europe.[25]

Japan's export-oriented manufacturing provided many job opportunities in the 1960s and had a strong impact on demographic changes. Among the major areas of the economic growth, it was the automobile industry that took the lead in the country's manufacturing during the 1960s–1970s. Japan manufactured 8,000 passenger cars in 1955. It produced 165,000 cars in the year of 1960. Its manufacturing of passenger cars totaled 3,178,000 in 1970 and increased to 6,176,000 in 1975.[26] Among the major reasons behind Japan's economic growth during this time period were the Japanese government's economic policies, an educated work force, international trade opportunities, and technological aid from the U.S.

22   Beasley, *The Rise of Modern Japan*, 259.

23   Gordon, "Society and Politics from Trans-war through Post-war Japan," 273.

24   Li, *Modern China*, 19.

25   Henshall, *A History of Japan*, 168.

26   Huffman, *Modern Japan*, 198.

To compete in the international market, Japan's key industries, like steel, iron, petro-chemicals, and electronics, began to merge into giant corporations with mass production. The super-sized steel mills were completed with an annual production capacity of over 10 million tons of steel each after 1965. The huge steel complexes significantly increased the nation's steel products from 41 million tons in 1965 to 120 million tons in 1973. During the same period, other industries had also been super-sized, with the huge shipyards building 500,000-ton capacity ships, giant petro-chemical facilities producing 300,000 tons of ethylene and polythene annually per factory, and super power generators producing 500,000 kW of electricity annually per plant. Its heavy and chemical industries increased from 42.7 percent of the nation's industries in 1955, to 51.1 percent in 1965, and to 68.9 percent of total industry in 1970. By 1970 Japan became number one or two among the advanced countries in steel production, electric power production, automobile manufacturing, shipbuilding, and plastic production.[27]

While continuing to import new technologies from other advanced countries that numbered fifteen thousand between 1965 and 1973, Japan also began to focus on expanding its domestic research and development. It is true that Japan was, for the most part, a copier and reproducer of existing Western technologies in the early 1950s and an adapter and modifier in the late 1950s and early 1960s, but the country engaged in technological innovations at a global level in the late 1960s and early 1970s. From 1966 to 1973, research and development funds increased three times.[28] And by the early 1970s, there were twenty-one scientific researchers per every ten thousand Japanese people, the second highest research personnel rate in the world after

only the United States. Japan began to demonstrate its capacities for designing and producing relatively advanced new technologies and manufacturing systems, especially in high-quality home appliances, such as color televisions, watches, cameras, tape recorders, and electron microscopes with high magnifications. Japan appeared to have strong potential indigenous technological capabilities to compete with the advanced countries including the United States. By the early 1970s, Japan's productive quality had become one of the best in the world. The perfectionization of manufacturing also improved labor productive efficiency with an increase of 12.4 percent between 1966 and 1973.[29]

Japan's export trade continued to grow rapidly in 1966–1973. After 1965 Japan had maintained a surplus in its international trade with most trading partners in the world including the United States. Its exportation totaled $8.32 billion in 1965 with a surplus of $1.9 billion that year. By 1972 its exportation had increased to $28.03 billion, more than triple that of 1965, with a surplus of $8.97 billion, more than four times that of 1965. Among the major exports, industrial items increased rapidly from 62.4 percent of the total exports in 1965, to 73 percent in 1970, and up to 84 percent of the total exports in 1977.[30] The steady growth of trade surplus brought in a huge amount of hard currency to Japan and increased the nation's gold reserves. The international status of Japanese yen improved, and its strong financial status had made Japan a wealthy country with a huge capital surplus and many overseas investment opportunities. In 1961 Japan's overseas investment totaled $381 million. Its total foreign investment increased to $1,066.8 million in 1965 with a majority of the investments in textile, mining, and chemical industry in the

---

27 Huffman, *Modern Japan*, 166.

28 McClain, *Japan*, 575.

29 Huffman, *Modern Japan*, 188.

30 Henshall, *A History of Japan*, 167.

Third World countries in Asia, Africa, and Latin America.[31] After the 1970s, however, Japanese direct investments entered the United States and other industrialized countries in Europe.

Remarkably, Japan maintained balanced development in 1966–1973 between agriculture and industry; between the big corporations and small- and medium-sized factories; and between manufacturing and service industries. With a rapid growth of industry, Japanese farmers lost two-thirds of their labor force to the industry in the 1960s. The farming labor decreased from 41 percent of the entire labor force in 1955, went down to 24.6 percent in 1965, and continued to decrease to only 13.8 percent of the national total by 1975. Nevertheless, the Japanese government continued to advance the agriculture sector and support local farmers. In 1961 the Basic Agricultural Laws were promulgated, increasing farmers' loans and governmental subsidies. By 1973 Japanese agriculture had modernized, with machineries, new irrigation systems, and fertilization.[32] In the industrial sector, small- and medium-sized companies were threatened by the formation of huge conglomerates in the 1950s. The government modified industrial structure during the merging and supersizing of the late 1960s so that the small- and medium-sized companies operated as satellites around the large enterprises to provide parts, service, and supportive roles. Through the reorganization, these small- and medium-sized companies became cooperative and enjoyed mutual benefit with the large enterprises. They enjoyed an average annual increase of their production of more than 17 percent between 1966 and 1973. During the same period, Japan's service industries, including public utilities, transportation and communication, finance and banking, commerce and retails, and medical and legal services, also had a tremendous development. The total service labor force increased from 35.1 percent in 1955, to 43.4 percent in 1965, and up to 52.1 percent of the national total labor force in 1975.

Last but not the least, Japan's minimum spending on its defense through the Cold War because of the protective American "nuclear umbrella" and mutual defense treaty contributed to Japan's economic advancement, even though the country had established a small armed force, the Self Defense Forces (including army, naval, and air forces), in 1954. The cost of this force was very low, about 1 percent of Japan's GNP through the 1960s to the 1980s. In 1974, for example, Japan spent only $1.9 billion on its defense, while the United States spent $63.3 billion, the Soviet Union $61.9 billion, and West Germany $7.8 billion. The Japanese Self Defense Forces were not deployed outside Japan until the First Persian Gulf War in 1991.[33]

The annual average Japanese GNP growth rate remained at 10.5 percent between 1966 and 1973. After its GNP exceeded the British and French in 1967, it went ahead of that of Germany in 1968, becoming the third largest economy in the world only after the United States and the Soviet Union. Its economy in 1973 was as much as 2.4 times that of 1964. By 1980 Japan's annual GNP consisted of 13.3 percent of the world total among the industrial countries, and it became the second largest economy in the world only after the United States. In 1985 Japan's GNP totaled $1,329 billion, compared to $3,988 billion for the United States, $2,063 billion for the Soviet Union, $354 billion for China, and $190 billion for India. In 1988 Japan's GNP increased to $2,792 billion, and its per capita GNP was higher than the equivalent American figure.[34]

---

31   Gordon, "Society and Politics from Trans-war through Post-war Japan," 262.

32   Beasley, *The Rise of Modern Japan*, 255.

33   Huffman, *Modern Japan*, 192; Henshall, *A History of Japan*, 155–6.

34   Gordon, "Society and Politics from Trans-war through Post-war Japan," 294.

It should be noted that Japan's economic growth has not been entirely steady because of its energy dependence on foreign oil and natural gas. Japan's energy system shifted from coal production to oil importation and consumption, and in the early 1950s, oil production experienced tremendous development in the Middle East, while the United States and other oil-importing countries were able to control the oil price for their low-cost importation. Since the cost of importing oil from the Middle East was lower than producing coal in Japan, the country began to import crude oil and change its energy consumption structure. In 1956 coal consumption consisted of more than 50 percent of the nation's energy total, while oil was only 21.9 percent. However, by 1964, oil consumption increased to 55.7 percent of the nation's total, while coal decreased to 29.2 percent.[35] Oil importation helped keep the cost of production low, and supported the petro-chemical, shipbuilding, steel, iron, and harbor construction industries. The 1973 Oil Crisis, in which the Arab countries in OPEC (Organization of the Petroleum Exporting Countries) placed an oil embargo against the United States and its allies for their support of Israel, had an adverse impact on Japan. The dramatic rise of oil prices from three to eleven dollars a barrel was a wake-up call for the oil-dependent Japanese industries and caused a temporary slow-down of their growth. More importantly, Japan quickly adapted to the new international environment in the late 1970 and early 1980s by reorienting its economic policies, initiating conservation programs, switching to the manufacturing of small and light products that were less dependent on oil, and developing passenger cars with much higher gas mileage than their American counterparts.

As stated previously, the combination of governmental policies, social and cultural factors, and a favorable international climate, especially the easy availability of American technology and markets, along with the promise of military protection, collectively propelled Japan's phenomenal growth. Ironically, the American efforts at restoring Japan's economic power and enhancing its profile in Asia, which were largely due to Cold War calculations, would later backfire. By the 1980s, a rising Japan was perceived as a threat to American economic supremacy. Notably, the "economic miracle" transformed the country into a world-class economic power. The Japanese people, proud of their heritage and conscious of their newfound economic muscle, desired for their country to claim a more prominent place in world affairs. While Japan's close alliance with the United States had paid dividends in that Washington seemed eager to restore Japan's power status in East Asia and Western Pacific, much to the dismay and irritation to China, the Koreas, and Vietnam. Ironically, such a stand seemed to backfire by the 1980s as growing trade imbalance led to increasing frictions between Tokyo and Washington.

New Foreign Policy and Japan-US Relations (1965–1988)

For Japan, as for most other East Asian countries during the Cold War, foreign policy developed within the nuclear balance between the United States and the Soviet Union. Edwin Reischauer and Craig Albert point out that "throughout this era and beyond, the central principle of Japan's foreign policy was to maintain close ties to the United States."[36] Washington had made efforts to persuade Japan and South Korea to come to a settlement in

---

35 Xiaobing Li and Michael Molina, "Japan," in *Oil: A Cultural and Geographic Encyclopedia of Black Gold*, eds. Xiaobing Li and Michael Molina (Santa Barbara, CA: ABC-CLIO, 2014), vol. 2: 563–9.

36 Edwin Reischauer and Craig Albert, *Japan: Tradition and Transformation*, revised ed. (Boston, MA: Houghton Mifflin, 1989), 314.

the 1950s to complete the normalization of the Japan-Korean relations. As discussed in chapter five, this was vital to America's strategic interests in East Asia. Moreover, as South Korea remained far from reaching a self-sustaining economy, Washington was eager to share the cost with an increasingly prosperous Japan. In a sense, the United States was anxious to relinquish its role as South Korea's sole financial supporter. Thus, Washington actively pursued an avenue for placing South Korea under the joint custody of the Unites States and Japan. On the other hand, Japan was hardly in a position to overlook Washington's wish, as its rapidly expanding industrial economy needed continued access to the vast consumer market as well as the capital and technology pool in America.

The Eisaku Sato administrations (1964–1972) desired to resolve the unpleasant past by opening a new chapter of neighborly cooperation. The Japanese were anxious to secure the Korean market for their industrial products. They were also observant of the opportunity to exploit South Korea's abundant and highly educated labor force. Aggressive business leaders of both countries exerted pressure on their respective governments for an early conclusion of normalization talks in 1964. The ensuing developments proved that the judgement of these business communities was generally correct and justifiable. By 1965 the treaty was concluded between the two countries, and Japan normalized its diplomatic relationship with South Korea. Japanese business reentered the Korean market after twenty years, since it was forced to withdraw from the peninsula at the end of the Pacific War.

Japan made major changes in its foreign policy-making in the late 1960s and early 1970 after the Nixon shock in 1969 and the first oil shock in 1973. After winning the election of 1968, President Richard Nixon carried out his new policy toward the Vietnam War, including Vietnamization, to build up the South Vietnamese armed forces so that American forces could withdraw, as he had promised to the American voters during his presidential campaign, without the Communists overrunning the South. In his Guam Doctrine, or the Nixon Doctrine, the president asked all the American allies, including Japan, to take on a greater role in or increase their responsibility for regional defense against Communist aggression. Historians likely agree that Japan exploited the opportunity offered by the US alliance system to pursue improved relations with the Communist states like China.[37] Glenn D. Hook, Julie Gilson, Christopher W. Hughes, and Hugo Dobson point out that "what is more, Japanese policy-makers became less consistent in following U.S. foreign policy goals as the strength of U.S. global hegemony began to wane and multi-polarity in the international system started to wax in the early 1970s."[38]

Although there was a fear among Japanese that the United States might use Japan as a bargaining chip for a Sino-American rapprochement, the Japanese government moved forward to improve its relations with Communist China. Following Washington's policy toward the Beijing, Japan had established diplomatic relations with Taiwan but not mainland China since 1949. In 1952 Yoshida signed a peace treaty with the Taiwanese government since the latter was not among the forty-six signatories of the peace treaty at San Francisco in 1951. In the 1960s the economic and cultural relations between Tokyo and Beijing improved when trade began between the two countries. Then, Japan voted with the United States in the UN for replacing Taiwan with China in 1970 and 1971.

Although Tokyo was "completely caught off guard" in the summer of 1971 when Washington suddenly announced Nixon's plan to visit Beijing

---

37   Chalmers Johnson, *Japan: Who Governs? The Rise of the Developmental State* (New York: W. W. Norton, 1995), 235–63.

38   Hook, Gilson, Hughes, and Dobson, *Japan's International Relations*, 33.

in February 1972, Japanese leaders followed suit quickly.[39] In that September, only months after Nixon's visit to Beijing, Japan and China established a formal diplomatic relationship. (The diplomatic relationship between Beijing and Washington was not established until January 1, 1979.) Trade between China and Japan increased from $1.1 billion in 1972 to $3.8 billion in 1975.[40] The trading amount between the two countries in 1975 was 25 percent of China's total foreign trade. Reischauer and Albert point out that "China was attracted by Japanese technology but had little to offer in return and it was reluctant to be simply a supplier of oil and other raw materials."[41] Then, the two countries went further and signed a peace treaty of friendship and mutual cooperation in 1978. When China's "Reform and Opening" process began to unfold in the late 1970s and early 1980s, Japan was the first among all major industrial/capitalist countries to provide China with substantial technological and financial support.

Within the context of President Richard Nixon's détente policy and the withdrawal of American forces from Southeast Asia in 1972–1973, Tokyo received the new doctrine with mixed emotions. In 1972 the United States returned administrative control of Okinawa and the Ryukyu Islands to Japan. In the same year, Nixon visited Beijing to carry out the Nixon Doctrine; he was the first US president to visit the Communist state since its founding in 1949. The Nixon Doctrine was born against the backdrop of political uncertainty in East Asia. By then the United States was not expected to achieve a clean victory in Vietnam; the nation with the most modern weaponry and tactics but which was politically divided and unsure of its mission in the region failed to subjugate the ill-equipped but determined North Vietnamese forces. Confronted by the prospect of a long military stalemate and worsening antiwar sentiments at home, the Nixon administration was anxious to end the war by withdrawing its forces. Such a policy change affected Nixon's decision to reach out to the Chinese, but it also caused consternation and a sense of betrayal among the Japanese. Another abrupt shift in US policy was the imposition of a 10 percent surcharge on Japanese exports, which is sometimes referred to as a second Nixon shock. Kenneth Henshall points out that "the Nixon Shocks were not as damaging as the Oil Shock, but they were disturbing to the Japanese. They clearly signaled a cooling in American attitudes and goodwill towards Japan. Nevertheless, Japan rode them all out, and by the end of the 1970s many Japanese were starting to wonder if they needed American good will anyway."[42]

The Japanese government's close tie to the United States came with some inherent risks. Japan's foreign relations are intimately bound up with its economic ups and downs. The major change in its foreign policy took place in the early 1970s. Japan was admitted as a full member to the Asian Development Bank and then to the International Development Bank. The United States sponsored Japan's reentry into the UN and World Bank. In April 1973, in a major speech in New York, Henry Kissinger, then secretary of the state in the Nixon administration, proposed "a new Atlantic Charter." Arguably, without the US patronage, it would have been more difficult for Japan to become a member of these important international organizations. In addition, as explained previously, the American consumer market as well as its technological aid and military protection of Japan all contributed to Japan's sustainable economic growth.

---

39   Hane and Perez, *Modern Japan*, 401.

40   Gordon, "Society and Politics from Trans-war through Post-war Japan," 264; Henshall, *A History of Japan*, 167.

41   Reischauer and Albert, *Japan*, 319.

42   Henshall, *A History of Japan*, 168.

However, the close Tokyo-Washington alliance also came with problems. More than anything else, it was complicated by the growing trade imbalance between the two countries. Japan's protectionist policies and intricate marketing network made it extremely difficult for American products to find inroads into the Japanese market. As the Japanese economy continued to surge ahead while the Unites States suffered periodic economic downturns, Japan's trade surplus began to rattle American politicians and the public. When Japanese companies, armed with seemingly infinite resources, went on a buying spree in the United States during the 1980s, Americans incurred a great deal of anxiety. A devalued yen and a strong dollar further boosted the Japanese buying power. Japanese purchases of factories, real estate, sports teams, and movie companies in the United States gave rise to not only economic resentment but also renewed racial tensions. A *New York Times* editorial in March 1981 pleaded, dripping sarcasm, "Please, Japan, Return the Favor: Occupy Us." In 1982 Vincent Chin, a young Chinese-American man, was severely beaten in a club brawl by two Chrysler employees who mistook him as Japanese, and he died as a result. The perpetrators reportedly blamed Chin for having stolen American automakers' jobs. Mutual distrust between Japan and United States grew, especially when Japanese cars took about one-third of the American automobile market by the mid-1980s. The Plaza Accord signed among the United States, Japan, and several European countries in 1985 pressured the Japanese government to raise the value of yen against the American dollar in order to make it cheaper for the Japanese to purchase American products. As it turned out, the accord became a double-edged sword. While it led to increased US exports to Japan, it also created "bargains" for the Japanese, companies and wealthy individuals alike, within the

Unites States, hence the continuing buying frenzy until the economic recession hit Japan in the early 1990s. Japan can share. The United States was Japan's largest single market and the source for most of its technology.

Social Changes and Economic Crisis (1980s–2000s)

The late 1970s saw the emergence of an era in Japan with a new and different character. McClain points out that "the unprecedented economic boom changed life dramatically for Japan's citizens."[43] In the late 1980s, the government changed policy so that Japanese people received more benefits from the nation's wealth, including improving public health, social welfare, and retirement.

The LDP enjoyed considerable popular support from the constituencies that received benefits from LDP legislation and domestic policies. In the early 1980s, however, more Japanese began to criticize LDP political dominance, personal networking, and scandal and corruption. Later in the decade, the party was beset by several exposed cases of corruption, including political bribery, sex scandals, and mismanagement. It was also undermined by the defection of a number of party elites who had been part of the political establishment. In the election of 1993, the LDP failed to gain the majority for the first time in thirty-eight years.[44] The New Party won a governing majority in the Diet, and its leader, Hosokawa Morihiro, assumed the position of the prime minister in 1993, thus ending LDP's dominance since 1955.

The debate within the conservative camp over how to position Japan to meet the challenges of the twenty-first century was gaining a great deal of steam. This debate was sparked by a new awareness that Japan could no longer look to foreign models

---

43 McClain, *Japan*, 572.
44 Gordon, "Society and Politics from Trans-war through Post-war Japan," 294; Beasley, *The Rise of Modern Japan*, 253–4.

and that henceforth it would have to define its own future goals. On January 7, 1989, Emperor Hirohito died. Having been emperor since 1926, he was the longest-reigning monarch in the nation's history.[45] Just as the death of Emperor Meiji that signified the end of a pivotal era, the passing of Hirohito also conveniently bracketed the end of Showa Japan, one that had witnessed wars, reconstruction, and phenomenal economic growth. His eldest son Akihito ascended the throne as Japan's 125th emperor, Emperor Heisei, on November 12, 1990.

The country had also experienced tremendous social changes from the 1970s to the 1990s. In the patterns of marriage, postwar changes reached into the eighties. In the early postwar period, most marriages were still arranged by go-betweens with the approval of the parents. This gave way in the 1960s and 1970s to "love marriages," in which the partners made their own arrangements, although sometimes asking an office superior or teacher to serve as an honorary go-between. During this time most young couples lived apart from their parents, and by the eighties almost four out of five marriages were of this new type. In addition, more and more women began opting to delay their marriage from the mid-twenties to the late twenties or early thirties due largely to their desire to stay longer in the work force, as many women are still expected to leave their jobs after marriage, especially after having children. The famed "M" curve still exists in that women's participation in the paid labor force is higher before marriage, declines after marriage and during their childbearing years, and then rises again when their children reach school age. Notably, in recent years, the Shino Abe administration has adopted policies to raise the female labor participation rate by encouraging gender equality in the work place and by extending the hours of daycare centers.

Enticing women to have a longer work life outside of the home sphere can partially help to remedy the existing problem of labor shortage. Population growth in Japan has been rather slow despite its economic prosperity, with the population increasing from about 122 million in the 1980s to 127 million presently. During the late 1980s, the Japanese were already living longer than any other peoples in the world; women had gained four years for an average lifespan of eighty-one years, and men's average lifespan had gone up by three years to seventy-five.[46]

Because WWII and the postwar baby boom affected the age distribution in Japan, the new longevity also portended a serious futue problem: at the turn of the century, Japan would have a higher percentage of nonworking old people than would any other country. The combination of a rapidly expanding economy and a slowly growing population produced a serious labor shortage in the late 1970s and early 1990s. A well-functioning national health care system notwithstanding, other forms of social welfare, including retirement benefits and elderly care, were still lacking. So much of Japan's economic surplus was put back into new investment that little remained for social programs. Welfare for the sick and old was minimal.

Another issue that confronted Japan for several decades after the war was its environmental problems. With the world's attention focused on China's air and water pollution in recent years, it is easy to overlook the fact that Japan wrestled with a similar predicament when the country was undergoing rapid economic development. By the 1980s the greatest domestic problem was pollution.

The social challenges aside, by far the biggest challenge facing Japan during the last quarter of a century has been its prolonged economic stagnation. As the Showa era ended in 1989, Japan soon found itself in an unexpected economic recession. In 1993

---

45   Herbert P. Bix, *Hirohito and the Making of Modern Japan* (New York: Perennial, 2000), 3.

46   Beasley, ibid., 253–4;

the production of four-wheeled vehicles fell by 12 percent and exports fell by over 18 percent, while Toyota announced a reduction in profits of nearly 35 percent in 1992.[47]

Some of the large companies began to move their manufacturing capacity to Japanese-owned factories overseas, the so-called "hollowing-out" of Japanese industry. These transfers were largely for the sake of market access: to circumvent the threats of protectionism directed from time to time against Japanese goods. They were accomplished most successfully in China and the countries of Southeast Asia, which found themselves able as a result not only to take over certain Japanese export markets but also to penetrate the Japanese market itself.

Another consequence of the Japanese economic downturn was that even the giants began labor cuts, including companies like the electronic powerhouse Hitachi, the computer titan Fujitsu, and the communications combine NTT. Traditional lifetime employment could no longer be guaranteed nor could pensions. Some companies even found it difficult to keep the retirement age at sixty-five. Increasingly they turned to a compulsory retiring age of sixty for men and fifty-five for women. The government also made new policies to reduce annual working hours to move Japan away from its reputation as a country of workaholics. However, many observers believed that the change was best explained by economic crisis. A report at the end of the 1990s showed no significant reduction in the number of employees who worked over sixty hours a week.

The government responses to recessions had usually been a series of economic rescue packages, designed to act as a stimulus to consumer spending. For example, in August 1992, the Miyazawa cabinet announced a spending program of 10,700 billion yen for public works, loans to small- and medium-sized business, and help to banks in disposing of real estate. In February 1994, the Hosokawa cabinet decided to stimulate the economy by spending 15,300 billion yen, including an income tax cut of 5,500 billion yen in the coming year.[48] After the mid-1990s, the government also began its "Restructuring and Deregulation" policy, which was to reduce the government intervention in business such as to give less protection to Japanese firms in the domestic market and open it more fully to foreign goods. The new policy would break down some of the traditional relationship between business and government.

Then, in the second half of the 1990s, a major economic crisis swept Asian countries and to some extent, Japan bored the brunt of further economic decline. Before the crisis of 1997 and 1998, Asia had been known for the robustness of its economy, its high exports, its attractiveness to foreign investors, and its increasing wages. Rather than being the darling of capitalists, Asia faltered in 1997 and 1998. In 1996 and 1997 industrial productivity fell 50 percent in Thailand. These years suggest that the Asian Economic Crisis may have begun in Thailand. In 1997 Thailand had a $10 billion deficit, though by December, possibly through austerity, it reduced its deficit to $40 million. In 1997 in Thailand, the sale of cars, steel, electronics and other goods fell between 35 and 75 percent. By 1998 unemployment stood at 6 percent. In 1997 and 1998 South Korean businesses went bankrupt, pushing unemployment upward. In November 1998 South Korea posted 5 percent unemployment, a high number for this country. In 1998 South Korean GNP weakened by 6.7 percent. Indonesia's GNP fell 13 percent in 1998, and its stock market plummeted by as much as 84 percent. In 1998 unemployment increased the number of poor Indonesians from twenty-three

---

47 Beasley, *The Rise of Modern Japan*, 285–6.

48 Gordon, "Society and Politics from Trans-war through Post-war Japan," 294.

million to forty million. Overall, the collective GDP declined 7 percent in East Asia in 1998.[49]

Japan saw its GDP fall additional 2 percent in that year. In the late 1990s, the country's trade surplus became smaller, as imports grew faster than exports. The changing balance sheet of Japanese trade also resulted from a series of diplomatic attempts to reduce the bilateral trade imbalance between Japan and the United States under the Bush and Clinton administrations. Some agreements in principle to increase Japanese purchases in automobiles and auto parts had been reached. Automobiles and auto parts were the largest item in dispute between the two countries, since they were accounting for about two-thirds of America's $60–80 billion annual trade deficits from the 1980s to the 2000s.

As a result, business culture and social value continued to change through the 2000s. For several decades Japan's economic success had rested on the manufacturing of high-quality goods at low prices through mass production and heavy investment in technology. The achievements were also made possible by the so-called "company-centered" approach that emphasized long working hours, low dividends, and restrictive arrangements between employees and management. In the 2000s, attitudes changed among workers, especially the young people, who were no longer wholly satisfied with a workaholic way of life. The country went through a grave period from the 2000s–2010s, when instability in the energy market and financial system came to the surface. In 2000 Japan's GNP stood at 511 trillion yen ($4.7 trillion), while that of the United States was $9 trillion. In the same year, its per capita GNP was $37,560, and the United States' was $33,000.[50] The 2011 Tohoku earthquake and tsunami hit Japan's economic recovery from the 2000s recession, and China replaced Japan as the second largest economy in the world in 2012.

Two Koreas

When Vietnam and China underwent revolutionary reforms and transformations, Kim Il-Sung's North Korea greeted the emerging political reality in the Socialist and Communist world with typical disdain. Naturally, the dictatorial regime, which had pursued the highly unrealistic dream of building a socialist paradise with the self-sufficient *Juche* idea, saw the revolutions in Eastern European countries as more of a threat than a benevolent transformation. Having enforced rigid political regimentation for most of the post-Korean War period, the Kim regime harbored an intense fear of reforms that might eventually cause its own demise. Categorically rejecting the seemingly irresistible currency of wholesale reforms in the Communist camp, the North Korean leadership elected to continue the course maintained for decades, namely its own brand of isolated socialism. It showed no inclination of modifying its dictatorial leadership, which was characterized by the intense personality cult of Kim Il-sung and his family.

Nothing is more characteristic of Kim's old-fashioned politics than his succession scheme. From the early 1970s Kim undertook various political maneuvers to gain a legal as well as political sanction to designate his son Kim Jong-Il, a man known for limited experience and unknown leadership quality, as his successor. The elder Kim's archaic succession scheme, deftly packaged on the pretext of "carrying through the revolution generation after generation," was to ensure the survival of his political legacy. His scheme to perpetuate his family's political monopoly encountered little domestic resistance, at least in

---

49   Walter Jung, "Asia's Crisis and New Opportunity," in *Asia's Crisis and New Paradigm*, eds. Walter Jung and Xiaobing Li (Lanham, MD: University Press of America, 2000), 1–3.

50   Henshall, *A History of Japan*, 173–4.

public. Kim's brutal politics in treating potential opponents may have been the primary reason for this apparent acquiescence. As early as 1974 North Korea's Kim dynasty was already operational; Kim Jong-Il took over the daily operation of the Workers' Party but under his father's close supervision. Nevertheless, the elder Kim continued a relentless, highly organized campaign to consolidate his son's political power throughout the 1970s. Gradually, Kim Jong-Il succeeded his father as the leader of North Korea. His ascendancy, although he was unable to claim the presidency outright, greatly benefitted from the fact that there was no political faction in North Korea capable of foiling the succession scheme the two Kims worked on for so long and so hard. Kim Jong-Il in the North-South equation presented a dimension that was quite different from the one his father represented.

After General Park Chung Hee was elected as the fifth president of the ROK (Republic of Korea) in 1963, the political tasks facing South Korea were formidable, even for the highly dedicated and energetic president. In addition to the nation's faltering economy, which demanded not only immediate but also comprehensive attention, the new administration had to confront several major tasks in both domestic and international areas. Foremost, it had to devise a long-term strategy for the ever-present military threat of North Korea. In foreign relations, it had to revise its relations with the United States to fit the evolving international political climate. The new government faced such intimidating problems without matching national strength. Moreover, it could expect no outpouring of international goodwill form the Western community, to which South Korea remained a hermit kingdom representing nothing but bitter memories of the war and poverty.

First of all, as discussed in chapter seven, the Park administration normalized its relations with Japan in 1965. One of the most compelling factors that helped complete the normalization of the Japan-Korea relationship was the strong political pressure exerted by the United States. In the meantime, Seoul also answered the Johnson administration's call for a military coalition in Vietnam and sent two infantry divisions and one marine brigade, the second largest foreign force among those participating in the coalition, to the Vietnam War in 1965. Nevertheless, Park's priority went to building an industrial infrastructure for a self-sustained, growth-oriented economy. His plan called for extensive utilization of foreign input, including capital, raw materials, and technology. To facilitate the free movement of capital and technology, he initiated many new fiscal policies, including participation in GATT and the adjustment of exchange rates. The government was mobilizing every available resource to accelerate the nation's economic revitalization. South Korea's economy entered its taking-off stage by the late 1960s. Led by Park's focused leadership, it undertook a rapid import-substitution drive as its export-led industrial expansion was shaping up. During this period, multinational corporations started to enter the South Korean market, providing the domestic economy with a growing influx of foreign capital and technology transfer. The nation's industrial development proceeded at such a rate and scope that it even changed the people's pessimistic attitude. The new promising chapter of a modern, industrial Korea was beginning to unfold. By the 1970s the South Korean export economy had passed its incubation period and entered the world market, concentrating on its strategic sector of labor intensive, low technology products.

The close US-South Korea collaboration in Vietnam and their warm bilateral relations encountered a sudden chill in 1971 with the Nixon Doctrine, which included the withdrawal of the remaining US ground forces from South Korea. The full implementation of the doctrine meant that the US East Asian policy was undergoing a fundamental shift; no longer could any nation expect a full and automatic intervention by US forces against Communist aggression in the region. Under the framework of "Asian defense by Asian forces," the Nixon administration was willing to offer its Asian allies only logistical support. South Koreans had not expected the American forces to become a permanent fixture of the Korean landscape. Yet they earnestly wished the US military to remain until the ROK military completed an extensive modernization program, which was needed to strengthen its still inadequately equipped forces to a level at which they could face the North's forces alone. The modernization of ROK forces, a pledge that the Johnson administration made in 1965, had not progressed much by 1969. Over Seoul's protest, Washington had withdrawn its twenty thousand troops from South Korea by early 1971. The withdrawal forced the ROK army to assume the defense of the entire western front along the DMZ, thus making almost a complete front defense by South Korea itself. The United States left one last combat division as a symbol of its security commitment over the peninsula.

In many ways, the 1971 presidential election was an epochal point in South Korea's political maturity. For the first time in history, the government permitted open political forums, although in a limited fashion. It even engaged in a public discussion of the merits of nationalistic unification, the notion that the nation should undertake steps toward the unification process unfettered by political ideology. The new approach represented a radical departure from the stereotypical ideological unification in each side's image. The main opposition candidate, Kim Dae-Jung, insisted that national unification was feasible not by military means but by the political guaranty of the four powers, namely China, Japan, the United States, and the Soviet Union. Kim's bold idea was, in spirit, compatible with Nixon's East Asian approach, which argued that the justified interests of the four powers be respected. Although his progressive proposal was largely

election material, that such a revolutionary idea surfaced in a nation where extreme rightists prevailed was a significant development.

On July 4, 1972, the governments in Seoul and Pyongyang simultaneously issued an extraordinary joint communique. In it both governments declared that they would seek national unification in a spirit of independence, peaceful unification, and greater national unity. However, intermittent talks that followed the joint communique produced no tangible results. Neither the North nor the South was ready to negotiate anything of substantial value. Talks did not even contribute to the stability of the peninsula's military confrontation. Dialogue served the political purpose of the dictatorial regimes on both sides of the DMZ. President Park's most profound contribution to his country was his successful expansion and upgrading of the nation's defense industry before he was assassinated by his security chief on October 26, 1979.

After the assassination of the president, South Korea experienced the installation of the Yushin Constitution, the Kwangju uprising of 1980, and General Chun Doo Hwan's election of 1981. Walter B. Jung states, "General Chun added another sad chapter to South Korea's already tainted history of political transition, one that had earned the hermit kingdom a much- disparaged reputation in the eyes of the world community."[51] Like General Park, President Chun exploited the public's fear of weakening national defense and their desire to continue the nation's economic expansion. These two overriding concerns still remained decisive, although it was debatable whether they were sufficient to give Chun an excuse for dashing the nation's long-standing desire to move toward the democratization of the political process. Contrary to its generally negative political image, the Chun administration provided focused leadership in the nation's drive for economic development. During President Chun's tenure the

---

51   Walter B. Jung, *Nation Building: The Geopolitical History of Korea* (Lanham, MD: University Press of America, 1998), 319.

nation experienced its first true economic buoyancy, illustrated in the milestone of its first current account surplus in 1986. Under the guidance of the Chun regime the exuberant export sector spearheaded the nation's hyperactive economic expansion. On December 16, 1987, South Korea held its first direct presidential election in sixteen years. Then, in 1992, the nation elected Kim Young Sam as its president, the first nonmilitary president in three decades.

By the mid-1980s, South Korea had made further adjustments in its export economy. It reduced its heavy export dependence on predominantly low-technology, labor intensive products by expanding the strategic export sectors to medium-technology, capital intensive products, including automobiles, electronics, and supertankers. The country recorded its first trade surplus in 1986–1988 when its exports grew at a phenomenal rate of 26 percent per year. Its total export reached $60 billion with a positive trade balance of over $11 billion in 1988. In the meantime, it also reduced its export dependency on the US market from 35 percent of its total international trade in 1988 to 30 percent in 1990. Its stable export performance during the 1980s and early 1990s was largely responsible for the nation reaching its economic objectives: a high growth rate with price stability and a current account surplus. It also secured a coveted place among a small bank of nations by being recognized as one of the newly industrialized countries and one of four of Asia's economic "tigers" (Hong Kong, Taiwan, and Singapore).

The IOC (International Olympic Committee) decision to award the 1988 summer Olympic Games to Seoul galvanized South Koreans. The Seoul Olympics helped elevate the prestige of industrial South Korea worldwide. The government and Korean people were eager to show their progress and success to the international community. They were sanguine about their accomplishment of conquering age-old poverty and rebuilding the nation over devastated war ruins in less than three decades. They were proud of their "Miracle of the Han River." The games were overwhelmed by the far-reaching political ramifications of the participation of the People's Republic of China, which sent a large delegation to Seoul unhampered by the lack of diplomatic relations between the two nations. It was the Communist giant's first open indication that it was serious in upgrading its relations with South Korea. The Chinese participation totally eclipsed North Korea's absence from the games and was the first tangible success for South Korea's persistent pursuit of nonpolitical contacts with China.

Entering the 1990s, South Korea's export economy was performing at a pace that should enable the hermit kingdom to achieve the desired status of a mature industrial power.[52] In the late 1980s South Korea agreed to accommodate the increasingly vocal demands of its major trading partners. As a step toward free trade, it reduced the rate of import protection by 95 percent in 1988 and by 98 percent by 1990 to open domestic markets to foreign goods. The Uruguay Round and the GATT negotiation of 1994 opened the nation's strategic domestic market to foreign products. Another historic shift in the international arena, inaugurated by China's experimentation with a market economy, and a bold initiative of Soviet president Gorbachev, provided further momentum to South Korea's drive. In 1990 South Korea's two-way trade with the East bloc countries and China reached $5 billion, recording a yearly growth rate of over 23 percent. Its trade with China had grown to $10 billion by 1994, making China South Korea's third largest trading partner.

Nowadays most South Koreans live in cities, where crowded space makes it difficult to maintain

---

52   The state-run Korea Institute for International Economic Policy (KIEP) reported that by 1996, South Korea's total trade had reached $240 billion, making the nation one of the world's top ten trade nations.

the structure of an extended family. As a result, the so-called "nuclear family" has long become the norm. Meanwhile, the traditional arranged marriages have ceased to exist, even though parents and relatives still tend to play a bigger role in "matchmaking" and are more involved in the marriage decision than what is common in Western societies. It is true that young men today share more household chores with their wives and in child rearing, but in general the division of labor within the family still assigns more responsibilities to women, especially compared with their Western counterparts, even though a great many young women also work outside of the home.

If the push for women's rights at the turn of the century was guided by national interests, then during the post-WWII era, Korea began to see a new kind of women's movement that was largely synchronized with the bourgeoning feminism elsewhere in East Asia and the world. Religious groups' advocacy for women's rights became eclipsed by that of liberal feminists, who addressed not only gender issues but also urban-rural and other social inequalities.[53] As in Japan, when images of the "new women" took hold of the society's imagination, Korea saw a similar emergence of such women in research for individual freedom. "Few social changes marked a greater break with tradition than those that concerned women. Many Korean women embraced new ideas and opportunities presented by a modernizing society."[54] Among other things, they began to promote birth control as means of alleviating their burdens of taking care of a large family and rendering seemingly endless household chores. They sought opportunities to work outside of their home sphere, pursue modernity through fashion, and articulate feminist ideas in women's magazines.

The evolving experiences of South Korean women are not dissimilar to those of other East Asian women. The phenomenal economic growth during the past six and half decades has generated both new opportunities and challenges for women. During the 1960s and 1970s, an ever-increasing number of women participated in both the paid, urban labor force and in labor in rural areas. It should be noted that postwar Korean feminism became energized by and interlaced with the labor movements. Working in the industrial sector was both liberating and constraining. It was in the factories where women workers organized themselves to assert their rights. With the increase in urbanization that attracted rural residents to the cities in search of job opportunities in the 1960s and early 1970s, Korean agriculture became feminized, as many rural women were left behind to attend to farming in addition to taking care of their families.[55]

The existing gender inequalities notwithstanding, South Korean women have made tremendous strides in fighting for their rights and freedoms. The legacy of student and labor activism against political authoritarianism in the 1960s and 1970s and against economic inequality in subsequent decades has lent itself to sustained feminist movements to the present day, despite some setbacks. South Korean women have organized themselves in their struggle for political and social rights through the League of Women Voters and the Korean Family Law Reform movement. They have also played an active role in gaining environmental protection for the broader society and in sustaining the peace movement in the post-Korean War world.

Changes in South Korean women's lives were closely intertwined with the country's changing economic landscape. The 1980s saw strenuous efforts

---

53   Ibid.

54   Seth, *A History of Korea*, 287.

55   Miriam Ching Yoon Louie, "Minjung Feminism: Korean Women's Movement for Gender and Class Liberation" in *Global Feminism since 1945*, ed. Bonnie Smith (New York: Routledge, 2000), 119.

on the part of the South Korean government to restructure its industries, necessitated by an economic recession in the midst of political instability. Severe inflation also caused widespread public discontent with the government. As a result, the reform to veer away from heavy industrial manufacturing to focus on light industrial production and the service sector gave rise to more opportunities for women workers in the latter two arenas, especially in the service industry. However, such opportunities were also accompanied by the fact that women remained in lower-paying positions in the midst of "labor market segregation."[56]

Similarly, economic globalization during the past several decades has also been a double-edged sword for South Korean women. While generating more employment opportunities along global assembly lines, the increased demands of multinational corporations have not alleviated the double burden for women, who have had to shoulder the dual responsibilities both in the paid work force and at home. Meanwhile, as an increasing number of women work in factories run by multinational corporations, they also have had to deal with increased sexual discrimination in the workplace, leading some feminist scholars to conclude that South Korean women have, by and large, been "the victim of both colonialism and globalization."[57]

---

56   Scott M. Fuess, Jr. and Bun Song Lee, "Government Reforms, Economic Reconstructuring, and the Employment of Women: South Korea, 1980–92" in *Women in the Age of Economic transformation: Gender Impact of Reforms in Post-Socialist States and Developing Countries*, eds. Nahid Aslanbeigui, Steven Pressman, and Gale Summerfield (New York: Routledge, 1994), 158.

57   Miriam Ching Yoon Louis, "Minjung Feminism," 119.

Chapter 12

The Second Indochina War (1954-1975)

The Geneva Accords (1954)

When Dien Bien Phu fell on May 7, 1954, the timing could not have been more inconvenient for French negotiations. Discussions to end the First Indochina War were set to begin the very next day in Geneva, Switzerland. The French and the Viet Minh both yearned to end the war. From the perspective of Pham Van Dong (1906–2000), the head of the Viet Minh delegation to the Geneva Conference, the strategically important victory at Dien Bien Phu had been achieved only at the expense of a great deal of blood and treasure. Viet Minh leadership wished to avert a major battle for the Red River delta.[1] In France, Prime Minister Joseph Laniel (1889–1975) and the French political right were hoping to find a way "to bring an end to the war on terms that could be profitable to French interests in Indochina and could still be made to look honorable."[2] However, the debacle at Dien Bien Phu collapsed the Laniel government. On June 18, 1954, leftist Pierre Mendès France (1907–1982) replaced him as prime minister. He insisted that the

negotiators at the Geneva Conference produce an agreement to end the war within thirty days.[3]

The other important actors at the Geneva Conference were the People's Republic of China, represented by Premier Zhou Enlai (1898–1975), the Soviet Union represented by Minister of Foreign Affairs Vyacheslav Mikhailovich Molotov (1890–1986), and the United Kingdom, represented by Secretary of State for Foreign Affairs Anthony Eden (1897–1977). The United States, which was represented by Secretary of State John Foster Dulles (1888–1959), largely stayed on the sidelines of these discussions.[4]

The main interest of the major powers at the conference was to keep a civil war in Vietnam from arising and escalating into a major Cold War battlefront—in other words, to avoid precisely the events that actually occurred during the 1960s. It is an important but infrequently noted fact that a resolution of the Indochina question was but one aim of the Geneva Conference. The other was to resolve the remaining outstanding issues in the wake of the Korean War, which had ended in an armistice in 1953

---

1   Fredrik Logevall, *Embers of War* (New York: Random House, 2014), 561.

2   Ibid., 489.

3   Edward Miller, *Misalliance* (Cambridge, MA: Harvard University Press), 89.

4   Keith W. Taylor, *History of the Vietnamese* (New York: Cambridge University Press), 560.

but has not formally been ended by treaty even to the present day.

All sides were wary of repeating the experience of Korea in Vietnam. The Soviet Union was only a little more than a year removed from the death of Joseph Stalin, and First Secretary Nikita Khrushchev's position in power was still far from secure. The People's Republic of China had lost more than 180,000 soldiers in the Korean War, less than a year before the Geneva negotiations. China's First Five-Year Plan (1953–1957) required soldiers to perform key land reform and industrial tasks that made a protracted conflict in Vietnam unpalatable to China.[5]

Given the geopolitical situation at the time, the most prudent course for the major powers was to partition Vietnam. However, the Vietnamese representatives at the conference were universally opposed to partition of the country. Agreement required some convenient way to placate Vietnamese parties—especially the Viet Minh—on the partition issue. Therefore, the cease-fire agreement at Geneva called for a line of demarcation "to be fixed" at the seventeenth parallel, and for the North Vietnamese forces to withdraw to the north of that line while the French Union forces withdrew to the south.[6] A declaration at the end of the conference, which was not signed by anyone, indicated that "general elections shall be held in July 1956" to guarantee "territorial integrity" to Vietnam.[7]

These 1956 elections were never held. Historians opposed to US intervention in Vietnam regularly cite this fact to prove that the Republic of Vietnam, the non-Communist state that emerged in the South, was illegitimate from the start.[8] However, it appears clear that the major players at the Geneva Conference knew at the time of the final declaration that no such election was likely to ever occur. Its occurrence was a low priority for those involved in any case. Most likely, the general elections provision was added to the final declaration as a kind of window dressing to persuade the Viet Minh forces to agree to sign the cease-fire's seventeenth parallel provision.

This explanation would shed light on why the Soviet Union pushed for the agreement for elections to be extended out to two years, rather than the original eighteen months. It would also explain why the United Kingdom's and United States' representatives affirmed that the outcome of the Geneva Conference would bear no risk of the non-Communist area coming under later communist control.[9] Since partition was specifically designed to reduce tensions between the two sides, and an attempt to unify the country through elections was likely to exacerbate Cold War tensions, it was likely that not

---

5   Xiaobing Li, *China's Battle for Korea* (Bloomington: Indiana University Press, 2014), 239; Meg E. Rithmire, *Land Bargains and Chinese Capitalism: The Politics of Property Rights under Reform* (New York: Cambridge University Press, 2015), 37.

6   "Agreement on the Cessation of Hostilities in Vietnam," *Foreign Relations of the United States, 1952–1954* Volume XVI (The Geneva Conference), Document 1044, accessed April 11, 2016. https://history.state.gov/historicaldocuments/frus1952-54v16/d1044

7   "The Final Declaration on Indochina," *Foreign Relations of the United States, 1952–1954* Volume XVI (The Geneva Conference), Document 1047, accessed April 11, 2016. https://history.state.gov/historicaldocuments/frus1952-54v16/d1047

8   Robert Buzzanco, "Military Dissent and the Legacy of the Vietnam War," in *The War that Never Ends: New Perspectives on the Vietnam War*, eds. David L. Anderson and John Ernst (Lexington, KY: University Press of Kentucky, 2007), 196; James M. Carter, *Inventing Vietnam: The United States and State Building, 1954–1968* (New York: Cambridge University Press, 2008), 48.

9   Keith W. Taylor, "China and Vietnam: Looking for a New Version of an Old Relationship," in *The Vietnam War: Vietnamese and American Perspectives*, eds. Jayne Werner and Luu Doan Huynh (Armonk, NY: M. E. Sharpe, 1993), 278.

only the United States but also Britain, the Soviet Union, and maybe even the People's Republic of China favored a partition of Vietnam that was a de facto permanent one.[10] The Viet Minh were given little choice but to accept this situation; the Bao Dai government, though present for the negotiations, was allowed very little input into the final result. Finally, this explains why, after South Vietnam refused to hold reunification elections in 1956 on the grounds that it had not been present at the Geneva Conference, the Soviet Union did not isolate South Vietnam. Instead, in 1957, just months after the South refused such elections, the Soviets "indirectly recognized the Republic of South Vietnam and signaled its acceptance of two independent states in Vietnam."[11]

North Vietnam from "North-first" to "South-first" (1953–1960)

The government of the Democratic Republic of Vietnam in the North appealed to the party elite to support the Geneva negotiations. Some party leaders remembered the failed negotiations in 1946. They were hesitant to support an agreement made through negotiations with the French. Having lost a great deal of territory that they controlled south of the seventeenth parallel, the DRV leadership would have to convince other party members and the general public to accept a de facto long-term partition. To do so, they argued for a "North-first"

line: a policy aimed at modernizing and developing North Vietnam's industry and agriculture, in the hope that in the meantime, the government of South Vietnam would collapse or a peaceful and negotiated settlement and reunification agreement could eventually be reached. Ho Chi Minh, General Secretary Truong Chinh (1907–1988), Pham Van Dong, who in 1955 would succeed Ho as prime minister, and Minister of Defense Vo Nguyen Giap all probably advocated for a North-first position.[12]

In the 1950s, the North-first strategy had two major prongs. The first was the land reform program (1953–1957). This program continued efforts already underway before the Geneva agreements to redistribute land away from landlords and give it to landless peasants. The second prong was industrial development. This goal was to be achieved through North Vietnam's three-year plan (1958–1960) to nationalize and expand industrial production and also to work to collectivize the agricultural sector in the wake of the land reform.[13]

The mid-1950s were one of two periods in which the government in North Vietnam, the Democratic Republic of Vietnam (DRV), was heavily influenced by developments and advisors from the People's Republic of China. Even before the land reform program, from 1951 to 1953, the Viet Minh prepared the ground for the land reform by forcing intellectuals to participate in rectification campaigns in which they denounced bourgeois writings they had published before joining the party. The mid-1950s

---

10   Robert F. Randle, *Geneva 1954: The Settlement of the Indochinese War* (Princeton, NJ: Princeton University Press, 1969), 202.

11   Mari Olsen, *Soviet-Vietnam Relations and the Role of China, 1949–64: Changing Alliances* (New York: Taylor and Francis, 2006), 75.

12   Ang Cheng Guan, *The Vietnam War from the Other Side* (New York: Routledge, 2013), 24; Pierre Asselin, *Hanoi's Road to the Vietnam War, 1954–1965* (Berkeley, CA: University of California Press, 2013); Lien-Hang Nguyen, *Hanoi's War: An International History of the War for Peace in Vietnam* (Chapel Hill: University of North Carolina Press, 2012), 42. Lien-Hang Nguyen is much more hesitant to identify specifically which members of the leadership actually espoused the North-first position.

13   Asselin, *Hanoi's Road*, 48.

were, for this reason, "a high point of Maoist influence and of Party authority."[14]

By 1952 the time was ripe for the Viet Minh to shift from seeking alliances with landlords and reducing rent to neutralizing and "expelling" landlords. To accomplish land reform, the party leadership turned to Luo Guibo (1907–1995), the Chinese ambassador to the DRV. In the fall of 1952, Luo submitted a detailed plan for land reform in Vietnam. This document called on the Vietnamese Communist Party to remove landlords through trials, replace them with party cadres, reorganize rule systems, and use the land reform as a means to consolidate power. Using this document as a framework, Vietnamese Communist leaders elaborated a strategy of having cadres trained to classify rural people into categories. Cadres divided the population into landlords, rich peasants, strong, average, and weak middle peasants, poor peasants, and landless peasants. Once cadres were trained in these classifications, they were sent to local villages to find peasants who were willing to denounce landlords and set up public trials in which landlords would be accused of a certain set of stock crimes.[15] They were asked to proceed on a five-step program of living with villagers and collecting data, presenting findings at public assemblies at which people could "speak bitterness" about landlords, putting landlords on trial and subjecting them to a range of punishments, including execution, redistribution of property, and the creation of new peasant associations to replace the old elite Councils of Notables.[16]

The land reform program was designed to kill significant numbers of predesignated landowners and agitate peasants. Cadres were given a minimum quota of landlords that were to receive a death sentence in every village.[17] They arrived at the village and immediately began to teach peasants how landlords had cheated and abused them, giving each a list of the common crimes of which the landlords were guilty. To avoid participating in criticizing these landlords was to be opposed to the revolution. It was therefore very dangerous. Families of landlords were shunned from society and prevented from working. Many of them died of starvation.[18] Though the question of how many died as a direct result of the land reform is a matter of serious historiographical dispute, estimates range from three thousand to two hundred thousand people.[19]

General Secretary Truong Chinh, who was regarded as the political leader most fond of Maoist strategies—his name means "Long March" in Sino-Vietnamese—has been understood to have been the major enthusiast of Vietnamese land reform activities, and thus, when the DRV was forced to admit "errors" had occurred in the

---

14 Shawn McHale, "Freedom, Violence, and the Struggle over the Public Arena in the Democratic Republic of Vietnam, 1945–1958," in *Naissance d'un État-Parti/Birth of the Party State: Vietnam since 1945*, eds. Christopher E. Goscha and Benoît de Trégoldé (Paris: Les Indes Savantes, 2004), 94–5.

15 Alex-Thai D. Vo, "Nguyen Thi Nam and the Land Reform in North Vietnam, 1953," *Journal of Vietnamese Studies* 10, no. 1 (Winter 2015): 19–25; Hoang Van Chi, *From Colonialism to Communism: A Case History of North Vietnam* (New York: Praeger, 1964), 163–4.

16 Ken MacLean, *The Government of Mistrust: Illegibility and Bureaucratic Power in Socialist Vietnam* (Madison: University of Wisconsin Press, 2013), 44–5.

17 Chi, *From Colonialism to Communism*, 212.

18 Vo, "Nguyen Thi Nam," 25–9.

19 For a discussion of the range of estimates, see ibid., 4–15. See also Edwin E. Moise, *Land Reform in China and North Vietnam: Consolidating the Revolution at the Village Level* (Chapel Hill: University of North Carolina Press, 1983), 217–18.

campaign in 1956, he was the one who was forced out of his post as general secretary.[20] However, as Alex-Thai Vo has recently shown, there is considerable evidence that others in high-level leadership positions, including Ho Chi Minh and Vo Nguyen Giap, were also complicit in the land reform's excess. In 1952 Ho Chi Minh personally sought out the blessing of Liu Shaoqi and Joseph Stalin for Luo Guibo's blueprint for land reform. After the trial and death sentence of the controversial landlord Nguyen Thi Nam in 1953, Ho Chi Minh penned an article under the pseudonym "C.B." in the official newspaper *Nhan Dan* (The People) condemning the "miserable old hag" for her crimes, and he may have even been present for her public trial.[21]

In 1956 Vo Nguyen Giap issued a public apology for the excesses of the land reform. In that year the Communist world was in the midst of de-Stalinization. Three years after Stalin's death, Nikita Khrushchev consolidated his power in the Soviet Union through the so-called "secret speech."[22] Khrushchev's efforts to open up limited criticisms of the Stalin years spurred de-Stalinization efforts around the Communist world. Chinese experienced the Hundred Flowers movement. North Vietnam's version of this was the Nhan Van-Giai Pham affair of 1956, in which intellectuals published critiques of the regime in two prominent journals, *Nhan Van* (Humanism), and *Giai Pham* (Masterworks). These works critiqued land reform. They also criticized the "culture of land reform" that allowed party elites to accumulate power and

presented no effective means for people to lodge criticisms against the party.[23]

DRV leaders censored their critics. They shuttered the journals and stripped intellectuals and writers of their professional memberships. They subjected them to self-criticism, hard labor, and even long prison terms, even though they were mostly reformists rather than anti-Communist dissidents.[24] The journalist, poet, and literary critic Phan Khoi (1887–1959), the philosopher Tran Duc Thao (1917–1993), the novelist Tran Dan (1926–1997), and even Van Cao (1923–1995), the composer of Communist Vietnam's national anthem, were among those intellectuals forced to undergo self-criticism or punishment during the Nhan Van-Giai Pham affair.

Gradually, members of the Vietnamese Communist Party became disillusioned with the North-first strategy, the premises of which were increasingly tenuous by 1957. The first premise was that by building Socialism, the DRV could rapidly become a successful state that would attract support from southerners who would want to reunify under DRV auspices. The second was that this reunification would happen organically because the south was in such political tatters as of 1954 that it would not survive for long. The deeply problematic land reform and the dissent of prominent and generally pro-Socialist intellectuals revealed the idea of a rapidly transformed Socialist republic to be nothing more than a pipe dream. What is more, these two events revealed gaping cleavages

---

20 Qiang Zhai, *China and the Vietnam Wars, 1950–1975* (Chapel Hill: University of North Carolina Press, 2005), 75; Nguyen, *Hanoi's War*, 34–5.

21 Vo, "Nguyen Thi Nam," 40–1.

22 Richard Saull, *Rethinking Theory and History in the Cold War: The State, Military Power, and Social Revolution* (London: Frank Cass, 2001), 144.

23 Kim N.B. Ninh, *A World Transformed: The Politics of Culture in Revolutionary Vietnam, 1945–1965* (Ann Arbor: University of Michigan Press, 2002), 145.

24 Peter Zinoman, "Nhan Van-Giai Pham and Vietnamese 'Reform Communism' in the 1950s: A Revisionist Interpretation," *Journal of Cold War Studies* 13, no. 1 (Winter 2011): 60–4.

in the nascent Socialist society in the North. The Socialist vision of development was premised on mass mobilization, and widespread dissent made prospects for the success of such a common effort less likely. Moreover, by 1957 South Vietnam was strengthening, not collapsing. The point in favor of the North-first argument was industrial production—the second prong of the North-first strategy. Industrial production was bolstered by massive Chinese and Soviet aid. According to Soviet advisors, the goals for the development of the national economy under the three-year plan were met by 1960.[25]

In contrast, by 1957 South-first supporters rallied the party to their cause. While the land reform divided a society, unification with the South motivated Northerners to stand with their government in the name of nationalism. South-firsters skillfully portrayed the cause of reunification as an extension of the original anticolonial enterprise of the Viet Minh. By framing a war with the South as an anti-imperialist war against American aggression and for the national unification of Vietnam, the party could galvanize broad support for their aims. At least in the realm of industrial production and infrastructure, the war could also serve the aims of development, as the DRV could use foreign aid from China or the Soviet Union to develop armaments and to repair the roads and rail networks necessary to produce them and get them to the front. The downside of this plan was evident: it would cost many lives, and given the possibility of formidable opposition from the United States, it would be a war that would be difficult to win. By the late 1950s, however, the North-first strategy had been tried, and it appeared to be failing. A gradual but perceptible shift was in order.

The primary figures precipitating this shift were Le Duan and Le Duc Tho. These two critical figures took similar routes to power. Neither one of these men was from the far South. Le Duan was from Quang Tri province in central Vietnam, while Le Duc Tho hailed from Ha Nam province in the Red River delta. Nevertheless, Le Duan and his trusted deputy Le Duc Tho had risen in the eyes of the party through their leadership in the South. Each of these men started to rise in prominence in 1951, the year in which the commander of Viet Minh activities in the south, Nguyen Binh, died under suspicious circumstances and the year in which Le Duan became the head of the Central Office of South Vietnam (COSVN), and therefore the leader of Communist operations in the South.[26]

In 1956 when Truong Chinh was dismissed from office and Vo Nguyen Giap was forced to issue a public apology for the land reform, Le Duan and Le Duc Tho were in an excellent position to take advantage. When it became plain to the party that they were losing control of the countryside, Le Duc Tho was appointed to oversee the rectification of the land reform, and he too was given a position on the Politburo and made the organizational chief of the party.[27] By 1957 the die was cast. Le Duan was made acting general secretary of the party.[28] Those senior party leaders who had made up the party's well-educated elite who had been tainted by the failures of the mid-1950s would be marginalized. Ho Chi Minh would be of use to the party as a diplomatic liaison between other Communist countries and as powerful symbol of national unity. Leaders of the party such as Truong Chinh and Pham Van Dong and military leader Vo Nguyen Giap would remain influential voices but would be increasingly marginalized in day-to-day decision

25 Olsen, *Soviet-Vietnam Relations*, 79.

26 Nguyen, *Hanoi's War*, 17–25.

27 Ibid., 35.

28 Asselin, *Hanoi's Road to the Vietnam War*, 47.

making. By the late 1950s, de facto military leadership had passed from Giap to Nguyen Chi Thanh (1914–1967), a fellow Central Vietnamese and ally of Le Duan.[29]

However, after the 1957 changing of the political guard, the party did not immediately abandon the North-first strategy. That shift was gradual. By suggesting in the United Nations that both North and South Vietnam be recognized, the Soviet Union clearly indicated its willingness to accept the legitimacy of a permanent division.[30] Given this atmosphere, in 1957 and 1958 the new northern leadership sought a peaceful negotiation for rapprochement with Ngo Dinh Diem's administration in South Vietnam while continuing to build up industry and infrastructure in the North. They embarked upon a three-year plan (1958–1960) to modernize industry and create new state-owned enterprises with the help of Soviet and Chinese experts.[31]

At the fifteenth plenum of the Communist Party in January 1959, Le Duan, who had even in his elevated political position been repeatedly traveling to the South to investigate conditions there, reported to the plenum that the prospect of success of the existing revolutionaries fighting against the Diem government was very slim. Emboldened by political victories and bolstered by American support, the Diem regime was increasingly able to flex its muscles against the outgunned guerilla fighters being supported by the North. The plenum decided that more decisive action was necessary. Without further support, the window of opportunity for any effective action in the South would close. Accordingly, they passed Resolution 15, calling for the southern revolutionaries to use "armed propaganda" and

force to augment the nonviolent "political struggle" that they had been waging in previous years.[32] In May 1959 this decision was underscored when the Military Transportation Group 559 was initialized to create a road to the South and to facilitate the transfer of supplies and weapons. By July Group 759 was formed with a similar purpose: to find a means to transfer weapons and equipment South via a maritime route.[33]

In 1960 the gradual shift in power that had begun in 1957 was finally completed. At the Third Party Congress, Le Duan replaced Ho Chi Minh as general secretary, and in the immediate aftermath of the Congress, in December 1960, the party announced the formation of the National Liberation Front (NLF), which was designed to be a new broad-based organization in the South modeled on the Viet Minh. The NLF united southern Vietnamese who opposed the Ngo Dinh Diem regime and opposed United States intervention in Vietnam under one umbrella organization, which, like the Viet Minh, would be under the de facto leadership of the Communist Party.

The foundation of the NLF could be read as an indication of the North's commitment to a protracted struggle in the South. In reality, the situation was more complicated. The party remained divided. In addition to the division between North-first and South-first philosophies, the Vietnamese party was increasingly being pulled into the Sino-Soviet rift, which was already emerging by the late 1950s. Moreover, the Third Party Congress had passed a new five-year plan for industrial development, which was to produce economic gains by freeing up additional resources and manpower by *reducing* the size and budget of the army.

---

29 Taylor, *History of the Vietnamese*, 570.

30 Asselin, *Hanoi's Road to the Vietnam War*, 45.

31 Olsen, *Soviet-Vietnam Relations and the Role of China*, 79.

32 Asselin, *Hanoi's Road*, 59.

33 Guan, *The Vietnam War from the Other Side*, 34–5.

In fact, perhaps Hanoi's creation of NLF was a way to send a signal to southern revolutionaries that the liberation of the South would be had primarily through their efforts, and not through the efforts of the North.[34] In 1960, despite the changing of the political guard, the North was still basically in a North-first strategy, which explains their active interest in French-brokered proposals for the neutralization of the Vietnam conflict in 1962. But by the end of 1959 a protracted shift was already afoot, and so was a protracted war.

The First Republic in South Vietnam (1955–1963)

The State of Vietnam emerged from the Geneva Accords having been handed all of the land below the seventeenth parallel, giving them not only control over the southern part of Vietnam but also over the vast majority of central Vietnam as well. Having actual political authority over this territory was another matter. Head of State Bao Dai and his new prime minister, Ngo Dinh Diem, had little control over the territorial mandate that the Geneva Accords gave. This was not merely a matter of Communist guerillas holding land in the Mekong delta. In the South, Bao Dai and Diem faced a host of divisions. The Binh Xuyen mafia, under the direction of the charismatic underworld figure Bay Vien, controlled gambling, opium, and prostitution. The mafia had even been afforded de facto authority over large parts of Saigon and Cholon. Bao Dai appeased Bay Vien by granting him control over the police force, and even went as far as making him a brigadier general in the Vietnamese National Army (VNA).[35]

Moreover, not only did the Cao Dai army control Tay Ninh province to the northwest of Saigon, but Cao Dai factions that had split from the main temple also controlled areas in the delta. The Hoa Hao armies held sway over much of the delta territory closer to the Cambodian border. In accepting the prime ministership, Diem inherited a country that might well have been on its way to independence from the French but which appeared to have bleak prospects for long-term success.

Set in this context, the Saigon government achieved astounding political, economic, and military successes in 1954–1955. Diem managed to affirm an agreement with Bao Dai giving him total political authority. He convinced one powerful Hoa Hao general to lay down his arms, and captured, prosecuted, and eventually executed the other. He negotiated terms that allowed the generals of the Cao Dai militia to integrate their troops into the VNA. He even defeated the Binh Xuyen, his most intractable foe. After shuttering their casinos and closing operations, Diem had to fight the Binh Xuyen in the streets in the Battle of Saigon. After a month of close combat in Cho Lon in April and May of 1955, the remnants of the Binh Xuyen scattered and Bay Vien was forced to flee to Paris.[36] Somehow, by the summer of 1955, Ngo Dinh Diem had emerged from the chaos with political control firmly in his grasp.

Having gained military control of the VNA, Cholon, and the countryside, Diem now moved to eliminate the lingering political authority of Bao Dai and the Cao Dai, both of whom were attempting to negotiate political power. On July 7, 1955, Diem announced that a referendum would be held on whether Bao Dai should be removed from power and Diem made president of a new Vietnamese republic. Ngo Dinh Diem then delayed until October 6, to announce that the referendum would be held on October 23, leaving Bao Dai with insufficient time to return from his home in France to contest the

---

34 Asselin, *Hanoi's Road to the Vietnam War*, 84–6.

35 Miller, *Misalliance*, 93; Chapman, *Cauldron of Resistance*, 74.

36 Logevall, *Embers of War*, 644–5.

election. He then unleashed an unrelenting public relations campaign against the former emperor in the press. He also created a ballot that presented the emperor in an unfavorable light and strongly suggested to voters that voting for him was the better choice. Amid an election tainted by questionable voting procedures, Diem won an overwhelming and suspicious 98 percent of the vote.[37]

Whatever the results of a fair referendum would have been, it would be a mistake to assume that Diem was unpopular. The election was a powerful statement of the end of French influence in Vietnam, which was associated in many Vietnamese eyes with the figure of Bao Dai. And it was a clear statement that the new Republic of Vietnam would resist any efforts to create national unification elections in 1956. Ngo Dinh Diem was now president of the Republic of Vietnam, and he was going to assert his authority as a leading anti-Communist voice in Vietnam and beyond.

Throughout the course of the next several years, with the help of the United States, the Republic of Vietnam entered a course of cultural, political, and military nation building. Bolstered by an influx of largely Catholic intellectuals from North Vietnam who fled Communist rule between 1954 and 1956, Vietnamese universities and public agencies expanded during the First Republic (1955–1963). Journals, magazines, and newspapers, which had been a bulwark of modernist urban culture in Vietnam prior to the French War, now proliferated again in Saigon and Hue. In the North, intellectuals took on the work of creating a new national history and culture. State-sponsored journals and institutes supported writers who created an image of the Vietnamese nation as emerging courageously from millennia of fighting against foreign aggression—from the Chinese, from the Mongols, from the French, and most recently from the Americans.[38]

In the South, intellectuals sought to construct a vision of a cosmopolitan Vietnam, one that was open to ideas and people from around the world and was influenced by a unique blend of indigenous, Chinese, Indian, Southeast Asian, and Western elements. Southern journals emphasized Vietnamese contacts with Western nations and also focused on the developments of ideas about science, technology, and culture, from Buckminster Fuller to Jean-Paul Sartre, from around the world. The Diem regime, not to be left out of this project, also engaged in cultural nation-building projects. Through the RVN's ministries of Education and Civil Affairs, they sought to place emphasis on Southern Vietnamese theatrical forms, cosmopolitanism in the arts, and a more nationalist-centered version that offered an anticolonial version of resistance against foreigners.[39]

In addition, the Diem regime embraced personalism as a philosophy of the Republic. Though not always clearly articulated or implemented in the Republic, personalism was in fact a widespread worldview in the mid-twentieth century, deeply influential in the lives of figures from Margaret Sanger to Martin Luther King, Jr. It emerged out of the efforts of the French Catholic philosopher Emmanuel Mounier to marshal the phenomenological insights of Martin Heidegger in a way that was less hostile to Catholicism than was the existentialist philosophy associated with figures such as Jean-Paul Sartre. His philosophy focused on the development of the idea of a society based on "the person." Mounier conceptualized "the person" not as an autonomous individual. Instead, the person

---

37   Chapman, "Staging Democracy," 697–8.

38   See Patricia Pelley, *Postcolonial Vietnam: New Histories of the National Past* (Durham, NC: Duke University Press, 2002).

39   Matthew Masur, "Exhibiting Signs of Resistance: South Vietnam's Struggle for Legitimacy, 1954–1960," *Diplomatic History* 33, no. 2 (April 2009): 292–313.

was one who could be free from excessive incursions of the state but was still defined by a responsibility to others and to a wider society to maintain and preserve human dignity.

In the economic realm, nation building focused on the same ideas that were the impetus for reform in the North: rural land reform and urban development. The Southern land reform, of course, operated differently than in the north. Under the tutelage of US agriculture expert Wolf Ladejinsky, the Diem administration produced a scheme in which wealthy landowners were compensated the fair market value for a portion of their lands, which were then turned over to poor or landless peasants for cultivation. This program of land redistribution was coupled with existing efforts to develop new villages in the Mekong delta, to be settled in part with new Catholic migrants from the North as a bulwark against Communist infiltration.[40] Though this version of land reform did not produce the mass death and rural unrest as the Northern land reform, it was also not completely effective, as many wealthy families were able to find loopholes to help them avoid giving up their land.

Urban areas in particular experienced economic prosperity in the First Republic period. Aided by the United States Agency for International Development's Commodity Import Program, the Southern Vietnamese middle class was able to enjoy access to more durable goods. Even if the availability of those goods might have the negative effect of delaying the indigenous production of goods and destabilizing the Vietnamese currency, the ultimate effect on GDP was positive.

This trajectory continued until the North Vietnamese began to actively support war efforts against the South in 1959. The Diem government was quick to respond in ways that might have proved militarily effective but also tended to increase resentment and resistance against the regime. In the wake of the creation of units 559 and 759 in the North, the RVN National Assembly passed Decree 10/59, which greatly expanded existing laws providing trials for treason of those suspected of supporting Communism, expanding it to cover more types of opposition and streamlining judicial procedures to produce faster prison sentences and even faster executions.[41]

On July 7, 1959, on the fifth anniversary of Diem's coming to office as prime minister, he announced a new program of rural concentration centers that would come to be known as "agrovilles."[42] Notably, Diem did not consult US advisors before announcing this program.[43] The agrovilles would serve several purposes. First, they would concentrate the most remote parts of the rural population in centers, thus allowing the government to prevent the peasants in these areas from succumbing to Communist infiltration. However, the agrovilles were also a rural development policy, a continuation of the earlier land reform efforts. Diem hoped that the agrovilles would provide their rural inhabitants with new schools, new methods of agriculture, electricity, maternity clinics, and new medical facilities, in addition to being an effective strategy against

---

40   Miller, *Misalliance*, 78–80, 158–160; Biggs, *Quagmire*, 158–164; Tran Quang Minh, "A Decade of Public Service: Nation-building during the Interregnum and Second Republic," in *Voices from the Second Republic of South Vietnam (1967–1975)*, ed. Keith W. Taylor (Ithaca, NY: Cornell Southeast Asia Program Publications, 2014), 52–4.

41   David W. P. Elliott, *The Vietnamese War: Revolution and Social Change in the Mekong Delta*. Concise Edition. (Armonk, NY: M. E. Sharpe, 2007), 102.

42   Joseph J. Zazloff, "Rural Resettlement in South Vietnam: the Agroville Program," *Pacific Affairs* 35, no. 4 (Winter 1962): 327.

43   Philip Catton, *Diem's Final Failure: Prelude to America's War in Vietnam* (Lawrence, KS: University Press of Kansas, 2002), 63.

increasingly brazen infiltration by Communist forces.[44]

Unfortunately, the agroville policy failed. Local officials, who were motivated to please the central government of the republic, coerced local villagers to resettle against their will. Their heavy-handedness only increased the resistance of villagers. Even if there had been no coercion, it is unlikely that a program of forced resettlement would have generated much rural support for the regime.[45] The NLF and North Vietnamese troops were able to take advantage of the failure of the agrovilles to further intensify the war in the countryside. Only twenty agrovilles had been constructed by the time the program was abandoned.[46]

The failure of the agroville program emboldened critics of the Diem regime both in Vietnam and in the United States. US policy was influenced by increasing calls for reform from the Elbridge Durbrow (1903–1997), the United States ambassador to South Vietnam between 1957 and 1961. Durbrow believed that the Diem regime needed to answer to its critics for its own sake and to increase the perception that US operations on behalf of Diem were legitimate. Responding to pressure from Ladejinsky and South Vietnam's vice president, Nguyen Ngoc Tho, in 1960 Durbrow pressured Diem to reduce the influence of his brother Ngo Dinh Nhu and his wife Madame Nhu, to give the National Assembly powers to investigate and reduce corruption, to reduce censorship of the press, and

to afford villagers greater self-determination in the wake of the collapse of the agroville experiment.[47]

Perhaps emboldened by this US pressure, South Vietnamese critics of Diem's administration pushed the case for reform. In April 1960 some liberal intellectuals met at the Caravelle Hotel in downtown Saigon and drafted a letter critical of Diem's policies and urging him to "liberalize the regime, promote democracy, guarantee minimum civil rights," and "recognize the opposition."[48] They did not, however, call for Diem to step down. In November 1960 elements of the army attempted a coup against Diem that failed. Many liberal intellectuals, including some of the people who had signed the Caravelle Manifesto, supported them.[49] Durbrow, for his part, adopted an attitude of neutrality toward the coup and suggested that Diem negotiate with the coup leaders to prevent an escalation of violence.[50]

From that point on, relations between the United States and Diem began to deteriorate, as the trust between Diem and the embassy had been permanently broken. Relations continued to unravel despite a change in the executive branch in the United States that on paper appears to have been to Diem's possible advantage. In 1961 John F. Kennedy (1917–1963) assumed the presidency, succeeding Dwight Eisenhower. Kennedy was interested in being viewed as tough on Communism and employed people such as General Maxwell Taylor, who were interested in focusing on local counterinsurgency efforts and in solving security problems

---

44   Zazloff, "Rural Resettlement," 327.

45   Catton, *Diem's Final Failure*, 69.

46   Taylor, *History of the Vietnamese*, 517.

47   Ronald Bruce Frankum, Jr., *Vietnam's Year of the Rat: Elbridge Durbrow, Ngo Dinh Diem, and the Turn in U.S. Relations, 1959–1961* (Jefferson, NC: MacFarland, 2014), 87.

48   Diem, *In the Jaws of History*, 93.

49   Frankum, *Vietnam's Year of the Rat*, 4.

50   Miller, *Misalliance*, 212.

through supporting allies by increasing military assistance.[51]

On January 19, 1961, Eisenhower and Kennedy held a meeting to discuss key foreign policy matters. In that meeting, Eisenhower argued that "the key to the entire area of Southeast Asia" was not Vietnam, but Laos.[52] Kennedy appears to have taken this seriously, but he took the question of Laos in a policy direction completely different than that taken during the Eisenhower administration. W. Averell Harriman (1891–1986), a veteran diplomat and bureaucrat that had served in the cabinet of President Harry S. Truman, influenced Kennedy's Laos policy. Harriman became the secretary of state for Far Eastern affairs in the Kennedy administration. He had Kennedy's ear and his confidence. He tended to support policies that attempted to reduce Cold War conflicts through great power negotiations. It would then be up to those powers, in particular the Soviet Union, the United States, and the People's Republic of China, to enforce those agreements by reigning in the actions of allies in smaller states.[53]

By 1962, under Harriman's direction, the United States and the Soviet Union, along with the governments of Poland, China, Britain, Burma, Thailand, Cambodia, South Vietnam, North Vietnam, and the Royal Lao Government, entered into an agreement specifying the withdrawal of all foreign troops—Chinese, North Vietnamese, South Vietnamese, Soviet, American—from Laos. This neutralization agreement included a provision that they "would not use the territory of the Kingdom of Laos for interference in the internal affairs of other countries."[54] Since a cease-fire between the non-Communist forces and the Pathet Lao (the Lao Communist organization) was already in place in Laos, this agreement would basically allow Pathet Lao areas in eastern Laos to remain in Communist hands, and areas controlled by the Royal Lao Government in western Laos to remain in government hands. The agreement also reflected the short-lived reality that Laos in 1962 had agreed on a coalition government led by neutralists.[55]

The decision to neutralize Laos was premised on two false assumptions. The first was that Lao neutralist forces could help contain Communism in Laos. In reality "the Neutralist center was neither politically nor militarily strong enough to withstand the determination of both the political Left and Right to destroy it."[56] The neutralist coalition broke down in 1963 and fighting began again. The second false assumption was that the Soviet Union could prevent North Vietnam from using Pathet Lao-controlled territory in eastern Laos as a conduit for fighters heading to the South to support the NLF. Harriman apparently took at face value the guarantees of Soviet ambassador Georgy Pushkin (1909–1963), that the Soviets would prevent the continued infiltration into Laos by North Vietnamese troops along the nascent Ho Chi Minh trail.[57] In reality, the entire NLF-based South-first strategy was premised on infiltration into South Vietnam through the Ho Chi Minh Trail, so it is inconceivable that the North would

---

51 Taylor, *History of the Vietnamese*, 579.

52 "Memorandum of Conference on January 19, 1961 between President Eisenhower and President-Elect Kennedy on the Subject of Laos," *The Pentagon Papers*, Gravel Edition, vol. 2 (Boston, MA: Beacon Press, 1972), 636.

53 Taylor, *History of the Vietnamese*, 578.

54 "Declaration on the Neutrality of Laos. Signed at Geneva, on 23 July 1962," accessed May 11, 2016. https://treaties.un.org/doc/Publication/UNTS/Volume%20456/volume-456-I-6564-English.pdf

55 Martin Stuart-Fox, *Historical Dictionary of Laos* (Metuchen, NJ: Scarecrow Press, 1992), 119.

56 Ibid., 120.

57 Dommen, *The Indochinese Experience of the French and the Americans*, 479.

honor an agreement that gave up a cornerstone of their strategy. In the meantime, the United States was also "unofficially" involved in Laos, using Air America, a CIA-sponsored airline, to transport supplied munitions and troops to CIA-trained members of the Hmong ethnic minority who were fighting the Communists.[58]

The failure of neutralization in Laos was one of the critical US policy mistakes of the Vietnam War. The neutralization precluded strategies that would have made South Vietnam easier to defend. In the words of C. Dale Walton:

> It was naïve of policymakers to believe that the Laos Accords would meaningfully curtail North Vietnamese infiltration of that country and obtuse of Washington to continue to present that Laos was a neutral country long after extensive North Vietnamese use of that state was obvious. The United States attempted to guarantee that Indochina would not be a unified theater, but even the most cursory examination of Hanoi's behavior should have made it obvious that the North Vietnamese were too shrewd politically to obey the Laos Accords.[59]

Meanwhile, in South Vietnam, the Kennedy administration, operating under the advice of Maxwell Taylor, began implementing a strategic hamlet program in the context a considerable escalation of its commitment to pacifying the situation in rural areas in the Mekong delta. This commitment led to clashes between the Military Assistance Advisory Group (MAAG) and the Diem regime. Diem wanted to start afresh after the failure of the agroville program and designed a new program to be carried out with minimal interference from the United States. MAAG wanted a program that was much more centralized and that would include more US control.

Diem's vision prevailed. He was attracted to efforts by local officials who created watchtowers near villages and organized local militia to police the villages against Communist incursions. By February 1962, an Interministerial Committee for Strategic Hamlets, with Ngo Dinh Nhu as de facto leader, was organized and the Strategic Hamlet program was officially underway.[60] By that time, the program had already grown in informal popularity so there were already hundreds of strategic hamlets in operation.[61] Initially, the Strategic Hamlet program's effectiveness posed a problem for the NLF and the North, which only spurred the Diem regime to construct more hamlets. As the pace of the program exploded in late 1962 and early 1963, it caused friction between Diem and US advisors, who thought that the growth of strategic hamlets was unsustainable, and caused considerable peasant discontent, which led to a decline in popular commitment to the survival of the hamlets.[62]

Meanwhile, in 1963, the Diem regime was faced with a more profound crisis, centered on the complaints of Buddhist monks. Although Diem had curried favor with Buddhist leaders since the beginning of his regime, he had gained power with the help of an "inner circle of allies and advisors [that] continued to be dominated by Catholics and especially by members and longtime friends of the Ngo family."[63] Therefore, some Buddhists argued that Diem favored Catholics at their expense.

---

58   William M. Leary, "Air America," in *The Encyclopedia of the Vietnam War: A Political, Social, and Military History*, 2nd ed., ed. Spencer C. Tucker (Santa Barbara, CA: ABC-Clio, 2011), 14.

59   C. Wale Walton, *The Myth of Inevitable US defeat in Vietnam* (Portland, OR: Frank Cass, 2002), 156.

60   Catton, *Diem's Final Failure*, 90–7.

61   Taylor, *History of the Vietnamese*, 581.

62   Catton, *Diem's Final Failure*, 170–6.

63   Miller, *Misalliance*, 33.

On May 4, 1963, Catholic groups in Hue had displayed the white and gold Catholic flag in celebration of the silver jubilee anniversary of Diem's older brother Ngo Dinh Thuc's being consecrated as a Bishop. Two days later, on May 6, an official telegram from the president's office indicated that no religious flags or banners would be displayed at such festivals. The ban appears to have been ironically motivated by Diem's annoyance at the pomp and circumstance surrounding his elder brother's celebration. Unfortunately for him, Buddhists regarded it as an attempt to disrupt their Vesak celebrations—a festival in honor of the birth and attainment of enlightenment of Siddhartha Gautama, the historical Buddha—which had been initiated at a conference in Sri Lanka in 1950 to promote Buddhism in the context of modern nationalism.[64]

The conflict came to a head on May 8, 1963. In Hue, Vesak had been marked by the prominent display of the red, blue, and saffron-yellow striped Buddhist flags. This prompted government officials to order that either they be displayed below a flag of the Republic of Vietnam, or the flags be taken down. When the RVN flag was not displayed, troops from the Army of the Republic of Vietnam (ARVN) ripped down the Buddhist flags. Three thousand people celebrating Vesak in Hue proceeded to the local radio station to protest. They demanded that the radio station broadcast a program about the Vesak events. They were met with ARVN troops, who fired on the demonstrators and used tear gas grenades, killing eight people and beginning Vietnam's Buddhist crisis of 1963.[65]

The most prominent leader of the Buddhist crisis at this time was Thich Tri Quang (b. 1924). While in Sri Lanka, he had been influenced by the effort to modernize Buddhism to bring it in line with the events of decolonization and the rise of nationalism. He had become a member of the Vietnam General Buddhist Association, an organization tied to these efforts, and had risen to become one of its leaders. After the collapse of the Vesak celebrations, Thich Tri Quang and other Buddhists demanded that the government accept responsibility for the incident and the revocation of a law that only Catholics could call their organizations a "church." When those demands were not met, Buddhists first organized a mass fasting to protest.[66] Then, on June 11, 1963, sixty-six-year old Thich Quang Duc had fellow monks douse him with gasoline on a crowded Saigon street and burned himself to death in protest. This act "galvanized world opinion and became, throughout the world, a poignant example of South Vietnamese resistance to Diem."[67]

The Buddhist crisis extended into the summer of 1963 and intensified. In July, Nhat Linh, one of Vietnam's most famous writers and activists, committed suicide in protest to the Diem government's action and left a note pleading the case of the Buddhists. Then, on August 20, 1963, the regime raided pagodas in Saigon, Hue, and Danang, damaging them and arresting monks.[68]

The crisis strengthened the hands of those US policymakers and South Vietnamese military leaders who were opposed to Diem. The anti-Diem faction in the United States had already been emboldened when in the spring of 1963, Diem had

---

64   Ibid.,266. See also Charles A. Joiner, "South Vietnam's Buddhist Crisis: Organization for Charity, Dissidence, and Unity," *Asian Survey* 4, no. 7 (July 1964): 915; Taylor, *History of the Vietnamese,* 567.

65   Joiner, "South Vietnam's Buddhist Crisis," 915–16.

66   Ibid., 917–18; Taylor, *History of the Vietnamese,* 587. See also Dommen, *The Indochinese Experience,* 508–9.

67   Robert J. Topmiller, *The Lotus Unleashed: The Buddhist Peace Movement in South Vietnam, 1964–1966* (Lexington: University Press of Kentucky, 2002), 3.

68   Miller, *Misalliance,* 275.

demonstrated a willingness to work with Polish and French diplomats to negotiate a peaceful unification with the North, bypassing his American patrons in the process.[69] The American press was also increasing the pressure on the Kennedy administration to remove Diem. Thich Quang Duc's immolations had been seen on national television, and *New York Times* reporter David Halberstam subjected the Diem regime to a nearly daily barrage of criticism.[70]

Already in July, the United States Central Intelligence Agency (CIA) was motivated by the discontentment with Diem to identify several groups of potential RVN government officials and military leaders who might be willing to orchestrate a coup against the regime. One of these, which was led by three very senior military officials, Lieutenant Generals Tran Van Don and Duong Van Minh and Major General Le Van Kim, each of whom had been transferred to meaningless noncombat positions by the regime in order to neutralize them.[71] Several US leaders who had come to believe that Diem had to go encouraged them. The most important of these figures were Roger Hilsman (1919–2014), assistant secretary of state for Far Eastern affairs, and Henry Cabot Lodge Jr. (1902–1985), who had just arrived as the new US ambassador to South Vietnam. Slowly, over the course of the summer and early fall, those advocating for the removal of Diem got the upper hand over the calmer heads in the Kennedy administration.[72] On November 1, 1963, with the assent of the United States, Diem and his brother Nhu were captured, and the next day, they were killed on orders of General Duong Van Minh. Ambassador Henry Cabot Lodge, knowing that Diem and Nhu's murder was imminent, did nothing to stop it from occurring.[73]

In neutralizing Laos and participating in the assassination of Ngo Dinh Diem, the United States promulgated an inept policy that made it very difficult for a non-Communist state in South Vietnam to succeed. The failure of the neutralization of Laos meant that the South Vietnamese would be powerless to stop the continuous infiltration of their country by North Vietnamese troops. The assassination of Diem deprived South Vietnam of a capable, if repressive, leader. It placed power in the hands of generals who had no political experience and whose power base was tenuous even within the ARVN. It alienated supporters of Diem and further divided the population, making effective governance impossible. Under these conditions, American policymakers made US military escalation a self-fulfilling prophecy.

Escalation of the Second Indochina War (1963–1967)

In North Vietnam, Diem's assassination emboldened leaders who favored an aggressive war against the south. By this time, the Sino-Soviet rift was dividing party leaders. The North-first moderate faction, including President Ho Chi Minh, Defense Minister Vo Nguyen Giap, Vice President Ton Duc Thang, and Foreign Minister Ung Van Khiem, was also generally pro-Soviet and relatively moderate. The South-first militant faction was generally pro-Chinese. It included Prime Minister Le Duan, general political department chairman General Nguyen Chi Thanh; Chairman of the Party Organization Committee Le Duc Tho; and Chairman of the National Assembly Standing Committee Truong Chinh.

---

69   Dommen, *The Indochinese Experience*, 531–3.

70   Ibid., 539.

71   Miller, *Misalliance*, 280–2.

72   Dommen, *The Indochinese Expeirnce*, 552–6.

73   Ibid., 556.

In the spring of 1963, the moderates, urged on by the Soviet Union, sought diplomatic negotiations with the South as means of easing pressures.[74] Militants, on the other hand, were emboldened by Communist successes at the Battle of Ap Bac in January 1963, which convinced them that a guerilla strategy in the South could be successful. Diem's assassination prompted a special meeting of the Central Committee of the Communist Party, which became their ninth plenum. Le Duan and his allies emerged from that meeting with a decisive victory, which allowed them to take over "party-decision making, staging a coup of sorts of their own."[75] At the ninth plenum, they passed Resolution 9, which reads as a repudiation of the Soviet line and an endorsement of the policies of Mao Zedong, including the idea of using a mass offensive to spark popular uprisings.

Subsequently, they were able to gradually purge party members who disagreed with their views, and isolate those, like Giap and Ho, who were too powerful to be subjected to purging.[76] Le Duan sidelined Ho Chi Minh by arguing to party members that he was responsible for "the two mistakes." These two mistakes showed Ho Chi Minh to be too conciliatory and too quick to avoid necessary war. They were allowing the French back into the North in 1946 and consenting to the cease-fire and partition of the country in the Geneva Accords of 1954.[77] Ho Chi Minh, who becoming increasingly feeble in any case, was made as a symbolic figure for the regime, fortifying an already existing cult of personality for Ho into a powerful ideological weapon for the regime—a cult Ho Chi Minh himself was instrumental in creating and perpetuating.[78]

In choosing targets of an antimoderate purge, Le Duan and his militant colleagues focused in particular on the friends, associates, and colleagues of the head of the Institute of Philosophy in Hanoi, Hoang Minh Chinh (1922–2008). In a report circulated prior to the ninth plenum, Hoang Minh Chinh had indicted North Vietnamese policy as being too aggressive and too Maoist and argued that the party needed to hew closer to the Soviet line.[79] Soon, civil servants, public figures, and intellectuals who had made statements supportive of Hoang Minh Chinh's views were targeted and moderates remaining on the Central Committee were demoted.[80]

In the fall of 1964, Le Duan named General Nguyen Chi Thanh as the new head of COSVN. This move guaranteed that a Chinese-oriented mobilization strategy would be pursued in the South. It also guaranteed that the North, not the NLF or other southerners, would have control over military decision-making in the war. This move northernized the struggle in the South and paved the way for a critical turning point in the war: the Tet offensive of 1968.[81]

Meanwhile, after the November 1963 coup, the government in South Vietnam began to unravel

---

74 Asselin, *Hanoi's Road to the Vietnam War*, 156–7.

75 Ibid., 145–52.

76 Ibid.

77 Asselin, *Hanoi's Road*, 171; Nguyen, *Hanoi's War*, 66–7.

78 Asselin, *Hanoi's Road*, 171. On Ho Chi Minh's health and mental fitness, see Brocheux, *Ho Chi Minh*, 173–4; Duiker, *Ho Chi Minh*, 554 (discussing the state of Ho Chi Minh's mental and physical fitness in 1965). On the Ho Chi Minh cult, see Olga Dror, "Establishing Ho Chi Minh's Cult: Vietnamese Traditions and their Transformation," *Journal of Asian Studies* 75:2 (May 2016): 433–466.

79 Asselin, *Hanoi's Road*, 170; Nguyen, *Hanoi's War*, 48.

80 Asselin, *Hanoi's Road*, 170.

81 Ibid., 199; Nguyen, *Hanoi's War*, 73.

quickly. General Duong Van Minh became the president, serving as "first among equals" with the other military officers who had supported the coup against Diem. General Minh was not particularly well prepared for the demands of politics, and indeed appeared to be someone more interested in playing tennis and tending to his orchid garden and aquarium than in policy matters.[82]

United States policy was in turmoil as well. Diem's removal was carried out, in spite of the objection of influential figures like General Maxwell Taylor and Secretary of Defense Robert McNamara, because it had at least the tacit support of President Kennedy. Three weeks later, however, Kennedy was himself assassinated. The new president, Lyndon Johnson, had been opposed to Diem's removal.[83] United States policymakers became increasingly alarmed after it became clear that Duong Van Minh could not be counted on to toe the American line. Instead, he was at least potentially sympathetic to neutralization and to a peaceful settlement with the North that Cambodian leader Prince Norodom Sihanouk (1922–2012) and French president Charles de Gaulle (1890–1970) were trying to broker.[84]

With the help of MAAG commander General Paul Harkins (1904–1984), the United States therefore supported a bloodless coup that led to the toppling of Duong Van Minh in January 1964, only three months after the coup against Diem. Harkins had not supported the coup against Diem and did not trust Duong Van Minh. He believed that another general, Nguyen Khanh (1927–2013) would

prove to be a reliable ally that could be counted on to endorse US policies in Vietnam.[85]

What Harkins failed to realize, however, was that this was precisely the quality that would render Nguyen Khanh unpalatable to nationalists in South Vietnam. Khanh was without a power base, and American efforts coordinated by Lodge to launch a public relations campaign on his behalf failed.[86] Meanwhile, the Buddhist movement continued, and the ARVN was increasingly divided between disaffected supporters of this or that faction. ARVN morale plummeted, and the desertion rate became dangerously high.[87]

By the summer of 1964, South Vietnam was descending into chaos, and American policymakers began to believe that the country could only be defended with massive United States intervention. Such intervention was made increasingly possible after the Gulf of Tonkin incident in August 1964, in which the crew of the destroyer USS *Maddox* believed that North Vietnamese patrol boats fired on them. In actuality, the *Maddox* was conducting audio surveillance fifteen miles from the North Vietnamese coast to gain basic intelligence on troop movements, and the patrol boats were attempting the prevent the *Maddox* from intimidating local fishing vessels. The best evidence seems to indicate that the *Maddox* was not actually attacked by torpedo boats, and this perception was a result of a misreading of radar signals. The *Maddox* fired warning shots that were then answered with fire from the North Vietnamese.

As a result, on August 5, the United States launched a campaign of airstrikes against North

82   Dommen, *Indochinese Experience*, 538.

83   George McT. Kahin, *Intervention: How America Became Involved in Vietnam* (New York: Alfred P. Knopf, 1986), 194.

84   Ibid., 198; Taylor, *History of the Vietnamese*, 590–1.

85   Taylor, *History of the Vietnamese*, 591.

86   Kahin, *Intervention*, 205–7.

87   Nguyen Cong Luan, *Nationalist in the Viet Nam Wars* (Bloomington: Indiana University Press, 2012), 242.

Vietnam, and on August 7, congress authorized President Johnson to take "all necessary measures" to prevent North Vietnamese aggression.[88] Acting under the authority of the Tonkin Gulf resolution, by March 1965, the first US Marine combat soldiers arrived in Da Nang. Prior to that, though there were more than twenty thousand US troops in Vietnam, their role was advisory in nature; they were not engaging in direct combat. These events would trigger an escalation of the US military role that would eventually lead to a buildup of around five hundred thousand US troops in Vietnam.

Meanwhile, the political situation continued to deteriorate. Faced with Nguyen Khanh's growing unpopularity, Maxwell Taylor, now the ambassador to South Vietnam, forced him to move toward a civilian government. As a result, he nominated the elderly liberal politician Phan Khac Suu (1893–1970), who had signed the Caravelle Manifesto, as the president of a new High Council and chief of state. This move set off a political crisis when Phan Khac Suu refused to authorize Nguyen Khanh's effort to formally retire the older generals who had been involved in the anti-Diem coup. This move was an effort to placate the Young Turks, a group of up-and-coming military officers led by Nguyen Cao Ky (1930–2011), and Nguyen Van Thieu (1923–2001). But when the Young Turks decided to take matters into their own hands by kidnapping the older generals, Nguyen Khanh lost whatever loyalty the Americans continued to have for him. On February 14, as a last-ditch attempt to hold onto power, he asked Phan Huy Quat (1908–1979),

another Caravelle Manifesto signer, to form a new civilian government. Khanh was then deposed by yet another military coup.[89]

In the spring of 1965, South Vietnam would have a civilian government. However, this government would not last. As a northern Buddhist, potential supporter of the Buddhist protest movement, and former member of the Dai Viet Party, Catholics and conservatives mistrusted Phan Huy Quat. This limited his legitimacy, and some southerners did not trust having a northerner in power.[90] By June 1965 the government ground to a halt when Phan Huy Quat and Head of State Phan Khac Suu could not agree on a cabinet.[91] Quat was forced to step down, and the Young Turks put in place a military regime, with Nguyen Van Thieu as chief of state and Nguyen Cao Ky as prime minister.[92] In the meantime, the United States began assuming nearly total control over the actual fighting of the war. In March 1965 they began Operation Rolling Thunder, a massive bombing campaign.

American officials, however, realized that they could not achieve success in the South unless they stabilized the political situation. In the spring of 1966, President Johnson called Nguyen Cao Ky to a conference on Vietnam in Honolulu. Out of this conference emerged the Declaration of Honolulu, which specified that the Thieu/Ky government would create a social revolution and "formulate a democratic constitution in the months ahead, including an electoral law," and create, on the basis of that constitution, an elected government."[93]

---

88 For a thorough and detailed account of these events, see Edwin E. Moise, *Tonkin Gulf and the Escalation of the Vietnam War* (Chapel Hill: University of North Carolina Press, 1996), especially, xi–xii.

89 Bui Diem, *In the Jaws of History* (Bloomington: Indiana University Press), 121–3.

90 Taylor, *History of the Vietnamese*, 596; Bui Diem, *In the Jaws of History*, 146.

91 Taylor, *History of the Vietnamese*, 596.

92 Bui Diem, *In the Jaws of History*, 146; Nguyen Cong Luan, *Nationalist in the Viet Nam Wars*, 281.

93 United States Information Service, *The Declaration of Honolulu* (London, UK: The American Embassy, 1966), 9. Douglas Pike Collection, Virtual Vietnam Archive, accessed May 12, 2016. http://www.virtualarchive.vietnam.ttu.edu/; Nguyen

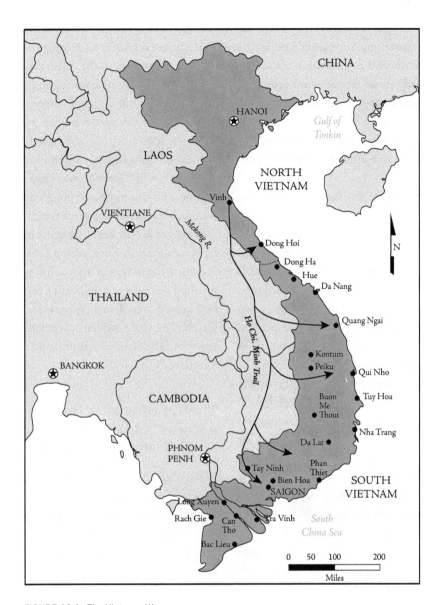

FIGURE 12.1 The Vietnam War

However, the situation would get more unstable before it got better. In early March 1966, Nguyen Cao Ky fired General Nguyen Chanh Thi (1923–2007), an original conspirator in the 1960 coup attempt against Diem who was from Hue and was viewed as aligned with the Buddhist movement.

Though General Thi appears to have been removed for petty reasons, Thich Tri Quang and others in the Buddhist movement took it as an action against them and took to the streets demanding democratic reforms and an end to the war. A major crisis was only averted when Ky reaffirmed his commitment

---

Cao Ky, *How We Lost the Vietnam War* (Lanham, MD: Rowman and Littlefield, 2002), 80–4.

to the process of convening an assembly to draft a constitution.[94] However, a considerable amount of damage was already done. Some members of the Buddhist movement in Hue were not willing to be reconciled with the Thieu/Ky regime. They fled into the mountains to join the Communist forces and came back with them to fight during the Tet offensive in 1968.[95]

Meanwhile, the war became increasingly bloody. The North's strategy involved an ideological struggle premised on mobilizing peasants to join in the war effort.[96] The very premise of such a war effort was that there would be no distinction between civilians and the military. As American casualties mounted and stories of civilians being killed by American troops multiplied, the war gradually became less popular in the United States, and European allies began openly questioning US actions.[97]

Fortunately, politics and government in the South were beginning to stabilize. In April 1966 the South Vietnamese government convened a National Political Congress that included major religious and political leaders as well as chairs of provincial and municipal councils in order to encourage candidates to run for the constitutional assembly. Elections were held for that purpose in September 1966, creating a broad-based Constituent Assembly, which produced a draft constitution.[98] The United States assisted in producing this constitution, which was originally premised on a strong executive. US

diplomats even delivered copies of the *Federalist Papers* to members of the Assembly.

Ultimately, a draft constitution was formulated in April 1967 in which the executive powers of the president were shared with a prime minister and which guaranteed the independence of the judiciary.[99] As a result, on September 3, 1967, the first presidential election was held since the Diem regime, and this election, though it excluded Communists, was by all accounts much fairer than the 1955 election had been. In fact, the ticket headed by Truong Dinh Dzu, which favored immediate American withdrawal and negotiations for peace, finished second in the balloting. But a coalition led by Nguyen Van Thieu (as president) and Nguyen Cao Ky (as vice president) won with 35 percent of the vote. The Second Republic was born in South Vietnam.[100]

The Tet Offensive, the Paris Peace Accords, and the Second Republic in South Vietnam (1967–1975)

Meanwhile, North Vietnam was still caught up in the vagaries of the Sino-Soviet rift. In a way, this disagreement between their two patrons had helped the North Vietnamese in their fight in the south in the mid-1960s. The Soviet Union did not want to lose all influence over Vietnamese policy, and accordingly, the North Vietnamese were able to play China and the Soviets against one another to maintain

---

94   Sophie Quinn-Judge, "The Search for a Third Force in Vietnam: From the Quiet American to the Paris Peace Agreement," in *Vietnam and the West: New Approaches*, ed. Wynn Wilcox (Ithaca, NY: Cornell Southeast Asia Program Publications, 2010), 167–8; Topmiller, *Lotus Unleashed*, 33; Bui Diem, *In the Jaws of History*, 166–7.

95   Olga Dror, "Introduction," in Nha Ca, *Mourning Headband for Hue* (Bloomington, IN: Indiana University Press, 2014), xxv.

96   Vo Nguyen Giap, *The Military Art of People's War: Selected Writings of Vo Nguyen Giap* (New York: NYU Press, 1970), 104–5.

97   Bui Diem, *In the Jaws of History*, 169.

98   Pham Cong Tue, "From the First to the Second Republic: From Scylla to Charybdis," in *Voices from the Second Republic*, ed. K. W. Taylor (Ithaca, NY: Cornell Southeast Asia Publications, 2015), 122.

99   Mark Sidel, *The Constitution of Vietnam: A Contextual Analysis* (Portland, OR: Hart Publishing, 2009), 22–3.

100   Pham Cong Tue, "From the First to the Second Republic," 123; Bui Diem, *In the Jaws of History*, 207–8.

generous aid from both.[101] Nevertheless, the start of the Cultural Revolution in China in 1966 raised the stakes of the Sino-Soviet dispute considerably.

The mid-1960s saw a two fateful events that would expose the cracks and fissures in Hanoi and destabilize military strategy: the suspicious death of General Nguyen Chi Thanh and the Anti-Party affair, in which Hoang Minh Chinh, the strategist who had been criticized for arguing for the Soviet line back in 1963, was arrested. These two events were very likely linked and originated with disputes over the planning of the Tet Offensive in 1968, which began in the spring of 1967. The Tet offensive sought a once-and-for-all turning point in the war, a massive victory that would either defeat the United States or lead them to the bargaining table in a very disadvantaged position.

The initial plan was "an all-out political-military attack aimed at the cities while the big communist main force units focused their efforts on luring enemy forces away from the cities and pinning them down for long enough to allow the attacks in the cities to succeed in toppling the RVN government."[102] The plan was later modified to include the element of a "General Offensive and General Uprising," which meant that the purpose of the Tet offensive was to spark a general uprising against the US and the regime in South Vietnam, as had been specified as a strategic goal by Resolution 9, passed in the aftermath of Diem's assassination as a blueprint for the war.[103]

This plan was clearly opposed by the moderates, still led by Ho Chi Minh and Vo Nguyen Giap, who considered it to be impractical and dangerous.[104] Vo Nguyen Giap preferred a strategy of protracted guerilla warfare to wear down opponents. In fact, in this period, he and Nguyen Chi Thanh engaged in a very public debate on this issue in the press, with Giap arguing that direct engagements in large-unit warfare, such as that proposed in the Tet Offensive, wasted forces and were suicide missions against the better-equipped Americans, and Thanh retorting that Giap was out of touch and no longer in the field.[105] In reality, Giap had already been sidelined in the mid-1960s and his views did not prevail. Giap spent the second half of 1967 "resting" in Hungary, and did not come back until after the Tet offensive.[106] Whether he did so voluntarily to protest the Tet offensive or was forced to leave is not clear.

On July 6, 1967, General Nguyen Chi Thanh, the head of military operations in South Vietnam and the main strategist behind the Tet offensive, died of a heart attack. This immediately raised suspicions, as he was only fifty-three years old and had shown no previous signs of ill health.[107] Less than a month later, in what would come to the known as the Anti-Party Affair, security forces arrested Hoang Minh Chinh along with around three hundred other people, more than thirty of whom were high-level generals, professors, writers, and journalists who were suspected of sympathy with the Soviets, which also implied a less aggressive, more

---

101   Nguyen, *Hanoi's War*, 194–5.

102   Merle Pribbenow, "General Vo Nguyen Giap and the Mysterious Evolution of the Plan for the 1968 Tet Offensive," *Journal of Vietnamese Studies* 3, no. 2 (2008): 16.

103   Ibid., 3.

104   Ibid., 16–17.

105   Lien-Hang Nguyen, "The War Politburo: North Vietnam's Diplomatic and Political Road to the Tet Offensive," *Journal of Vietnamese Studies* 1, nos. 1–2 (2006): 22.

106   Pribbenow, "General Vo Nguyen Giap," 18.

107   Nguyen, *Hanoi's War*, 88.

conciliatory approach to the war.[108] Various explanations for the crackdown of the Anti-Party Affair are possible. Perhaps Le Duan felt that the easing of the hard anti-Soviet line of Resolution 9 in 1965–1966 (which may have been a result of the need for Soviet anti-aircraft guns) needed to be corrected; perhaps it was a statement against the possible Soviet-US rapprochement over Vietnam that was apparently being pursued in the summer of 1967; or perhaps it was in retaliation for the suspected complicity of the pro-Soviet element in the possible poisoning of Nguyen Chi Thanh.[109]

Whatever the reason, the Anti-Party affair was a clear message that the Tet offensive was to go ahead as a general offensive leading to an imagined general uprising of the South, as planned, even after the death of one of its planners. Van Tien Dung, an ambitious general, was tapped by Le Duan to continue planning. By the end of the summer, a plan was devised to have the main force units of the North Vietnamese Army (NVA) troops occupy American troops in the countryside while the NLF and other NVA units attacked the city and town centers throughout the South. They hoped this would create mass demonstrations in support of the Communist efforts, thus bringing down the Saigon regime.[110]

The Tet offensive went badly from the point of view of the North. In order to preserve secrecy, members of the NLF were given less than two weeks to prepare for the battle. Additionally, due to the last-minute preparations and confusion about the start date, some units in central Vietnam actually started the Tet offensive a day early, eliminating the element of surprise and forcing other units to act before they were prepared to do so.[111] Though initially on January 30, 1968, the offensive took control of the center of dozens of cities and towns throughout the south, they were able to hold only one for more than forty-eight hours. The general uprising of the urban population of the South that was purportedly sympathetic to the Communist cause never occurred.

Moreover, the events in the one city that was held, the former imperial capital at Hue, served to galvanize the urban population of the South against the Communists. In that location, the NVA forces were able to establish firm control everywhere by February 1, 1968, except for one ARVN compound and one compound housing US forces. They would hold the area for nearly a month, until they were pushed out on February 26. In the aftermath, more than three-quarters of the city of Hue was left in ruins. The Communists rounded up foreigners (not only Americans, but also Germans, Filipinos, and Koreans) and those who were thought to have ties to the Saigon regime. Some were subjected to show trials and then executed; others were summarily executed in secret; still others were witnesses executed to cover up these earlier crimes. As many as 2,800 people may have perished as a result.[112] The Saigon regime was able to produce propaganda based on these killings as proof that a bloodbath would result from a Communist takeover.[113] However, these killings failed to make a dent in American public opinion because the depth of the violence in Hue

---

108   Sophie Quinn-Judge, "The Ideological Significance in the DRV and the Significance of the Anti-Party Affair, 1967–68," *Cold War History* 5, no. 4 (November 2005): 480–2.

109   Ibid., 484–5; Nguyen, *Hanoi's War*, 91–4.

110   Nguyen, *Hanoi's War*, 101.

111   Ibid., 108.

112   Olga Dror, "Introduction," xxvi–xxxi.

113   Ministry of Foreign Affairs, Republic of Vietnam, *The War in Vietnam: Liberation of Aggression?* (Saigon, South Vietnam: Ministry of Foreign Affairs, 1968), 9–10.

was not uncovered for several months, by which time American atrocities had captured the headlines.

In a way, despite the tactical debacle of the Tet offensive, the North did meet certain strategic goals. One of Le Duan's main purposes for the offensive was to weaken the Johnson administration's position in an election year and embolden the antiwar movement in the United States. From this point of view, the Tet offensive was a strategic success. CBS news anchor Walter Cronkite famously argued that the war was unwinnable, leading Johnson to quip: "if I've lost Cronkite, I've lost middle America."[114] In March 1968 President Johnson made the decision not to seek reelection, largely because of the albatross of the war. In the meantime, on March 16, 1968, three platoons entered a village they called My Lai, on the central coast about fifteen kilometers to the northwest of the city of Quang Ngai. They lined up and killed more than three hundred villagers, including a significant number of children. This event would not come to be widely known until Seymour Hersh's reporting about the incident in November 1968, by which time it was only a coda to the other aspects of the war that had become a major issue in the 1968 presidential election.[115] The eventual winner, Republican Richard Nixon of California, pledged that he had a secret plan to end the war.

Though it has never become clear what Nixon's "secret plan" actually was, perhaps it may be derived from the policies put into effect when Nixon assumed office in January 1969. Nixon's policies deviated from those of the Johnson administration in several ways. First, Nixon was open about expanding the theater of war into Laos and Cambodia, expanding bombing raids and reconnaissance missions into those countries openly, whereas the official policy of the Johnson administration was not to violate the neutrality of the other two Indochinese countries. Nixon took a broader view of the war in Vietnam, seeing it as a symptom of a larger problem of relations with Cold War adversaries. He grasped that by taking an international view of the war, by taking advantage of the Sino-Soviet rift, and by attempting to improve relations with the USSR and China, he could substantially affect negotiations over the future of Vietnam.

Though the extent of direct US involvement in this coup is unclear, it was also very convenient that in 1970 Cambodia's neutralist prime minister, Prince Sihanouk, was deposed by his rival, right-wing military leader Lon Nol (1913–1985), particularly because Lon Nol was more than willing to take US aid and to allow US bombing in Cambodian territory. It is likely that US military forces—though not the CIA—were involved in this coup.[116] Additionally, the United States committed to a policy of Vietnamization, under which the US military trained the ARVN and provided them with better equipment. This allowed the ARVN to have a more active role in planning and fighting the war. It was also an attractive way of escalating the war while still potentially saving American money and lives.[117]

---

114 Nancy J. Woodhull and Robert W. Snyder, eds., *Defining Moments in Journalism* (New Brunswick, NJ: Transaction Publishers, 1998), 162.

115 Heonik Kwon, *After the Massacre: Commemoration and Consolidation in Ha My and My Lai* (Berkeley, CA: University of California Press, 2006), 2–3; Kendrick Oliver, *The My Lai Massacre in American History and Memory* (Manchester, UK: Manchester University Press, 2006), 1–5.

116 Ben Kiernan, "The Impact of Cambodia on US Intervention in Vietnam," in *The Vietnam War: Vietnamese and American Perspectives*, eds. Jayne Werner and Luu Doan Huynh (Armonk, NY: M. E. Sharpe, 1993), 216–32.

117 See Ngo Vinh Long's critique of Vietnamization in "Legacies Foretold: Excavating the Roots of Postwar Vietnam," in Scott Laderman and Edwin A. Martini, *Four Decades On: Vietnam, the United States, and the Legacies of the Second Indochina War* (Durham, NC: Duke University Press, 2013), 20–2.

Integral to Nixon's strategy were the ideas of his national security advisor, and later secretary of state, Henry Kissinger (b. 1923). Kissinger was a bookish former Harvard government professor who had arrived in New York when his family fled the Nazis in 1938. In 1951 he had written a nearly four hundred-page undergraduate honors thesis on nineteenth-century European historiography, essentially siding with the famed historian Oswald Spengler in holding that human beings were a product of their times, rather than the other way around, but that this should not entice people to submit blindly to history.[118] In his doctoral dissertation, Kissinger advocated applying this idea to international relations, arguing that statesmen operate within the confines of an international order but that by recognizing "the real relationship between forces" and using them to "serve his ends," the diplomat could change these circumstances.[119] These ideas are often glossed under the rubric of *realpolitik*, though Kissinger does not himself use the word.

Kissinger placed an emphasis on manipulating existing circumstances and actors to maximize the result for the United States, preferably without hindrance from "a cumbersome government bureaucracy, a shortsighted Congress, or the vagaries of public opinion."[120] Accordingly, the Nixon administration fought a "war for peace." Kissinger started negotiating in secret with Le Duc Tho in 1969, and the United States sought the upper hand in these negotiations with increasingly brutal bombings in Laos and Cambodia, and on targets in Hanoi.[121] Achieving such a peace agreement became more important for Nixon's domestic popularity; after 1968 the war became increasingly unpopular.

Meanwhile, the political and social situation in South Vietnam improved considerably in the late 1960s and early 1970s. The Second Republic featured two more democratic elections, a senate election in 1970 and a presidential election in 1972. The Second Republic was also blessed with a host of talented advisors, many of whom had advanced graduate training in the United States, who embarked on a number of successful programs to reform the economy, produce agricultural and land reforms, and produce a genuine dialogue and a true oppositional politics.[122]

In addition, American counterculture was overlaid on the urban culture of South Vietnam, which still reflected the influences of a Buddhist-tinged cosmopolitan existentialism that had prevailed since the late 1950s. The folk-tinged guitar music of Trinh Cong Son reflected existentialist themes and decried the war that was turning Vietnam into "a forest of dry bones" and "a mountain of graves."[123] By the early 1970s, the South had a hippie youth culture, particularly among urban youth of relatively well-to-do families, who sported long hair and embraced the credo of "make love, not war."[124]

---

118   Henry Kissinger, *The Meaning of History: Reflections on Spengler, Toynbee, and Kant* (Undergraduate Honors Thesis, Harvard University, 1951); Harvey Starr, *Henry Kissinger: Perceptions of International Politics* (Lexington: University Press of Kentucky, 2015), 63.

119   Henry Kissinger, *A World Restored: Metternich, Castlereigh and the Problems of Peace*; Quoted in Starr, *Henry Kissinger*, 53.

120   Nguyen, *Hanoi's War*, 133.

121   Ibid., 10.

122   For examples of these US trained bureaucrats, see Taylor, *Voices of the Vietnam War*.

123   John C. Schafer, "Death, Buddhism, and Existentialism in the Songs of Trinh Cong Son," *Journal of Vietnamese Studies* 2, no. 1 (2007): 167.

124   Olga Dror, "Raising Vietnamese: War and Youth in the South in the Early 1970s," *Journal of Southeast Asian Studies* 44, no. 1 (February 2013): 86–90.

As the war dragged into this early 1970s, the ARVN also performed well even as US troops began a rapid withdrawal of forces. A key benchmark for this program was the 1972 spring-summer offensive, in which the North tried to take advantage of the US weariness of the war and calculated that the ARVN would be weak because of the recent and considerable withdrawal of US troops. The NVA launched a general attack with conventional forces across the seventeenth parallel. Though they initially gained ground in Quang Tri province, ARVN forces, fighting with only US air support as assistance, beat back the NVA and prevented them from achieving a decisive victory.[125]

This ARVN success forced the north, represented by Le Duc Tho at the Paris talks, to become more engaged in diplomatic negotiations to end the war. In addition to concerns about the failure of NVA forces in 1972, party leaders in the North also worried about the rapid rapprochement between the United States and the People's Republic of China that was facilitated by President Richard Nixon's visit to that country in February 1972. Though those negotiations did not produce any concrete promises for the PRC to help the United States end the Vietnam War, the thawing of relations between these two enemies was disconcerting for North Vietnamese negotiators.[126] In December 1972 the Nixon administration launched the massive "Christmas bombing" campaign against Hanoi, which was designed to extract more concessions

from the North but had mixed results: it may have kick-started negotiations, but it led to more criticism of the United States' actions from the international community.[127]

In January 1973, nearly four years of negotiations between Kissinger and Le Duc Tho resulted in the Paris Peace Accords. This agreement specified that the United States would totally withdraw its military forces in sixty days, by the end of March 1973. In exchange, all US prisoners of war would be repatriated. However, the North Vietnamese Army would not have to withdraw from South Vietnam at all. The sovereignty of the Second Republic in South Vietnam was virtually rejected by the document. Not only was the Second Republic excluded from all negotiations, the agreement placed them on theoretically equal footing with the Provisional Revolutionary Government (PRG), a shadow government set up by the NLF in 1969 to administer areas under Communist control.[128] Nguyen Van Thieu, the president of South Vietnam, was only coerced into going along with the agreement because President Nixon made it very clear that all US aid to Vietnam would be cut off if he did not agree, and that the United States would ensure that North Vietnam would adhere to the terms of the agreement, including assurances that the United States would act if North Vietnam attacked across the seventeenth parallel and that substantial military aid would be forthcoming if Thieu agreed.[129]

125   Nguyen, *Hanoi's War*, 258; George J. Veith, *Black April: The Fall of South Vietnam, 1973–1975* (New York: Encounter Books, 2012), 85–7.

126   Pierre Asselin, *A Bitter Peace: Washington, Hanoi, and the Making of the Paris Agreement* (Chapel Hill: University of North Carolina Press, 2002), 36–7.

127   Nguyen, *Hanoi's War*, 296–7.

128   "Agreement on Ending the War and Restoring Peace in Viet-Nam, Signed in Paris and Entered into Force January 17, 1973," accessed May 20, 2016, https://www.mtholyoke.edu/acad/intrel/vietnam/treaty.htm

129   Nguyen Phu Duc, *The Viet-Nam Peace Negotiations: Saigon's Side of the Story* (Christiansburg, VA: Dalley Book Service, 2005), 372–9; Bui Diem, *In the Jaws of History*, 317; Van Nguyen Duong, *The Tragedy of the Vietnam War: A South Vietnamese Officer's Analysis* (Jefferson, NC: McFarland, 2008), 172.

As the Americans disengaged from South Vietnam at a rapid pace, the South Vietnamese economy was thrown into turmoil. By the fall of 1973, the Arab-Israeli War destabilized prices for oil in South Vietnam and caused perilous inflation. In the meantime, whatever attention the United States paid to Vietnam was now distracted by the priority of defending Israel.[130] The Organization of Petroleum Exporting Countries' oil embargo, which produced gasoline shortages in the United States and elsewhere, had a particularly devastating effect on Vietnamese oil imports, raising the cost of oil in South Vietnam by 400 percent. In 1973 inflation of more than 65 percent was coupled with rapid reductions in US economic and military aid pushed for by an increasingly antiwar congress in the United States. This forced South Vietnam to devalue its currency, the piaster, eight times between 1973 and 1975.[131]

These developments rendered the ARVN, which had built itself into a formidable fighting force as shown by the fighting in Quang Tri in 1972, a shadow of its former self by 1974. Tires, batteries, and M-16 rifle parts were all in short supply. ARVN units were forced to ration ammunition. Moreover, during the rapid US withdrawal, American forces took with them everything on military bases.[132] In some cases, they forced the ARVN to purchase their military bases from the US Army and then ripped out electrical wiring and took even the generators with them.[133]

In December 1974 the NVA decided to test whether the United States would maintain its commitment to aiding South Vietnam in the case of a violation of the Geneva Accords. They attacked Phuoc Long, a strategically important town near the Cambodian border, and managed to seize the area by January 1975. More importantly, the lack of an American response convinced officials in Hanoi that in the aftermath of the Watergate scandal and the resignation of President Nixon, the United States was not going to honor their commitment to President Thieu to enforce the Paris accords. The North could attack the South with impunity and without any fear of an American reprisal. As a result, by January 19, 1975, the leadership in Hanoi had decided on a final direct invasion to liberate South Vietnam.[134]

The North had benefitted from a massive increase in supplies from the Soviet Union. For years, the rivals in the Sino-Soviet rift had competed for Hanoi's favor. Now, however, they could supply North Vietnam directly through Haiphong harbor and by railroad without fear of American bombing. In March 1975, the NVA, led by General Van Tien Dung, began an assault on the central highlands in preparation for an extended campaign to take Saigon that the North assumed would not be finished until well into 1976. However, by mid-March, President Nguyen Van Thieu made the decision to pull out ARVN forces from the central highlands. It would prove to be a crucial mistake. The abandonment of this critical region caused widespread panic, increased the desertion of ARVN soldiers concerned for their families, and sparked a refugee crisis, with tens of thousands of people crowding the main outlets to the coasts to flee the Communists. As the end of March neared, South Vietnam's forces

---

130 Van Nguyen Duong, *The Tragedy of the Vietnam War*, 180.

131 Nguyen Phu Duc, *The Viet Nam Peace Negotiations*, 419; Nguyen Duc Cung, "Building a Market Economy during Wartime," in Taylor, *Voices from the Second Republic*, 101–3.

132 Nguyen Phu Duc, *The Viet Nam Peace Negotiations*, 419.

133 I am indebted to David Biggs for this information. He briefly discusses the case of Camp Eagle, which was to the southeast of Hue, in David Biggs, "Frame DS1050-1006DF129: March 20, 1969," *Environmental History* 19, (April 2014): 4–5.

134 Van Nguyen Duong, *The Tragedy of the Vietnam War*, 184–5.

collapsed around the defense of Saigon, and Hue and Quang Tri were ceded to Communist forces.[135] Under pressure, Nguyen Van Thieu resigned as president on April 21, 1975; a week later, in an effort to spur negotiations as anticipated by the Paris Peace Accords, Duong Van Minh became president on the hope that the PRG, which had expressed a willingness to negotiate, might be persuaded to find a neutral solution. However, the North was not interested in extending actual governance and control to their southern NLF/PRG allies; some PRG leaders, feeling betrayed, actually joined the exodus of Vietnamese refugees from a united Communist Vietnam.[136]

On April 30, 1975, Saigon fell to the Communist forces, and Vietnam was reunited under Communist rule. This meant an end to two decades of US intervention in Vietnam and at least a temporary peace. In the aftermath of this event, conditions changed rapidly. Street names in southern cities were changed to reflect the national heroes of the Communist pantheon. The Communists constructed camps for the "socialist reeducation" of those who were prominent members of the republic, or of the ARVN, or who had been employed by Americans or other forces allied with them. In total, perhaps more than one million people underwent socialist reeducation.[137] For some, this experience meant nothing worse than repeating the party line on Vietnamese history, even though it was being taught to them by an illiterate peasant. For others it meant starvation and beatings.[138] For perhaps as many as sixty-five thousand, it meant death.[139] As a result, many Vietnamese, especially from the South, fled on boats to refugee camps in Malaysia, Thailand, and Hong Kong, from whence they would be resettled in France, Germany, Canada, and the United States, among other countries. In 1975 alone, more than 125,000 Vietnamese were resettled in the United States.[140] This process would expand in the years to come, reproducing the cultural attributes of the Republic of Vietnam in the Vietnamese diaspora.

---

135 Ibid., 185–96; Veith, *Black April*, 299–382.

136 Nguyen Phu Duc, *Viet-Nam's Peace Negotiations*, 438–41.

137 Nathalie Huynh Chau Nguyen, *Memory is Another Country: Women of the Vietnamese Diaspora* (Santa Barbara, CA: ABC-Clio, 2009), 30.

138 Huynh Sanh Thong, "Introduction," in *To Be Made Over: Tales of Socialist Reeducation in Vietnam* (New Haven, CT: Yale Council on Southeast Asia Studies, 1988), vii–xiii.

139 Nathalie Huynh Chau Nguyen, *Memory is Another Country*, 30.

140 Karin Aguilar-San Juan, *Little Saigons: Staying Vietnamese in America* (Minneapolis: University of Minnesota Press, 2009), 19.

Chapter 13

China and Vietnam

Reforms, Crises, and War (1976–1990)

After Mao's death in 1976 and on his third return, Deng Xiaoping launched an unprecedented seismic reform in 1978 and opened China to the outside world in order to expand the Four Modernizations. Reformers emerged in large numbers with popular support and soon overthrew the Maoists. During 1986–1991, most Communist countries, including the Soviet Union, underwent political reforms and economic transformations. The epochal developments were spurred by Soviet leader Mikhail Gorbachev's bold reform programs, *glasnost* (policy reform, including openness and government transparency) and *perestroika* (economic reform), which helped to release the eastern bloc countries from the long Kremlin control. It was an open admission that economic stagnation in the Communist camp reached a point where it threatened national survival itself. In turn, freed former Soviet satellite countries in Eastern Europe adopted various political measures pursuing society-wide democratization and institutional pluralism. This effectively terminated not only the Soviet-led communist movement in the world but also the traditional East-West rivalry. China and Vietnam faced similar challenges and made their own choices during the worldwide Communist crisis.

Deng Xiaoping, as the leading figure of the second-generation leadership (1978–1989), took control and launched a wave of tremendous change, particularly in the evolution from a centrally planned economy to a free-market system seeking global inclusion and in meeting an increasingly popular demand for economic modernization along with improvement in the general standard of living. Deng adapted to the changing circumstances and prevented the CCP and the PRC from becoming financially insolvent, as happened in the Soviet Union a few years later. The economic reforms in the 1980s were, in Deng's words, comparable to "crossing the river by feeling the stepping stones." In other words, they were tentative and experimental in nature. These reforms have successfully transformed China from an agrarian economy to one of booming industry, which has in turn transformed its political structure from a communistic totalitarian government to one that remains centralized but with inherent self-balancing mechanisms that draw in factional and regional interests.

Even though the Cultural Revolution was said to have "crucially weakened the CCP's efficiency and morale," the party survived after Mao's death in 1976.[1] Spence points out that in the 1980s, "with the suppression

---

1   Spence, *The Search for Modern China*, 3rd ed. (New York: Norton, 2013), 551.

of the broad-based pleas for greater democratic participation, the party reconsolidated its power." Richard McGregor attributes the party's survival to leaders who had been able "to maintain the political institutions and authoritarian powers of old-style communism, while dumping the ideological straitjacket that inspired them."[2] According to Patrick Fuliang Shan's argument, the party's association with Chinese grass-roots society "in a total native social setting" guaranteed its flexibility and adaptation to the ever-changing China during the continuing revolution.[3] Our findings suggest that the CCP has grown beyond the Leninist party system, which depended on secrecy and institutional control, and has developed a self-improvement mechanism and functionality, which can adapt to a new environment and allow changes within the party. David Shambaugh concludes: "the CCP has exhibited many classic symptoms of an atrophying and decaying Leninist party—but, at the same time, it is also showing itself capable of significant adaptation and reform in a number of key areas."[4]

These changes are not without challenges, and more often than not the reforms contain issues of contradiction, uncertainty, and clashes that are inherent in the intermingling of tradition and modernity. Deng was required to make many promises by revising the constitution for more civil rights, institutionalizing the bureaucracy, and establishing checks and balances by giving more power to the National People's Congress (NPC).

After the national reunification in 1976, the Vietnamese government faced tremendous economic difficulties, refugee problems, social issues, and the war with Cambodia in 1977–1978. To make matters worse, the yearlong Sino-Vietnamese War in early 1979, in which Vietnam had to fight off 220,000 Chinese troops, took a toll on its economy. Known also as the Third Indochina War, it started when Deng Xiaoping decided to send the Chinese soldiers across the Sino-Vietnamese border in response to Hanoi's occupation of Cambodia, which was supported by China. Plagued by a multitude of pressing challenges, Hanoi decided in 1986 to change its economic policy by launching a reform movement, known as *doi moi* (or renovation). Among other important initiatives were the de facto decollectivization of agriculture, elimination of most price controls, and encouragement of small private companies. The following year, the government issued a new directive allowing foreign companies to invest, operate, and produce in Vietnam and offering favorable foreign investment acts.

The *doi moi* movement shifted the Vietnamese economy from state control to a market economy, resulting in an average annual growth rate of 8 percent from 1991 to 1996. After adopting its own "open door" policy with the West, cheap labor and cost production soon became attractive to foreign investments and manufacturing companies like Honda, Sony, Nike, and Wal-Mart. Vietnam's international trade and exchanges also led to the normalization of its diplomatic relationship with the United States in December 1995, twenty years after the end of the Vietnam War. In the late 1990s, however, the country continued to experience protests from various social groups such as the Protestant Montagnard ethnic minorities of the Central Highland and the Hoa Hao Buddhists in the south.

---

2   Richard McGregor, *The Party: the Secret World of China's Communist Rulers* (New York: Harper/Perennial, 2012), 26.

3   Patrick Fuliang Shan, "Local Revolution, Grassroots Mobilization and Wartime Power Shift to the Rise of Communism," in *Evolution of Power: China's Struggle, Survival, and Success*, eds. Xiaobing Li and Xiansheng Tian (Lanham, MD: Lexington Books, 2014), chapter 1.

4   Shambaugh, *China's Communist Party*, (Berkeley: University of California Press, 2008), 5.

Deng Xiaoping's Returns and Reforms

During the Chinese Cultural Revolution, Deng Xiaoping and many other old guard leaders were purged by Mao and his loyalists like the Gang of Four. The Gang of Four, however, lacked the administrative experience and any military background. Mao feared that the Gang of Four would plunge the country into new disturbance as they tried to achieve their revolutionary objectives. Mao in his last year rehabilitated several national leaders to assist the Gang of Four. Among the others was Deng Xiaoping, who was appointed by Mao a member of the CCP Central Committee in 1973 and vice chairman of the CMC in 1975.[5] When Mao and Zhou Enlai were both seriously ill, Deng began to direct the daily work of the party, government, and military. He tried to correct the wrongdoing of the Cultural Revolution and tackled all kinds of problems that involved economic development. After his return, however, Deng found himself in a new political struggle with Jiang Qing and the Gang of Four over his new economic and military reform programs. Jiang Qing began to criticize Deng's reform efforts and accused him of destroying the Cultural Revolution and returning to old capitalist lines. Mao soon dismissed Deng Xiaoping from the leadership positions in April 1976. Deng's second return was short and unsuccessful.

After Hua Guofeng purged the Gang of Four, he brought Deng Xiaoping back to power again in 1977. Hua, however, was a receiver of the Cultural Revolution and designated for prominence just by Mao himself. Hua reached the top through good fortune because he served Mao's home province of Hunan for more than two decades and through his loyalty to Mao. He found it difficult to separate himself from the past ten years when he was carrying out Mao's policies loyally. Deng rejected Mao's theory of continuing revolution, which had been endorsed by Hua. Eventually, Deng took over Beijing as the new paramount leader.[6] In 1978 Deng made his historic speech, "Emancipate the Mind," at the Third Plenary Session of the CCP Eleventh Party Central Committee. His speech declared an unprecedented seismic reform and an opening to the outside world so as to bring the "Four Modernizations" to China, including industry, agriculture, science and technology, and national defense.[7]

The desire for change helped bring about an important shift in fundamental economic philosophy in China. For the decades of Mao's era, state planning dominated China's economic life. It was

---

5 Ding Wei, "The 1975 CMC Enlarged Meeting," in Military History Research Division, China Academy of Military Science (CAMS), *Junqi piaopiao; xinzhongguo 50 nian junshi dashi shushi, 1949–1999* [PLA Flag Fluttering; Facts of China's Major Military Events in the Past Fifty Years, 1949–1999] (Beijing: Jiefangjun chubanshe [PLA Press], 1999), 2: 591; Merle Goldman and Roderick MacFarquhar, "Dynamic Economy, Declining Party-State," in *The Paradox of China's Post-Mao Reforms*, eds. Goldman and MacFarquhar (Cambridge, MA: Harvard University Press, 1999), 4.

6 Deng became the second generation of the CCP political and military leadership. See Li Cheng, *China's Leaders*, (Lanham, MD: Rowman & Littlefield, 2001), 7–9.

7 Deng, "Emancipate the Mind, Seek Truth from Facts, and Unite as One in Looking to the Future, December 13, 1978," speech as the closing session of the CCP Central Conference. This speech was prepared for the Third Plenary Session of the CCP Eleventh Central Committee. In fact, this speech served as the keynote address for the Third Plenary Session. See Deng Xiaoping, *Selected Works of Deng*, (Beijing: Foreign Languages Press, 1994) vol. 2: 150–63; and CCP Central Committee, "Communiqué of the Third Plenary Session of the CCP Eleventh Central Committee," adopted on December 22, 1978. The Party document is included in Research Department of Party Literature, CCP Central Committee, ed., *Major Documents of the People's Republic of China—Selected Important Documents since the Third Plenary Session of the Eleventh CCP Central Committee* (Beijing: Foreign Languages Press, 1991), 20–2.

Deng who brought the idea and practice of market economy into his reform plan. He carried out the economic reform through a series of gradual changes and created a more market-oriented economy. Deng explained in a talk when he was on his inspection tour in Southern China that it was crucial for China to rely on reform to liberate productive forces.[8] Challenging the ideology and practice of traditional state planning economy, Deng called for the stimulation of the economy by opening China to the outside world and the adoption of the Western model and technology in economic activities to mend problems China confronted. "We must learn to manage the economy by economic means," he suggested.[9] There were hurdles in the process of modernization yet "the reforms are irreversible in their direction," he continued.[10]

Deng achieved his goal in economic reform through a number of specific reform policies, all of which came together to form a more capitalist market economy. For instance, he created "Special Economic Zones" (SEZ), urban areas open to free trade to attract foreign businesses and investment. The joint ventures soon became practical for foreign investors in the SEZs, looking for a Chinese partner, setting up a joint company or a project through agreements, and then carrying out operations by both parties. Cheap labor, low-cost facilities, and huge domestic markets were attractive for foreign investors. He later expanded the experience to the rest of the country. Among the first group of SEZs were Shenzhen, Zhuhai, and Xiamen.

In Shenzhen, the manufacturing factories increased from twenty-six in 1980 to five hundred in 1984. In that year, this previously underdeveloped Chinese town had fulfilled over three thousand business agreements with foreign investors from fifty countries, with a total value of $2.3 billion. In 1991 the four SEZ cities accounted for 14.32 percent of the national export value. In the 1980s Deng opened fourteen more cities along China's coast for foreign investments and joint ventures. SEZs were so successful that they became an economic reform engine and played an instrumental role in integrating China into the global economy.

In the countryside, Deng instituted a set of new land reforms, also known as the "Household Production Responsibility System" (HPRS) in 1979. The policy of individual responsibility implemented first in Sichuan and Anhui provinces that allowed peasants to own land temporarily under contract and to decide for themselves what might be able to increase their production directly linked agricultural production to the wealth of peasants. Essentially, the HPRS kept land under the state's permanent ownership, but leased it to private citizens for long periods of time. The expansion of the scope of private markets that provided peasants with an opportunity for commercial activities to sell their profitable crops in free markets ensured the improvement in the quality of life for peasants. The word "rich" was no longer associated with "capitalism." Instead, to strike it rich became the ultimate goal for peasants. Harrison Salisbury described the change between Mao's era and Deng's era in this way: "Mao helped the peasants seize the land from the rich and then took it back for the communes" while "Deng gave the land back

---

8 Deng, *Deng Xiaoping Nan Xun Jiang Hua (Talks Made on Southern China Inspection Tours) 1992, Zhongguo Jingjiwang*, *http//:www.ce.cn.com* accessed on January 15, 2012.

9 Deng, *Deng Xiaoping Wenxuan* (Selected Works of Deng Xiaoping), 1975–1982 (Beijing: Xinhua Chubanshe, 1983), 2: 119–20; Michael E.Marti, *China and the Legacy of Deng Xiaoping: From Communist Revolution to Capitalist Evolution* (New York: Potomac Book, 2002), 2.

10 Richard Nixon, *In the Arena* (New York: Simon and Schuster, 1990), 60; Michael E.Marti, *China and the Legacy of Deng Xiaoping*, 19.

to the peasants, demolished the commune structure, and watched the rice bowls overflow. He put money into people's pockets, money they earned themselves."[11]

The primary focus of Deng's reform is China's modernization, including economic development, the opening of China to the outside world, prospering within the current world system, and pragmatism as his political philosophy. He knew that some of China's neighboring countries like Japan, South Korea, and Singapore had experienced a period of rapid economic growth. As a result, these nations successfully joined the ranks of the developed countries. Deng's concern with the economic inefficiency in state enterprises under the central government helped him to rethink and develop a scheme to turn inefficiency into efficiency by subjection to market forces. He promised that China should follow the East Asian model and also maintain an accelerated economic growth rate. He stated, "… it is now both possible and necessary for us to bring about, in the prolonged process of modernization, several periods of rapid growth with good economic returns. We must have this ambition." Deng continued, "In developing the economy, we should strive to reach a higher level every few years. … Guangdong, for example, should try to mount several steps and catch up with the 'four little dragons' of Asia in twenty years."[12]

Nevertheless, Deng still believed that only socialism could save China. Yet he also contended that Marxism stressed the importance of dynamics and change. An important part of Deng's theory lies in his exploration of the theory of socialism: Why must China have a socialist system? Do the planning systems and market mechanisms really distinguish socialism from capitalism? These ideological questions directly affected the direction of China's development. Under Deng's idea of socialism, China gradually moved toward a market economy with both state and private sectors. He encouraged the practice of provincial and private enterprises in their choices of capital allocation for profitable production. Commenting on the theory and practice of socialism with Chinese characteristics, Richard McGregor, an Australian born reporter for the *Financial Times*, remarked that "far from harming socialism … the unprecedented partnership between a communist party and capitalist business" worked well. He concluded that "… entrepreneurs, properly managed and leashed to the state [local], are the key to keep communist rule afloat."[13]

Deng further explained that the reason that China lagged behind the developed capitalist countries in its economy, technology, and culture was not due to the socialist system, but basically to China's history prior to 1949, when the People's Republic was established. Deng was confident that China would "develop more rapidly than the economy of any capitalist country."[14] The creation of a Chinese style of socialism demonstrated Deng's practical understanding of Marxism and his pragmatic method to build the country for a better future. Because of Deng, the free market faith took root. Market mechanisms, individual property rights, and less central government interference with enterprises became the driving forces to revitalize China's economy. The shifting of powers from the central government to local governments in economic reforms and the acceptance of private enterprises received public support and appreciation.

---

11 Harrison Salisbury, *The New Emperors: China in the Era of Mao and Deng* (New York: Harper Perennial, 1993), 392.

12 Deng, *Selected Works*, 3: 363, 365.

13 Richard McGregor, *The Party: The Secret World of China's Communist Rulers* (New York: HarperCollins Publisher, 2010), 198.

14 Deng, *Selected Works*, 2: 174–5

Economic Growth and Opening to the West

As a traditional agrarian country since ancient times, agriculture has played a crucial role in China's economy and its social stability. Its current agricultural production must meet the food needs of 1.3 billion people, over 20 percent of the world's total population. The grain crops, about 80 percent of total farming acreage in 1978, included wheat, corn (maize), soybean, millet, and tubers. The total grain outputs increased from 113.2 million tons in 1949 when the PRC was founded, to 304.8 million tons in 1978, and to 508.4 million tons in 1999. They were about 83 percent of the gross value of the total agricultural outputs in 1949, 64 percent in 1978, and 51 percent in 1999.[15] The rural sideline products, accounting for 4.3 percent of the total agricultural output value in 1949, increased to 17.1 percent in 1980. Village- and town-run enterprises included medical herb farms, botanical gardens, silkworm and mulberry farms, and food processing. Over 1.48 million rural sideline enterprises hired more than thirty million workers in 1980. The state supported the growth of the sideline enterprises in the rural areas.

The tertiary industries, such as real estate, finance, insurance, accounting, legal service, tourism, entertainment, public transportation, postal service, commerce, and telecom services, have undergone significant growth in China since the 1980s. The market-oriented economic reform focused on an open-trade and consumer-oriented growth strategy that encouraged service sectors with favorable policy support. From 1978 to 1988, the Chinese government invested $175.9 billion in capital construction of basic infrastructure, more than 1.5 times of the total investment in the previous years, from 1952 to 1977. As a result, the service industry grew much faster than the rest of the economy from 1979–1991; while the GDP grew 7–9.4 percent annually, the service sectors grew in double digits.[16]

In 1983 the centralized, state-owned and operated financial institutions began their reforms by moving to exercising monetary control though setting reserve requirements, managing credit funds, and granting more loans to the private sector, similar to the operation of monetary mechanisms in the West. The banks were also decentralized by separating from PBC (People's Bank of China) and specializing in their particular spheres of influence: ABC (Agricultural Bank of China) handles financial needs in agriculture; CCB (China's Construction Bank) and CBC (China's Bank of Communication) focus on domestic transactions; ICBC (Industrial and Commercial Bank of China), CDB (China Development Bank), and CIB (China Investment Bank) work with loans and lending activities; and BOC (Bank of China) specializes in international transactions, having numerous branch offices in many countries. Since the mid-1980s, a secondary financial market has gradually developed for government bonds. In August 1986 the Shenyang Trust and Investment Company first began with over-the-counter trading, then the Shanghai Stock Exchange (SSE) opened in December 1990, and the Shenzhen Stock Exchange (SZSE) opened in July 1991, creating a bond market to generate new financial resources from the society.[17]

During his economic reform, Deng continued to open China to the outside world, especially the West. He summarized the foreign-policy guideline

---

15   Susan Whiting, *Power and Wealth in Rural China: The Political Economy of Institutional Change* (Cambridge, UK: Cambridge University Press, 2006), introduction and chapter 1.

16   Michael Pettis, *Avoiding the Fall: China's Economic Restructuring* (New York: Carnegie Endowment Publishing, 2013), sections 1–2.

17   Xiaobing Li, "Financial Institutions," in *Modern China*, 131–3.

as "observe patiently, respond sensibly, consolidate our own footing, be skillful in hiding one's capacities and biding one's time, be good at the tactics of low profile diplomacy, never take the lead, and take proper initiatives."[18] The open door economic policy reflected a fundamental change in China's developmental strategy. From 1978 to 1981, a drive to improve relations with the United States was an important component of China's opening to the outside world. The United States had financial resources and technology China needed for its economic growth and four modernizations.[19] A better and closer relationship with Washington would bring in direct investment, new technology, and international market share. Deng sought every opportunity to improve the Sino-U.S. relationship after the normalization of Beijing-Washington diplomacy on January 1, 1979. As the result, the U.S. accepted China as the Most Favored Nation in trading status in July 1979, and signed a new Shanghai Communique with China when President Ronald Reagan met Deng Xiaoping in August 1982.[20] Then, the U.S. Department of State changed the PRC status to the category of "friendly, non-allied" country in May 1983.

Low labor costs have made China one of the major sources for low-priced manufactured products across the world, particularly for the United States during the 1980s. The new international trade policies have been extraordinarily successful at transforming China from a closed economy to a major trading nation in a relatively short time. In 1987 China resumed its status as a member of the General Agreement on Tariffs and Trade (GATT). China's total foreign trade rose from $21 billion in 1978 to over $80 billion in 1988, a fourfold increase within ten years. China's exports to the United States and other countries significantly increased in the 1990s and included miscellaneous manufactured articles such as toys, games, clothing and apparel, as well as footwear and domestic products. Since the 1990s China has expanded the exports and moved far beyond cheap manufacturing by including petrochemicals, fertilizers, polymers, machine tools, shipping, and electric appliances in their exports.

During Deng's economic reform, China's GDP increased about 7–9 percent annually from $58 billion in 1979 to $356 million in 1989. The GDP per capita increased from $180 in 1979 to $323 in 1989. Automobile manufacturing grew from 443,400 vehicles in 1985 to 1.1 million vehicles in 1992. During the 1980s, the service industry, including tourism, entertainment, public transportation, post, commerce, and telecom services, has seen significant growth in the country. Deng's market-oriented economic reform focused on an open-trade and consumer-oriented growth strategy that encouraged served sectors with favorable policy support. As a result, the service industry grew much faster than the whole economy from 1979 to 2000.[21]

18 Qu Xing, "China's Foreign Policy since the Radical Changes in Eastern Europe and the Disintegration of the USSR," *Waijiao Xueyuan Xuekan* [Journal of Foreign Affairs Collage] 4 (1994), 19–22.

19 Among the recent publications in English on the Sino-American rapprochement are William Burr, ed., *The Kissinger Transcripts: The Top-Secret Talks with Beijing and Moscow* (New York: New Press, 1999); Jim Mann, *About Face: A History of America's Curious Relationship with China, from Nixon to Clinton* (New York: Knopf, 1999); Rosemary Foot, *The Practice of Power: U.S. Relations with China since 1949* (Oxford, England: Oxford University Press, 1997); Ross, *Negotiating Co-operation: The United States and China, 1969–1989*.

20 Cohen, *America's Response to China* 5th ed. (New York: Columbia University Press, 2010), 206–7.

21 Jing Luo, "Deng Xiaoping's Reforms," in Luo ed., *China Today*, 1: 121.

Foreign Policy Initiatives: Vietnam, Hong Kong, and Macao

Deng Xiaoping's pragmatism also caused a major shift of China's foreign policy from revolutionary, communist ideology to nationalist interests and domestic development. Although Deng changed China's status in the late 1970s from an isolated outsider to an actively engaged insider of the international community, he tried to keep China in a low profile as one of the third-world developing countries to create a "peaceful international environment" for his economic reform and opening to the Western world. Deng, however, did not miss any opportunity to eliminate any potential national security threat and gain new territory with national sovereignty. His decision to go to war against Vietnam in 1979 and negotiating efforts for the return of Hong Kong and Macao revealed his active participation in the Asian-Pacific affairs.

After the Vietnam War ended in 1975, Hanoi had allied with the Soviet Union against China in Southeast Asia. In 1978, Vietnam invaded Cambodia and occupied the capital city. In the meantime, other issues between Beijing and Hanoi also reached the brink of war, including disputed border areas and islands in the South China Sea, expelling 300,000 Chinese Vietnamese refugees, and attacks on the border villages on Chinese side. China closed the Sino-Vietnamese border on December 25, 1978 and deployed more than 200,000 troops along the border.[22]

On February 17, 1979, Deng issued the order to his generals to invade Vietnam. More than 220,000 PLA troops crossed the border and attacked the Vietnamese Army. By February 26, the PLA occupied Lao Cai, Cao Bang, and Ha Jiang. By March 5, the Chinese also took over Mong Cai, Cam Duon, and Lang Son. Nevertheless, the PLA troops suffered very heavy casualties more than 1,300 soldiers killed every day. The poor discipline, low morale, combat ineffectiveness, and the high casualties on the part of Chinese troops in the 1979 Sino-Vietnam War shocked many of the PLA's commanding officers.

On March 5, the Chinese government decided to stop the invasion of Vietnam and began to withdraw the PLA troops to China. Although the Chinese troops returned by March 16, the Sino-Vietnamese border conflict continued from 1979 to 1992. Among the large-scale battles were the PLA attacks on Vietnamese positions in the mountains near Lao Son in April-May 1984. More than 1,000 Chinese soldiers were killed during the five-week attack. By the end of the 1980s, tension eased along the border, and the two nations normalized their diplomatic relationship. In 1992, all the PLA troops withdrew from their positions at Lao Son in Vietnam.

In the 1980s, Deng Xiaoping began negotiations with the British government for the return of Hong Kong, and with the Portuguese government for the return of Macao. After the Qing Dynasty (1644–1911) lost the First Opium War (1839–1841) to Great Britain, the Chinese government was forced to sign the humiliating Treaty of Nanjing (1842), ceding Hong Kong to the British in perpetuity. After the Second Opium War, the British acquired Kowloon in 1860 and subsequently the New Territories in 1898, as part of a ninety-nine-year lease agreement. In the 1970s Hong Kong's economy took off with an annual growth rate between 6 and 8 percent. In the 1980s its exports reached $73 billion. Deng Xiaoping developed a theory of "one country, two systems" to apply to the territories under European colonial administrations. In 1984 the PRC and UK governments signed an agreement for China to resume its sovereignty over Hong Kong. On July 1, 1997, Britain returned Hong Kong to China, and Beijing established the Hong Kong

---

22   Xie Guojun, "The Sino-Vietnamese Border War of Self-defense and Counter-offense," in CAMS, *Junqi piaopiao* [PLA Flag Fluttering], 624–5.

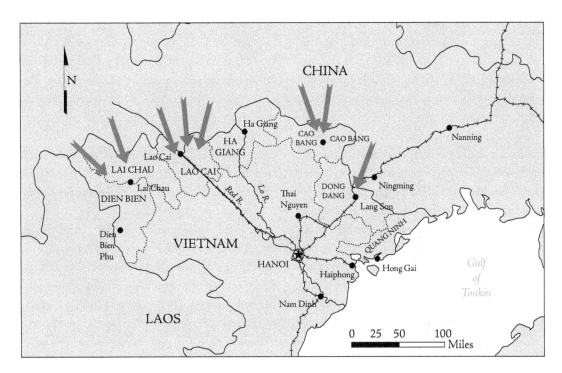

FIGURE 13.1 The Sino-Vietnam War

Special Administrative Region (HKSAR) as an autonomous government. Chee-hwa Tung was elected as the first Hong Kong chief executive in July 1997. More than two years later, in December 1999, successful negotiations with the Portuguese, who had controlled Macao since the mid-sixteenth century, led to the latter's return to China. Like its neighbor Hong Kong, Macao became another special administrative region in accordance with the "one country, two systems" policy.

The 1989 Tiananmen Square Incident

However, the capitalist market-economy tested the limit of Deng Xiaoping's reform under the CCP leadership. China's reform was different from that in the Soviet Union in the 1980s. Soviet leader Mikhail Gorbachev launched both economic and political reforms as *glasnost* and *perestroika*

by providing some autonomy and freedom to the local economy and government to save the USSR. Deng Xiaoping was afraid of political instability and social disorder so he focused on liberal economic reform while discouraging and even stifling political reform.[23] He proved his strategy working since Gorbachev's political reform undermined the people's support to communism as a state ideology and led to the collapse of the Soviet Union in 1991. To save the state and the party, Deng insisted on the "Four Cardinal Principles"—keeping to the Socialist road, upholding the people's democratic dictatorship, abiding the CCP's leadership, and adhering to Marxism-Leninism and Maoist thought. Deng believed that, while China must keep its door open to the world, stability must be stressed; to guarantee stability, the party must be in control.[24]

Therefore, Deng Xiaoping was unwilling and unable to carry out political reform in China since he

---

23   Xiaosi Yang, "Politics of Deng Xiaoping," in Luo ed., *China Today*, 1: 115.

24   Anita Chan, "The Social Origins and Consequences of the Tiananmen Crisis," 105.

needed the party's support. Nevertheless, the CCP began a major change in the 1980s. The political tradition of the CCP as a peasant/worker party was dropped, and the party's policy suffered under many of Deng's compromises he needed to have to strike with business leaders, social elite, and military leaders. It became a new political culture to use public resources to cater to particularistic loyalty, even if the same activities would be perceived as corrupt in the West. In particular, the norm of reciprocity embedded in CCP political culture socialized people to treat corrupt exchanges as neutral and acceptable. Moreover, the Chinese culture emphasizes hierarchical relationships, order and harmony, which might also consolidate Chinese people's trust in political party and government. The Party still controlled the government, economy, media, and military. Privileged interest groups and individuals, who had a position or connection in the government, dominated market and economy. By the 1990s, the CCP transformed into a party dominated by elite and power-interest groups, who works for the upper social class, rather than peasants and workers.

To secure the military support to his reform policy, Deng also allowed the PLA to run business like manufacturing, transportation, agriculture, mass media, and service industry including banks, hotels, and restaurants. General Xiong Guangkai, deputy chief of the PLA General Staff, believed PLA-owned enterprises as a double-edged sword, it could help military financially, but at the same time it could hurt the PLA militarily and politically.[25]

Thus, Deng could not reach the goal of his reform that socialist China would realize common prosperity among all people. Many people, who lived at the bottom of the society, particularly the peasants, did not share much of the fruit from Deng's economic reform. Through these years, it seemed that more policies were employed to protect the rights of rich people. The issue of income disparity resulted from Deng's decision to let a few people get rich first. Since he did not mention who were these people, the powerful and well-connected people were really getting rich fast.

In 1987–1989, more and more people began to complain about power abuse, mismanagement, official corruption, and economic scandals in the party and government.[26] While public opinion was turning increasingly critical of the CCP's handling of economy, Beijing's leadership became polarized between the old-guard conservatives and reforming leaders like Hu Yaobang and Zhao Ziyang. In 1988, Hu lost his fight and was dismissed from his position as the CCP Secretary General. On April 15, 1989, Hu died in Beijing. Soon his memorial activities turned into a widespread movement led by the college students against the bureaucracy, corruption, and one-party government. The conservative leaders, including China's President Yang Shangkun and Premier Li Peng, denounced the students' protesting in Beijing as an anti-government movement.[27]

The denouncement from the authority did not scare the students, and instead hundreds of thousands of students came to the Tiananmen Square (Beijing's Washington Mall) and launched a large-scale demonstration in early May. Many citizens in the capital city joined their pro-democracy

---

25   General Xiong Guangkai, *International Strategy and Revolution in Military Affairs* (Beijing: Tsinghua University Press, 2003), 180.

26   Xiaobing Li, "Introduction: Social-Economic Transition and Cultural Reconstruction in China," in *Social Transition in China*, eds. Jie Zhang and Xiaobing Li (Lanham, MD: University Press of America, 1998), 1–18.

27   Deng's views were reflected in an April 26, 1989, editorial in the *Renmin ribao* (People's Daily). See Zhang Liang, ed., *The Tiananmen Papers; The Chinese Leadership's Decision to Use Force against Their Own People—in Their Own Words* (New York: Public Affairs, 2001), 71–5.

demonstration against corruption and party-state government. The movement soon spread to 116 cities in China, including the major cities like Shanghai, Tianjin, Chongqing, Guangzhou, and Wuhan. On May 6–16, the students camped at the Tiananmen Square and demanded a dialogue with the government officials. Some of them began their hunger strike to show their determination to promote democracy and to root out corruption.[28]

The conservative leaders blamed the nationwide demonstrations to the reformist leaders like Zhao Ziyang and kept the Party Elders on their side, including Li Xiannin, Bo Yibo, and Wang Zhen. Although Deng Xiaoping was at Wuhan in May–June, he also supported the conservative leaders' position against the Tiananmen movement. With Deng's agreement, President Yang Shangkun issued martial law in Beijing on May 13 in order to end the students' occupation of the Tiananmen Square.[29] Martial law, however, did not work at all. On May 23, the students who remained in the square organized the largest demonstration in Beijing. Many teachers, workers, peasants, professionals, and city residents supported their demonstration. After he talked to Deng on the phone, Yang met the top military leaders next day and decided to employ military measures to stop the Tiananmen Square demonstration.[30] The PLA sent twenty-two infantry divisions from thirteen different armies to Beijing under the "Martial Law Force Command." Since the party and military had been polarized over the students' demonstration in May, Yang and the PLA high command were not sure about each army's loyalty to the Party Center and attitude toward the event.[31]

In late May, while the PLA troops moved into the city, they faced strong resistance of the students and city residents with mostly non-violent activities, like tailgate parties and street cooking, but the others involved in burning furniture and turned over buses as roadblocks. Many of the PLA troops were stopped in the suburbs of Beijing, and their vehicles were blocked in the city street. Some of them felt "varying degrees of sympathy for the students." After the event, the PLA carried out investigations against those who questioned martial law and refused to follow their orders. Among the punished were 111 PLA officers who had "breached discipline in a serious way and 1,400 soldiers shed their weapons and ran away."[32] The majority of them were reprimanded or charged thereafter, and a number of high-level military officials lost their positions in the aftermath. General Xu Qinxian, for example, feigned illness to avoid commanding his troops against the demonstrators in Beijing.[33]

On June 2, the party leaders issued the order to open fire on the crowds "put a quick end to the turmoil and restore order in the capital."[34] When some troops hesitated, the Party Center called all the troops on June 3 to use all necessary means, including tanks and machine guns, to put down the "counter-revolutionary riot" by force.

In the evening of June 3, the PLA troops forced their way through the city streets of Beijing. They shot those who tried to stop the troop movements. About 1:00 a.m. on June 4, they arrived at the Tiananmen Square and confronted with tens of thousands of students. The troops opened fire on the crowds, and their tanks and armored vehicles

---

28 Ibid., 121–2.

29 Ibid.

30 Zhang, ed., ibid., 287–8, 302–3.

31 Martial Law Troop Command, "Martial Law Situation Report, no. 3, May 19," in Zhang, ed., ibid., 227.

32 Extracts from military security report are included in a CMC document, dated December 29, 1989.

33 Harlan Jencks, "Civil-Military Relations in China: Tiananmen and After," *Problems of Communism* 40 (May–June 1991), 22.

34 For more details on the Tiananmen Incident, see Zhang, ed., ibid; Goodman and Segal, eds., *China in the Nineties*.

ran through the students' tents. By 6:00 a.m. next morning, the troops cleared the square.[35] At least one thousand students were killed at the Tiananmen Square that night. Red Cross estimated at least 3,000 civilian casualties on June 3–4 in Beijing.[36] It also became known as the "Tiananmen Square Massacre" or "June 4 Event."

The Tiananmen Square Event was a major setback of Deng Xiaoping's reform movement. It tested the limit of CCP political adaptation and democratization, and revealed the restraint of the one-party system from cooperating with various political and social groups in achieving economic growth. Law enforcement, military power, and use of force still played the indispensable roles in Deng's China as it did during Mao's era. After June 1989, the international community condemned Beijing's use of military force to kill students and civilians in the streets. U.S. President George H. W. Bush suspended all official exchanges with China and joined Western countries to impose economic sanctions on China. Deng retired from his official positions in 1989, and died on February 28, 1997.[37]

One scholar points out, "If Mao Zedong is remembered as the founder of the People's Republic of China, as well as the source of wave after wave of nerve-wracking political campaigns, Deng Xiaoping is remembered for deprogramming Mao's system and for leading China onto the road of economic prosperity."[38] His reform, however, succeeded at high costs, including losing the party's political control, decentralizing the government,

increasing stratification and inequalities in the society, and the declining status of the military. The military elites patiently waited for the party to reward their loyalty and support during the Tiananmen Square crackdown, as promised by the paramount leader. After Deng Xiaoping's passing, they expected a big payback from his successor Jiang Zemin, the new third generation of the Chinese Communist leadership.

The Third Indochina War and Economic Failure in a Unified Vietnam

In the decade after its reunification (which formally occurred in 1976), the Vietnamese government also grappled with many difficult issues, including a refugee crisis, a failed attempt to collectivize agriculture in the south, and the Third Indochina War, which is a term for the interrelated conflicts of the late 1970s that involved a border conflict with China and a war between Vietnam and Cambodia in which the China became heavily involved.

In the late 1970s, the Hanoi government's main priority was to rebuild the newly united country. They had to assert their unquestioned will over political affairs. The need to exercise control meant making sure that their allies in the former GVN did not challenge them. Members of the former NLF/GVN movement were therefore removed from political authority in the years after 1975.[39] In addition, cadres running reeducation camps attempted to

---

35 Party Central Office Secretariat, "Minutes of the Politburo Standing Committee Meeting, June 3, 1989," in Zhang, ed., ibid., 368–70.

36 The official statistics listed 264 deaths, including twenty-three college students and twenty PLA soldiers and officers. The Beijing Red Cross estimated 2,600 deaths, and China Radio International reported in Beijing on June 4 that "several thousand people, mostly innocent citizens" had been killed by "heavily armed soldiers." See Zhang, ed., ibid., 385, 389.

37 Xiaobing Li, "Reforming the People's Army: Military Modernization in China," *Journal of Southwest Conference on Asian Studies* 5 (2005), 17.

38 Jing Luo, "Reform of Deng Xiaoping," in Luo, ed., *China Today*, 1: 121.

39 Truong Nhu Tang, "The Myth of a Liberation," *New York Review of Books* (October 21, 1982), 31–36.

ensure the ideological purity of those remaining in the former South Vietnam.

In agricultural policy, Hanoi sought a quick transformation of Southern lands. Party leaders believed that it was imperative to remove all vestiges of feudal land ownership from the Mekong delta and other southern areas. Therefore, by 1976, the party embarked upon a bold strategy of collectivization. This process differed markedly from land reform, in which farmers would be categorized and land redistributed based on wealth. Instead, under collectivization, lands were immediately taken by the state in order to create advantageous economies of scale. Party leaders assumed that collectivization would help align southern peasants with Communism.

That effort did not succeed. In 1978 Vietnam faced devastating famine from the lack of production on collectivized farms and the scarcity of basic goods.[40] By 1980 many of the collective farms that had been set up in the south were no longer functioning.[41] There are several possible explanations for this failure. First, perhaps southern Vietnamese farmers were unwilling to cede property control to the state as obediently as their northern counterparts had. Second, the southern economy had already been decimated by the pre-1975 inflation. It had lost a substantial portion of its population as refugees fled. Finally, since Northern cadres were responsible for the collectivization efforts, some southern farmers saw their organizing efforts as a kind of carpet-bagging.

The failed collectivization contributed to a decimation of the Vietnamese economy in the early 1980s. Other reasons for this decline included the rapid depopulation of some southern areas, the increasing difficulty of maintaining the levels of foreign aid to which Vietnam had become accustomed in earlier decades, particularly from China and the Soviet Union, and the increasing expense, in both blood and treasure, of the Third Indochina War.

Meanwhile, the refugee crisis continued unabated. Whereas in 1975 and 1976, most refugees fled southern Vietnam to avoid political persecution, some refugees also continued to flee Vietnam in the late 1970s and 1980s because of the increasingly dire state of the economy. By the spring of 1978, the outflow of refugees had hit more than 1,500 per month.[42] By 1979 the number was in the tens of thousands per month. Moreover, of the more than 550,000 refugees that arrived in camps in such places as Malaysia or Hong Kong, only about one-third had been resettled to their final destinations in Europe or North America.[43]

In that year, after a conference in Geneva and in consultation with the United States and Vietnamese governments, the United Nations Office of the High Commissioner for Human Rights announced the Orderly Departure Program, under which Vietnamese could be preapproved to leave legally and resettlements would be streamlined. From 1979 to the mid-1990s, when the program was closed in the face of normalizing relations between Vietnam in the United States, more than 600,000 Vietnamese

---

40   Danielle Labbé, *Land Politics and Livelihoods on the Margins of Hanoi, 1920–2010* (Vancouver: University of British Columbia Press, 2014), 95.

41   Benedict J. Kerkvliet, *The Power of Everyday Politics: How Vietnamese Peasants Transformed National Policy* (Ithaca, NY: Cornell University Press, 2005), 178.

42   Sucheng Chan, *The Vietnamese American 1.5 Generation: Stories of War, Revolution, Flight, and New Beginnings* (Philadelphia, PA: Temple University Press, 2006), 68.

43   Yen Le Espiritu, *Body Counts: The Vietnam War and Militarized Refugees* (Berkeley, CA: University of California Press, 2014), 52.

settled abroad under the program, more than 450,000 of whom settled in the United States.[44]

In the context of the chaos of collectivization and fleeing refugees, Vietnam was facing an increasingly bellicose threat from Cambodia. As we saw in chapter eleven, in 1970 Prince Sihanouk was overthrown by a military coup led by General Lon Nol, who set up the Khmer Republic (1970–1975). One of Lon Nol's first actions was to issue an ultimatum for all Vietnamese Communist forces to leave the territory they were occupying in eastern Cambodia within forty-eight hours—a demand that was popular among the Cambodian population. This announcement allowed Lon Nol to justify his encouragement of heavy American bombing of eastern Cambodia. This US B-52 bombing, which continued until August 1973, allowed his regime to persist until 1975.[45]

The bombing exacerbated the fault lines of an already fractured Cambodian politics. Eastern Cambodians harbored deep resentment for the Vietnamese. Over the course of the 1960s and early 1970s, the NVA had trampled their fields and occupied their lands. By 1970 ARVN troops began occupying areas of eastern Cambodia as well, and with them came reports of South Vietnamese troops looting and pillaging villages in eastern Cambodia.[46] These actions made the Lon Nol government vulnerable, particularly after the end of the US bombing campaign. It also played into the hands of Saloth Sar, a former teacher who went by the *nom de guerre* Pol Pot (1925–1998). Pol Pot led the Communist Party of Kampuchea

(CPK), better known by their informal name, the Khmer Rouge. From the 1960s, the Khmer Rouge was committed to a Maoist version of Communism based on the Cultural Revolution. They aimed to eliminate bourgeois and colonialist elements of Cambodian society to return the land to Khmer (ethnically Cambodian) farmers. A central point of their ideology was the restoration of the greatness of Cambodia as it existed during the powerful classical Angkor Empire (802–1431). Though a number of other Cambodian politicians shared this goal, including Lon Nol, only Pol Pot's CPK wished to accomplish it by attacking Vietnamese areas that had formerly been Cambodian and cleansing them of their non-Khmer population.[47]

In late April 1975, in the context of the destabilization of Indochina and the impending North Vietnamese conquest of the South, Pol Pot arrived in Phnom Penh with Khmer Rouge forces. By May 1975 the Khmer Rouge had created an eight-point plan of action that called for the evacuation of major cities, the abolition of markets, the withholding of all currency, the defrocking of monks, who were to be put to work growing rice, the execution of all leaders associated with the Lon Nol regime, and the establishment of cooperative farming throughout the country, along with communal eating, the expulsion of Vietnamese from the country, and the amassing of troops at the Vietnamese border.[48]

Pol Pot followed up on this plan by stationing massive numbers of troops at the Vietnamese border by 1977. In response, in July of that year, Le Duan made an attempt to stage a pro-Vietnamese coup

44   Jonathan H.X. Lee, *Chinese Americans: The History and Culture of a People* (Santa Barbara: ABC-Clio, 2015), xlii.

45   David Chandler, *A History of Cambodia* (Boulder, CO: Westview Press, 1992), 206; Ben Kiernan, *How Pol Pot Came to Power: Colonialism, Nationalism, and Communism in Cambodia, 1930–1975* (New Haven, CT: Yale University Press, 2004), xxiv.

46   Ben Kiernan, *How Pol Pot Came to Power*, 307.

47   Wilfred G. Burchett, *The Cambodia-China-Vietnam Triangle* (Chicago, IL: Vanguard Books, 1981), 58.

48   Ben Kiernan, *The Pol Pot Regime: Race, Power, and Genocide in Cambodia under the Khmer Rouge, 1975–79*, revised ed. (New Haven, CT: Yale University Press, 2014), 55.

within the CPK that failed.[49] He ordered Vietnamese troops to amass at the Cambodian border and began fighting skirmishes on the Cambodian side. In response to these decisions, the PRC made it clear that it would support the Pol Pot regime against what it perceived to be the aggressions of the Soviet-backed Le Duan regime in Vietnam. A clandestine war broke out and continued through 1978 on the Cambodian-Vietnamese border. This war burst into the open in December 1978, when the Vietnamese launched a massive counterattack into Cambodia. By January 1979 the Vietnamese had established a pro-Vietnamese and pro-Soviet People's Republic of Kampuchea, under the de facto leadership of Hun Sen (b. 1952), who is, as of 2019, still Cambodia's prime minister.

PRC leader Deng Xiaoping was in the middle of normalizing relations with the United States and did not want Vietnam's strategic position in the Communist world challenged by Soviet satellites. He sought to contain the Vietnamese, calling them "the Cubans of the Orient." If the Vietnamese were not taught "some necessary lessons," Deng said at a press conference in Washington, DC, "their provocations will increase."[50] He attacked Vietnamese towns on the Vietnam-China border, resulting in a massively destructive war that left chaos and suffering in its wake but was ultimately inconclusive. Chinese troops were eventually forced to retreat, but not before decimating Vietnamese towns near the Chinese border.[51]

Doi Moi in Vietnam (1986–2000)

By 1986 Vietnam was at a turning point. The collectivization of the South had not been successful, and the Third Indochina War took a toll on the economy. In 1982 Le Duan crushed what he perceived to be opposition from local officials in the South, including moderates who simply wished to reopen factories and feed a population that by the early 1980s was on a path to starvation. He worried cadres were turning the South into "another Yugoslavia"—in other words, that they were pursuing a capitalist economic deviation from the Soviet line. In 1983, when Le Duan was conveniently away on a trip to Moscow, party leaders met with cadres in the South in Dalat and asked them to speak freely about developments. This meeting, known as the Dalat affair, began to convince certain party leaders, chief among them Truong Chinh and Premier Pham Van Dong, of the dire economic situation, especially in the South. They concluded that a change of economic policy might be necessary.[52]

Two other developments allowed Vietnamese economic policy to change. The first was that the winds were shifting decidedly in favor of economic reform among Communist countries internationally. By the early 1980s, China was pursuing a path of economic reform directed by Premier Zhao Ziyang. Vietnam had become much closer to the Soviet Union and much more dependent on Soviet than on Chinese aid. But by 1985, Soviet policy was changing as well. In that year, Mikhail Gorbachev (b. 1931) had become the de facto leader and was embracing *perestroika*, a "restructuring" of the economic and political system in the face of lagging economic growth in the Soviet Union. The second development that precipitated change in Vietnam was the death of Le Duan in July 1986. Le Duan had been firmly at the helm in the early 1960s, and had been the major obstacle to a more flexible economic policy before 1986. When political and economic

---

49 King C. Chen, *China's War with Vietnam, 1979: Issues, Decisions, and Implications* (Stanford, CA: Hoover Institution Press, 1987), 34.

50 Quoted in Nayan Chanda, *Brother Enemy: The War after the War* (New York: Harcourt Brace Jovanovich, 1986), 354.

51 Ibid., 357–8.

52 Elliott, *Changing Worlds: Vietnam's Transition from Cold War to Globalization*, 43–6.

discontent reached its height in 1982, Le Duan sent investigative teams to the South to shut it down. His death allowed other party leaders to pursue reform.

The opportunity for such reform was the Sixth Party Congress in December 1986, when the party decided on a radical new direction. The Sixth Party Congress set into motion a series of new policies to be implemented by the end of the 1980s. Together, these reforms were known as *doi moi*, or renovation. By the late 1980s numerous reform measures had been implemented. These included allowing the payment of wages and salaries in cash, allowing small private companies, abolishing internal checkpoints between provinces, revising the foreign investment laws to allow non-Vietnamese companies to invest in joint ventures with Vietnamese firms, the de facto de-collectivizing of agriculture, eliminating most price controls to allow foreign participation in banking, and creating special "export processing zones" on the model of the special economic zones in China, in which 100 percent foreign-owned enterprises would be allowed to do business. Together, these policy changes represented a "dramatic shift toward a market economy."[53]

These reforms led to a gradual *rapprochement* between the Communist government of Vietnam and the forces that had once opposed it. The party worked to sign economic agreements with other non-Communist countries, including the United States, to increase foreign investment. This led to a number of agreements and to progress in diplomatic relations. By 1995, twenty years after the fall of Saigon, the United States and Vietnam established normal diplomatic relations. Realizing the economic power of remittances sent from refugees abroad, the Vietnamese government encouraged refugees to reestablish ties with their home country and to visit or even return to Vietnam.

Renovation rapidly changed the Vietnamese economy. From 1991 to 1996, the Vietnamese economy grew at an average annual rate of 8 percent.[54] The state became far more dependent on private business revenues and far less dependent on foreign aid. These changes led to predictable effects, such as the rise of billboard advertisements by multinational firms such as Coca-Cola, Honda, and Sony, the importation and widespread popularity of foreign films, and the growth of tourism. Young people in the 1990s began to carry mix tapes of their favorite heavy metal and grunge bands, such as Black Sabbath, Nirvana, or Metallica, along with them, and the popular press translated the lyrics into Vietnamese for the consumption of young people.[55]

However, the party made—and tolerated—political changes at a much slower rate. In the early years of the renovation policy, innovative writers such as Nguyen Huy Thiep (b. 1950) and Duong Thu Huong (b. 1947) stormed onto the scene. They offered criticisms of the party and exposed the starvation of the late 1970s and early 1980s. They criticized earlier party miscues such as the land reform. Filmmakers portrayed the party critically in cinema. In particular, the documentary films of Tran Van Thuy (b. 1940) led to reevaluations of the party. There were even efforts to have real debates in electing members of the national assembly. Ultimately, though, that assembly continues to be dominated by properly vetted members of the Vietnamese Communist Party. Vietnam remains a state tightly controlled by the party.

Just as in China, the road to economic reform in Vietnam has not always been smooth. In the

---

53 William S. Turley and Mark Selden, eds., *Reinventing Vietnamese Socialism: Doi Moi in Comparative Perspective* (Boulder, CO: Westview Press, 1993), 7.

54 Zachary Abuza, "The Politics of Reform in Vietnam, 1986–2000," in *Vietnam: Current Issues and Historical Background*, ed. V. Largo (Hauppauge, NY: Nova Science Publishers, 2002), 4.

55 David Marr, "Vietnamese Youth in the 1990s," *The Vietnam Review* 2 (1997): 294.

mid-1990s, the party and some journalists became increasingly concerned with "social evils": the negative social effects of economic expansion, such as increasing heroin use, the prevalence of HIV/AIDS, and perceived increases in prostitution and sex tourism. In December of 1995, Prime Minister Vo Van Kiet announced a new initiative to eliminate "social evils" and "poisonous culture." The bureaucracy and local police mobilized to protect young people from drugs and prostitution by raiding massage parlors, karaoke bars, and video stores and by campaigning against shops with "foreign words," as foreign investment was seen as a cause of these problems.[56] In the twenty-first century, the discourse of "social evils" was picked up by a muckraking press as a way to sell papers through the interest in the public in salacious stories and by capitalizing on public fears surrounding migration and development, particularly in Saigon (renamed Ho Chi Minh City after 1975).[57]

Another political issue that emerged out of renovation was the control of rampant political corruption. With the emergence of joint Vietnamese enterprises with foreign firms and competition for party approval of new businesses, as well as pressure to maintain certain state enterprises, the renovation period brought not only an infusion of money into Vietnam but also an expansion of opportunities for graft. The low salaries of civil servants in Vietnam perpetuated the problem of corruption. In an atmosphere of rising prices and middle-class expectations, these low salaries put pressure on civil servants to supplement their income through extralegal means.[58]

Under the leadership of General Secretary Do Muoi (1917–2018) from 1991 to 1997, the party sought consensus about economic reform but achieved little advancement on the corruption issue. His protégé, Le Kha Phieu (b. 1931), focused on attempting to rid the bureaucracy of corruption, even going so far as to say that the root of such problems lay in the "illness of Partyization," in which the party dominated too much of Vietnamese political life.[59] Because of his firm approach, however, he managed to alienate almost all of his constituencies in the party and was in office for less than four years, from 1997 to 2001.[60]

In this period of time, the Chinese and Vietnamese leaders learned several lessons that have helped to redefine the parties' characteristics and changed them in numerous ways. The CCP and VCP acted according to their own consistent inner logics in their political agenda, changing from a peasant/military elite-led, rural-centered armed uprising party in the 1940s–1960s to an urban-centered political party in the 1970s–1990s. The successions and power transitions of the late 1980s show that new generations, facing varied social conditions, adjusted to the social climate of their time. The successions of power in the PRC and SRV (Socialist Republic of Vietnam) took place within a single party system. Thus the supreme leaders chose their heir-apparent and selected their successors while still living. Some Western historians have overlooked the complex nature of the tremendous changes in these Communist Parties from one generation to the next. The patterns examined in this chapter illuminate previous party experiences and possibly predict the political future of China and Vietnam.

56   Ibid., 331–3; see also Wynn Wilcox, "In their Image: The Vietnamese Communist Party, the "West," and the Social Evils Campaign of 1996," *Bulletin of Concerned Asian Scholars* 32, no. 4 (December 2000): 15–24; Christophe Robert, "'Social Evils' and the Question of Youth" (PhD Dissertation, Cornell University, 2005).

57   Erik Harms, *Saigon's Edge: On the Margins of Ho Chi Minh City* (Minneapolis: University of Minnesota Press, 2011), 43.

58   Martin Gainsborough, *Vietnam: Rethinking the State* (New York: Zed Books, 2010), 53–4.

59   Ibid., 137.

60   Taylor, *History of the Vietnamese*, 618.

Chapter 14

China

Evolving Economic Superpower

The year 1991 witnessed the collapse of the Soviet Union and the end of the global Cold War. Nevertheless, China stayed on its course by continuing to promote the party's modernization policy and agenda through the last decade of the twentieth century. We examine the CCP not only as a political institution but also as a social institution, which endorses many social values and popular ideas, such as nationalism. Chinese nationalism, which is deeply rooted in the heart of several generations, has risen significantly since the 1990s because of explosive economic growth. In these years, adopting a pragmatic nationalism has allowed the CCP's national leadership to improve its position in the society. This government has effectively promoted nationalism to emphasize China's unity, strength, prosperity, and dignity over the core values of human rights and democracy. This kind of nationalism emphasizes the loyalty of the community to the state, rather than holding human rights as its fundamental value and democracy as its desired result. Oftentimes the government has

even called on individuals to sacrifice personal rights for the national interest.

After the Tiananmen Square Movement, China continued its economic reforms. In the 1990s, the country became industrialized when its manufactured goods consisted of 52 percent of the country's total. Then, in the mid-2000s, China became urbanized when more than 50 percent of its population lived in cities. Clearly, the party did not want urbanization to make it lose control of the cities, as it did from 1966–1976 during the Cultural Revolution and again in 1989 during the Tiananmen Incident.[1] It intended to lead the urban movement by making new policies, empowering pro-party interest groups, controlling the legal system, and putting more pressure on the middle class, which was campaigning for civil liberties, freedom, and democracy.

The unprecedented historical transition of the CCP after 1989 has also drawn attention from other political scientists and legal scholars. In 2000 Bruce Dickson offered "a useful framework for analyzing CCP's policies of co-opting new elites and forging links with

---

1   For more details on the Cultural Revolution, see Sun and Li, "Mao Zedong and the CCP: Adaptation, Centralization, and Success," in *Evolution of Power: China's Struggle, Survival, and Success*, eds. Xiaobing Li and Xiansheng Tian (Lanham, MD: Lexington Books, 2014), 46–55.

non-party organizations, as well as understanding the problems that have arisen as a consequence."[2] After Deng Xiaoping's tenure (1978–1989), both Jiang Zemin (1990–2002) and Hu Jintao (2002–2012) were willing to share power. They provided moderate leadership of the new generations. In other words, the new leaders in Beijing were able to share their governance with the executive, legislative, and judicial branches by empowering congressional committees, ministries of the State Council, courts, and law enforcement. Their practical and inclusive politics reflects the shift of the party's ideology and political goals from radical Communism to moderate nationalism. Dickson, however, concludes in his 2008 book that to share the economic benefits, the private entrepreneurs support the party's agenda rather than promoting democratization in China.[3] He then predicts that if the CCP succeeds, it may be able to "preempt or postpone" political reforms.[4]

Jiang's China: Political and Legal Reform

Before his retirement, Deng Xiaoping chose Jiang Zemin (b. 1926) as his successor. Jiang was a technocratic leader with a bachelor degree in electrical engineering from the prestigious Shanghai Jiaotong University in 1947. He served as an engineer of a factory after 1949 and was sent to the Soviet Union for training at the Stalin Automobile Factory in 1955. After his return, Jiang became deputy director and director of factories and research institutes. Speaking some English and Russian, he worked as deputy director and director of the Foreign Affairs Department of the First Ministry of Machine-building Industry in Beijing. Then, Jiang became the Minister of the Electronics Industry. During Deng's reform movement, Jiang Zemin served as mayor of Shenzhen, the first Special Economic Zone (SEZ) in China. His successful experience in Shenzhen earned his place in the CCP Twelfth Central Committee in 1982. Then, he was appointed as mayor of Shanghai in 1985. In June 1989, Jiang Zemin became a member of the Standing Committee of the Politburo and General Secretary of the CCP Central Committee. In November he became chairman of the CMC at the Fifth Plenary Session of the Thirteenth Central Committee.[5]

At the Eighth National People's Congress held in March 1993, Jiang was elected president of the PRC and chairman of the government's CMC. In the 1990s Jiang gradually shifted the party's ideology and political goals from radical Communism to moderate nationalism in order to unite China, lending one more source of legitimacy for the CCP as the country's ruling party. He developed his own theoretical principles, the Three Represents, that the CCP should represent "the development of China's advanced productive forces, the orientation of the development of China's advanced culture, and the fundamental interests of the broadest masses of the Chinese people."[6] The Three Represents became the most essential requirements for officials and officers to fulfill their obligations and duties during Jiang's tenure from 1990 to 2002, as well as his most potent legacy.

---

2 Bruce J. Dickson, "Cooptation and Corporatism in China: The Logic of Party Adaptation," *Political Science Quarterly* 115, no. 4 (2000): 517–43.

3 Bruce J. Dickson, *Wealth into Power: The Communist Party's Embrace of China's Private Sector* (Cambridge, UK: Cambridge University Press, 2008), Introduction.

4 Bruce J. Dickson, "Updating the China Model," *The Washington Quarterly* 34, no. 4 (Fall 2011): 39–58.

5 New Star Publisher, ed., *Selected Documents of the Fifteenth CCP National Congress* (Beijing: New Star, 1997), 104–6.

6 Jiang Zemin, "How Our Party Is to Attain the 'Three Represents' under the New Historical Conditions," in *On the "Three Represents*," Jiang Zemin (Beijing: Foreign Languages Press, 2003), 8.

Based on his political experience since the reform and opening up, Jiang also developed the Twelve Relations. According to Jiang, these Twelve Relations need to be handled correctly in China's economic and social development. Report at the Fifteenth CCP National Congress, he made a series of major planning for the 21st century to build socialism with Chinese characteristics. Jiang Zemin pointed out that significant progress has been made in the reform of the economic system. It is certain that the common development of various economic components with public ownership is the basic economic system in the primary stage of Chinese socialism. The realization of public ownership can be diversified, and the non-public economy is an important part of the socialist market economy. In the aspect of political system reform, to further expand the democracy, to better guarantee the people's democratic election and democratic policy-making democratic management and democratic supervision, and adhere to lawfully, strive to build a democratic politics of socialism with Chinese characteristics.

Jiang continued the reform movement by carrying it into the arenas of criminal justice and the legal system. From 1995 the NPC and its Standing Committee began to amend the Criminal Law by adding more punishable acts, due to an increase of crime in the country. The current PRC Criminal Law has ten chapters and 452 articles and has increased publishable crimes by the death penalty from twenty-six in 1976, to sixty in 1995, and to sixty-eight in 1997.[7] Capital punishment for some crimes, including tax fraud, passing fake negotiable notes, and the illegal "pooling" of funds, is unique to the Chinese judicial system. The government claims that this level of punishment is necessary to combat increasing corruption. The 1997 legislation also further decentralized the appeals process, giving final authority to the provincial courts rather than the Supreme Court. Both of these measures have increased the number of executions in recent years. Executions are often carried out on the same day as the sentencing.

During the 1990s reforms, the legal system was revived, and many law schools reopened. More textbooks and legal magazines are being published, and lawyers have once again begun to practice law. The courts have handled more cases than at any time in the past, with more than 2.5 million lawsuits reported in 1986, 3.85 million legal cases in 1994, and 6 million cases in 1999. By the early 2000s, there was a modest fluctuation in the number of cases heard in the court. For example, 5.58 million were brought forward in 2002, and this number dropped to 5.54 million, but it rose again in 2006 to 5.7 million.[8] The Ministry of Justice has been reestablished under the State Council, and in public discourse slogans such as "rule the country by law" and "rule the country according to law" have increasingly been used. During Jiang's tenure, the constitution has had important changes and revisions in 1993 and 1999. Even though some civil rights and legal codes were provided by the constitution, many have not been enacted until recent years.

In 1995 the Supreme Court issued its first five-year plan for reforming the country's courts. It addressed problems such as competence, fairness, judicial training, and regularity in court procedures. The plan embraced some important reforms such as the creation of rules regarding the use of evidence and the separation of cases from adjudication and adjudication from enforcement.[9] Since then, the legal profession has become increasingly

---

7   Klaus Mühlhahn, *Criminal Justice in China: A History* (Cambridge, MA: Harvard University Press, 2009), 217–19.

8   Ministry of Justice, PRC, *Zhongguo falu nianjian, 1994–2005* [China Law Yearbook, 1994–2006] (Beijing: Falu chubanshe [Law Publishing], 2004–2008). Statistics tables.

9   Ronald Keith, Zhiqiu Lin, and Shumei Hou, *China's Supreme Court* (London: Routledge, 2013), 121–2, 187–90.

institutionalized, marked by an expansion in legal education and an increasing awareness on the part of the citizenry as to their rights under the law.

China has one of the largest law-enforcement bodies in the world.[10] As a rule, police officers in China do not perform static guard duty but are tasked with controlling the population, fighting crime, and maintaining safety. Some urban centers have antiriot units equipped with a few armored cars. Previously, those involved in law enforcement went unarmed, but since late 1994, circumstances have required them to carry side arms more often. The official Chinese newspaper reported that more than five hundred police officers have been killed each year since 1993. In January 1996 new rules were issued concerning the use of batons, tear gas, handcuffs, water cannons, firearms, and explosives. These regulations updated the 1980 guidelines and were a response to the rise in crime. Despite these new adjustments, police forces are not considered part of the armed forces of China as defined by the *National Security Law*. As part of Jiang's legal reforms, China strengthened the People's Armed

People (PAP) in the 1990s. This national organization was established in 1983 and has regular troops, something like a combination of the National Guard with SWAT (Special Weapons and Tactics) teams in the United States. In late 1996 the Chinese government transferred fourteen infantry divisions of PLA regular soldiers, totaling 150,000 men, to the PAP force. In 2000 PAP was comprised of one million members.[11]

Banking Reforms, Foreign Investment, and Urbanization

Throughout the 1990s, China entered the period of Jiang Zemin, who is often referred to as the Communist Party's Third-generation Core Leadership.[12] Jiang was also the principal founder of Three Represents Theory.[13] Under his leadership, China's reform and opening up and modernization continue to move forward. Modernization construction has made rapid development in the 1990s, by 2000 the GDP reached more than one trillion US dollars, per capita gross domestic product of about $800.[14] In

---

10   Estimates of the total of China's law-enforcement forces may vary but are usually in the vicinity of 2.4 million. There are 640,000 police and 250,000 detectives and investigators under the control of the Ministry of Public Security (MPS) in Beijing. This ministry has a bureau of public security in each province and county, a metropolitan police department in each city, and precinct offices in each district. In 2008 this top-down centralized police system had 31 provincial bureaus of public security; 356 metropolitan police departments; 2,972 county police headquarters; and 41,941 local police stations. There are also more than 350,000 traffic cops.

11   As part of the national law enforcement, the PAP or CPAPF (officially Chinese People's Armed Police Force) was established in 1982 as a paramilitary force, similar to a combination of the National Guards with SWAT (Special Weapons and Tactics) teams in the United States. In 2000 the PAP was comprised of one million men in thirty-one armies, including 508 armed police regiments and 42 special regiments, such as helicopter, artillery, tank, chemical, and engineering regiments. The PAP also had thirty-two command academies and twenty-nine hospitals across the country.

12   Please refer to *Jiang Zemin*, The Central People's Government official website of the People's Republic of China, http://www.gov.cn/test/2007-11/21/content_811768.htm [Reference date 2017-10-25]; *Resume of Jiang Zemin*, Xinhua Net [Reference date 2015-3-25]; *Resume of Jiang Zemin*, People.com.cn [Reference date 2015-3-25].

13   Hu Jintao, *Address on the Semina of studying SELECTED WORKS OF JIANG ZEMIN*, Xinhua Net [Reference date 2015-3-25].

14   Lengrong, *China under Jiang Zemin's leadership (serial 1)*, Perple.com.cn [Reference date 2001-7-06)], http://www.people.com.cn/GB/guandian/29/173/20010706/505085.html.

1994 a new state budget law separated the banking system from the government by establishing bank autonomy, prohibiting government offices from borrowing from the banks. The major banks are responsible for their own profits and losses. In 1995 the government issued the Commercial Bank Law, allowing state-owned banks to be commercialized, and commercial banks were established. Many much smaller, local banks had been established, and stock market trading was booming. More private-sector firms had access to commercial loans, domestic stock markets, and foreign investment. To clear the entanglement of poorly performing SOEs and inefficient debt-ridden state banks, the CCP Fifteenth National Congress announced an initiative in 1997 that provided for the sale of most of the SOEs.[15] In 1999 Jiang set up four state asset management agencies to purchase, manage, and dispose of the bad loans of state banks. Instead of paying banks interest, the debtor SOEs paid dividends to the asset agency. Those loans were then sold as initial public offerings or transfers of ownership.

As a result, the share of government-invested enterprises produced by SOEs has decreased from 77.6 percent in 1966 to 17.5 percent in 2010, while the number of large-sized SOEs declined from 118,000 in 1995 to 46,800 in 2010.

During the late 1990s and early 2000s, China became one of the world's manufacturing centers, due to its low cost of production and participation in international trade organizations such as the WTO (World Trade Organization). China's manufacturing includes metals, machinery, transportation, petrochemicals, defense, electronics, and textile industries. It also can be divided into heavy industries such as steel, machinery, automobiles, and shipbuilding, and light industries such as electronics, instruments, tools, and consumer products. Its steel outputs increased from 64.3 million tons in 1980, to 140 million tons in 2000, to 419 million tons in 2006. Automobile manufacturing increased from 443,400 in 1985, to 1.1 million in 1992, to 2.3 million in 2001, and 4.44 million in 2003.[16] China's industrialization in the 1990s was based partly on low-cost production, including low wages paid to workers and minimum workplace safety standards. Many full-time, part-time, and rural migrant workers continue to confront safety problems, such as a dangerous working condition, toxic environments, and lack of protection and safety education, as well as forced and uncompensated overtime.

Jiang expanded China's foreign trade by adopting new policies to promote international economic relations, such as the Maritime Commerce Law enacted in 1993, Anti-Subsidy Rules issued in 1997, and the Foreign Investment Law revised in 2001. Hong Kong then became part of China, and Taiwan had developed extensive trade relations with the mainland. China's total foreign trade had risen from $80 billion in 1988 to $300 billion by 1997, a threefold increase in less than ten years. China's entry into the WTO in 2001 further promoted its international trade. By 2002 China's exports to the United States exceeded that of Japan. China's total foreign trade rose from $300 million in 1997 to $620 billion in 2002, more than doubling in five years. In 2002 the ranking of China in the world's trading nations jumped from thirty-second to sixth.[17]

The annual total was $39 billion FDI in 1999 and $41 billion FDI in 2000. More than three hundred enterprises belonging to the Fortune Global 500 invested in China by 2000.[18] Foreign investment

---

15   New Star Publisher, ed., *Selected Documents of the Fifteenth CCP National Congress*, 23–5.

16   Li, *Modern China*, 139–40.

17   Robert G. Sutter, *Chinese Foreign Relations: Power and Policy since the Cold War*, 4th ed. (Lanham, MD: Rowman & Littlefield, 2016), 63.

18   Sutter, *Chinese Foreign Relations*, 64.

accelerated industrialization in the 1990s by establishing various industries that absorbed a large proportion of the low-wage rural labor force.

In 1978 the farming workforce composition was reduced to 67.4 percent. It continued to drop to 55.8 percent in 1988, 44 percent in 1999, 40.3 percent in 2004, and an estimated 36 percent in 2014. The country has more than three hundred million farm workers today, and agriculture constituted 13 percent of China's GDP in the 2000s.[19]

The number of Chinese cities increased from 223 in 1981 to 663 by the end of 2000.[20] From 1989 to 2001, a total of $781.5 billion was invested in urban development, an increase of more than ten times that of the previous decade. Of that amount, 37 percent went into the transportation, post, and telecom sectors, 35 percent into energy supply facilities, and 12 percent into public utilities. As a result, the service industry grew much faster than the overall economy from 1979–2001, when the GDP climbed 7–9.4 percent annually, and the service sectors grew in double digits, per annum. From 1991 to 1997, China's GDP rose an average of 11 percent annually, totaling $559 billion in 1994 and reaching $1,083 billion in 1999. Its GDP rose 8 and 7.3 percent in 2000–2001 and increased to $1.9 trillion in 2004.[21] Its GDP per capita was only $469 in 1994, but it almost doubled by 1999, reaching $865, and increasing to $1,490 in 2004.

In the meantime, Jiang Zemin also faced old issues like official corruption. Corruption is a social and historical phenomenon. From the point of view of world history, almost all countries have corruption, also have anti-corruption. However, different countries, different historical periods, due to differences in economic development, political systems, historical and cultural traditions and other aspects, the manifestation and characteristics of corruption are different. Same as any other countries, corruption is an encumber on China's economic development and a disaster of social stability. Because corruption distorts economic decisions and undermines social law. And these two points for a stable and prosperous society are crucial. Therefore, corruption is intolerable behavior. In his career of a lifetime, Jiang Zemin fought against corruption in one way or another. He believed that corruption would not only erode people's morale, but also is the biggest stumbling block to China's full potential as a great power. Jiang Zemin stepped up the fight against corruption during his tenure, and some powerful figures were caught. The director of one of China's most popular cigarette producers, Chu Shijian, known as king of China's tobacco, was sentenced to life imprisonment for embezzling 3.5 million dollars; a deputy Minister of Public Security, the head of the anti-smuggling operation, was arrested on suspicion of colluding with smugglers. The vice governor of Jiangxi province received bribes 90 times, the amount of up to $ 650,000, becoming the highest-ranking official to be executed in China since 1949.

Hu's China: Economic Superpower

After Jiang retired, Hu Jintao (b. 1942) became the party chairman in November 2002 and the country's president in March 2003. He was deputy director of the committee and later secretary of the Gansu Provincial Committee of CCYL (Chinese Communist Youth League) in 1975–1980. Then, he became a member of the Secretariat of the CCYL

---

19 Whiting, *Power and Wealth in Rural China*, (Cambridge, UK: Cambrdige University Press, 2006), introduction.

20 *Zhongguo chengshi jingji shehui nianjian, 1985* [Almanac of Chinese Urban Economy and Society, 1985], 39; and *Zhongguo chengshi tongji nianjian, 2000* [China's Urban Statistical Yearbook, 2000] (Beijing: Zhongguo tongji chubanshe [China Statistics Publishing], 2001), 3.

21 Ebrey and Walthall, *Modern East Asia*, 3rd ed. (Boston, Ma: Wadworth, 2014), 581–2.

Central Committee in 1982, and the first secretary of the Secretariat in 1983. Then, Hu Jintao served as the Provincial Secretary of the Party Committee of Guizhou in 1985, and Secretary of the Party Committee in Tibet in 1988–1992. During his four years in Tibet, Hu successfully suppressed Tibetan independence movement and Buddhist rebellions by sending PLA troops to the streets of Lhasa, the capital of Tibet. His hardline policy and toughness against religious and social movements won him the membership of the Standing Committee of the Politburo of the Fourteenth CCP Central Committee in 1992. Then, Deng Xiaoping decided Hu to succeed Jiang Zemin. In 1997, Hu Jintao became a member of the Secretariat Committee.[22]

During his early years in power, Hu designed his "scientific development" concept, entrenching it in the party's constitution as an official guiding ideology. He emphasized political and social harmony by nurturing good relations with central and local governments as well as supporting the growing professionalism and interest groups inside and outside the government. To deal with the problems left behind by Jiang, Hu made certain important changes in China's economic, military, social, and political policies. Hu and Premier Wen Jiabao (b. 1942), employed macroeconomic control policies over the rapidly growing economy.

In 2010 China had 19.8 percent of the world's total manufacturing output and became the largest manufacturer in the world.[23] Its manufacturing accounted for 31.6 percent of China's GDP in 2013, an increase of 7.6 percent from 2012, and it is the largest GDP contributor in the country. It hires more than four hundred million manufacturing workers, about 52.3 percent of the labor force in the industries. China's steel output increased from 64.3 million tons in 1980, to 140 million tons in 2000, to 419 million tons in 2006, and to 683 million tons in 2011, which was an increase of 9 percent from 2010. As the largest steel supplier in the world, China produced 45 percent of the world's steel in 2011. China's automobile manufacturing increased from 1.1 million in 1992, to 2.3 million in 2001, 4.44 million in 2003, and 5.71 million in 2005. By 2006 China became the third largest automotive manufacturer (after the United States and Japan), and the second largest vehicle consumer (only after the United States) in the world. Automobile production continues to grow, from 8.88 million in 2007, to 9.35 million in 2008, and to 13.83 million in 2009, when China became the largest automaker in the world. By 2010 China had also become the largest vehicle consumer in the world when 18 million new cars were sold that year.[24]

Amounting to about 25–28 percent of the country's industrial value, China's energy industry, including crude oil, natural gas, coal, electricity, and nuclear energy, has become one of the fastest-growing sectors in the past twenty-five years. Energy production and consumption taken together can be regarded as a sign of how the national economy operates. China ranked fifth in world oil production and produced 4,090 thousand barrels a day in 2011, accounting for 5.1 percent of that year's world total and an increase of 23.56 percent from 2001.[25] Since the 2000s Beijing has encouraged and emphasized the importance of major Chinese state-owned oil

---

22 For more information on Hu's political career, see Joseph Fewsmith, *China since Tiananmen: From Deng Xiaoping to Hu Jintao*, 2nd ed. (Cambridge, UK: Cambridge University Press, 2008).

23 Xiaobing Li, *Modern China*, (Santa Barbara, CA: ABC-CLIO, 2015), 121.

24 Shaun Rein, *The End of Cheap China: Economic and Cultural Trends That Will Disrupt the World* (Hoboken, NJ: Wiley-Blackwell, 2014), chapters 1 and 4.

25 Xiaobing Li and Michael Molina, "China" in *Oil: A Cultural and Geographic Encyclopedia of Black Gold*, eds. Li and Molina, vol. 2: 462–72.

companies going abroad to seek development and cooperation opportunities.

Furthermore, the defense industry plays an important role not only in manufacturing, but also in technology research and development. Out of the annual military spending of $189 billion in 2013, an increase of 14 percent from 2012, an estimated 37.5 percent went to the defense industry for manufacturing weapons, ammunition, military vehicles, and communication equipment. China has also begun to export weapon systems, including missiles, to foreign countries. Most of the defense enterprises are located in the remote, mountainous areas. Other heavy and light industries such as construction materials, electronics, computer technology, textiles, food processing, and plastic products are distributed in the coastal and urban areas.

By 2010 China established the third largest service industry in the world (only after the United States and Japan). The service industry produced 43 percent of the country's annual GDP, second only to manufacturing. Among the service sectors, telecom service has shown a rapid development by establishing numerous communications systems that link all parts of the country by internet, telephone, telegraph, radio, and television. In 2003, when the number of mobile phone users increased to 268.7 million, China became one of the leaders in terms of communications development. By 2006 the number of fixed-lines, mainly in the countryside, increased by 79 percent. Approximately 100 million cell phones were sold in 2006, and in 2007, 190 million were sold, an increase of 74 percent. In 2007 more than 600 million mobile phones were manufactured in China, more than 50 percent of the world's total production. Many companies, such as China Telecom, CNC, China Mobile, China Unicom, and China Satcom, have shared China's telecom market. The tremendous changes in communications technology, particularly the transition from printed mediums to more rapid digital formats, are challenging the authority of official Chinese political and social institutions.

Many Western Internet service providers such as Yahoo, AOL, and others have entered the Chinese market. In 2003 more than eighty million households were logged into the Internet. By 2009 the number of domestic websites grew to 3.23 million, an annual increase of 12.3 percent. Internet users grew to 137 million in 2006, 162 million in 2007, and 618 million in 2014.[26] While encouraging Internet use for business and educational purposes, the government has kept tight controls on its use for political discussion. At a Politburo meeting in January 2007, Hu Jintao said that the Internet was related to the country's safety, security, and source of sensitive information. As a result, the State Council established the Bureau of Internet within the State Council's Media Department, while a mirror organization, the Bureau of Internet Propaganda, was formed in the office of External Propaganda in the CCP Central Committee.

Although the Hu-Wen administration in 2002–2012 strategically shifted China's economic development from a global oriented policy to a more regionally balanced one, they continued to support the joint ventures and to encourage foreign investment. By 2003 the government had approved establishment of five hundred thousand joint ventures. In 2004 the United States had forty-five thousand joint ventures in China with a total investment of $48 billion. Among the major American companies in China are Boeing, General Motors, ExxonMobil, Chevron, ConocoPhillips, IBM, and General Electric. Because of the development of joint ventures, China and the outside world have become truly interdependent.

---

26   Information Office, State Council of the PRC, "The Internet in China, 2010," in *White Papers of the Chinese Government, 2009–2011*, ed. Information Office, State Council of the PRC (Beijing: Foreign Languages Press, 2012), 231–2.

Since the 2000s the Hu-Wen government expanded the exports and moved far beyond cheap manufacturing such as toys, games, shoes, and cloth by adding petrochemicals, fertilizers, polymers, machine tools, shipping, and electric appliances in their exports. By 2005 China replaced the United States as Japan's main trading partner. In the following year, China's total international trade reached $1.4 trillion, of which $762 billion was with the United States. As of 2013 China's leading export partners were the United States (20 percent), Hong Kong (12 percent), Japan (9 percent), South Korea (8 percent), and Germany (5 percent). China imported electrical machinery, optical and medical equipment, organic chemicals, and telecommunications and sound equipment, as well as oil and mineral fuels. China's leading import partners were Japan (16 percent), Hong Kong (12 percent), South Korea (12 percent), the United States (9 percent), Taiwan (8 percent), and Germany (7 percent). China's total foreign trade rose from $1.15 trillion in 2004, to $2.17 trillion in 2007, to $3.64 trillion in 2011, and to $4.16 trillion in 2013, more than tripling in less than ten years.[27]

Foreign investment was a central component of China's continuing economic growth. In 2002 China became the top recipient of foreign investment in the world. It received $80 billion FDI in 2005 and $69.5 billion FDI in 2006. In September 2013 China established the Shanghai Free Trade Zone as a new effort to attract more foreign investment, which now has access to almost all sectors in the metropolitan economy.

After 2000 China's foreign exchange reserves increased significantly, from $0.8 billion in 1979, to $165.6 billion in 2000, and $346.5 billion by 2003,

when its reserves were higher than its outstanding debt ($182.6 billion). Its surplus on trade had significantly contributed to the increase of its foreign exchange reserves. China's foreign exchange reserves reached $470.6 billion in mid-2004 and continued to increase to $711 billion in 2005, $941.1 billion in 2006, $1,332.6 billion in 2007, and $1,808.8 billion by June 2008, making it the highest foreign exchange reserve in the world.[28] It was equal to nearly $1,500 per person for the entire Chinese population of 1.3 billion.

China became the second-largest economy in the world by 2011, following only the United States, and for the first time in its history exceeded Japan. Its GDP increased from $1 trillion in 1999 to $8.2 trillion in 2008, with an average annual growth rate over 13 percent; it rose from $9 trillion in 2009 to $10 trillion in 2010, with a growth rate of 10.4 percent; and from $11.3 trillion in 2011 to $12.6 trillion in 2012, with 7.8 percent growth. In 2002–2014, China's GDP rose between 7 and 9.4 percent each year.[29] Despite some slowdown in recent years, China has still scored impressive growth, with its GDP standing at 11.2 trillion as of the end of 2016.

Such phenomenal economic development has instilled a heightened sense of nationalism in the Chinese populace. Nationalist pride was most evident in the 2008 summer Olympic Games held from August 8, through August 24, in Beijing. It was the first time for China to host the Olympics and the third time for Asian countries to hold the summer Olympics; Japan held it at Tokyo in 1964 and Korea at Seoul in 1988. China became the eighteenth nation to host a summer Olympic Games, and the twenty-second to hold the Olympic Games overall. The 2008 Beijing Olympics became

27 Sutter, *Chinese Foreign Relations*, 63–5.

28 For more details of foreign exchange reserve in China, see Yasheng Huang, *Selling China: Foreign Direct Investment during the Reform Era* (Cambridge, UK: Cambridge University Press, 2005).

29 Information Office, State Council of the PRC, "China's Peaceful Development, 2011," in *White Papers of the Chinese Government, 2009–2011*, ed. Information Office, State Council of the PRC (Beijing: Foreign Languages Press, 2012), 507–8.

the most-watched of international events in sports history with 4.7 billion viewers, about 70 percent of the total world population, and more than the 3.9 billion viewers of the 2004 Olympics in Athens.[30] More than one hundred heads of state from all over the world attended the opening ceremony and the games in Beijing, including US president George W. Bush and the first lady. The reported total costs of the 2008 Olympics were between $40 billion and $44 billion, vastly more than the total costs of $15 billion of the 2004 Olympics at Athens. Critiques included limited access for the international media and air and water pollution in Beijing, as well as human and civil rights conditions, which had not been improved upon in China as the Chinese government had promised.

As a new member of the global community, however, the PRC has not always followed every international standard but has adapted the regulations selectively. While Hu Jintao was cooperative on certain issues, his government did not always agree with the West, especially not with the United States. President Bush, trying to include China in the war against terror after September 11, 2001, as well as coordinate responses to the crises with North Korea, asked China to be a "responsible stakeholder" in multilateral national efforts. Beijing considers many matters, including human rights and civil liberties, to be domestic problems, and believes that no foreign government or organization should interfere in its internal affairs. The Confucian heritage that emphasizes the paternalistic role of the state has lent itself to the Chinese government's belief that individual interests and rights should be subordinate to those of the state. Such a concept

runs counter to that in Western countries, where individual rights are deemed as inalienable. As a result, China and the West, especially the United States, have often been on a course of conflict when it comes to human rights issues.

In addition, China's implementation of international laws and agreements in the area of trade, such as the WTO, depends largely on its understanding of and governmental capabilities in local communities. The country continues to face criticism over its unwillingness and ability to meet international obligations, especially in applying global standards in areas such as labor, public health, gender, discrimination, and especially in human rights. As previously mentioned, the Chinese government's statements on human rights differ from international norms, particularly in its focus on hierarchies of rights and local conditions of development. Its reliance on the right to participate in the development of global legal standards has been used to justify its selective adoption and frequent rejections of international norms. The country has its own normative principles, which have been described as "Chinese characteristics."

Even though China also joined the Agreement on Trade-Related Aspects of Intellectual Property Rights (TRIPS) and other international organizations in the 1980s, pirating intellectual property and violations of copyright extended in the PRC during the 1990s and 2000s. Chinese courts had received 87,420 civil lawsuits of intellectual property rights (IPR) violations in 2012, an increase of 46 percent from 2011, and handled 83,850 cases during that year, an increase of 44 percent from the previous year. About 60,000 suspects were arrested, and

---

30 Beijing won the bid at the International Olympics Committee (IOC) meeting in Moscow in July 2001, winning over other applicants on the final list, which included Toronto, Paris, Istanbul, and Osaka, to host the Game of the XXIX Olympiad (or the 2008 Summer Olympic Games). More than 11,400 athletes, including 4,637 women and 6,305 men, from 204 countries and regions which had National Olympic Committees (NOCs), traveled to Beijing and competed in twenty-eight sports and 302 events, more than those for the 2004 Games. China had the largest participating team with a total of 639 athletes, and the United States was second with 596.

29,852 of them were convicted for crimes of IPR infringement and producing and selling substandard commodities, with a total value of $1.83 billion. China has 2,731 IPR judges sitting on 420 courts. Still, China continues to remain a major risk for IPR. In 2007 US trade representatives announced that the United States would begin WTO dispute settlement consultations with the PRC over deficiencies in China's protection and enforcement of copyrights and trademarks on a wide range of products. The Office of the US Trade Representative in 2014 has put China on its Priority Watch List for a tenth consecutive year.

New Challenges: The Power of Party vs. the Rule of Law

Although the judicial reform continued through Hu Jintao's years of 2002–2012, the Chinese legal system has not yet been able to protect individual rights and civil liberties rather than enforce punitive measures as the core purpose of law. All local and special courts have a two-hearing system, except for the two special regions of Hong Kong and Macau, which have their own judicial systems and are not under the jurisdiction of the Supreme People's Court in Beijing. Chinese citizens have few rights to a fair trial, or retaining a lawyer, or appellate review, and little freedom from unfair interrogation, torture, and cruel and unusual punishment. Defendants' rights have only recently become an indispensable part of the criminal justice system. In 2006 only 30 percent of all prisoners had a lawyer or legal consultant for their case. Defense attorneys often face chronic difficulties in accessing information for

clients. Among 933,156 defendants tried that year, only 1,147 were found not guilty. The conviction rate was, and still is, more than 99 percent.[31]

In 2003 the high court formulated twenty documents of judicial interpretation of criminal, civil, and administrative law enforcement and regulation on legal aid as part of the court reform. To improve the legal service, the higher court developed a human network for the country's legal service system and defined a scale of citizens' rights to such services. The number of legal aid offices had increased from 2,418 in 2002, to 2,774 in 2003, from serving 129,775 individuals in 2002, to 166,433 cases in 2003.[32] In 2005 the Supreme Court created its third five-year plan designed to strengthen the courts. The plan laid out fifty goals, including the improvement of court finances, the appointment of judges, and the reform of procedures for the prosecution of capital cases. Furthermore, the plan sought to break the link with local CCP authorities, who usually control court appointments and judges through the annual budget. The same year, the Supreme Court also instructed all sitting judges below the age of forty that they must get a college degree within five years or risk losing their jobs. As a result, by 2006, for the first time, more than 50 percent of Chinese judges had college degrees. This was a substantial increase from the 6 percent of judges who had college degrees in 1995 and the 20 percent of judges who did in 2000.[33]

The Chinese government often launches "strike hard" campaigns against crime. During these times, the police force vigorously combats crime, including organized and gang-related offenses, murder, rape, kidnapping, and other serious violent actions. These campaigns result in severe punishments and mass

---

31 Xiaobing Li, "The Dragon's Tale: China's Efforts toward the Rule of Law," in *Modern Chinese Legal Reform: New Perspectives*, eds. Xiaobing Li and Qiang Fang (Lexington: University Press of Kentucky, 2013), 95–6.

32 Information Office, State Council of the PRC, "Progress in China's Human Rights Cause in 2003," in *White Papers of the Chinese Government, 2002–2004*, ed. Information Office, State Council of the PRC (Beijing: Foreign Languages Press, 2005), 414.

33 Xiaobing Li, *Civil Liberties in China*, (Santa Barbara, CA: ABC-CLIO, 2010), 27.

executions. The public, however, supports these harsh measures. In 2009, for example, the Chinese police cracked 3.1 million criminal cases.[34] Law-enforcement officials continue to conduct illegal searches and to utilize extended detention, torture, and forced confessions. The rights of a defendant continue to be sharply limited and can be violated by law-enforcement agencies.

Authorities' attempts to expand the scale of capital punishment reflect the government's concerns over the increasing crime rate. This is inconsistent with the global trend of seeking to reduce or eliminate the death sentence altogether, despite China signing two key international human rights treaties in the 2000s that included articles against the death sentence.[35] China accounts for over 70 percent of criminals executed in the world per year, and some international human rights organizations put the number at between ten thousand and fifteen thousand a year, or around twenty to thirty per day, more than the rest of the world combined.[36] The Supreme Court only regained the right to review all death penalty decisions on January 1, 2007. Even though a debate continues concerning the death sentence, and criticism has increased within the legal circle, there is no plan to abolish the practice. The ultra-emphasis on punishment reflects China's legal tradition that the core purpose of law is to enforce punitive measures, rather than to protect rights. This also reflects the traditional view that the state's authority to maintain social order, wherein all people can benefit, should always be preserved. The extensive use of capital punishment clearly represents the government's intent to maintain political stability and social order. Guided by legal instrumentalism, China has perpetuated the tradition that the nation's collective interests transcend individual rights.

In 2004, Xu Shuangfu, leader of an underground church known as the Three Grades of Servant, was arrested. Some Westerners consider it to be an orthodox Christian house church network, which is an unofficial church based in China's northeast and claims millions of followers. In July 2006 the Heilongjiang Provincial High Court sentenced Xu to death and immediately executed him.[37] In 2005 Wu Weihan was arrested and charged with conducting espionage for Taiwan. At the time of his arrest, he had received his PhD in Germany in the 1990s and worked in an Austrian biomedical company as a researcher. Dr. Wu was sentenced to death in May 2007 by Beijing's court. No appeals and no family visits were allowed by the court during his entire prison time. One day before his execution, the court gave special permission for his daughter's visit. On November 28, 2008, Wu was executed by gunshot. In October 2009 British prime minister Gordon Brown condemned the Chinese government's decision to execute a British citizen in Xinjiang. Despite his request and the British family's appeals for clemency on the grounds of mental illness, Chinese authorities executed the British man by lethal injection on December 29.[38]

In Xinjiang, most of the eight million Uyghurs are Muslims, who face harsh religious policies. In June 2007, for example, during the traditional period for a pilgrimage to visit Mecca, Xinjiang authorities collected the passports of all Muslims to prevent any non-state-approved pilgrimage. In early July

34 Information Office, State Council of the PRC, "Progress in China's Human Rights Cause in 2003," 411.

35 The two key international rights organizations are Amnesty International (www.amnesty.org) and Human Rights Watch (www.hrw.org).

36 In March 2005, a senior member of the NPC announced that China executes approximately ten thousand people per year.

37 The Heilongjiang Provincial High Court also gave death sentences to three other church leaders, and eleven church members received various sentences from three to fifteen years in prison.

38 Li, *Modern China*, 98.

2009, tens of thousands of Uyghur demonstrators gathered at Urumqi, and confronted police, because two young Uyghur workers died and the government refused to conduct any investigation. Then, the peaceful demonstration escalated into riots on July 5–7. The government reported that 197 people were killed and 1,721 others were injured during the two-day riot.[39] The World Uyghur Congress reported a much higher tally, at approximately six hundred deaths. The official confirmed that on July 18, more than 1,500 Uyghurs were arrested. By December 2009 authorities had sentenced twenty-two Uyghurs to death for their participation in the July 5 religious and ethnic rioting.[40]

Although the Constitution recognizes that religious worship is part of a citizen's rights, it requires respect for those who do not have a religious belief. Since the ruling CCP is an atheistic party, it must protect its political base. The church or temple can conduct only government-approved worship and activities. The growth of religious groups in China is tempered by state control and persecution. Reprisals against unregistered groups have primarily focused on the Christians who, for various reasons, choose to attend "house churches" or "underground churches." For these reasons, many Catholics choose to worship outside the state-controlled congregations. Officially, there are about five million Catholics in China; according to the Vatican and other Catholic sources, the number is closer to ten million, with half of them worshipping outside the state-managed churches. The official number of Protestants is twenty-three million to twenty-five million, but unofficial estimates indicate that there are more than thirty million Protestants in China today.[41]

The Chinese government dislikes having religious groups and activities outside the system, especially with connections to foreign religious groups. Yao Liang, a Catholic bishop of an underground church, was arrested in 2006 in Hebei Province and was sentenced to seven years in prison. In December 2009 Yao died in jail. In 2007 authorities arrested 270 priests of the underground Christian churches. Many of them received prison sentences. The government continues to suppress the larger and most popular religious groups such as Falun Gong, one of the Buddhist groups. The organization estimated that nearly ninety thousand members were arrested, sixty thousand of whom were tortured in prison, and three thousand of whom died during or after their incarceration or forced labor.[42]

In Tibet political authorities continue to control Buddhist activities, and repression of religious freedom remains commonplace. In March 2008 a Buddhist demonstration took place and turned violent on the 14th. Many Tibetan monks were shot to death during the clash with armed police. They demanded freedom of religion and protested against official control and suppression of Tibetan Buddhism. After the "March 14 Riot," the government reported that 28 Tibetans were killed and one police officer was dead, plus 325 civilians were wounded, 58 of whom were in critical condition.

The freedoms of speech, political expression, the press, association, assembly, and peaceful demonstrations are all limited in China. Beijing continues

---

39   Information Office, State Council of the PRC, "Development and Progress in Xinjiang, 2009," in *White Papers of the Chinese Government, 2009–2011*, ed. Information Office, State Council of the PRC (Beijing: Foreign Languages Press, 2012), 177.

40   Information Office, State Council of the PRC, "Development and Progress in Xinjiang, 2009," in *White Papers of the Chinese Government, 2009–2011*, ed. Information Office, State Council of the PRC (Beijing: Foreign Languages Press, 2012), 177.

41   Zhaohui Hong, Lu Cao, and Jiamin Yan, "The Protestant Church Shortage and Religious Market in China: Spatial and Statistical Perspectives," in *Ethnic China: Identity, Assimilation, and Resistance*, eds. Xiaobing Li and Patrick Fuliang Shan (Lanham, MD: Lexington Books, 2015), 141.

42   Xiaobing Li, *Civil Liberties in China*, 61.

to restrict some of its citizens' fundamental rights by targeting unregistered organizations and unauthorized activities. Chinese journalists, lawyers, intellectuals, and activists who raise issues of official corruption, public health, and environmental crises face persecution, prosecution, harassment, detention, torture, and imprisonment. In 2006 Dr. Gao Yaojie (b. 1927), an eighty-year-old physician, was fighting the spread of AIDS in China's countryside when she was named to receive a Human Rights Award from an international women's organization in the United States. At the award ceremony, Gao criticized Chinese policies and the lack of health care in rural areas. After her return to China, she was arrested for "violating the rights of other citizens." From May–June 2007, authorities arrested some members of the Pan-Blue Alliance, which recognized the Chinese Nationalist Party in Taiwan, and promoted the Three Principles of the People. Because of its political orientation, the alliance could not get registered and became an illegal organization. Most of its leaders were arrested or sent to the labor camps or mental hospitals, while the government shut down its websites and newsletters.

Liu Xiaobo (1955–2017), professor of Beijing Normal University with a PhD in literature (1988), served as president (2003–2007) of the Independent Chinese Pen Society. In 2008 he co-authored the "Charter 08" manifesto and posted it online, calling for increased political freedoms and human rights in China. He was arrested in 2009 and sentenced to eleven years of imprisonment on December 23, 2009, for "the crime of inciting subversion of state power." Due to the nature of the charges, Liu is described as a political prisoner. In October 2010 Liu was awarded the Nobel Peace Prize for his "long and non-violent struggle for fundamental human rights in China."[43] The Nobel Committee is still waiting for him to collect his medal, pick up his prize money, and give his Nobel lecture.

In 2006 Gao Zhisheng (b. 1964), a human rights attorney in Beijing, was arrested and tortured by the secret police and sentenced to five years in jail for "disturbing public order." In 2008 Guo Quan (b. 1968), professor at Nanjing Normal University with a PhD in sociology (1999), was arrested for founding a democratic party and was sentenced to ten years in prison for "subversion of state power." In 2010 Tan Zuoren (b. 1954), an editor of a local journal in Chengdu, Sichuan province, and an environmentalist writer, was sentenced to another imprisonment of five years after being released on parole for a three-year imprisonment for "inciting subversion of state power" since he criticized the government environmental policy. In 2011 Ai Weiwei (b. 1957), a visual artist, was arrested at Beijing International Airport. Ai had led a "citizens' investigation team" to Sichuan after the earthquake on May 12, 2008, in response to the government's lack of transparency. He began blogging and turned out a steady stream of "scathing social commentary and criticism of government policy."[44] The blog was soon shut down due to its popularity and Ai's outspoken criticism on the Sichuan earthquake and the Beijing Olympic Games. Even though he was charged with an economic crime, Ai was imprisoned as a political prisoner. The authorities, if they believe it necessary, bar political dissidents from going overseas or returning home.

Authorities continue to use political dissidents as hostages in domestic and international politics. In March 2004 the Chinese government released dissident Wang Youcai (b. 1966) in response to repeated requests by the US government. Wang

---

43 Jean-Philippe Beja and Eva Pils, *Liu Xiaobo, Charter 08 and the Challenges of Political Reform in China* (Hong Kong: Hong Kong University Press, 2012), 2–4.

44 Guobin Yang, *The Power of the Internet in China: Citizen Activism Online* (New York: Columbia University Press, 2011), 11–13.

had been serving an eleven-year sentence for founding the China Democracy Party. Before the NPC national convention, he was released and allowed to travel to the United States on medical parole. In March 2006 the Chinese authorities released Tong Shidong, a seventy-two-year-old political dissident, before President Hu Jintao's visit to the United States. Tong was a retired physics professor in central Hunan province and was first arrested in 1999, then again in 2002. He was sentenced to six years in jail in June 2005 for helping to organize a would-be opposition party, the China Democracy Party. In 2013 the US Department of State issued its annual report on Chinese people's rights and stated that the condition of civil rights in China "remained poor."[45]

The power of the party and the rule of law are still locked in constant conflicts in contemporary China. Many civil rights that are enshrined in the Chinese Constitution are upheld only selectively in actual practice. China's economic modernization has not given rise to meaningful political democratization. Contrary to the historical experiences in the West where a growing middle class often demanded broader political participation, the Chinese middle class has been, as beneficiaries of the economic development, generally content with the social stability and political order.

---

45   US Department of State, *China (Tibet, Hong Kong, Macau): Human Rights, 2013* (Washington, DC: Government Printing Office, 2014), 2.

Conclusion to Part Five

By the twenty-first century, the East wind was prevailing over the West wind. Western imperialism and economic domination appear to be on the wane, while East Asian countries appear to be ascendant. Leading the charge is China, where economic growth has been remarkably consistent since the 1980s, and where urban areas are increasingly developed. China continues to be an ascendant military power as well, and its influence in international affairs continues to increase. Vietnam has also experienced considerable economic growth since the 1980s. While the Asian Financial Crisis of the late 1990s wounded the economies of South Korea and Japan, their economies remain among the largest in the world.

This economic ascendancy came to Asian countries only after considerable episodes of twentieth-century turmoil. Much of Japan was physically destroyed by the end of WWII and Japan's development was only possible after Japanese people constructed a new society and new political systems out of the embers of war. South Korea emerged as an economic dynamo as a phoenix out of the ashes of the Korean War. Vietnam's economic development was triggered by a policy of economic reform that came in the wake of three major wars and a failed attempt at creating a unified socialist economy in the late 1970s. Finally, China's economy emerged from the reforms of the 1980s, which were possible only when the last vestiges of the Maoist social and economic changes of the Cultural Revolution were eliminated after the death of Mao Zedong in 1976.

Despite the economic, political, and military might of East Asia today, significant challenges remain. Powerful environmental challenges, from pollution to desertification to climate change, confront East Asian societies, as they do the entire world. Throughout East Asia, income inequality remains a reality. In Vietnam and China, labor exploitation, human rights, and the maintenance of the rule of law present persistent challenges.

East Asia and the West, in modern times, became entwined with one another. This entanglement remains and is perhaps more profound than ever, as we will see in the Conclusion. However, what became clear in part five is that in the twenty-first century, the relationship between East Asia and the West will be one of much greater parity than in the past.

Conclusion

East Asia in the Twenty-first Century

In the new century, East Asia is a powerhouse of most dynamic growth, and the region is playing a crucial role in the recovery and development of global economy. Sustainable development in China, Vietnam, Korea, and Japan is improving security and stability in post-Cold War East Asia. The region has been drawing growing attention in the world since it has highlighted the diversity of world civilizations and development patterns as an intersection of interests of major powers. The security and development of East Asia has captured the interests of the world. Major countries have shifted their focuses toward East Asia and the Pacific with juxtaposition of cooperation and competition among them. Meanwhile, however, East Asians find themselves confronting their own complex historical legacy that is squarely rooted in both their own traditions and their troubled encounters with one another and collectively with the West. Additionally, East Asia strives to meet the multifaceted challenges of the present that encompass economic cooperation, strategic competition, regional security, and threats of global terrorism. Historical factors and present disputes appear to be mutually reinforcing. Territorial disputes in the South China Sea and over the Jiaoyu/Senkaku Islands threaten to upset the regional peace; American military presence in East Asia and the Pacific continues to complicate the geopolitical balance of power in that area; North Korea's looming nuclear capacity poses grave threats to not only neighborly relations but also global security. Historical grievances and current conflicts are intertwined, making East Asia a hotbed for both constructive and destructive changes.

The destabilizing factors in the region largely came from the East Asian countries themselves. First, China's political situation and reform have produced uncertainties and instability. The PRC today has little in common with Cold War China of 1949 to 1979. The government has brought back Confucianism and nationalism—subjects that had been destroyed during the revolution of the CCP in the 1950s–1970s—as ruling philosophies and ideologies. Randall Peerenboom considers this development as China's path forward rather than as a problem, "or at least that it is too early to tell."[1] He believes that "China is now following the path of other East Asian countries that have achieved sustained economic growth, established the rule of law, and developed constitutional or rights-based

---

1   Randall Peerenboom, "Law and Development of Constitutional Democracy: Is China a Problem Case?" *The Annals of the American Academy, AAPSS*, 603 (January 2006): 192.

democracies, albeit not necessarily liberal rights-based democracies."[2] Nevertheless, China's policy toward East Asia allows for a plurality of political systems and swift adjustments to changes in the international context. The drawback to this type of order is that it does not clarify Beijing's long-term objectives. Insofar as China achieves full-blown global power status, we still do not know what kind of global power China will be. Many strategic calculations and predictions depend on the CCP's current agenda to maintain both economic growth and social stability.

Among other major domestic issues, since the 2000s, corruption has become one of the key elements of the power-capital institution with three ways of connecting politics and business: making money through abusing power, seeking power through paying bribery, and pursuing power and/or wealth by pawning intellectual capital. Consequently, the power-interest groups have gradually spread from the upper class to the middle class, demonstrated by the "gray" income of 6.2 trillion yuan RMB (about $1 trillion), which was 12 percent of the GDP in 2011. The growth of gray income represents the extensive scope of corruption in China. The amount of cash that flowed overseas from China increased from $48 billion in 2000 to $65 billion in 2011, and China had become the fourth largest country in the world that had witnessed massive outflow of capital. The People's Bank of China (PBC, China's central bank) reported that more than eighteen thousand government officials and state-owned enterprise CEOs escaped from China in 2008, taking 800 billion yuan RMB (about $133 billion) in cash to foreign countries since the mid-1990s.[3]

Hu Jintao (r. 2002–2012) paid special attention to political scandals, corruption, and mismanagement in the government and in the party. Many cases involved the collection of bribes for the procurement of licenses or the manipulation of regulations. In 2005–2006, more than six thousand officials were investigated, detained, and sentenced by prosecutors. Hu fought back against the "Shanghai Gang," first in 2006–2008 by arresting and sentencing Chen Liangyu (b. 1946), mayor and party committee secretary of Shanghai and CCP Politburo member, to eighteen years in jail. Chen was charged with corruption and misuse of the city's pension fund. He was responsible for 3.45 billion yuan RMB ($439.4 million) from funds that had been siphoned off from the Shanghai Social Security Pension Fund for illicit loans and investments.[4] Then, Hu arrested Bo Xilai, mayor and party committee secretary of Chongqing and CCP Politburo member, in 2012.[5] Hu's victories over Chen and Bo protected his power base through his tenure.

After Hu retired, Xi Jinping (b. 1953) was elected party chairman and the country's president in November 2012. His political career began when he was appointed as vice mayor of the city of Xiamen in 1985. Xi was promoted to the office of lieutenant governor of Fujian in 1995, acting governor in 1999, and governor in 2000. He was then transferred to Zhejiang, and served as acting governor in 2002, governor in 2003, and provincial party committee secretary in 2003. Xi was appointed as party secretary of the Shanghai Municipal Committee in 2007, one of the most important local positions in the CCP. Xi became an alternate member of the CCP Fifteenth Central Committee in 1997 and a member

---

2   Ibid., 193.

3   Andrew Wedeman, *Double Paradox: Rapid Growth and Rising Corruption in China* (Ithaca, NY: Cornell University Press, 2012), introduction and chapter 4.

4   David Shambaugh, *China's Communist Party* (Berkeley: University of California Press, 2008), 154.

5   Rowan Callick, *The Party Forever: Inside China's Modern Communist Elite* (London: Palgrave Macmillan, 2013), chapters 1 and 5.

of the Sixteenth Central Committee in 2002. He entered the nine-man Standing Committee of the Politburo at the Seventeenth CCP National Congress in 2007 and became a national leader.[6] Since taking office, Xi has made it clear that China is a superpower, and that it wants to be treated as such. The new leader made some important policy changes to fit nationalist ideas and popular social movements, continuing to employ nationalism as an ideology to unite China and to fight for its superpower status, perhaps resulting in one more source of legitimacy for the CCP as the country's ruling party. Xi has been taking tougher positions on political control, the anticorruption movement, national defense, and military modernization, as well as territorial issues such as the disputed islands in the South China Sea.[7]

The pragmatic nationalism dictated by the Xi government through the 2010s pursues China's unity, strength, prosperity, and dignity rather than choosing civil and human rights as its core. This brand of nationalism emphasizes a common goal rather than holding individual rights as its fundamental value or democracy as its desired result. The government frequently calls on individuals to sacrifice personal rights for the national interest and has its own normative principles, which have been described as the "Chinese characteristics." As a new member of the global community, moreover, the PRC has not always followed all international standards but has adapted regulations selectively. Beijing considers many matters, including human rights, to be domestic problems, and believes no foreign government or organization should interfere in its internal affairs.

On the other hand, the domestic and international policies of the Xi administration have not solved the multitude of social and economic problems in China. The country has become polarized between its urban life and rural existence, and between the new economic elites and the working class. Among many pressing issues are the ones related to the massive number of migrant laborers. China's economic growth is based on its low production costs. The problems of Chinese labor have become serious in terms of low wages, poor working conditions, and human rights. By 2006 more than 160 million peasants had left their farms and sought work in cities, resulting in problems related to employment, housing, public health, transportation, and law enforcement. About 74 percent of migrant laborers, working ten to twelve hours a day, earn only $80–200 a month, about 12–30 percent of the average urban salary.[8] Full-time workers continue to confront many problems, such as safety in the workplace; coal mining is still the most dangerous profession in China. Official statistics show that the number of mineworker fatalities increased from 3,082 in 2000, to 3,790 in 2002, to 4,143 in 2003; and in 2004 and 2005, fatalities reached a horrendous high of more than 6,000 miners each year. According to a report by the World Federation of Trade Unions in 2006, some Chinese manufacturing companies hire child laborers between the ages of twelve and fifteen during the summer and winter breaks as full-time workers.[9] These child laborers are paid much less than the minimum wage and are

---

6 Jonathan Sharp, ed., *The China Renaissance: The Rise of Xi Jinping and the 18th Communist Party Congress* (Singapore: World Scientific, 2014), introduction.

7 Xiaoxiao Li, "Unity and Stability: Xi Jinping's Promise and the CCP's Future," in *Evolution of Power: China's Struggle, Survival, and Success*, eds. Xiaobing Li and Xiansheng Tian (Lanham, MD: Lexington Books, 2014), 351–66.

8 For more information on the migrant workers, see Michelle Loyalka, *Eating Bitterness: Stories from the Front Lines of China's Great Urban Migration* (Berkeley: University of California Press, 2013).

9 See Leslie Chang, *Factory Girls: From Village to City in a Changing China* (New York: Spiegel & Grau, 2009).

required to work as many hours a day as adult workers. Migrant women who make up the majority of the work force in the textile industry have also experienced harsh work-related treatments, including long hours, crowded dorms, low wages and delayed pay, and sexual harassment. Violation of labor laws has posed grave hazards to the workers. China's economic growth, as impressive as it has been, has come at tremendous human and social cost. While such problems have plagued all industrialized countries in the past, they do pose alarming challenges for China as its economic development continues in the twenty-first century. Child labor, human trafficking, prostitution, and drug addiction, as well as domestic violence and abuse are entrenched and very resistant to change.

The Ministry of Public Security of the PRC has estimated that twenty thousand women and children are abducted and sold each year, and some NGOs estimate that between thirty thousand and fifty thousand have been trafficked annually. The ministry reported approximately 2,500 trafficking cases during 2008, although experts claim the number is much higher. The estimated number of sex workers ranges from four million to as many as ten million.[10] Subsequent to the first HIV case being diagnosed in 1985, the official number of infected people reached 22,517 in 2000, 40,560 in 2002, and 840,000 in 2003. Intravenous drug use reportedly accounted for between 60 and 70 percent of these cases. Before 1985 there were very few female drug users, but the figure escalated quickly in the 1990s and 2000s. The number of registered female drug users reached

118,000 in 1999, climbed to 138,000 in 2000, and was estimated to represent roughly 16 percent of all drug users (more than 1.1 million) nationwide in both 2002 and 2003. By 2006 more than 30.7 million Chinese people were living below the poverty line ($1 a day), without sufficient food and clothing. Nearly 20 million urban residents were dependent on government and social welfare. Susan Trevaskes, Elisa Nesossi, Flora Sapio, and Sarah Biddulph conclude, "Uneven distribution of wealth, unequal access to justice, and corruption—entrenched throughout a political system characterized by weak oversight mechanism—have inspired widespread discontent. Many increasingly feel that their health, property and wages are no longer adequately protected by the legal system or government."[11]

Similar to the Chinese experience, Vietnam also faces tremendous challenges in its economic reform and social transition. In 2001 Nong Duc Manh became the general secretary of the Vietnamese Communist Party. Widely rumored to be Ho Chi Minh's illegitimate son, he moved political reforms at a much slower pace than his predecessors in Vietnam and was able to achieve greater consensus during his time as general secretary, which lasted until 2011.[12] Under his leadership, in 2007, Vietnam became a member of the World Trade Organization (WTO), despite ongoing concerns about protectionist policies, corruption, and internet censorship.[13]

Religious freedom also remains a concern in Vietnam. Buddhist monks are only allowed to operate under the officially sanctioned Buddhist organization, and the Vietnamese state continues to

---

10 Bin Liang and Liqun Cao, "China's Policies toward Illegal Drugs and Prostitution in the New Era: Struggle within the Global Context," in *Modern Chinese Legal Reform: New Perspectives*, eds. Xiaobing Li and Qiang Fang (Lexington: University Press of Kentucky, 2013): 189–214.

11 Susan Trevaskes, Elisa Nesossi, Flora Sapio, and Sarah Biddulph, "Stability and the Law," in *The Politics of Law and Stability in China*, eds. Susan Trevaskes, Elisa Nesossi, Flora Sapio, and Sarah Biddulph (Cheltenham, UK: Edward Elgar, 2914), 5.

12 See Sophie Quinn-Judge, "History of the Vietnamese Communist Party," in *Rethinking Vietnam*, ed. Duncan McCargo (New York: Routledge, 2004), 37.

13 Sarah Joseph, *Blame it on the WTO? A Human Rights Critique* (New York: Oxford University Press, 2011), 171–4, 200.

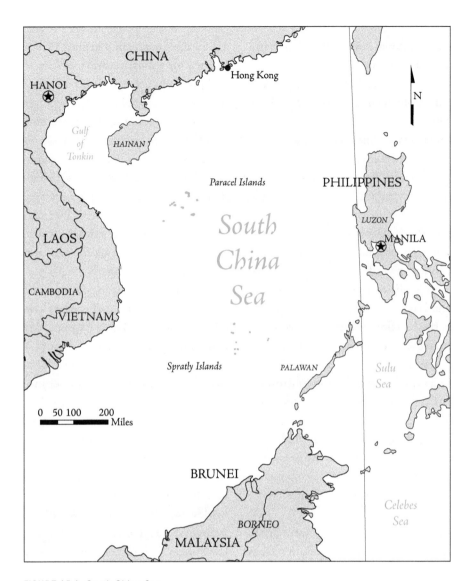

FIGURE 15.1 South China Sea

(ironically) restrict the freedom of expression of former members of the 1960s "third force" Buddhist movement that contributed to the demise of Ngo Dinh Diem in 1963. Leaders of the Hoa Hao, the Cao Dai, and of Protestant groups also report government infringement on religious freedom.[14]

Vietnam continues to have a culture that respects and even lionizes the scions of innovation in the global neoliberal economy. When Microsoft cofounder Bill Gates visited Hanoi in 2006, thousands of young students hung from trees and off balconies to get a view of him.[15] Nevertheless, under the leadership of current general secretary Nguyen Phu Trong (b. 1944) since 2011, the Vietnamese public has been increasingly concerned with the impact of neoliberal economic expansion on the

---

14   Edward P. Lipton, *Religious Freedom in Asia* (Hauppague, NY: Nova Science Publishers, 2002), 196–7.

15   "Vietnam Gives Gates a Star Welcome," *BBC News*, accessed June 2, 2016. http://news.bbc.co.uk/2/hi/asia-pacific/4933290.stm

environment and national sovereignty. Vietnamese have been catalyzed over Chinese attempts to assert sovereignty over the Paracel and Spratly island chains, both of which have historically been claimed by Vietnam among other countries. This is not a new dispute; in fact, China had first seized the Paracel Islands from Vietnam in 1974 over concerns that South Vietnamese attempts to explore for oil in the islands would lead to the discoveries that would benefit the Vietnamese.[16] Over the course of the last several years, these concerns became more pronounced as China has expanded reefs into artificial islands through using sand to create landfills for airstrips and port facilities in the Spratly Islands.[17]

Environmental concerns merged with those over sovereignty in the bauxite mining controversy. In 2007 the Vietnamese government allowed the state-owned mining company, Vinacomin, to mine for bauxite in the Central Highlands. The controversy arose because a Chinese company, Chalco, was actually doing much of the mining. Given the political sensitivity of mining and of the Central Highlands region, this spurred a controversy in the press, and even the aging war hero Vo Nguyen Giap spoke out against what he perceived to be Chinese interference in Vietnamese affairs.[18]

The environment and sovereignty were again linked in 2016 when environmental pollution from a Taiwanese company, Formosa Plastics Group, was blamed for a massive death of fish, clams, whales, and possibly even sea birds on the central coast of Vietnam that would have a negative effect on the livelihoods of countless fishing communities in that area.[19] These protests came at an inconvenient time, right before a major visit to Vietnam by US president Barack Obama, which was to highlight the new Trans-Pacific Partnership removing trade barriers between the United States, Vietnam, and several other Pacific rim countries, as well as removing a decades-old embargo on the sale of most military equipment to Vietnam.[20]

This episode perfectly captures Vietnam's balancing act. Internally, there has always been not one Vietnam but many. Regional identities differ considerably from north, to central, to south, and these cultural and ideological fault lines were made manifest in the Second Indochina War. These regional orientations influence the way that the Vietnamese have related to the larger world. Keith Taylor has said that the Hai Van Pass in Central Vietnam marks the dividing line between East and Southeast Asia.[21] North-central and northern Vietnam have always been more attracted to a Sinitic worldview, albeit with occasionally significant episodes of regional resistance to it; southern Vietnam has always shared more with its Southeast Asian

16   Nguyen Duc Cuong, "Building a Market Economy during Wartime," in Taylor, *Voices from the Second Republic*, 111–13; Ho van Ky-Thoai, "Naval Battle of the Paracels," in Taylor, *Voices from the Second Republic*, 153–8; Bill Hayton, *The South China Sea: The Struggle for Power in Asia* (New Haven: Yale University Press, 2014).

17   Derek Watkins, "What China Has Been Building in the South China Sea," *New York Times*, October 2015, accessed June 3, 2016. www.nytimes.com

18   Andrew Wells-Dang, "The Political Influence of Civil Society in Vietnam," in Jonathan D. London, ed., *Politics in Contemporary Vietnam: Party, State, and Authority Relations* (Basingstoke: Palgrave Macmillan, 2014), 171–2.

19   Scott Duke Harris, "Millions of Dead Fish on Vietnam's Shores Raise Industrial Pollution Fears," *Los Angeles Times*, May 4, 2016, accessed June 3, 2016, http://www.latimes.com/world/asia/la-fg-vietnam-fish-20160504-story.html

20   Gardiner Harris, "Vietnam Arms Embargo to Be Fully Lifted, Obama Says in Hanoi," *New York Times*, May 23, 2016, accessed June 3, 2016, http://www.nytimes.com/2016/05/24/world/asia/vietnam-us-arms-embargo-obama.html?_r=0

21   K. W. Taylor, "Surface Orientations in Vietnam: Beyond Histories of Nation and Region," *Journal of Asian Studies* 57, no. 4 (November 1998): 972.

neighbors, including a cosmopolitan ecumenism and extensive interactions with the world beyond Southeast Asia. Today, Vietnam is again at a crossroads, as tensions over economic expansion, environmental concerns, and national sovereignty are testing both Vietnam's relation to its East Asian neighbors to the north and to the wider world beyond them.

Third, tension on the Korean Peninsula creates another hot spot in East Asia.[22] By the early 1980s the North Korean press began to acclaim the younger Kim as the "great thinker and theoretician, outstanding genius of leadership, boundlessly benevolent teacher of the people, and the great leader of the century," clearly indicating that the systematic transfer of the Pyongyang regime's leadership was under way.[23] The elder Kim turned the political spotlight toward his son, gradually transferring more authority for affairs of the state and the party to his son. The elder Kim's succession plot was nearly completed by 1993, when young Kim assumed the nation's highest military positions, chairman of the military commission of the party and commander in chief of armed forces.

Kim Il-Sung, the first Communist leader of North Korea, died in July 1994, leaving behind even more questions about the secretive regime. The world knew little about his son, Kim Jong-Il, and even less about the inner workings of the Pyongyang government. Still, North Korea without Kim Il-Sung was expected to be quite different, yet what his sudden death meant to intra-Korean relations remained unclear. Consequently, the question of whether Kim Jong-Il could someday gain the power and prestige his father had monopolized in North Korea was unanswered for a while.

Gradually, Kim Jong-Il succeeded his father to become the leader of North Korea. His ascendancy, although he was unable to claim the presidency outright, was greatly benefitted by the fact that there is no political faction in North Korea capable of foiling the succession scheme the two Kims worked on for so long and so hard. Kim Jong-Il in the North-South equation presented a dimension that was quite different from the one his father represented. The nuclear standoff on the peninsula since October 2002 has been mainly the consequences of both the Cold War framework and mentality. Nevertheless, Kim lacked the charisma and revolutionary credentials his father had and used so effectively. Kim inherited the troubled relations between North Korea and the West, which were only made worse by President George W. Bush's "Axis of Evil" speech in early 2002. The Clinton administration had almost achieved a diplomatic breakthrough with the Agreed Framework, which struck a deal with North Korea—in exchange for oil and two light water reactors, Pyongyang, would suspend its nuclear weapons program, so for a while the tensions seemed to be subsiding. However, President Bush's "Axis of Evil" speech, which linked North Korea with Iran and Iraq as three of the most dangerous countries in the world, to some extent prompted Kim Jong-Il to act aggressively in renewing North Korea's pursuit of nuclear power.

After Kim Jong-Il died in December 2011, his third son, Kim Jong-Un, succeeded him, continuing his father's policy, only with more vigor and determination, leading to the intensification of North Korea's conflicts with South Korea, Japan, and the United States. Recently Kim Jong-Un has ordered repeated missile tests in an effort to eventually succeed in producing a small warhead that can be carried on a long-range missile to maximize its destructive power. The threat posed by North Korea to regional security has compelled even China to take a tougher stand against Pyongyang, evidenced

---

22   Xia Liping, "The Korean Factor in China's Policy toward East Asia and the United States," *American Foreign Policy Interests* 27, no. 4 (August 2005): 241–58.

23   Walter B. Jung, *National Building: The Geopolitical History of Korea* (Lanham, MD: University Press of America, 1998), 342.

in its decision to suspend its importation of coal from North Korea. The situation on the Korean peninsula remains the most dangerous potential flashpoint in East Asia. The border between the two Koreas remains one of the world's most militarized. Diplomatic means for resolving Pyongyang's nuclear program are not producing results. Within the past few years, there have been significant breaches of the peace—incidents such as missile testing and the North's bombardment of the islands in the South. Both Seoul and Pyongyang clearly have survival-level national security interests hanging in the balance. Moreover, both the United States and China have major national security interests at stake. However, their security calculus of the regime in Pyongyang in particular is nearly unfathomable, and it is not entirely clear that the United States and China are discussing peninsular issues in anything but the most minimalist manner. Moreover, there is the nuclear factor. David M. Finkelstein warns, "For these and many other reasons, we can never discount or ignore this satiation. It is one that casts a large shadow over the entire region. Like a volcano—sometimes dormant and sometimes active—it always possesses high potential for major destruction and disruption."[24]

As far as Japan is concerned, despite some recent signs of recovery and rejuvenation of its economy, the fact remains that the country has experienced the longest and most troubling economic recessions in its post-WWII history. The "economic miracle" that instilled tremendous sense of pride in the Japanese populace from the 1960s to the early 1990s has, to a considerable extent, been deflated, especially in light of the rise of China as a global power, replacing Japan as the world's second largest economy in 2011. Even though Japan has maintained its impressive social stability despite the unsettling economic situation,

severe problems as a result of the aging population and labor shortage, its political landscape underwent some instability, seen in the constant changes of prime ministership from 2006–2012. In six years seven prime ministers had to resign due to their inability to establish a parliamentary majority, the mishandling of economic policies, and various scandals, until Shinzo Abe reclaimed the prime ministership in 2012 after having served one short term from 2006–2007.

The economic malaise has contributed to the ascendancy of Japanese nationalism. In recent years Japan's foreign policies have swung forcefully to the right, largely due to the influence of Japan's conservative parties. As pointed out by some scholars, while the Chinese government has encouraged popular nationalism by making the Chinese people "remember" their past grievances and humiliation going back to the Opium War, the Japanese government has fostered popular nationalism by making the Japanese people "forget" their own past aggressions and the suffering that the Japanese military had inflicted on people in other Asian countries. The white-washing of the military atrocities in the elementary and middle school textbooks with scanty coverage of events such as the Manchurian Incident, the Rape of Nanking, and "Comfort Women" means that the younger generations are not well informed of the seamy side of Japanese history, thus making it easier for nationalistic rhetoric to make a deeper impact. For instance, the conservative politicians have made use of the disputed Senkaku Islands (or Diaoyu Islands in Chinese) to set off a new nationalist wave against China. After the ship-collision incident near these islands in 2010, Japan put forward a new version of the National Defense Program Guideline, which links island disputes with military strategy for the first time. After the cataclysmic earthquake and subsequent nuclear disaster, under political pressure, the

---

24   David M. Finkelstein, "Three Key Issues Affecting Security in the Asia-Pacific Region," in *Asia-Pacific Security: New Issues and New Ideas*, compiled by International Military Committee, China Association for Military Science (Beijing: Military Science Publishing House, 2014), 113.

Japanese government had to purchase a batch of US F-35 fighters in 2012 and presses on with the building of various warships. In that October, the Japanese cabinet decided to appropriate 16.9 billion yen to purchase patrol ships, helicopters, and other equipment for the Japanese Coast Guard. Besides strengthening its National Self-Defense Forces, the Shino Abe Cabinet has also pushed for a revision of the pacifist 1947 Constitution. In 2015 Abe succeeded in obtaining the Diet approval that the Japanese troops would be able to engage in combat missions overseas as part of allied military undertakings, different from the previous stipulation that Japanese soldiers could only engage in noncombat support capacities. The Abe administration has announced plans to revise, by 2020, the Constitution that has outlawed war forever as a means of solving international disputes. Specific revisions remain to be seen, but the nationalistic tone in Abe's foreign policies has raised some alarm in Japan's Asian neighbors.

While Japan's actions demonstrate understandable concerns with the North Korean threats, they also reflect the overall change in its foreign policy orientations. Mounting tensions with China have led to an ever-closer Tokyo-Washington alliance, which has in turn strengthened Japan's nationalistic sentiment and policies. Its tenuous alliance with South Korea has also undergone some fluctuations. The Yasukuni shrine visits by various Japanese prime ministers in recent decades have given rise to diplomatic and public protests in both China and South Korea, because the shrine houses the "spirits" of Japan's war dead, including WWII criminals such as Tojo Hideki. However, those oppositions from its Asian neighbors have not swayed Japanese leaders' intentions to continue such visits.

On the other hand, it should be pointed out that the textbooks with much diluted references to WWII in Asia and the Pacific are not used nationwide, and some teachers have insisted on educating their students on the troubling legacies of WWII.

Furthermore, proposals for constitutional revision have typically met with public protests, including Abe's plan to revise some pacifist terms in the Constitution by 2020. Women, in particular, have taken the lead in the Peace Movement, the tradition of which can be traced back to their opposition to entangling Japan in the Vietnam War. It should also be noted that the anti-Japanese sentiment in China could be overblown. For instance, after some Japanese activists raised the Japanese flag on a disputed islet within the Senkaku/Diaoyu island chain, in several Chinese cities a number of Japanese cars were smashed, and one Chinese man driving a Japanese car in Xi'an was severely beaten. Irrational expressions of nationalism on the parts of both Chinese and Japanese have led to highly negative mutual perceptions.

Although East Asia faces many challenges, the integration of national interests among all countries keeps deepening, and most countries have steadily passed their economic transformation and social transition. While the center of world economies is moving toward the East Asia-Pacific region, stability and prosperity of the region are of great significance to maintaining world peace and development and are in the best interests of all East Asian countries as well. We should treasure the favorable and hard-won environment and momentum for growth, establish a new concept of common security, and work to build a new type of East Asian security relationship featuring mutual trust, cooperation, mutual benefit, democracy, and equality. The building of strategic mutual trust should follow East Asia's unique characteristics and its own rules of development, adhere to innovation, and actively learn from the experience of other regions. Then, based upon mutual trust, East Asian countries may develop their own security organization or mechanism in the Asia-Pacific region to build and maintain the regional peace and stability. East Asian peoples have been historically able to grasp opportunities, join hands, forge ahead, and achieve sound and sustainable development.

Selected Bibliography

Abrami, Regina, William Kirby, and Warren McFarlan. *Can China Lead? Reaching the Limits of Power and Growth.* Cambridge, MA: Harvard Business Review, 2014.

Abuza, Zachary. "The Politics of Reform in Vietnam, 1986–2000." In *Vietnam: Current Issues and Historical Background*, edited by V. Largo, 1–21. Hauppauge, NY: Nova Science Publishers, 2002.

Aikman, David. *Jesus in Beijing: How Christianity Is Transforming China and Changing the Global Balance of Power.* New York: Regnery, 2006.

Allan, Tony, and Charles Phillips. *Ancient China's Myths and Beliefs.* New York: Rosen, 2011.

Alexander, Bevin. *Korea: The First War We Lost.* Revised ed. New York: Hippocrene Books, 1998.

Amman, Gustav. *The Legacy of Sun Yat-sen: A History of the Chinese Revolution.* Whitefish, MT: Kessinger Publishing, 2004.

Anderson, David L., and John Ernst. *The War that Never Ends: New Perspectives on the Vietnam War.* Lexington: University Press of Kentucky, 2007.

Anderson, James Adams. "Creating a Border Between China and Vietnam." In *Eurasian Corridors of Interconnection: From the South China to the Caspian Sea*, edited by Susan M. Walcott and Corey Johnson, 18–36. New York and London, UK: Routledge, 2015.

——, and John K. Whitmore. *Chinese Encounters on the South and Southwest: Forging the Fiery Frontier over Two Millenia.* Leiden and Boston: Brill, 2015.

Andrews, Julia, and Kuiyi Shen. *The Art of Modern China.* Berkeley: University of California Press, 2012.

Andressen, Curtis. *A Short History of Japan: From Samurai to Sony.* Canberra, Australia: Allen & Unwin, 2002.

Angle, Stephen. *Human Rights in Chinese Thought: A Cross-Cultural Inquiry.* Cambridge, UK: Cambridge University Press, 2002.

Appleman, Roy E. *South to the Naktong, North to the Yalu (June–November 1950), U.S. Army in the Korean War.* Washington, D.C.: Office of the Chief of Military History and U.S. Government Printing Office, 1961.

Arima, Seiho. "The Western Influence on Japanese Military Science, Shipbuilding, and Navigation." *Monumenta Nipponica* 19, no. 3–4 (1964): 329–54.

Armstrong, Charles K. *The Koreas.* 2nd ed. London, UK: Routledge, 2014.

Arrighi, Giovanni, Takeshi Hamashita, and Mark Selden, eds. *The Resurgence of East Asia: 500, 150 and 50 Year Perspectives.* London, UK: Routledge, 2003.

Asselin, Pierre. *Hanoi's Road to the Vietnam War, 1954–1965.* Berkeley: University of California Press, 2013.

——. *A Bitter Peace: Washington, Hanoi, and the Making of the Paris Agreement.* Chapel Hill: University of North Carolina Press, 2002.

Bailey, Thomas A. *A Diplomatic History of the American People.* 10th ed. Englewood Cliffs, NJ: Prentice-Hall, 1980.

Baker, John, and David Wiencek, eds. *Cooperative Monitoring in the South China Sea: Satellite Imagery, Confidence-Building Measures, and the Spratly Islands Disputes.* New York: Praeger, 2002.

Bakken, Borge, ed. *Crime, Punishment, and Policing in China.* Boulder, CO: Rowman & Littlefield, 2007.

Bandurski, David. *Investigative Journalism in China: Eight Cases in Chinese Watchdog Journalism.* Hong Kong: Hong Kong University Press, 2010.

Barlow, Tani. *The Question of Women in Chinese Feminism.* Durham, NC: Duke University Press, 2004.

Beals, Z. Charles. *China and the Boxers: A Short History of the Boxer Outbreak.* New York: M. E. Munson, 1901.

Beasley, W. G. *The Rise of Modern Japan.* 2nd ed. New York: St. Martin's, 1995.

Beja, Jean-Philippe, and Eva Pils. *Liu Xiaobo, Charter 08 and the Challenges of Political Reform in China.* Hong Kong: Hong Kong University Press, 2012.

Bello, David A. *Opium and the Limits of Empire: Drug Prohibition in the Chinese Interior, 1729–1850.* Cambridge, MA: Harvard University Press, 2005.

Bell, Daniel, and Hahm Chaibong, eds. *Confucianism for the Modern World.* Cambridge, UK: Cambridge University Press, 2003.

Bergère, Marie-Claire, and Janet Lloyd. *Sun Yat-sen.* Stanford, CA: Stanford University Press, 1998.

Bernstein, Thomas P., and Hua-Yu Li, eds. *China Learns from the Soviet Union, 1949–Present.* Lanham, MD: Lexington Books, 2011.

Bianco, Lucian. *Origins of the Chinese Revolution.* Stanford, CA: Stanford University Press, 1971.

Bickers, Robert A., and R. G. Tiedemann, eds. *The Boxers, China, and the World.* Lanham, MD: Rowman & Littlefield, 2007.

Biddulph, Sarah. *Legal Reform and Administrative Detention Powers in China.* Cambridge, UK: Cambridge University Press, 2008.

Bix, Herbert P. *Hirohito and the Making of Modern Japan.* New York: Perennial, 2000.

Black, Jeremy. *The Cold War: A Military History.* London, UK: Bloomsbury Academic, 2015.

——, ed. *War in the Modern World since 1815.* London, UK: Routledge, 2003.

Blair, Clay. *The Forgotten War: America in Korea, 1950–1953.* New York: Times Books, 1987.

Bovingdon, Gardner. *The Uyghurs: Strangers in Their Own Land.* New York: Columbia University Press, 2010.

Bradley, Mark Philip. *Imagining Vietnam & America: The Making of Postcolonial Vietnam, 1919–1950.* Chapel Hill, NC: University of North Carolina Press, 2000.

Brocheux, Pierre. *Ho Chi Minh: A Biography.* New York: Cambridge University Press, 2007.

Brook, Timothy, and Bob Tadashi Wakabayashi. *Opium Regimes: China, Britain, and Japan, 1839–1952.* Berkeley: University of California Press, 2000.

Brown, Delmer M. "The Impact of Firearms on Japanese Warfare, 1543–1598." *Far Eastern Quarterly* 7, no. 3 (May 1948): 217–39.

Brown, Elizabeth A. R. "The Tyranny of a Construction: Feudalism and Historians of Medieval Europe." *American Historical Review* 79, no. 4 (October 1974): 1063–88.

Brown, Kerry. *Hu Jintao: China's Silent Ruler.* Singapore: World Scientific, 2012.

Brown, Melissa. *Is Taiwan Chinese? The Impact of Culture, Power, and Migration on Changing Identities.* Berkeley: University of California Press, 2004.

Burchett, Wilfred G. *The Cambodia-China-Vietnam Triangle.* Chicago, IL: Vanguard Books, 1981.

Bureau of the Historical and Political Compilations, Defense Department of the Republic of China (ROC). *Gu Zhutong jiangjun jinianji* [Recollection of General Gu Zhutong's Works]. Taipei, Taiwan: Bureau of the Historical and Political Compilations, ROC Defense Department, 1988.

Burr, William, ed. *The Kissinger Transcripts: The Top-Secret Talks with Beijing and Moscow.* New York: New Press, 1999.

Buyandelger, Manduhai. *Tragic Spirits: Shamanism, Memory, and Gender in Contemporary Mongolia.* Chicago: University of Chicago Press, 2013.

Buzzanco, Robert. "Military Dissent and the Legacy of the Vietnam War." In *The War that Never Ends:*

New Perspectives on the Vietnam War, edited by David L. Anderson and John Ernst, 172–98. Lexington: University Press of Kentucky, 2007.

Byrnes, Joseph F. *Catholic and French Forever: Religious and National Identity in Modern France.* State College: Pennsylvania State University Press, 2005.

Callick, Rowan. *The Party Forever: Inside China's Modern Communist Elite.* London, UK: Palgrave Macmillan, 2013.

Campanella, Thomas. *The Concrete Dragon: China's Urban Revolution and What It Means for the World.* Princeton, NJ: Princeton University Press, 2011.

Carter, James M. *Inventing Vietnam: The United States and State Building, 1954–1968.* New York: Cambridge University Press, 2008.

Catton, Philip. *Diem's Final Failure: Prelude to America's War in Vietnam.* Lawrence: University Press of Kansas, 2002.

CCP Central Archives, Central Archival and Manuscript Research Division, and CCP Organization Department, comps. *Zhongguo gongchandang zuzhishi ziliao, 1921–1997* [Documents of the CCP Organization's History, 1921–1997]. 14 vols. Beijing: Zhonggong dangshi chubanshe [CCP Central Committee's Party History Press], 2000.

CCP Central Committee, ed. *Major Documents of the People's Republic of China—Selected Important Documents since the Third Plenary Session of the Eleventh CCP Central Committee.* Beijing: Foreign Languages Press, 1991.

CCP Party History Research Division. *Zhongguo gongchandang lishi dashiji, 1919–1987* [Major Historical Events of the CCP, 1919–1987]. Beijing: Renmin chubanshe [People's Press], 1989.

Chai Chengwen, and Zhao Yongtian. *Banmendian tanpan* [The Panmunjom Negotiations]. 2nd ed. Beijing: Jiefangjun chubanshe [PLA Press], 1992.

Chan, Sucheng. *The Vietnamese American 1.5 Generation: Stories of War, Revolution, Flight, and New Beginnings.* Philadelphia, PA: Temple University Press, 2006.

Chanda, Nayan. *Brother Enemy: The War after the War.* New York: Harcourt Brace Jovanovich, 1986.

Chandler, David. *A History of Cambodia.* Boulder, CO: Westview, 1992.

Chang, Gordon H. *Friends and Enemies: The United States, China, and the Soviet Union.* Stanford, CA: Stanford University Press, 1990.

Chang, Iris. *The Rape of Nanking; The Forgotten Holocaust of World War II.* New York: Basic Books, 1997.

Chang Jui-te. "The National Army from Whampoa to 1949." In *A Military History of China*, updated ed., edited by David A. Graff and Robin Higham, 193–210. Lexington: University Press of Kentucky, 2012.

Chang, Jung, and Jon Halliday. *Mao: The Unknown Story.* New York: Knopf, 2005.

Chang, Leslie. *Factory Girls: From Village to City in a Changing China.* New York: Spiegel & Grau, 2009.

Chang, Maria Hsia. *Falun Gong: The End of Days.* New Haven, CT: Yale University Press, 2004.

Chapman, Jessica. *Cauldron of Resistance: Ngo Dinh Diem, the United States, and 1950s Southern Vietnam.* Ithaca, NY: Cornell University Press, 2013.

Chen Jian. *Mao's China and the Cold War.* Chapel Hill: University of North Carolina Press, 2001.

——, and Xiaobing Li. "China and the End of the Global Cold War." In *The Cold War: From Détente to the Soviet Collapse*, edited by Malcolm Muir, Jr., 120–32. Lexington: Virginia Military Institute Press, 2006.

Chen, Jie. *A Middle Class without Democracy: Economic Growth and the Prospects for Democratization in China.* Oxford, UK: Oxford University Press, 2014.

Chen, King C. *China's War with Vietnam, 1979: Issues, Decisions, and Implications.* Stanford, CA: Hoover Institution Press, 1987.

Chethan, Deirdre. *Before the Deluge: The Vanishing World of the Yangtze's Three Gorges.* London, UK: Palgrave Macmillan, 2004.

Chi, Hoang Van. *From Colonialism to Communism: A Case History of North Vietnam.* New York: Praeger, 1964.

Chin, Ko-lin and James Finckenauer. *Selling Sex Overseas: Chinese Women and the Realities of Prostitution and*

Global Sex Trafficking. New York: New York University Press, 2012.

China National Military Museum comps. *Zhongguo zhanzheng fazhanshi* [History of Chinese Warfare]. Beijing: Renmin chubanshe [People's Press], 2001.

China Academy of Military Science (CAMS). *Zhongguo renmin jiefangjun quanguo jiefang zhanzhengshi* [History of the PLA in the Civil War]

Cho, Mun Young. *The Specter of "the People": Urban Poverty in Northeast China.* Ithaca, NY: Cornell University Press, 2013.

Choi Byung Wook. *Southern Vietnam under the Reign of Minh Mạng: Central Policies and Local Response.* Ithaca, NY: Cornell Southeast Asia Publications, 2004.

Cohen, Jerome B. *Japan's Economy in War and Reconstruction.* Minneapolis: University of Minnesota Press, 1949.

Cohen, Paul A. *History in Three Keys: The Boxers as Event, Experience, and Myth.* New York: Columbia University Press, 1997.

——. "Humanizing the Boxers." In *The Boxers, China, and the World,* edited by Robert A. Bickers and R. G. Tiedemann, 179–98. Lanham, MD: Rowman & Littlefield, 2007.

Cohen, Warren I. *America's Response to China: A History of Sino-American Relations.* 5th ed. New York: Columbia University Press, 2010.

Cole, Bernard. *Asian Maritime Strategies: Navigating Troubled Waters.* Annapolis, MD: Naval Institute Press, 2013.

Compilation Committee of ROC History. *A Pictorial History of the Republic of China.* Taipei, Taiwan: Modern China Press, 1981.

Confucius. *Analects.* Translated by Edward Slingerland. Indianapolis, IN: Hackett, 2006.

Cooke, Nola. "Early Nineteenth-Century Vietnamese Catholics and Others in the Pages of 'Annales de la Propagation de la Foi." *Journal of Southeast Asian Studies* 35, no. 2 (June 2004): 259–72.

——. "Strange Brew: Global, Local, and Regional Factors behind the 1690 Prohibition of Christian Practice in Nguyễn Cochinchina." *Journal of Southeast Asian Studies* 39, no. 3 (October 2008): 383–88.

—— and Li Tana, and James A. Anderson, eds. *The Tongking Gulf through History.* Philadelphia: University of Pennsylvania Press, 2011.

——. Crossley, Pamela Kyle. *The Wobbling Pivot; China since 1800: An Interpretive History.* New York: Wiley-Blackwell, 2010.

Cordier, Henri. *A Summary of Recent Events in Tong-King.* Shanghai: American Presbyterian Mission Press, 1875.

——. *La France et la Cochinchine, 1852–1858: La mission du Catinat a Tourane (1856).* Leiden: Brill, 1906.

Cumings, Bruce. *Korea's Place in the Sun: A Modern History.* New York: Norton, 1997.

Dalai Lama. *Freedom in Exile: The Autobiography of the Dalai Lama.* New York: Harper Perennial, 2008.

Daniels, Christopher. *South China Sea: Energy and Security Conflicts.* Lanham, MD: Scarecrow, 2013.

Dargyay, Eva K. *Tibetan Village Community.* Warminster, UK: Aris and Phillips, 1982.

Daughton, J. P. *An Empire Divided: Religion, Republicanism, and the Making of French Colonialism, 1880–1914.* New York: Oxford University Press, 2006.

Davis, Bradley Camp. *States of Banditry: The Nguyen Government, Bandit Rule, and the Culture of Power in the post-Taiping China-Vietnam Borderlands.* PhD Dissertation, University of Washington, 2008.

Davis, Deborah, and Sara Friedman, eds. *Wives, Husbands, and Lovers: Marriage and Sexuality in Hong Kong, Taiwan, and Urban China.* Stanford, CA: Stanford University Press, 2014.

de Ven, Hans van. "Military Mobilization in China, 1840–1949." In *War in the Modern World since 1815,* edited by Jeremy Black. London, UK: Routledge, 2003.

——. "War in the Making of Modern China." *Modern Asian Studies* 30, no. 4 (October 1996): 737–56.

Deng, Rong. *Deng Xiaoping and the Cultural Revolution—A Daughter Recalls the Critical Years.* Translated by Sidney Shapiro. Beijing: Foreign Languages Press, 2002.

Deng Xiaoping. *Selected Works of Deng Xiaoping.* 3 vols. Beijing: Foreign Languages Press, 1994.

Devonshire-Ellis, Chris, Andy Scott, and Sam Woollard, eds. *Setting up Joint Ventures in China.* New York: Springer, 2011.

Dickson, Bruce J. "Cooptation and Corporatism in China: The Logic of Party Adaptation." *Political Science Quarterly* 115, no. 4 (2000): 517–43.

——. *Wealth into Power: The Communist Party's Embrace of China's Private Sector.* Cambridge, UK: Cambridge University Press, 2008.

Diem, Bui with David Chanoff. *In the Jaws of History.* Bloomington: Indiana University Press, 1987.

Dikotter, Frank. *Mao's Great Famine; The History of China's Most Devastating Catastrophe, 1958–1962.* New York: Walker, 2010.

Dimitrov, Martin. *Piracy and the State: The Politics of Intellectual Property Rights in China.* New York: Cambridge University Press, 2012.

Dittmer, Lowell. *Liu Shao-ch'i and the Chinese Cultural Revolution: The Politics of Mass Criticism.* Berkeley: University of California Press, 1974.

Dommen, Arthur. *The Indochinese Experience of the French and the Americans: Nationalism and Communism in Cambodia, Laos, and Vietnam.* Bloomington: Indiana University Press, 2002.

Dreyer, Edward L. *China at War, 1901–1949.* New York: Longman, 1995.

——. "Continuity and Chang." In *A Military History of China.* Updated ed., edited by David A. Graff and Robin Higham, 15–27. Lexington: University Press of Kentucky, 2012.

Dror, Olga. "Raising Vietnamese: War and Youth in the South in the Early 1970s." *Journal of Southeast Asian Studies* 44, no. 1 (February 2013): 86–90.

——, and Keith Weller Taylor, eds. *Views of Seventeenth-Century Vietnam: Christoforo Borri on Cochinchina & Samuel Baron on Tonkin.* Ithaca, NY: Cornell University Southeast Asia Program, 2006.

Duiker, William J. *Cultures in Collision: The Boxer Rebellion.* San Rafael, CA: Presidio Press, 1978.

——. *Ho Chi Minh: A Life.* New York: Hyperion, 2000.

——. *Sacred War; Nationalism and Revolution in a Divided Vietnam.* Boston, MA: McGraw-Hill, 1995.

——. "What is to be done? Ho Chi Minh's *Duong Kach Menh.*" In *Essays into Vietnamese Pasts*, edited by K.W. Taylor and John K. Whitmore, 207–20. Ithaca, NY: Cornell Southeast Asia Program Publications, 1995.

Duong Van Nguyen. *The Tragedy of the Vietnam War: A South Vietnamese Officer's Analysis.* Jefferson, NC: McFarland, 2008.

Dutton, George. *The Tay Son Uprising: Society and Rebellion in Eighteenth-Century Vietnam.* Honolulu: University of Hawai'i Press, 2006.

Duus, Peter. *Feudalism in Japan.* New York: McGraw Hill, 1993.

Ebon, Martin. *Lin Piao; The Life and Writings of China's New Ruler.* New York: Stein and Day Publishers, 1970.

Ebrey, Patricia, and Anne Walthall. *Modern East Asia: From 1600; A Cultural, Social, and Political History.* 3rd ed. Boston, MA: Wadsworth, 2014.

——. *Pre-Modern East Asia: to 1800.* 3rd ed. Boston, MA: Wadsworth Cengage Learning, 2014.

Economy, Elizabeth. *By All Means Necessary: How China's Resource Quest Is Changing the World.* Oxford, UK: Oxford University Press, 2014.

Elleman, Bruce A. *Modern Chinese Warfare, 1795–1989.* London, UK: Routledge, 2001.

——, Stephen Kotkin, and Clive Scholfield, eds. *Beijing's Power and China's Borders: Twenty Neighbors in Asia.* Armonk, NY: M. E. Sharpe, 2012.

Elliot, Mark C. *The Manchu Way: The Eight Banners and Ethnic Identity in Late Imperial China.* Stanford, CA: Stanford University Press, 2001.

Elliott, David W. P. *Changing Worlds: Vietnam's Transition from Cold War to Globalization.* New York: Oxford University Press, 2012.

——. *The Vietnamese War: Revolution and Social Change in the Mekong Delta.* Concise Edition. Armonk, NY: M. E. Sharpe, 2007.

Elman, Benjamin A. "Naval Warfare and Refraction of China's Self-Strengthening Reforms into Scientific and Technological Failure, 1865–1895." *Modern Asian Studies* 38, no. 2 (May 2004): 306–29.

Elvin, Mark. *The Retreat of the Elephants: An Environmental History of China.* Ithaca, NY: Cornell University Press, 2006.

Esherick, Joseph W. *The Origins of the Boxer Uprising.* Berkeley: University of California Press, 1987.

———. *English Lessons: The Pedagogy of Imperialism in Nineteenth-Century China.* Durham, NC: Duke University Press, 2003.

———. *Reform and Revolution in China: The 1911 Revolution in Hunan and Hubei.* Berkeley: University of California Press, 1976.

———. "Revolution in a Feudal Fortress." *Modern China* 24, no. 4 (October 1998): 366–79.

Espiritu, Yen Le. *Body Counts: The Vietnam War and Militarized Refugees.* Berkeley: University of California Press, 2014.

Fairbank, John K., Edwin O. Reischauer, and Albert M. Craig. *East Asia: Transition and Transformation.* Revised ed. Boston, MA: Houghton Mifflin, 1989.

Fairbank, John K., and Merle Goldman. *China: A New History.* Enlarged ed. Cambridge, MA: Harvard University Press, 1998.

Farquhar, Judith. *Appetites: Food and Sex in Post-Socialist China.* Durham, NC: Duke University Press, 2002.

Feng Chih. *Behind Enemy Lines.* Beijing: Foreign Languages Press, 1979.

Feng Xianzhi, and Li Jie. *Mao Zedong yu kangmei yuanchao* [Mao Zedong and the War of Resisting the U.S. and Aiding Korea]. Beijing: Zhongyang wenxian chubanshe [CCP Central Archival and Manuscript Press], 2000.

Fewsmith, Joseph. *China since Tiananmen: From Deng Xiaoping to Hu Jintao.* 2nd ed. Cambridge, UK: Cambridge University Press, 2008.

Folsom, Ralph. *Law and Politics in the People's Republic of China.* Boulder, CO: Westview, 1992.

Foot, Rosemary. *Rights beyond Borders: The Global Community and the Struggle over Human Rights in China.* Oxford, UK: Oxford University Press, 2001.

———. *The Practice of Power: U.S. Relations with China since 1949.* Oxford, England: Oxford University Press, 1997.

Frankum, Ronald Bruce, Jr. *Vietnam's Year of the Rat: Elbridge Durbrow, Ngo Dinh Diem, and the Turn in U.S. Relations, 1959–1961.* Jefferson, NC: MacFarland, 2014.

Freeman, Charles, Jr. "The Process of Rapprochement: Achievements and Problems." In *Sino-American Normalization and Its Policy Implications,* edited by Gene T. Hsiao and Michael Witunsky, 2–21. New York: Praeger, 1983.

Frinklestein, David. "Three Key Issues Affecting Security in the Asia-Pacific Region." In *Asia-Pacific Security: New Issues and New Ideas,* compiled by International Military Committee, China Association for Military Science, 105–21. Beijing: Military Science Publishing House, 2014.

———. *Washington's Taiwan Dilemma, 1949–1950: From Abandonment to Salvation.* Fairfax, VA: George Mason University Press, 1993.

Gaddis, John Lewis. *The Cold War: A New History.* New York: Penguin Books, 2005.

———. *We Know Now: Rethinking Cold War History.* New York: Oxford University Press, 1997.

Gadkar-Wilcox, Wynn, ed. *Vietnam and the West: New Approaches.* Ithaca, NY: Cornell University Southeast Asia Program Publications, 2010.

———. "French Imperialism and the Vietnamese Civil Service Examination, 1862–1919." *Journal of American-East Asian Relations* 21, (2014): 373–93.

Gainsborough, Martin. *Vietnam: Rethinking the State.* New York: Zed Books, 2010.

Gallagher, Kelly. *China Shifts Gears: Automakers, Oil, Pollution, and Development.* Cambridge, MA: MIT Press, 2006.

Gallagher, Mary. *Contagious Capitalism: Globalization and the Politics of Labor in China.* Princeton, NJ: Princeton University Press, 2007.

Gao Meng, and Yan Jiaqi. *Wenhua dageming shi nian shi* [Ten Years of the Cultural Revolution]. Tianjin: Tianjin renmin chubanshe [Tianjin People's Press], 1986.

Gao Wenqian. *Wannian Zhou Enlai* [Zhou Enlai's Later Years]. Hong Kong: Mingjing chubanshe [Bright Mirror Publishing], 2003.

Gifford, Rob. *China Road: A Journey into the Future of a Rising Power*. New York: Random House, 2008.

Gladney, Dru. *Dislocating China: Muslims, Minorities, and Other Subaltern Subjects*. Chicago: University of Chicago Press, 2004.

Goldman, Merle, and Andrew Gordon. *Historical Perspectives on Contemporary East Asia*. Cambridge, MA: Harvard University Press, 2000.

——, and Roderick MacFarquhar, eds. *The Paradox of China's Post-Mao Reforms*. Cambridge, MA: Harvard University Press, 1999.

Gong Li. *Kuayue honggou: 1969–1979 nian zhongmei guanxi de yanbian* [Bridging the Chasm: The Evolution of Sino-American Relations, 1969–1979]. Zhengzhou: Henan renmin chubanshe [Henan People's Publishing], 1992.

Gordon, Andrew. "Society and Politics from Trans-war through Post-war Japan." In *Historical Perspectives on Contemporary East Asia*, edited by Merle Goldman and Andrew Gordon, 251–86. Cambridge, MA: Harvard University Press, 2000.

Graff, David A., and Robin Higham. *A Military History of China*. Updated ed. Lexington: University Press of Kentucky, 2012.

Grasso, June, Jay Corrin, and Michael Kort. *Modernization and Revolution in China: From the Opium Wars to World Power*. 3rd ed. Armonk, NY: M. E. Sharpe, 2004.

Gray, Jack. *Rebellions and Revolutions: China from the 1800s to 2000*. Oxford, UK: Oxford University Press, 2002.

Greenhalgh, Susan. *Cultivating Global Citizens: Population in the Rise of China*. Cambridge, MA: Harvard University Press, 2010.

Gries, Peter, and Stanley Rosen, eds. *Chinese Politics: State, Society and the Market*. London, UK: Routledge, 2010.

Ang Cheng Guan. *The Vietnam War from the Other Side*. New York: Routledge, 2013.

Gunn, Geoffrey. "The Great Vietnamese Famine of 1945 Revised." *Asia-Pacific Journal* 9, no. 5 (January 2011): 1–15.

Haley, Usha, and George Haley. *Subsidies to Chinese Industry: State Capitalism, Business Strategy, and Trade Policy*. Oxford, UK: Oxford University Press, 2013.

Hamashita, Takeshi. "Tribute and Treaties: Maritime Asia and Treaty Port Networks in the Era of Negotiation, 1800–1900." In *The Resurgence of East Asia: 500, 150 and 50 Years Perspectives*, edited by Giovanni Arrighi, Takeshi Hamashita, and Mark Selden, 17–50. London, UK: Routledge, 2003.

Hammer, Ellen. *The Struggle for Indochina*. Stanford, CA: Stanford University Press, 1955.

Han Huaizhi. *Dangdai zhongguo jundui de junshi gongzuo* [Military Affairs of Contemporary China]. 2 vols. Beijing: Zhongguo shehui kexue chubanshe [China's Social Science Press], 1989.

Hane, Mikiso. *Eastern Phoenix: Japan since 1945*. Boulder, CO: Westview, 1996.

——. *Premodern Japan: A Historical Survey*. Boulder, CO: Westview, 1991.

——, and Louis G. Perez. *Modern Japan: A Historical Survey*. 4th ed. Boulder, CO: Westview, 2009.

Vo Duc Hanh, Etienne. *La place du catholicisme dans les relations entre la France et le Viet-Nam de 1851 à 1870*. Leiden: Brill, 1969.

Hannas, William, James Mulvenon, and Anna Puglisi. *Chinese Industrial Espionage: Technology Acquisition and Military Modernization*. London, UK: Routledge, 2013.

Harms, Erik. *Saigon's Edge: On the Margins of Ho Chi Minh City*. Minneapolis: University of Minnesota Press, 2011.

Hasegawa, Tsuyoshi, ed. *East Asia and the Cold War: 1945–1991*. Stanford, CA: Stanford University Press, 2011.

Hastings, Max. *The Korean War*. New York: Simon and Schuster, 1987.

Hellegers, Dale M. *We, the Japanese People: World War II and the Origins of the Japanese Constitution*. Stanford, CA: Stanford University Press, 2002.

Henshall, Kenneth. *A History of Japan: From Stone Age to Superpower*. 2nd ed. London, UK: Palgrave Macmillan, 2004.

Hevia, James L. *Cherishing Men from Afar: Qing Guest Ritual and the McCartney Embassy of 1793*. Durham, NC: Duke University Press, 1995.

Hirakawa, Sachiko. "Japan Living in and with Asia." In *Regional Community Building in East Asia*, edited by Lee Lai To and Zarina Othman, 224–51. London, UK: Routledge, 2017.

History Compilation and Translation Bureau, ROC Defense Ministry. *8–23 Paozhan shengli 30 zhounian jinian wenji* [Recollection for the 30th Anniversary of the Victorious August 23 Artillery Battle]. Taipei, Taiwan: Guofangbu yinzhichang [Defense Ministry Printing Office], 1989.

——. *English Lessons: The Pedagogy of Imperialism in Nineteenth-Century China*. Durham, NC: Duke University Press, 2003.

Hoang Anh Tuan. "Tonkin Rear for China Front: The Dutch East India Company's Strategy for the North-Eastern Vietnamese Ports in the 1660s." In *Pirates, Ports, and Coasts in Asia: Historical and Contemporary Perspectives*, edited by John Kleinen and Manon Osseweijer, 64–71. Singapore: Institute for Southeast Asian Studies, 2010.

Ho, Loretta Wing Wah. *Gay and Lesbian Subculture in Urban China*. London, UK: Routledge, 2011.

Hong Xuezhi. *Kangmei yuanchao zhanzheng huiyi* [Recollections of the War of Resisting the U.S. and Aiding Korea]. Beijing: Jiefangjun wenyi chubanshe [PLA Literature Press], 1990.

Hong, Zhaohui, Lu Cao, and Jiamin Yan. "The Protestant Church Shortage and Religious Market in China: Spatial and Statistical Perspectives." In *Ethnic China: Identity, Assimilation, and Resistance*, edited by Xiaobing Li and Patrick Fuliang Shan, 139–50. Lanham, MD: Lexington Books, 2015.

Hook, Glenn D., Julie Gilson, Christopher W. Hughes, and Hugo Dobson. *Japan's International Relations: Politics, Economics and Security*. 2nd ed. London, UK: Routledge, 2005.

Hoskins, Janet. *The Divine Eye and the Diaspora: Vietnamese Syncretism becomes Transpacific Caodaism*. Honolulu: University of Hawaii Press, 2015.

Hsiao, Gene T., and Michael Witunsky. *Sino-American Normalization and Its Policy Implications*. New York: Praeger, 1983.

Hsu, Immanuel C. Y. *The Rise of Modern China*. 6th ed. Oxford, UK: Oxford University Press, 2000.

Hsu, Stephen, ed. *Understanding China's Legal System*. New York: New York University Press, 2003.

Hsueh, Roselyn. *China's Regulatory State: A New Strategy for Globalization*. Ithaca, NY: Cornell University Press, 2011.

Huang, Ray. *1587, A Year of No Significance: The Ming Dynasty in Decline*. New Haven, CT: Yale University Press, 1981.

Huang Yao, and Yan Jingtang. *Lin Biao yisheng* [Lin Biao's Life]. Beijing: Jiefangjun wenyi chubanshe [PLA Literature Press], 2004.

Huang, Yasheng. *Selling China: Foreign Direct Investment during the Reform Era*. Cambridge, UK: Cambridge University Press, 2005.

Huffman, James L. *Modern Japan: A History in Documents*. New York: Oxford University Press, 2011.

Hunt, Michael H. *The Genesis of Chinese Communist Foreign Policy*. New York: Columbia University Press, 1996.

Hurst, William. *The Chinese Workers after Socialism*. Cambridge, UK: Cambridge University Press, 2012.

Hu Wenyan, et al. *Zhongguo lishi* [Chinese History]. Beijing: Renmin jiaoyu chubanshe [People's Education Press], 1986.

Huynh Sanh Thong. *To Be Made Over: Tales of Socialist Reeducation in Vietnam*. New Haven, CT: Yale University Council on Southeast Asia Studies, 1988.

Information Office, State Council of the PRC, ed. *White Papers of the Chinese Government, 2002–2004*. Beijing: Foreign Languages Press, 2005.

——. *White Papers of the Chinese Government, 2009–2011*. Beijing: Foreign Languages Press, 2012.

Institute of Historical Studies, China Academy of Social Sciences (CASS). *Jianming zhongguo lishi duben*

[Concise History of China]. Beijing: Shehui kexue chubanshe [China Social Sciences Press], 2012.

International Military Committee, China Association for Military Science, ed. *Asia-Pacific Security: New Issues and New Ideas*. Beijing: Military Science Publishing House, 2014.

Isaacs, Harold R. *The Tragedy of the Chinese Revolution*. 2nd ed. Stanford, CA: Stanford University Press, 1961.

Israeli, Raphael. *Islam in China: Religion, Ethnicity, Culture, and Politics*. Lanham, MD: Lexington Books, 2007.

James, Leslie, and Elisabeth Leake, eds. *Decolonization and the Cold War: Negotiating Independence*. London, UK: Bloomsbury Academic, 2015.

Jiang Zemin. *On the "Three Represents."* Beijing: Foreign Languages Press, 2003.

Jin Binggao. *Zhongguo minzu yu minzu zhengce* [China's Nationalities and Ethnic Policy]. Beijing: Guojia xingzheng xueyuan chubanshe [State Administrative Studies University Press], 2013.

Jin Hui, ed. *Social History of Tibet: Documented and Illustrated History*. Beijing: China Intercontinental Press, 1995.

Joffe, Ellis. *The Chinese Army after Mao*. Cambridge, MA: Harvard University Press, 1987.

Johnson, Chalmers. *Japan: Who Governs? The Rise of the Developmental State*. New York: Norton, 1995.

Joiner, Charles A. "South Vietnam's Buddhist Crisis: Organization for Charity, Dissidence, and Unity." *Asian Survey* 4, no. 7 (July 1964): 908–21.

Joseph, Sarah. *Blame it on the WTO? A Human Rights Critique*. New York: Oxford University Press, 2011.

San Juan, Karin Aguilar. *Little Saigons: Staying Vietnamese in America*. Minneapolis: University of Minnesota Press, 2009.

Jung, Walter B. "Asia's Crisis and New Opportunity." In *Asia's Crisis and New Paradigm*, edited by Walter Jung and Xiaobing Li, 1–16. Lanham, MD: University Press of America, 2000.

———. *National Building: The Geopolitical History of Korea*. Lanham, MD: University Press of America, 1998.

———, and Xiaobing Li. *Asia's Crisis and New Paradigm*. Lanham, MD: University Press of America, 2000.

Kahin, George McT. *Intervention: How America Became Involved in Vietnam*. New York: Alfred P. Knopf, 1986.

Kang, David C. *East Asia before the West: Five Centuries of Trade and Tribute*. New York: Columbia University Press, 2012.

Kang, Wenqing. *Obsession: Male Same-Sex Relations in China, 1900–1950*. Hong Kong: Hong Kong University Press, 2009.

Kaplan, Robert. *Asia's Cauldron: The South China Sea and the End of a Stable Pacific*. New York: Random House, 2014.

Kau, Michael Y. M., ed. *The Lin Biao Affair: Power Politics and Military Coup*. White Plains, NY: International Arts and Science Press, 1975.

Keith, Charles. *Catholic Vietnam: A Church from Empire to Nation*. Berkeley: University of California Press, 2012.

Keith, Ronald, Zhiqiu Lin, and Shumei Hou. *China's Supreme Court*. London, UK: Routledge, 2013.

Kelley, Liam C. "Constructing Local Narratives: Spirits, Dreams, and Prophecies in the Medieval Red River Delta." In *Chinese Encounters on the South and Southwest: Forging the Fiery Frontier over Two Millenia*, edited by James A. Anderson and John K. Whitmore, 78–105. Leiden and Boston: Brill, 2015.

Kemenade, Willem Van. *China, Hong Kong, Taiwan, Inc.* New York: Vintage Books, 1997.

Kerkvliet, Benedict J. *The Power of Everyday Politics: How Vietnamese Peasants Transformed National Policy*. Ithaca, NY: Cornell University Press, 2005.

Huynh Kim Khanh. *Vietnamese Communism, 1925–1945*. Ithaca, NY: Cornell University Press, 1982.

Khoo, Nicholas. *Collateral Damage: Sino-Soviet Rivalry and the Termination of the Sino-Vietnamese Alliance*. New York: Columbia University Press, 2011.

Le Thanh Khoi. *Le Viet-Nam: Histoire et Civilisation*. Paris: Éditions de Minuit, 1955.

Kiernan, Ben. *How Pol Pot Came to Power: Colonialism, Nationalism, and Communism in Cambodia, 1930–1975*. New Haven, CT: Yale University Press, 2004.

———. "The Impact of Cambodia on US Intervention in Vietnam." In *The Vietnam War: Vietnamese and American Perspectives*, edited by Jayne Werner and Luu Doan Huynh, 216–32. Armonk, NY: M. E. Sharpe, 1993.

———. *The Pol Pot Regime: Race, Power, and Genocide in Cambodia under the Khmer Rouge, 1975–79*. Revised ed. New Haven, CT: Yale University Press, 2014.

Kieschnick, John. *The Impact of Buddhism on Chinese Material Culture*. Princeton, NJ: Princeton University Press, 2003.

Kleinen, John, and Manon Osseweijer, eds. *Pirates, Ports, and Coasts in Asia: Historical and Contemporary Perspectives*. Singapore: Institute for Southeast Asian Studies, 2010.

Kuhn, Dieter. *The Age of Confucian Rule: The Song Transformation of China*. Cambridge, MA: Harvard University Press, 2011.

Kuhn, Robert. *The Man Who Changed China: The Life and Legacy of Jiang Zemin*. New York: Random House, 2005.

Kurlantzick, Joshua. *Charm Offensive: How China's Soft Power Is Transforming the World*. New Haven, CT: Yale University Press, 2007.

Kwon, Heonik. *After the Massacre: Commemoration and Consolidation in Ha My and My Lai*. Berkeley: University of California Press, 2006.

Labbé, Danielle. *Land Politics and Livelihoods on the Margins of Hanoi, 1920–2010*. Vancouver, BC: University of British Columbia Press, 2014.

Laderman, Scott, and Edwin A. Martini. *Four Decades On: Vietnam, the United States, and the Legacies of the Second Indochina War*. Durham, NC: Duke University Press, 2013.

Lam, Willy. *Chinese Politics in the Hu Jintao Era: New Leaders, New Challenges*. Armonk, NY: M. E. Sharpe, 2006.

Lamb, Alastair. *The Mandarin Road to Old Hué*. Hamden, CT: Archon Books, 1970.

Lampton, David. *Following the Leader: Ruling China, from Deng Xiaoping to Xi Jinping*. Berkeley: University of California Press, 2014.

Larcher-Goscha, Agathe. "Prince Cuong De and Franco–Vietnamese Competition for the Heritage of Gia Long." In *Viet Nam Exposé*, edited by Gisèle Luce Bousquet and Pierre Brocheux, 198–211. Ann Arbor: University of Michigan Press, 2002.

Launay, Adrien. *Les cinquante-deux serviteurs de Dieu*. Vol. 2. Paris: Téqui, 1893.

Lawrence, Mark Atwood. *The Vietnam War: A Concise International History*. New York: Oxford University Press, 2008.

Lee, Jonathan H. X. *Chinese Americans: The History and Culture of a People*. Santa Barbara: ABC-Clio, 2015.

Li Baozhong. *Zhongwei junshi zhidu bijiao* [Comparative Study of Chinese Military System]. Beijing: Shangwu yinshuguan [Shangwu Press], 2003.

Li, Cheng. *China's Leaders; The New Generation*. Lanham, MD: Rowman & Littlefield, 2001.

Li Danhui. "Conflicts between China and the Soviet Union in Their Efforts to Aid Vietnam and Resist America." In *Lengzhan yu zhongguo* [The Cold War and China], edited by Zhang Baijia and Niu Jun, 372–414. Beijing: Shijie zhishi chubanshe [World Knowledge Publishing], 2002.

Li, He. *From Revolution to Reform: A Comparative Study of China and Mexico*. Lanham, MD: University Press of America, 2004.

Li Huazi. *Qingchao yu Chaoxian Guanxishi* [Study of the Relations between the Qing Dynasty and Korea]. Hong Kong: Yazhou chubanshe [Asian Publishing House], 2006.

Li Ke, and Hao Shengzhang. *Wenhua dageming zhong de renmin jiefangjun* [The PLA during the Cultural Revolution]. Beijing: Zhonggong dangshi ziliao chubanshe [CCP Central Committee's Party Historical Document Press], 1989.

Li, Xiaobing. *A History of the Modern Chinese Army*. Lexington: University Press of Kentucky, 2007.

———. *China at War*. Santa Barbara, CA: ABC-CLIO, 2010.

———. *China's Battle for Korea: The 1951 Spring Offensive*. Bloomington: Indiana University Press, 2014.

——. *Civil Liberties in China*. Santa Barbara, CA: ABC-CLIO, 2010.

——. *Modern China: Understanding the Modern Nation*. Santa Barbara, CA: ABC-CLIO, 2015.

——. *Voices from the Vietnam War: Stories from American, Asian, and Russian Veterans*. Lexington: University Press of Kentucky, 2010.

——, Allan Millett, and Bin Yu, trans. and eds. *Mao's Generals Remember Korea*. Lawrence: University Press of Kansas, 2001.

——, and Michael Molina. "Taiwan." In *Oil: A Cultural and Geographic Encyclopedia of Black Gold*, edited by Xiaobing Li and Michael Molina, 2: 670–74. Santa Barbara, CA: ABC-CLIO, 2014.

——, and Qiang Fang. *Modern Chinese Legal Reform: New Perspectives*. Lexington: University Press of Kentucky, 2013.

——, and Xiansheng Tian, eds. *Evolution of Power: China's Struggle, Survival, and Success*. Lanham, MD: Lexington Books, 2014.

Li Zhisui. *The Private Life of Chairman Mao; The Memoirs of Mao's Personal Physician*. New York: Random House, 1994.

Lipton, Edward P. *Religious Freedom in Asia*. Hauppague, NY: Nova Science Publishers, 2002.

Liu, Xiaoyuan. *A Partnership for Disorder: China, the United States, and their Policies for the Postwar Disposition of the Japanese Empire, 1941–1945*. Cambridge, UK: Cambridge University Press, 1996.

——. "From Five 'Imperial Domains' to a 'Chinese Nation': A Perceptual and Political Transformation in Recent History." In *Ethnic China: Identity, Assimilation, and Resistance*, edited by Xiaobing Li and Patrick Fuliang Shan, 3–38. Lanham, MD: Lexington Books, 2015.

Lockhart, Bruce McFarland. *The End of the Vietnamese Monarchy*. New Haven, CT: Yale University Southeast Asia Studies, 1993.

Logevall, Fredrik. *Embers of War: The Fall of an Empire and the Making of America's Vietnam*. New York: Random House, 2014.

London, Jonathan D., ed. *Politics in Contemporary Vietnam: Party, State, and Authority Relations*. Basingstoke, UK: Palgrave Macmillan, 2014.

Loyalka, Michelle. *Eating Bitterness: Stories from the Front Lines of China's Great Urban Migration*. Berkeley: University of California Press, 2013.

Luthi, Lorenz M. *The Sino-Soviet Split: Cold War in the Communist World*. Princeton, NJ: Princeton University Press, 2008.

——, ed. *The Regional Cold Wars in Europe, East Asia, and the Middle East: Crucial Periods and Turning Points*. Stanford, CA: Stanford University Press, 2015.

MacLean, Ken. *The Government of Mistrust: Illegibility and Bureaucratic Power in Socialist Vietnam*. Madison: University of Wisconsin Press, 2013.

Maier, Charles S. "Consigning the Twentieth Century to History: Alternatives for the Modern Era." *American Historical Review* 105, no. 3 (June 2000): 807–31.

Manguin, Pierre-Yves. *Les Nguyen, le Macao et le Portugal: Aspects politiques et commerciaux d'une relation privilège en mer de Chine, 1773–1802*. Paris: École Française d'Extrême-Orient, 1984.

Mann, Jim. *About Face: A History of America's Curious Relationship with China, from Nixon to Clinton*. New York: Knopf, 1999.

Mao Zedong. *Jianguo yilai Mao Zedong wengao* [Mao Zedong's Manuscripts since the Founding of the State]. Thirteen vols. Beijing: Zhongyang wenxian chubanshe [CCP Central Archival and Manuscript Press], 1989–1993.

——. *Mao Zedong junshi wenji* [Collected Military Papers of Mao Zedong]. 6 vols. Beijing: Junshi kexue chubanshe [Military Science Press], 1993.

——. *Mao Zedong junshi wenxun: neibuben* [Selected Military Papers of Mao Zedong: Internal Edition]. 2 vols. Beijing: Jiefangjun chubanshe [PLA Press], 1981.

——. *Mao Zedong wenji* [Collected Works of Mao Zedong]. 8 vols. Beijing: Renmin chubanshe [People's Press], 1993–1999.

——. *Selected Works of Mao Zedong*. 4 vols. Beijing: Foreign Languages Press, 1977.

Marin, Catherine. *Le role des missionaries français en Cochinchine aux XVIIe & XVIIIe siècles*. Paris: Églises d'Asie, 1999.

Marr, David G. "Ho Chi Minh's Independence Declaration." In *Essays into Vietnamese Pasts*, edited by K. W. Taylor and John K. Whitmore, 211–30. Ithaca, NY: Cornell Southeast Asia Program, 1995.

———. *Vietnam 1945: The Quest for Power*. Berkeley: University of California Press, 1995.

———. *Vietnamese Anticolonialism, 1885–1925*. Berkeley: University of California Press, 1971.

———. *Vietnam: State, War, and Revolution, 1945–1946*. Berkeley: University of California Press, 2013.

———. *Vietnamese Tradition on Trial, 1925–1945*. Berkeley: University of California Press, 1981.

Marti, Michael E. *China and the Legacy of Deng Xiaoping: From Communist Revolution to Capitalist Evolution*. New York: Brassey's, 2001.

Masur, Matthew. "Exhibiting Signs of Resistance: South Vietnam's Struggle for Legitimacy, 1954–1960." *Diplomatic History* 33, no. 2 (April 2009): 292–313.

Matray, James I., and Donald W. Boose, Jr., eds. *Ashgate Research Companion to the Korean War*. Surrey, UK: Ashgate Publishing, 2014.

McClain, James L. *Japan: A Modern History*. New York: Norton, 2002.

McCord, Edward A. *The Power of the Gun: The Emergence of Modern Chinese Warlordism*. Berkeley: University of California Press, 1993.

McGregor, Richard. *The Party: The Secret World of China's Communist Rulers*. New York: Harper/Perennial, 2012.

McHale, Shawn. "Freedom, Violence, and the Struggle over the Public Arena in the Democratic Republic of Vietnam, 1945–1958." In *Naissance d'un État-Parti/Birth of the Party State: Vietnam since 1945*, edited by Christopher E. Goscha and Benoît de Trégoldé, 89–114. Paris: Les Indes Savantes, 2004.

———. *Print and Power: Confucianism, Communism, and Buddhism in the Making of Modern Vietnam*. Honolulu: University of Hawaii Press, 2008.

McLeod, Mark W. *The Vietnamese Response to French Intervention, 1862–1874*. New York: Praeger, 1991.

———. "Truong Dinh and Vietnamese Anti-Colonialism, 1859–1864: A Reappraisal." *Journal of Southeast Asian Studies* 24, no. 1 (March 1993): 86–101.

Meisner, Maurice. *Mao's China: A History of the People's Republic*. New York: The Free Press, 1977.

Menzies, Gavin. *1421: The Year China Discovered America*. New York: Perennial, 2003.

Meyer, Milton W. *Japan: A Concise History*. 4th ed. Lanham, MD: Rowman & Littlefield, 2013.

Military History Research Division, China Academy of Military Science (CAMS). *Junqi piaopiao; xinzhongguo 50 nian junshi dashi shushi, 1949–1999* [PLA Flag Fluttering; Facts of China's Major Military Events in the Past Fifty Years, 1949–1999]. 2 vols. Beijing: Jiefangjun chubanshe [PLA Press], 1999.

———. *Zhongguo renmin jiefangjun de qishinian, 1929–1997* [The Seventy Years of the PLA, 1929–1997]. Beijing: Junshi kexue chubanshe [Military Science Press], 1997.

———. *Zhongguo renmin jiefangjun quanguo jiefang zhanzhengshi* [History of the PLA in the Civil War] (Beijing: Junshi kexue chubanshe [Military Science Press], 1997.

———. *Zhongguo renmin zhiyuanjun kangmei yuanchao zhanshi* [Combat Experience of the CPVF in the War of Resisting the U.S. and Aiding Korea]. Beijing: Junshi kexue chubanshe [Military Science Press], 1990.

Miller, Edward. *Misalliance: Ngo Dinh Diem, the United States, and the Fate of South Vietnam*. Cambridge, MA: Harvard University Press, 2013.

Millett, Allan R. *The War for Korea, 1950–1951: They Came from the North*. Lawrence: University Press of Kansas, 2010.

Ministry of Foreign Affairs, Republic of Vietnam. *The War in Vietnam: Liberation of Aggression?* Saigon, South Vietnam: Ministry of Foreign Affairs, 1968.

Moise, Edwin E. *Land Reform in China and North Vietnam: Consolidating the Revolution at the Village Level*. Chapel Hill: University of North Carolina Press, 1983.

———. *Tonkin Gulf and the Escalation of the Vietnam War*. Chapel Hill: University of North Carolina Press, 1996.

Morgan, Joseph G. *The Vietnam Lobby: The American Friends of Vietnam, 1955–1975.* Chapel Hill: University of North Carolina Press, 1997.

Mühlhahn, Klaus. *Criminal Justice in China: A History.* Cambridge, MA: Harvard University Press, 2009.

Munemitsu, Mutsu, and Mark Berger Gordon. *Kenkenroku: A Diplomatic Record of the Sino-Japanese War: 1894–1895.* Princeton, NJ: Princeton University Press, 1982.

Mungello, D. E. *The Great Encounter of China and the West, 1500–1800.* 4th ed. Lanham, MD: Rowman & Littlefield, 2013.

Murphey, Rhoads. *A History of Asia.* 3rd ed. New York: Longman, 2000.

Mutsu, Munemitsu, and Mark Berger Gordon. *Kenkenroku: A Diplomatic Record of the Sino-Japanese War: 1894–1895.* Princeton, NJ: Princeton University Press, 1982.

Neiberg, Michael S. *Warfare in World History.* London, UK: Routledge, 2001.

New Star Publisher, ed. *Selected Documents of the Fifteenth CCP National Congress.* Beijing: New Star, 1997.

Ngo Si Lien, ed. *Dai Viet Su Kt Toan Thu* [Complete Record of the History of Dai Viet]. Hanoi: Khoa Hoc Xa Hoi, 1993.

Nguyen Anh. The *Monarchie et fait colonial au Viêt-Nam (1875–1925): le crepuscule d'un ordre traditionnel.* Paris: L'harmattan, 1992.

Nguyen Cao Ky. *How We Lost the Vietnam War.* Lanham, MD: Rowman and Littlefield, 2002.

Nguyen Cong Luan. *Nationalist in the Viet Nam Wars.* Bloomington: Indiana University Press, 2012.

Nguyen, Nathalie Huynh Chau. *Memory is Another Country: Women of the Vietnamese Diaspora.* Santa Barbara, CA: ABC-CLIO, 2009.

Nguyen, Lien-Hang. *Hanoi's War: An International History of the War for Peace in Vietnam.* Chapel Hill: University of North Carolina Press, 2012.

Nguyen Phan Quang, and Vo Xuan Dan. *Lich su Viet nam tu nguon goc den nam 1884* [History of Vietnam from its foundations to 1884]. Ho Chi Minh: NXB Tong Hop, 2011.

Nguyen Phu Duc. *The Viet-Nam Peace Negotiations: Saigon's Side of the Story.* Christiansburg, VA: Dalley Book Service, 2005.

Nguyen Q. Thang, and Nguyen Ba The. *Tu dien nhan vat lich su Viet nam* [Dictionary of Vietnamese Historical Figures]. Hanoi: Khoa hoc xa hoi, 1991.

Nha Ca. *Mourning Headband for Hue.* Bloomington: Indiana University Press, 2014.

Nie Rongzhen. *Nie Rongzhen huiyilu* [Memoir of Nie Rongzhen]. 2 vols. Beijing: Jiefangjun chubanshe [PLA Press], 1984.

Ninh, Kim N. B. *A World Transformed: The Politics of Culture in Revolutionary Vietnam, 1945–1965.* Ann Arbor: University of Michigan Press, 2002.

Nixon, Richard. *The Memoirs of Richard Nixon.* New York: Grosset & Dunlap, 1978.

Oliver, Kendrick. *The My Lai Massacre in American History and Memory.* Manchester, UK: Manchester University Press, 2006.

Olsen, Mari. *Soviet-Vietnam Relations and the Role of China, 1949–1964: Changing Alliances.* New York: Taylor and Francis, 2006.

Osborne, Milton. *The French Presence in Cochin China and Cambodia: Rule and Response (1859–1905).* Ithaca, NY: Cornell University Press, 1969.

Ostrowski, Brian Eugene. "The Nôm Works of Geronimo Maiorica, S.J. (1589–1656) and their Christology." PhD Dissertation, Cornell University, 2006.

——. "The Rise of Christian Nôm Literature in Seventeenth-Century Vietnam: Fusing European Content and Local Expression." In *Vietnam and the West: New Approaches,* edited by Wynn Wilcox, 19–40. Ithaca, NY: Cornell University Southeast Asia Program Publications, 2010.

Paine, S. C. M. *The Sino-Japanese War of 1894–1895: Perceptions, Power and Primacy.* Cambridge, UK: Cambridge University Press, 2005.

Palais, James. *Confucian Statecraft and Korean Institutions: Yu Hyongwon and the Late Choson Dynasty.* Seattle: University of Washington Press, 1996.

Parker, Edward Harper, and Yuan Wei. *Chinese Account of the Opium War.* Charleston, SC: Biblio Life, 2009.

Patti, Archimedes L. A. *Why Viet Nam? Prelude to America's Albatross*. Berkeley: University of California Press, 1980.

Pelley, Patricia. *Postcolonial Vietnam: New Histories of the National Past*. Durham, NC: Duke University Press, 2002.

Peng Dehuai. *Peng Dehuai junshi wenxuan* [Selected Military Papers of Peng Dehuai]. Beijing: Zhongyang wenxian chubanshe [CCP Central Archival and Manuscript Press], 1988.

Peng Dehuai Biography Compilation Team. *Yige zhanzheng de ren: Peng Dehuai* [A Real Man: Peng Dehuai]. Beijing: Renmin chubanshe [People's Press], 1994.

Pepper, Suzanne. *Civil War in China: The Political Struggle, 1945–1949*. Berkeley: University of California Press, 1978.

Peters, Richard, and Xiaobing Li. *Voices of the Korean War: Personal Stories of American, Korean, and Chinese Soldiers*. Lexington: University Press of Kentucky, 2003.

Pettis, Michael. *Avoiding the Fall: China's Economic Restructuring*. New York: Carnegie Endowment Publishing, 2013.

Phan, Peter C. *Mission and Catechesis: Alexandre de Rhodes & Enculturation in Seventeenth-Century Vietnam*. Maryknoll, NY: Orbis Books, 1998.

Phan Phat Huon. *Viet-nam giao su* [Vietnamese Religious History]. Saigon: Cuu The Tuung Thu, 1965.

Preston, Diana. *The Boxer Rebellion: The Dramatic Story of China's War on Foreigners That Shook the World in the Summer of 1900*. New York: Walker, 2000.

Pribbenow, Merle. "General Vo Nguyen Giap and the Mysterious Evolution of the Plan for the 1968 Tet Offensive." *Journal of Vietnamese Studies* 3, no. 2 (2008): 1–22.

Pye, Lucian W. *China: An Introduction*. 4th ed. New York: HarperCollins, 1991.

Qi Dexue. "Several Issues on the War of Resisting the U.S. and Aiding Korea." In *Zhonggong dangshi yanjiu* [CCP Party History Research] 1 (1998): 69–82.

Qian Haihao. *Jundui zuzhi bianzhixue jiaocheng* [Graduate School Curriculum, China Academy of Military Science (CAMS): Military Organization and Formation]. Beijing: Junshi kexue chubanshe [Military Science Press], 2001.

Quinn-Judge, Sophie. "History of the Vietnamese Communist Party." In *Rethinking Vietnam*, edited by Duncan McCargo, 21–48. New York: Routledge, 2004.

——. *Ho Chi Minh: The Missing Years*. Berkeley: University of California Press, 2003.

——. "The Ideological Significance in the DRV and the Significance of the Anti-Party Affair, 1967–68." *Cold War History* 5, no. 4 (November 2005): 470–82.

——. "The Search for a Third Force in Vietnam: From the Quiet American to the Paris Peace Agreement." In *Vietnam and the West: New Approaches*, edited by Wynn Wilcox, 151–75. Ithaca, NY: Cornell Southeast Asia Program Publications, 2010.

Ramsay, Jacob. *Mandarins and Martyrs: The Church and the Nguyen Dynasty in Early Nineteenth Century Vietnam*. Stanford, CA: Stanford University Press, 2008.

Rankin, Mary. "'Public Opinion' and Political Power: *Qingyi* in Late Nineteenth Century China." *The Journal of Asian Studies* 41, no. 3 (May 1982): 453–84.

Randle, Robert F. *Geneva 1954: The Settlement of the Indochinese War*. Princeton, NJ: Princeton University Press, 1969.

Rawlinson, John L. *China's Struggle for Naval Development: 1839–1895*. Cambridge, MA: Harvard University Press, 1967.

Reid, Anthony, ed. *Southeast Asia in the Early Modern Era*. Ithaca, NY: Cornell University Press, 1993.

Rein, Shaun. *The End of Cheap China: Economic and Cultural Trends That Will Disrupt the World*. Hoboken, NJ: Wiley-Blackwell, 2014.

Reischauer, Edwin. *Japan: The Story of a Nation*. 4th ed. New York: McGraw-Hill, 1990.

——, and Craig Albert. *Japan: Tradition and Transformation*. Revised ed. Boston, MA: Houghton Mifflin, 1989.

Research Department of Party Literature, CCP Central Committee, ed. *Major Documents of the People's*

Republic of China—Selected Important Documents since the Third Plenary Session of the Eleventh CCP Central Committee. Beijing: Foreign Languages Press, 1991.

Rettig, Tobias. "French Military Policies in the aftermath of the Yên Bay Mutiny." South East Asia Research 10, no. 3 (November 2002): 303–18.

Rithmire, Meg E. Land Bargains and Chinese Capitalism: The Politics of Property Rights under Reform. New York: Cambridge University Press, 2015.

Robinson, Thomas. "The Sino-Soviet Border Conflicts of 1969." In Chinese Warfighting; the PLA Experience since 1949, edited by Mark A. Ryan, David M. Finkelstein, and Michael A. McDevitt, 198–216. Armonk, NY: M. E. Sharpe, 2003.

Ross, Robert S., and Jiang Changbin, eds. Re-examining the Cold War: U.S.-China Diplomacy, 1954–1973. Cambridge, MA: Harvard University Press, 2001.

Rowe, William T. China's Last Empire: The Great Qing. Cambridge, MA: Harvard University Press, 2009.

Ryan, Mark A., David M. Finkelstein, and Michael A. McDevitt, eds. Chinese Warfighting; the PLA Experience since 1949. Armonk, NY: M. E. Sharpe, 2003.

SarDesai, D. R. Southeast Asia: Past and Present. 7th ed. Boulder, CO: Westview Press, 2013.

——. Vietnam: Past and Present. 4th ed. Boulder, CO: Westview, 2005.

Saull, Richard. Rethinking Theory and History in the Cold War: The State, Military Power, and Social Revolution. London, UK: Frank Cass, 2001.

Schafer, John C. "Death, Buddhism, and Existentialism in the Songs of Trinh Cong Son." Journal of Vietnamese Studies 2, no. 1 (2007): 150–69.

Schell, Orville. Mandate of Heaven: The Legacy of Tiananmen Square and the Next Generation of China's Leaders. New York: Simon & Schuster, 1994.

——, and David Shambaugh, eds. The China Reader; The Reform Era. New York: Vintage Books, 1999.

Schoppa, R. Keith. Revolution and Its Past: Identities and Change in Modern Chinese History. 3rd ed. New York: Prentice Hall, 2011.

Schwartz, Benjamin I. The World of Thought in Ancient China. Cambridge, MA: Harvard University Press, 1985.

Scobell, Andrew. China's Use of Military Force: Beyond the Great Wall and the Long March. Cambridge, UK: Cambridge University Press, 2003.

Seagrave, Sterling. Dragon Lady: The Life and Legend of the Last Empress of China. New York: Vintage, 1992.

Seth, Michael J. A Concise History of Korea: From the Neolithic Period through the Nineteenth Century. Boulder, CO: Rowman & Littlefield, 2006.

Shambaugh, David. China's Communist Party: Atrophy and Adaptation. Berkeley: University of California Press, 2008.

Shan, Patrick Fuliang. "Local Revolution, Grassroots Mobilization and Wartime Power Shift to the Rise of Communism." In Evolution of Power: China's Struggle, Survival, and Success, edited by Xiaobing Li and Xiansheng Tian, 3–26. Lanham, MD: Lexington Books, 2014.

Sharp, Jonathan, ed. The China Renaissance: The Rise of Xi Jinping and the 18th Communist Party Congress. Singapore: World Scientific, 2014.

Shen Weiping. 8–23 paoji Jinmen [Bombardment of Jinmen on 8/23]. Beijing: Huayi chubanshe [Huayi Publishers], 1999.

Shen, Zhihua. "China Sends Troops to Korea: Beijing's Policy-making Process." In China and the United States; A New Cold War History, edited by Xiaobing Li and Hongshan Li, 13–48. New York: University Press of America, 1998.

——. Mao Zedong, Stalin he chaoxian zhanzheng [Mao Zedong, Stalin, and the Korean War]. Guangzhou: Gunagdong renmin chubanshe [Guangdong People's Press], 2004.

——, and Yafeng Xia. Mao and the Sino-Soviet Partnership, 1945–1959: A New History. Lanham, MD: Lexington Books, 2015.

Sheng, Michael M. Battling Western Imperialism: Mao, Stalin, and the United States. Princeton, NJ: Princeton University Press, 1997.

Shi Duqiao. *Zhongguo jindai junshi sixiangshi* [History of Military Thoughts in Modern China]. Beijing: Guofang daxue chubanshe [National Defense University Press], 2000.

Sidel, Mark. *The Constitution of Vietnam: A Contextual Analysis.* Portland, OR: Hart Publishing, 2009.

Simons, Geoff. *Korea: The Search for Sovereignty.* New York: St. Martin's, 1995.

Smith, R. B. "Bui Quang Chiêu and the Colonialist Party in French Cochinchina, 1917–30." *Modern Asian Studies* 3, no. 2 (1969): 122–35.

——. *Communist Indochina.* New York: Routledge, 2012.

Song Enfan, and Li Jiasong, eds. *Zhonghua renmin gongheguo waijiao dashiji, 1957–1964* [Chronicle of the People's Republic of China's Diplomacy, 1957–1964]. 2 vols. Beijing: Shijie zhishi chubanshe [World Knowledge Press], 2001.

Spence, Jonathan D. *The Search for Modern China.* 3rd ed. New York: Norton, 2013.

Standing Committee, PRC National People's Congress (NPC). *The Constitution of the People's Republic of China* (Beijing: Renmin Chubanshe [People's Publishing], 2004.

Starr, Harvey. *Henry Kissinger: Perceptions of International Politics.* Lexington: University Press of Kentucky, 2015.

Sun, Yi. "Explaining Female Suicides: An Analytical Study of the Cases at the Maple Women's Hotline Center." *American Review of China Studies* 5, no. 1–2 (Spring and Fall 2004): 25–43.

——, and Xiaobing Li. "Mao Zedong and the CCP: Adaptation, Centralization, and Succession." In *Evolution of Power: China's Struggle, Survival, and Success,* edited by Xiaobing Li and Xiansheng Tian, 27–60. Lanham, MD: Lexington Books, 2014.

Sutter, Robert G. *Chinese Foreign Relations: Power and Policy since the Cold War.* 4th ed. Lanham, MD: Rowman & Littlefield, 2016.

Taboulet, Georges. *La geste française en Indochine: histoire par les textes de la France en Indochine des origines à 1914.* Paris: Adrien-Maisonneuve, 1955–1956.

Tai, Hue-Tam Ho. *Radicalism and the Origins of the Vietnamese Revolution.* Cambridge, MA: Harvard University Press, 1992.

Nguyen Phut Tan. *A Modern History of Viet Nam.* Saigon: Khai Tri, 1964.

Li Tana. *Nguyen Cochinchina: Southern Vietnam in the Seventeenth and Eighteenth Centuries.* Ithaca, NY: Cornell University Southeast Asia Program Publications, 1998.

Tang Xiuying. "A Sword Thrusting the Sky." In *Liangdan yixing; zhongguo hewuqi daodan weixing yu feichuan quanjishi* [A Complete Record of China's Nuclear Bombs, Missiles, Satellites, and Space Programs], edited by the Political Department of the PLA General Armaments Department. Beijing: Jiuzhou chubanshe [Jiuzhou Press], 2001.

Tanner, Harold M. *China: A History: From the Great Qing Empire through the People's Republic of China.* Indianapolis, IN: Hackett, 2010.

Tao Wenzhao. *Zhongmei guanxishi, 1949–1972* [PRC-US Relations, 1949–1972]. Shanghai: Shanghai renmin chubanshe [Shanghai People's Press], 1999.

Tarling, Nicholas. "British Relations with Vietnam, 1822–1858." *Journal of the Malaysian Branch of the Royal Asiatic Society* 39, no. 1 (July 1966): 30–8.

Taylor, Jay. *The Generalissimo: Chiang Kai-shek and the Struggle for Modern China.* Cambridge, MA: Harvard University Press, 2009.

Taylor, Keith W. *A History of the Vietnamese.* New York: Cambridge University Press, 2013.

——. "Authority and Legitimacy in 11th Century Vietnam." In *Southeast Asia in the 9th to 14th Centuries,* edited by David G. Marr and A.C. Milner, 130–48. Singapore: Institute of Southeast Asian Studies, 1986.

——. "China and Vietnam: Looking for a New Version of an Old Relationship." In *The Vietnam War: Vietnamese and American Perspectives,* edited by Jayne Werner and Luu Doan Huynh, 266–85. Armonk, NY: M. E. Sharpe, 1993.

——. "The Literati Revival in Seventeenth-Century Vietnam." *Journal of Southeast Asian Studies* 18, no. 1 (March 1987): 1–23.

——. "Nguyen Hoang and the Beginning of Viet Nam's Southward Expansion." In *Southeast Asia in the Early Modern Era*, edited by Anthony Reid, 42–65. Ithaca, NY: Cornell University Press, 1993.

——, and John K. Whitmore, eds. *Essays into Vietnamese Pasts*. Ithaca, NY: Cornell University Southeast Asia Program Publications, 1995.

——, ed. *Voices from the Second Republic of South Vietnam (1967–1975)*. Ithaca, NY: Cornell University Southeast Asia Program Publications, 2014.

Thompson, C. Michele. *Vietnamese Traditional Medicine: A Social History*. Singapore: National University of Singapore Press, 2015.

Tien, Hung-mao. *Asian-Pacific Collective Security in the Post–Cold War Era*. Taipei: National Policy Institute, 1996.

To, Lee Lai, and Zarina Othman. *Regional Community Building in East Asia*. London, UK: Routledge, 2017.

Tønneson, Stein. *Vietnam 1946: How the War Began*. Berkeley: University of California Press, 2010.

——. *The Vietnamese Revolution of 1945: Roosevelt, Ho Chi Minh, and De Gaulle in a World at War*. Oslo: International Peace Institute, 1991.

Topmiller, Robert J. *The Lotus Unleashed: The Buddhist Peace Movement in South Vietnam, 1964–1966*. Lexington: University Press of Kentucky, 2002.

Totman, Conrad. *Japan before Perry: A Short History*. Berkeley: University of California Press, 1981.

Trevaskes, Susan, Elisa Nesossi, Flora Sapio, and Sarah Biddulph, eds. *The Politics of Law and Stability in China*. Cheltenham, UK: Edward Elgar, 2014.

Truman, Harry S. *Memoirs*. Garden City, NY: Doubleday, 1956.

Truong Buu Lam. *Colonialism Experienced: Vietnamese Writings on Colonialism, 1900–1931*. Ann Arbor: University of Michigan Press, 2000.

Truong Vinh Ky. *Cours d'histoire Annamite*. Saigon: Imprimerie du Gouvernement, 1875.

Tran Quang Minh. "A Decade of Public Service: Nation-building during the Interregnum and Second Republic." In *Voices from the Second Republic of South Vietnam (1967–1975)*, edited by Keith W. Taylor,

37–60. Ithaca, NY: Cornell Southeast Asia Program Publications, 2014.

Tran My-Van. *A Vietnamese Royal Exile in Japan: Prince Cuong De, 1882–1951*. New York: Routledge, 2005.

Tuck, Patrick J. N. *French Catholic Missionaries and the Politics of Imperialism in Vietnam, 1857–1914*. Liverpool: Liverpool University Press, 1987.

Tucker, Nancy Bernkopf. *Strait Talk: United States-Taiwan Relations and the Crisis with China*. Cambridge, MA: Harvard University Press, 2009.

Tucker, Spencer C. *Encyclopedia of the Vietnam War: A Political, Social, and Military History*. Oxford, UK: Oxford University Press, 2000.

——. *Vietnam*. Lexington: University Press of Kentucky, 1999.

Pham Cong Tue. "From the First to the Second Republic: From Scylla to Charybdis." In *Voices from the Second Republic*, edited by K. W. Taylor, 95–128. Ithaca, NY: Cornell Southeast Asia Publications, 2015.

Turley, William S., and Mark Selden, eds. *Reinventing Vietnamese Socialism: Doi Moi in Comparative Perspective*. Boulder, CO: Westview, 1993.

US Department of State. *China (Tibet, Hong Kong, Macau): Human Rights, 2013*. Washington, DC: US Government Printing Office, 2014.

——. *Foreign Relations of the United States, 1945–1979*. 28 vols. Washington, DC: US Government Printing Office, 1961–1986. Also available online at: https://history.state.gov/historicaldocuments/frus1952-54v16/d1044

Veith, George J. *Black April: The Fall of South Vietnam, 1973–1975*. New York: Encounter Books, 2012.

Vinh Sinh, and Nicholas Wickenden. *Overturned Chariot: The Autobiography of Phan Boi Chau*. Honolulu: University of Hawaii Press, 1999.

Vinh Sinh, ed. *Phan Châu Trinh and His Political Writings*. Ithaca, NY: Cornell University Southeast Asia Publications, 2009.

Vo, Alex-Thai D. "Nguyen Thi Nam and the Land Reform in North Vietnam, 1953." *Journal of Vietnamese Studies* 10, no. 1 (Winter 2015): 19–25.

Vo Nguyen Giap. *The Military Art of People's War: Selected Writings of Vo Nguyen Giap*. New York: New York University Press, 1970.

Vu, Tuong. "'It's Time for the Indochinese Revolution to Show Its True Colors': The Radical Turn of Vietnamese Politics in 1948." *Journal of Southeast Asian Studies* 40, no. 3 (October 2009): 519–42.

Wakeman, Frederic Jr. *The Fall of Imperial China*. New York: The Free Press, 1975.

Walcott, Susan M., and Corey Johnson. *Eurasian Corridors of Interconnection: From the South China to the Caspian Sea*. London, UK: Routledge, 2015.

Walthall, Anne. *Japan: A Cultural, Social, and Political History*. Boston, MA: Houghton Mifflin, 2004.

Walton, C. Wale. *The Myth of Inevitable US defeat in Vietnam*. Portland, OR: Frank Cass, 2002.

Wang Dinglie. *Dongdai Zhongguo kongjun* [Contemporary Chinese Air Force]. Beijing: Zhongguo shehui kexue chubanshe [China Social Sciences Press], 1989.

Wang, Furen, and Suo Wenqing. *Highlights of Tibetan History*. Beijing: New World Press, 1984.

Wang Taiping, ed. *Zhonghua renmin gongheguo waijiaoshi, 1970–1978* [Diplomatic History of the PRC, 1970–1978]. Beijing: Shijie zhishi chubanshe [World Knowledge Press], 1999.

Wang Zhaojun. *Shui shale Lin Biao* [Who Killed Lin Biao]. Taipei: Shijie chubanshe [Global Publishing], 1994.

War History Division, National Defense University (NDU). *Zhongguo renmin jiefangjun zhanshi jianbian* [A Brief History of the PLA Revolutionary War]. Beijing: Jiefangjun chubanshe [PLA Press], 2001.

Wedeman, Andrew. *Double Paradox: Rapid Growth and Rising Corruption in China*. Ithaca, NY: Cornell University Press, 2012.

Wells-Dang, Andrew. "The Political Influence of Civil Society in Vietnam." In *Politics in Contemporary Vietnam: Party, State, and Authority Relations*, edited by Jonathan D. London, 150–83. Basingstoke: Palgrave Macmillan, 2014.

Werner, Jayne. *Peasant Politics and Religious Sectarianism: Peasant and Priest in the Cao Dai in Viet Nam*. New Haven, CT: Yale University Southeast Asia Studies, 1981.

——, and Luu Doan Huynh, eds. *The Vietnam War: Vietnamese and American Perspectives*. New York: M. E. Sharpe, 1993.

Westad, Odd Arne. *The Global Cold War: Third World Interventions and the Making of Our Times*. New York: Cambridge University Press, 2005.

——. *Decisive Encounters: The Chinese Civil War, 1946–1950*. Stanford, CA: Stanford University Press, 2003.

——, ed. *Brothers in Arms: The Rise and Fall of the Sino-Soviet Alliance, 1945–1963*. Washington, D.C. and Stanford, CA: Woodrow Wilson Center Press and Stanford University Press, 1998.

Whiting, Susan. *Power and Wealth in Rural China: The Political Economy of Institutional Change*. Cambridge, UK: Cambridge University Press, 2006.

Whitmore, John K. "An Outline of Vietnamese History before French Conquest." *Vietnam Forum* 8 (Summer-Fall 1986): 1–12.

——. "Literati Culture and Integration in Dai Viet, c. 1430-c. 1840." *Modern Asian Studies* 31, no. 3 (July 1997): 671–5.

——. "Văn Đon, the 'Mac Gap,' and the End of the Jiaozhi Ocean System: Trade and State in Đai Viet, Circa 1450–1550." In *The Tongking Gulf through History*, edited by Nola Cooke, Li Tana, and James A. Anderson, 83–115. Philadelphia: University of Pennsylvania Press, 2011.

Wilcox, Wynn. "Dang Duc Tuan and the Complexities of nineteenth-Century Vietnamese Christian Identity." In *Vietnam and the West: New Approaches*, edited by Wynn Wilcox, 71–90. Ithaca, NY: Cornell Southeast Asia Program Publications, 2010.

Woodhull, Nancy J., and Robert W. Snyder, eds. *Defining Moments in Journalism*. New Brunswick, NJ: Transaction Publishers, 1998.

Woodside, Alexander. *Vietnam and the Chinese Model*. Cambridge, MA: Harvard University Council on East Asian Studies, 1971.

World Military High-Tech Book Series Compilation Team. *Daguo yizh; Dakai heheixiang* [Powers' Will:

Opening the Nuclear Black-box]. Beijing: Haichao chubanshe [Haichao Publishing], 2000.

Worthing, Peter M. *A Military History of Modern China: From the Manchu Conquest to Tiananmen Square.* Westport, CT: Praeger Security International, 2007.

Xia, Yafeng. *Negotiating with the Enemy: U.S.-China Talks during the Cold War, 1949–1972.* Bloomington: Indiana University Press, 2006.

Xiang, Lanxin. *Recasting the Imperial Far East: Britain and America in China, 1945–1950.* Armonk, NY: M. E. Sharpe, 1995.

Xiao Dehao, and Huang Zheng, eds. *Zhong Yue Bianjie Lishi Ziliao Xuanbian* [Selected Historical Materials on the Chinese-Vietnamese Borders]. Beijing: Shehui kexue wenxian chubanshe [Social Science Manuscript and Archival Publishing], 1992.

Xiong, Guangkai. *International Strategy and Revolution in Military Affairs.* Beijing: Tsinghua University Press, 2003.

Xu Yan. "Chinese Forces and Their Casualties in the Korean War," Translated by Xiaobing Li. *Chinese Historians* 6, no. 2 (Fall 1993): 45–64.

———. *Diyici jiaoliang: kangmei yuanchao zhanzheng de lishi huigu yu fansi* [The First Encounter: A Historical Retrospective of the War of Resisting the U.S. and Aiding Korea]. Beijing: Zhongguo guangbo dianshi chubanshe [China's Radio and Television Press], 1990.

———. *Jinmen zhizhan* [Battle of Jinmen]. Beijing: Zhongguo guangbo dianshi chubanshe [China Broadcasting and Television Publishing House], 1992.

———. *Junshijia Mao Zedong* [Mao Zedong as a Military Leader]. Beijing: Zhongyang wenxian chubanshe [CCP Central Archival and Manuscript Press], 1995.

Yang, Guobin. *The Power of the Internet in China: Citizen Activism Online.* New York: Columbia University Press, 2011.

Yang, Kuisong. "From the Zhenbao Island Incident to Sino-American Rapprochement." *Dangshi yanjiu ziliao* [Party History Research Materials], 12 (1997): 1–14.

———. "Origins of the U.S.-Soviet Cold War and Its Impact on China's Revolution." In *Lengzhan yu zhongguo* [The Cold War and China], edited by Zhang Baijia and Niu Jun, 51–88. Beijing: Shijie Zhishi Chubanshe, 2002.

———. *Zouxiang polie; Mao Zedong yu Moscow de enen yuanyuan* [Road to the Split; Interests and Conflicts between Mao Zedong and Moscow]. Hong Kong: Sanlian Shudian [Three Alliance Books], 1999.

Ye Yonglie. *Gaoceng jiaoliang* [Power Struggle at the Top]. Urumqi: Xinjiang renmin chubanshe [Xinjiang People's Press], 2004.

Yoshiharu Tsuboi. *L'empire Vietnamese face à la France et à la Chine.* Paris: L'Harmattan, 1987.

You Ji. "Meeting the Challenge of Multi-polarity: China's Foreign Policy toward Post-Cold War Asia and the Pacific." In *Asian-Pacific Collective Security in the Post-Cold war Era*, edited by Hung-mao Tien, 233–73. Taipei, Taiwan: National Policy Institute, 1996.

Young, Ernest P. *Ecclesiastical Colony: China's Catholic Church and the French Religious Protectorate.* New York: Oxford University Press, 2013.

Yu, Maochun. "The Taiping Rebellion." In *A Military History of China*, updated ed., edited by David A. Graff and Robin Higham, 135–52. Lexington: University Press of Kentucky, 2012.

Yust, Charles H. "Japanese Ling Guns, 1539–1905." In *Gun Digest*, 11th annual edition, edited by John T. Amber, 78–91. Chicago: Gun Digest Company, 1957.

Zarrow, Peter. *China in War and Revolution, 1895–1949.* New York: Routledge, 2005.

Zazloff, Joseph J. "Rural Resettlement in South Vietnam: the Agroville Program." *Pacific Affairs* 35, no. 4 (Winter 1962): 310–32.

Zhai, Qiang. *China and the Vietnam Wars, 1950–1975.* Chapel Hill: University of North Carolina Press, 2005.

Zhang, Dainian with Edmund Ryden, trans. *Key Concepts in Chinese Philosophy.* Beijing: Foreign Languages Press and New Haven, CT: Yale University Press, 2005.

Zhang, Jie, and Xiaobing Li, eds. *Social Transition in China.* Lanham, MD: University Press of America, 1998.

Zhang, Liang, ed. *The Tiananmen Papers: The Chinese Leadership's Decision to Use Force against Their Own People—in Their Own Words.* New York: Public Affairs, 2001.

Zhang, Shuguang. *Mao's Military Romanticism; China and the Korean War, 1950–1953.* Lawrence: University Press of Kansas, 1995.

———, and Chen Jian, trans. and eds. *Chinese Communist Foreign Policy and the Cold War in Asia: New Documentary Evidence, 1944–1950.* Chicago: Imprint Publications, 1996.

Zhang, Yutian. *Zhongguo jindai junshishi* [Military History of Modern China]. Shenyang: Liaoning renmin chubanshe [Liaoning People's Press], 1983.

Zhu, Fang. *Gun Barrel Politics: Party-Army Relations in Mao's China.* Boulder, CO: Westview Press, 1998.

Zinoman, Peter. "Nhan Van-Giai Pham and Vietnamese 'Reform Communism' in the 1950s: A Revisionist Interpretation." *Journal of Cold War Studies* 13, no. 1 (Winter 2011): 60–4.

Zottoli, Brian A. "Reconceptualizing Southern Vietnamese History from the 15th to 18th Centuries: Competition along the Coasts from Guangdong to Cambodia." PhD Dissertation, University of Michigan, 2011.

Zubok, Vladislav, and Constantine Pleshakov. *Inside the Kremlin's Cold War: From Stalin to Khrushchev.* Cambridge, MA: Harvard University Press, 1996.

Note on Transliteration

The *Hanyu pinyin* Romanization system is applied to Chinese names of persons, places, and terms. The transliteration is also used for the titles of Chinese publications. A person's name is written in the Chinese way, the surname first, such as Mao Zedong. Some popular names have traditional Wade-Giles spellings appearing in parentheses after the first use of the *Hanyu pinyin*, such as Zhou Enlai (Chou En-lai), as do popular names of places like Guangzhou (Canton). The Japanese and Korean names of persons, places, and terms are also translated by following the traditional East Asian practice that the surname is usually written first, as in Kim Il-Sung and Yoshida Shigeru. Exceptions are made for a few figures whose names are widely known in reverse order, such as Syngman Rhee. If a place has different spellings in Korean and English literature, parentheses are used at its first appearance—for example, Hahwaokri (Hagaru-ri). The Vietnamese names follow the traditional way that the surname is written first, then middle name, and first name, as in Ngo Dinh Diem and Vo Nguyen Giap. Most people in Vietnam are referred to by their given names, therefore President Diem and General Giap. The exceptions are for a very few particularly illustrious persons, such as Ho Chi Minh, who was called President Ho.

List of Maps

Index

CPSIA information can be obtained
at www.ICGtesting.com
Printed in the USA
BVHW050138290121
598864BV00002B/30